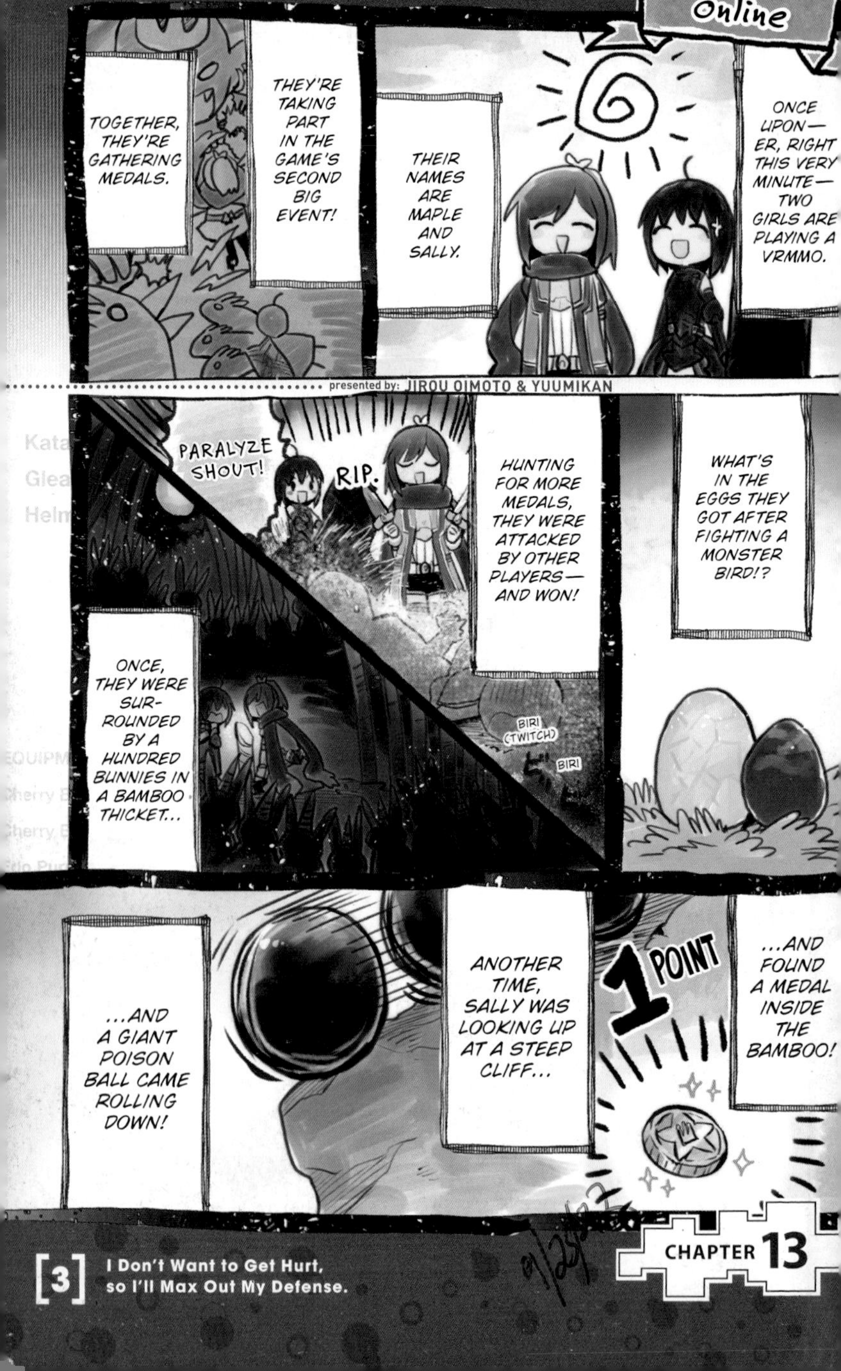
NewWorld Online
ONCE UPON— ER, RIGHT THIS VERY MINUTE— TWO GIRLS ARE PLAYING A VRMMO.
THEIR NAMES ARE MAPLE AND SALLY.
THEY'RE TAKING PART IN THE GAME'S SECOND BIG EVENT!
TOGETHER, THEY'RE GATHERING MEDALS.
presented by: JIROU OIMOTO & YUUMIKAN
WHAT'S IN THE EGGS THEY GOT AFTER FIGHTING A MONSTER BIRD!?
HUNTING FOR MORE MEDALS, THEY WERE ATTACKED BY OTHER PLAYERS— AND WON!
PARALYZE SHOUT!
RIP.
BIRI (TWITCH)
BIRI
ONCE, THEY WERE SURROUNDED BY A HUNDRED BUNNIES IN A BAMBOO THICKET...
...AND FOUND A MEDAL INSIDE THE BAMBOO!
1 POINT
ANOTHER TIME, SALLY WAS LOOKING UP AT A STEEP CLIFF...
...AND A GIANT POISON BALL CAME ROLLING DOWN!

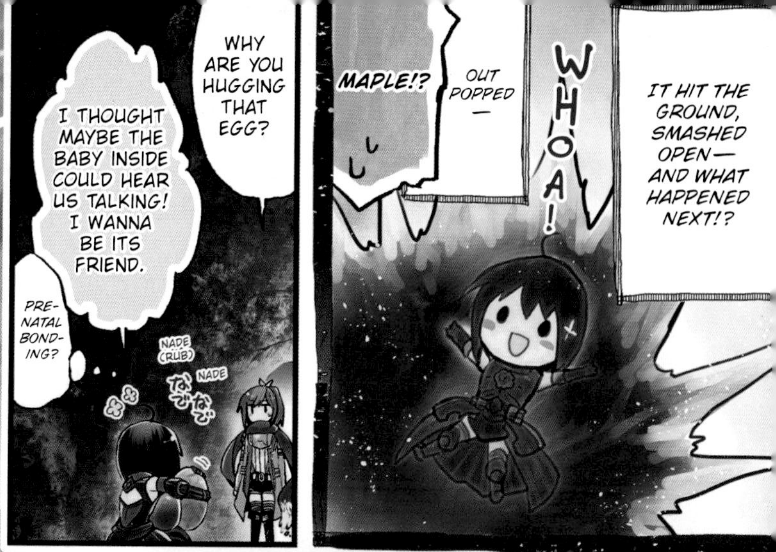
IT HIT THE GROUND, SMASHED OPEN— AND WHAT HAPPENED NEXT!?
WHOA!
OUT POPPED —
MAPLE!?
WHY ARE YOU HUGGING THAT EGG?
I THOUGHT MAYBE THE BABY INSIDE COULD HEAR US TALKING! I WANNA BE ITS FRIEND.
PRE-NATAL BOND-ING?
なでなで
NADE (RUB)
NADE

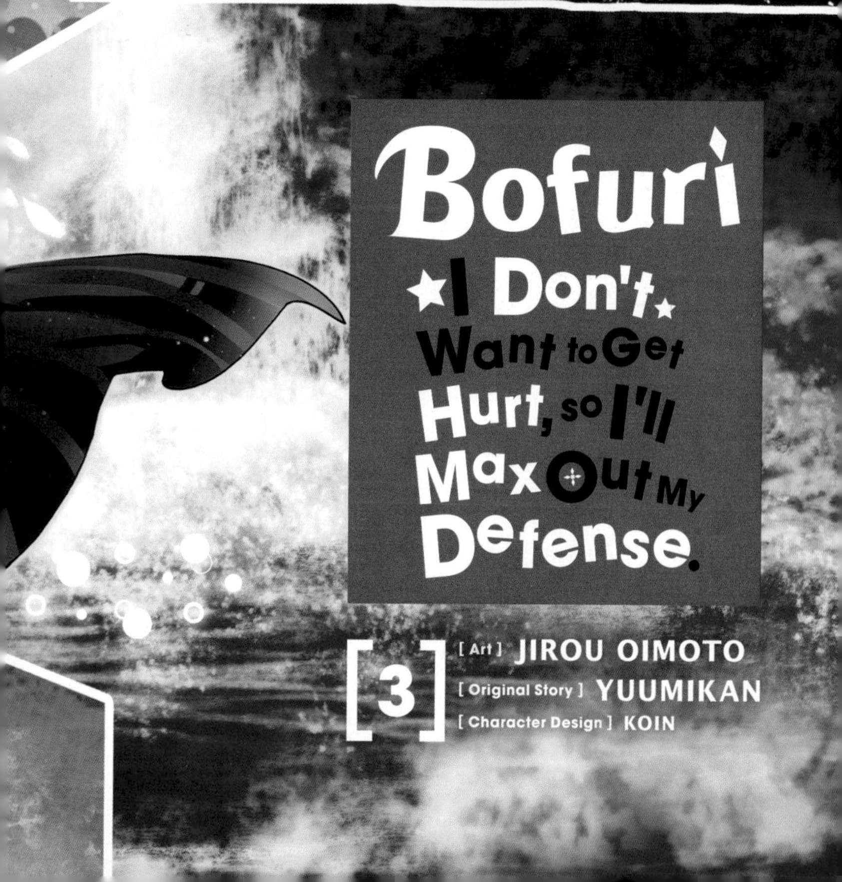
Bofuri
★I Don't Want to Get Hurt, so I'll Max Out My Defense.★
[3]
[Art] JIROU OIMOTO
[Original Story] YUUMIKAN
[Character Design] KOIN

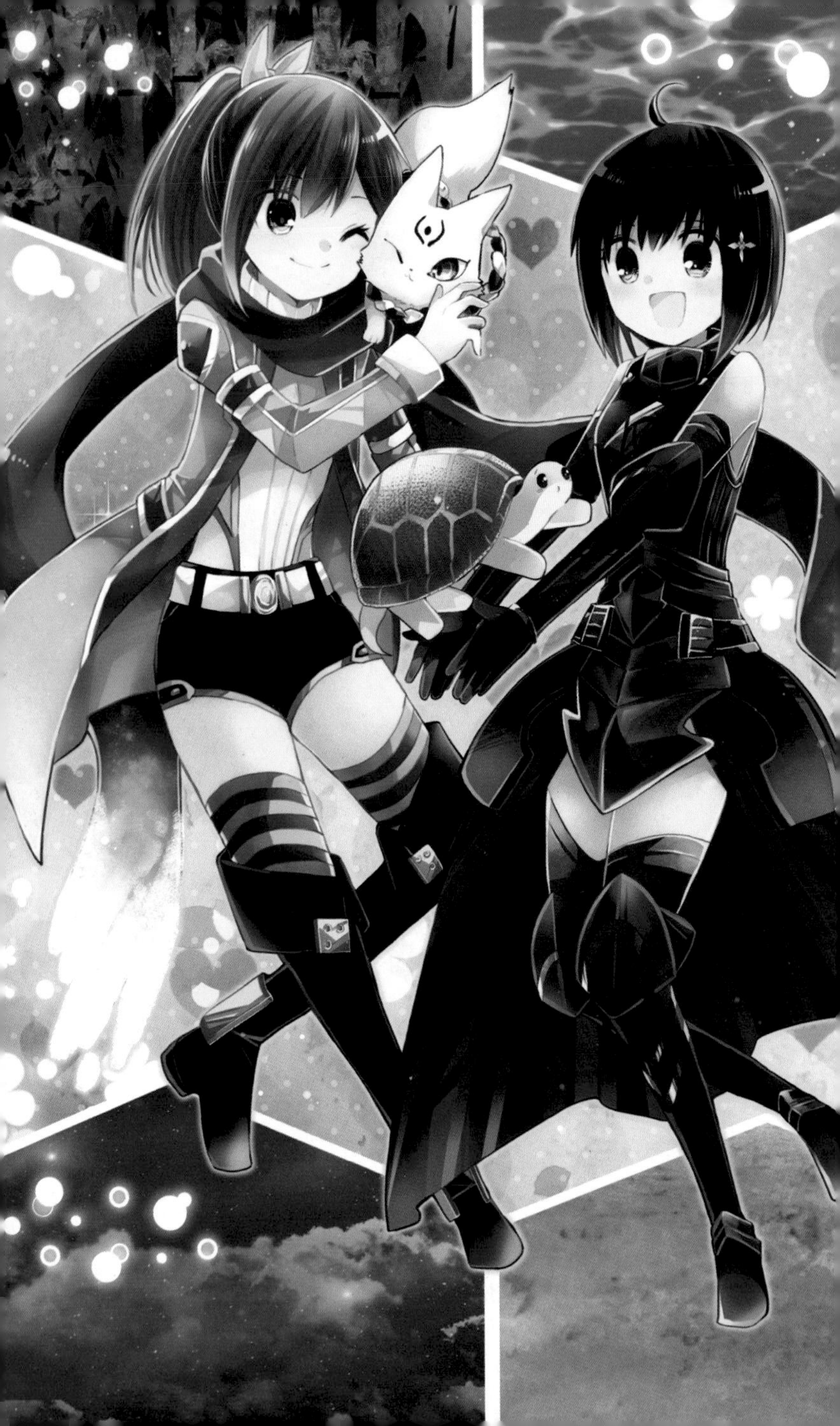

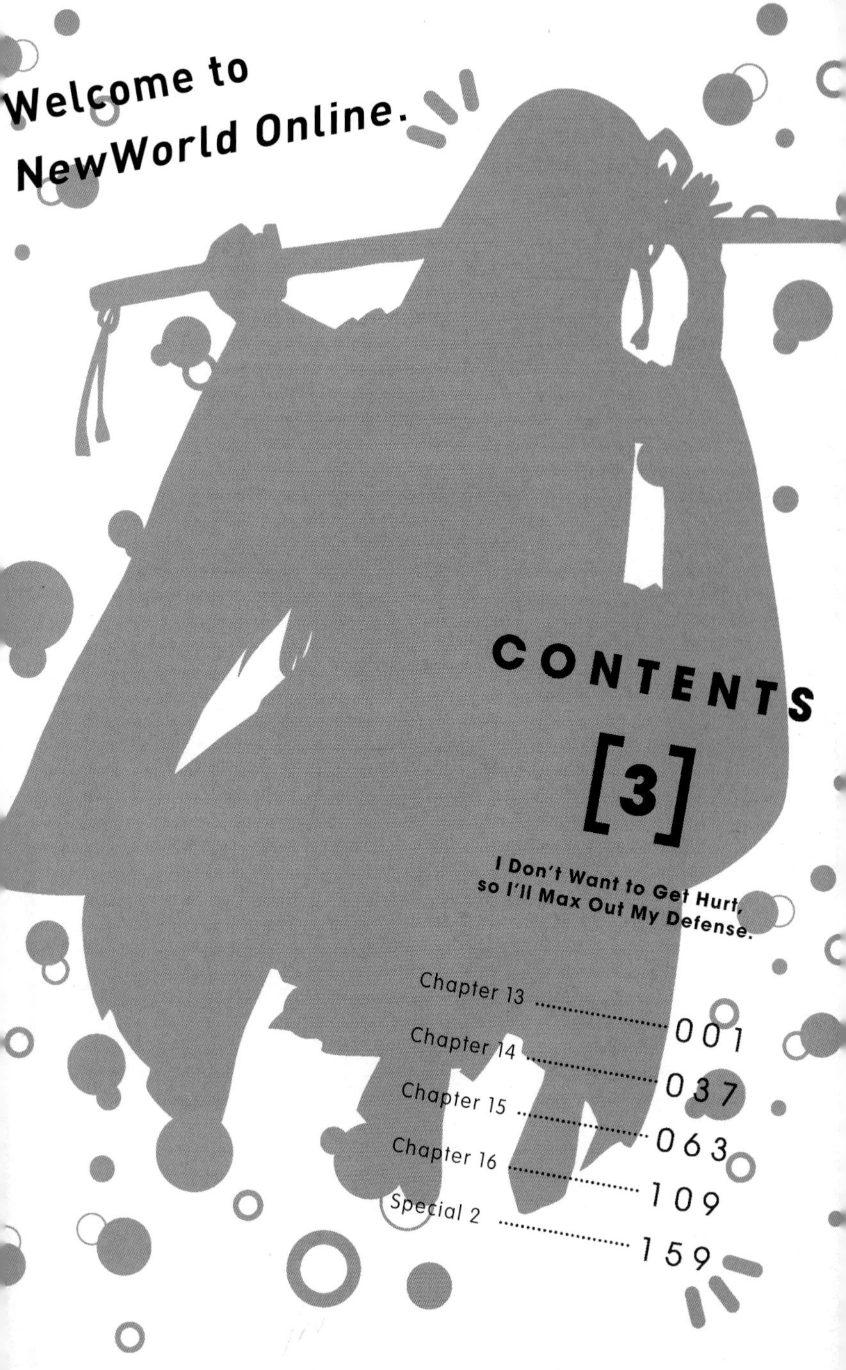

Welcome to NewWorld Online.

CONTENTS

[3]

I Don't Want to Get Hurt, so I'll Max Out My Defense.

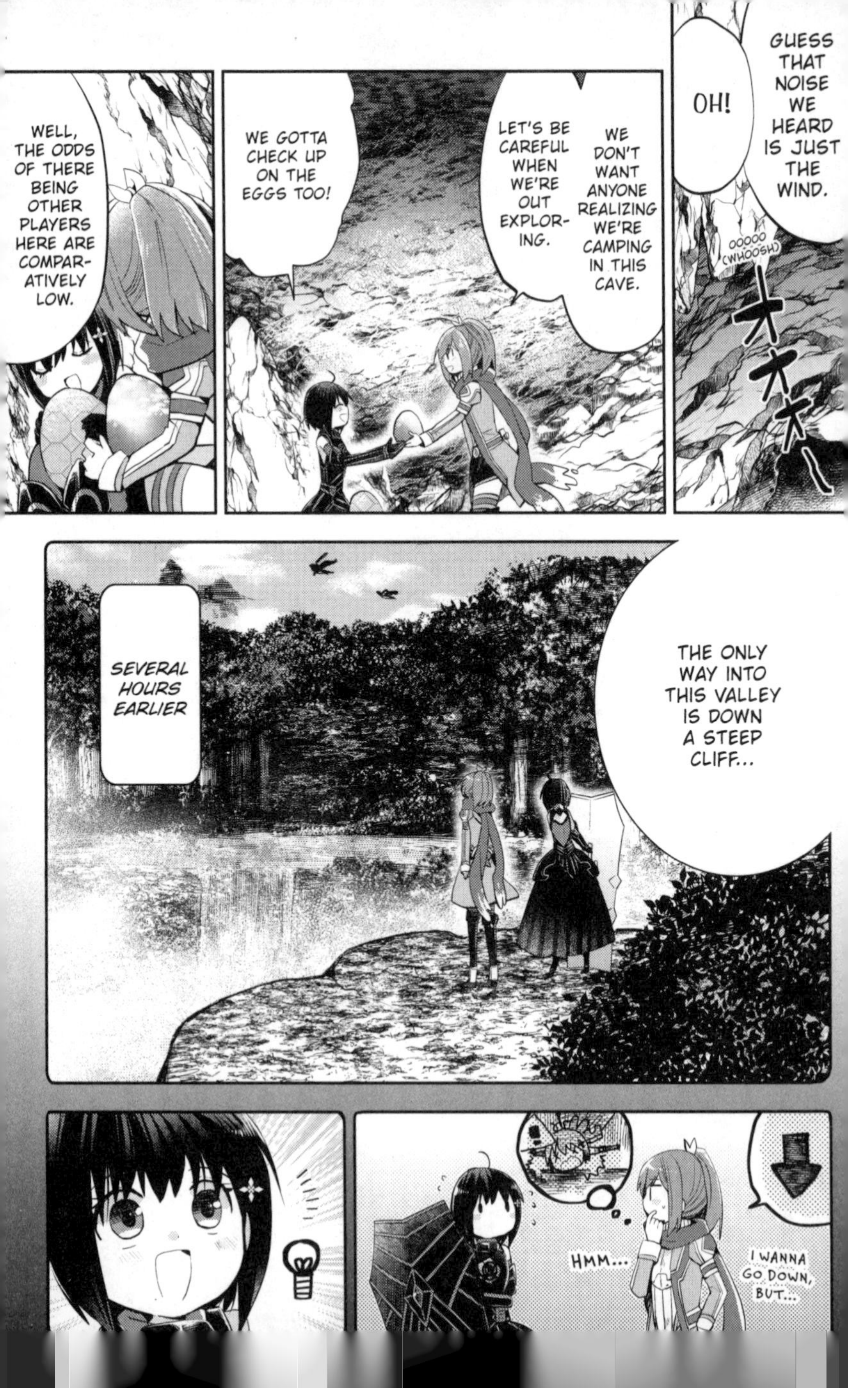
GUESS THAT NOISE WE HEARD IS JUST THE WIND.
OH!
OOOOO (WHOOSH)
LET'S BE CAREFUL WHEN WE'RE OUT EXPLORING.
WE DON'T WANT ANYONE REALIZING WE'RE CAMPING IN THIS CAVE.
WE GOTTA CHECK UP ON THE EGGS TOO!
WELL, THE ODDS OF THERE BEING OTHER PLAYERS HERE ARE COMPARATIVELY LOW.
THE ONLY WAY INTO THIS VALLEY IS DOWN A STEEP CLIFF...
SEVERAL HOURS EARLIER
I WANNA GO DOWN, BUT...
HMM...

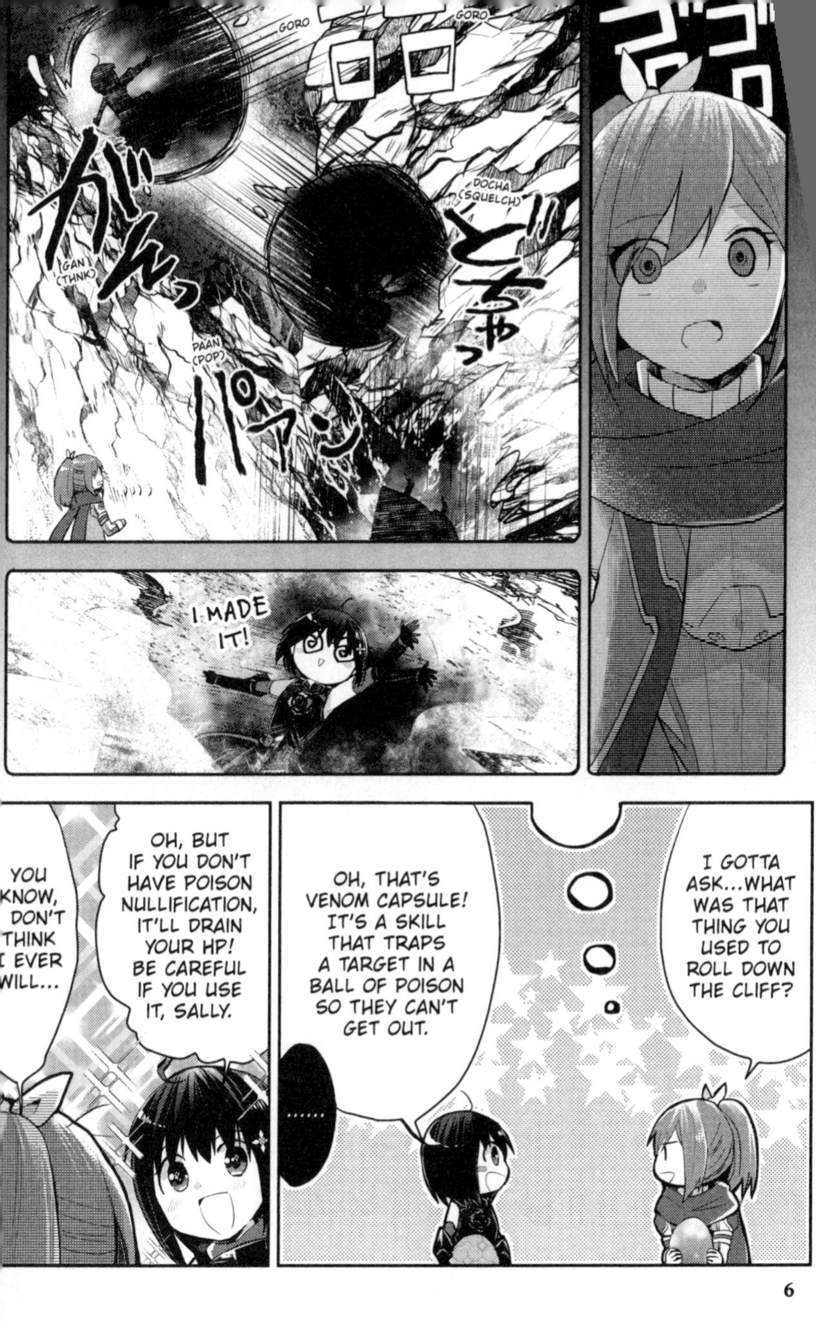
GORO
GORO
DOCHA (SQUELCH)
GAN (THNK)
PAAN (POP)
I MADE IT!
I GOTTA ASK...WHAT WAS THAT THING YOU USED TO ROLL DOWN THE CLIFF?
OH, THAT'S VENOM CAPSULE! IT'S A SKILL THAT TRAPS A TARGET IN A BALL OF POISON SO THEY CAN'T GET OUT.
......
OH, BUT IF YOU DON'T HAVE POISON NULLIFICATION, IT'LL DRAIN YOUR HP! BE CAREFUL IF YOU USE IT, SALLY.
YOU KNOW, DON'T THINK EVER WILL...

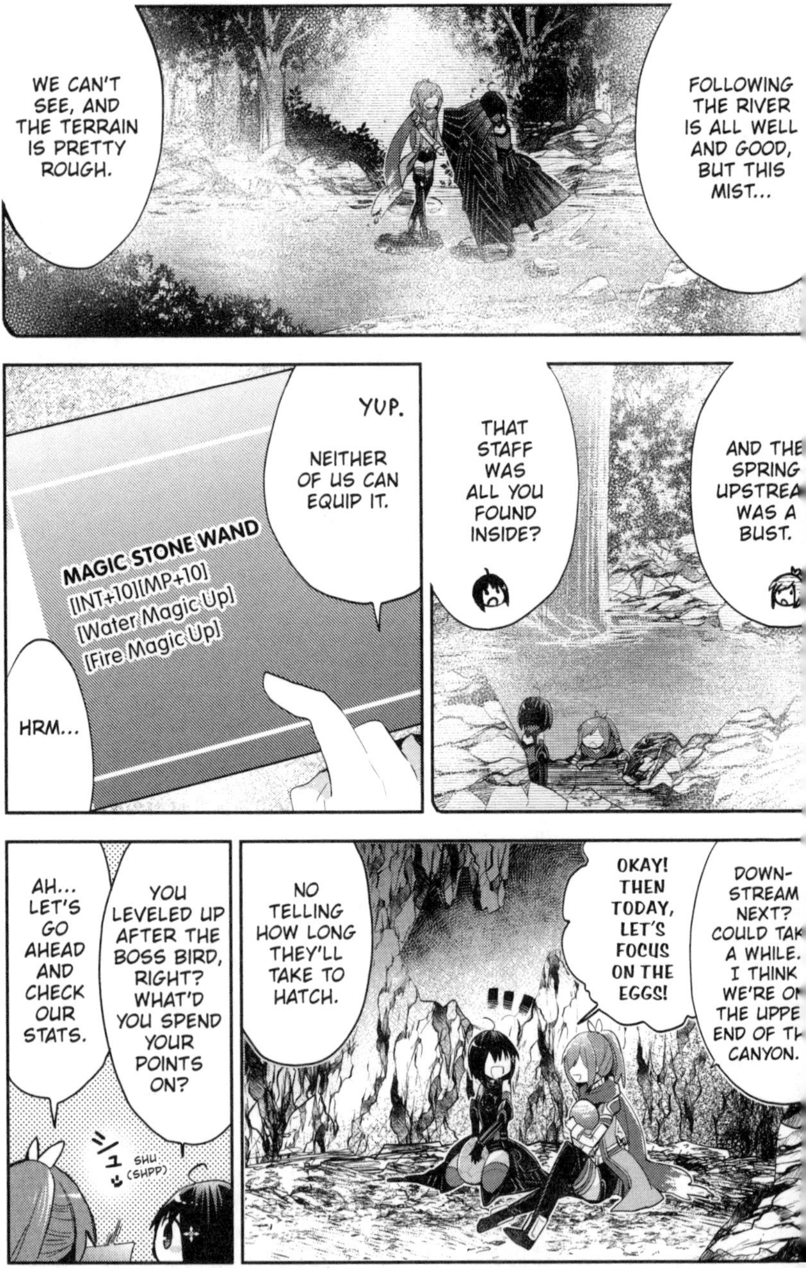
FOLLOWING THE RIVER IS ALL WELL AND GOOD, BUT THIS MIST...
WE CAN'T SEE, AND THE TERRAIN IS PRETTY ROUGH.
AND THE SPRING UPSTREA WAS A BUST.
THAT STAFF WAS ALL YOU FOUND INSIDE?
YUP.
NEITHER OF US CAN EQUIP IT.
MAGIC STONE WAND
[INT+10][MP+10]
[Water Magic Up]
[Fire Magic Up]
HRM...
DOWN-STREAM NEXT? COULD TAK A WHILE. I THINK WE'RE O THE UPPE END OF T CANYON.
OKAY! THEN TODAY, LET'S FOCUS ON THE EGGS!
NO TELLING HOW LONG THEY'LL TAKE TO HATCH.
YOU LEVELED UP AFTER THE BOSS BIRD, RIGHT? WHAT'D YOU SPEND YOUR POINTS ON?
AH... LET'S GO AHEAD AND CHECK OUR STATS.
SHU (SHPP)

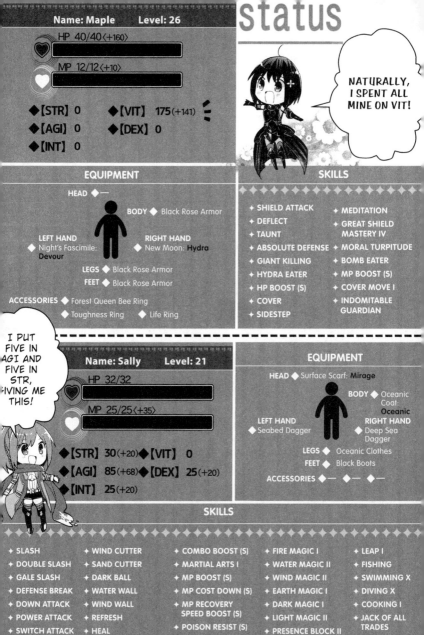

status

NATURALLY, I SPENT ALL MINE ON VIT!

Name: Maple **Level: 26**

HP 40/40〈+160〉

MP 12/12〈+10〉

◆【STR】 0 ◆【VIT】 175(+141)
◆【AGI】 0 ◆【DEX】 0
◆【INT】 0

EQUIPMENT

HEAD ◆—

BODY ◆ Black Rose Armor

LEFT HAND ◆ Night's Fascimile: **Devour**

RIGHT HAND ◆ New Moon: **Hydra**

LEGS ◆ Black Rose Armor

FEET ◆ Black Rose Armor

ACCESSORIES ◆ Forest Queen Bee Ring ◆ Toughness Ring ◆ Life Ring

SKILLS

- ✦ SHIELD ATTACK
- ✦ DEFLECT
- ✦ TAUNT
- ✦ ABSOLUTE DEFENSE
- ✦ GIANT KILLING
- ✦ HYDRA EATER
- ✦ HP BOOST (S)
- ✦ COVER
- ✦ SIDESTEP
- ✦ MEDITATION
- ✦ GREAT SHIELD MASTERY IV
- ✦ MORAL TURPITUDE
- ✦ BOMB EATER
- ✦ MP BOOST (S)
- ✦ COVER MOVE I
- ✦ INDOMITABLE GUARDIAN

I PUT FIVE IN AGI AND FIVE IN STR, GIVING ME THIS!

Name: Sally **Level: 21**

HP 32/32

MP 25/25〈+35〉

◆【STR】 30(+20) ◆【VIT】 0
◆【AGI】 85(+68) ◆【DEX】 25(+20)
◆【INT】 25(+20)

EQUIPMENT

HEAD ◆ Surface Scarf: **Mirage**

BODY ◆ Oceanic Coat: **Oceanic**

LEFT HAND ◆ Seabed Dagger

RIGHT HAND ◆ Deep Sea Dagger

LEGS ◆ Oceanic Clothes

FEET ◆ Black Boots

ACCESSORIES ◆— ◆— ◆—

SKILLS

- ✦ SLASH
- ✦ DOUBLE SLASH
- ✦ GALE SLASH
- ✦ DEFENSE BREAK
- ✦ DOWN ATTACK
- ✦ POWER ATTACK
- ✦ SWITCH ATTACK
- ✦ FIRE BALL
- ✦ WATER BALL
- ✦ WIND CUTTER
- ✦ SAND CUTTER
- ✦ DARK BALL
- ✦ WATER WALL
- ✦ WIND WALL
- ✦ REFRESH
- ✦ HEAL
- ✦ AFFLICTION III
- ✦ STRENGTH BOOST (S)
- ✦ COMBO BOOST (S)
- ✦ MARTIAL ARTS I
- ✦ MP BOOST (S)
- ✦ MP COST DOWN (S)
- ✦ MP RECOVERY SPEED BOOST (S)
- ✦ POISON RESIST (S)
- ✦ GATHERING SPEED BOOST (S)
- ✦ DAGGER MASTERY II
- ✦ MAGIC MASTERY II
- ✦ FIRE MAGIC I
- ✦ WATER MAGIC II
- ✦ WIND MAGIC II
- ✦ EARTH MAGIC I
- ✦ DARK MAGIC I
- ✦ LIGHT MAGIC II
- ✦ PRESENCE BLOCK II
- ✦ PRESENCE DETECT II
- ✦ SNEAKY STEPS I
- ✦ LEAP I
- ✦ FISHING
- ✦ SWIMMING X
- ✦ DIVING X
- ✦ COOKING I
- ✦ JACK OF ALL TRADES
- ✦ SUPERSPEED

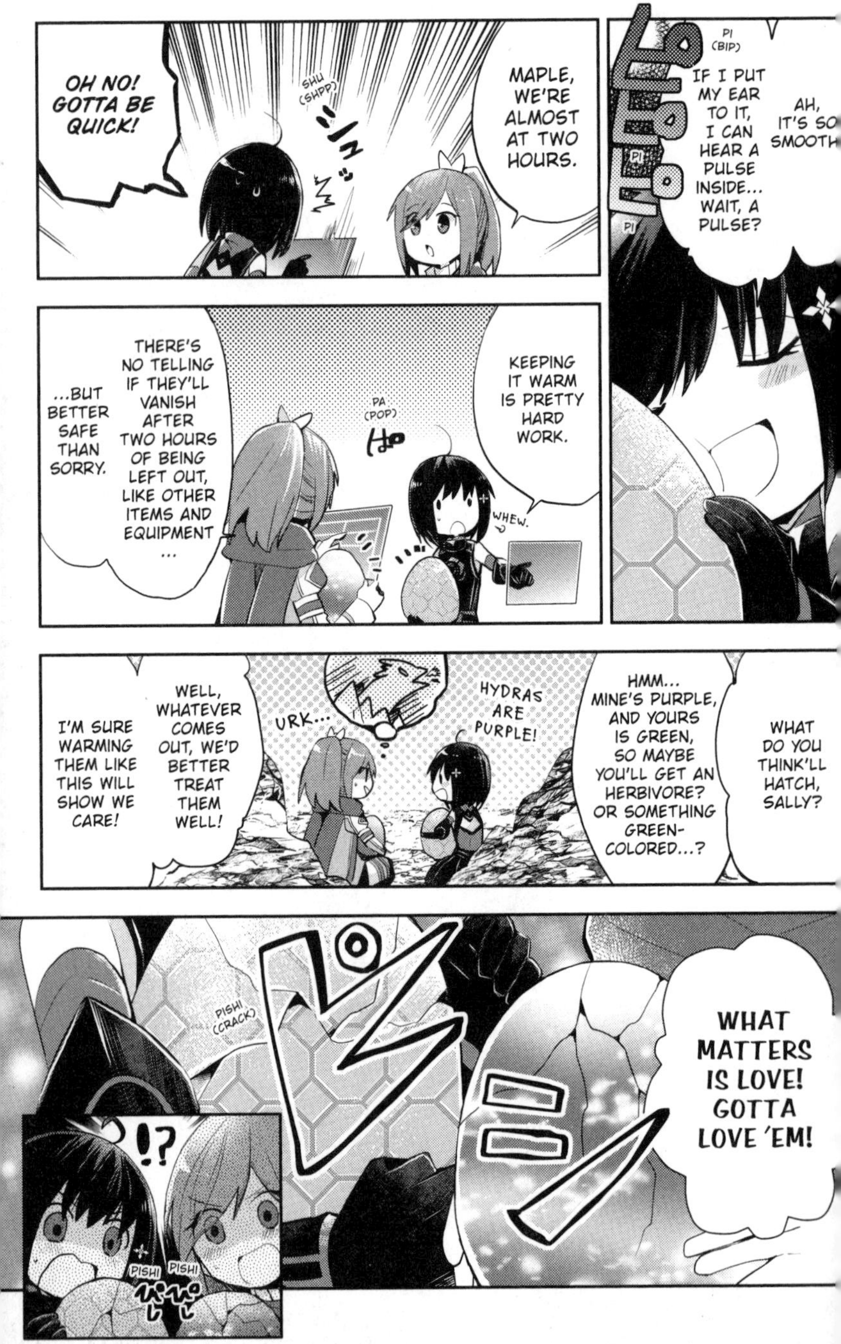
PI (BIP)
AH, IT'S SO SMOOTH
IF I PUT MY EAR TO IT, I CAN HEAR A PULSE INSIDE... WAIT, A PULSE?
PI
PI
MAPLE, WE'RE ALMOST AT TWO HOURS.
SHU (SHPP)
OH NO! GOTTA BE QUICK!
KEEPING IT WARM IS PRETTY HARD WORK.
WHEW.
PA (POP)
THERE'S NO TELLING IF THEY'LL VANISH AFTER TWO HOURS OF BEING LEFT OUT, LIKE OTHER ITEMS AND EQUIPMENT...
...BUT BETTER SAFE THAN SORRY.
WHAT DO YOU THINK'LL HATCH, SALLY?
HMM... MINE'S PURPLE, AND YOURS IS GREEN, SO MAYBE YOU'LL GET AN HERBIVORE? OR SOMETHING GREEN-COLORED...?
HYDRAS ARE PURPLE!
URK...
WELL, WHATEVER COMES OUT, WE'D BETTER TREAT THEM WELL!
I'M SURE WARMING THEM LIKE THIS WILL SHOW WE CARE!
WHAT MATTERS IS LOVE! GOTTA LOVE 'EM!
PISHI (CRACK)
!?
PISHI PISHI

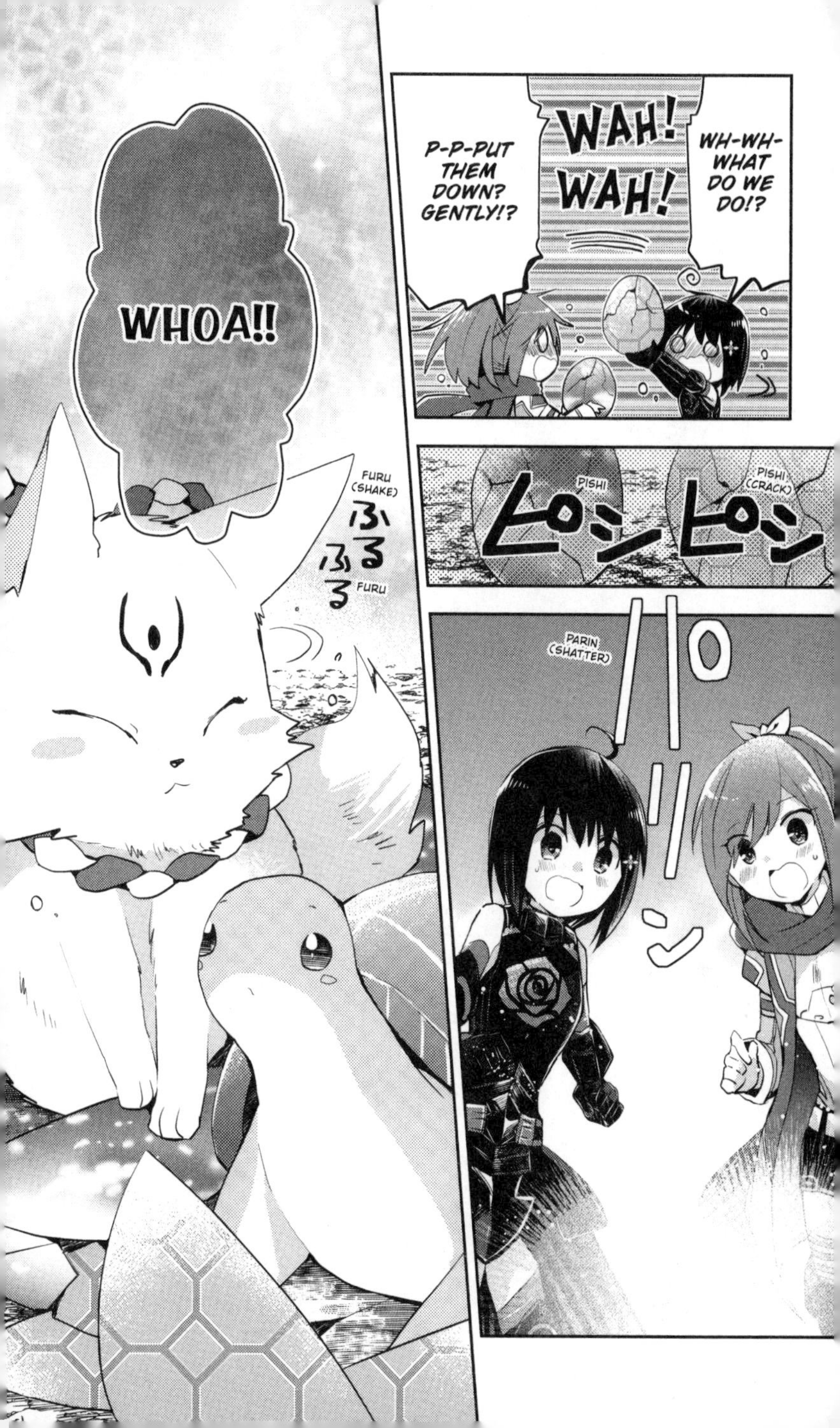
WH-WH-WHAT DO WE DO!?
WAH! WAH!
P-P-PUT THEM DOWN? GENTLY!?
PISHI (CRACK)
PISHI
PARIN (SHATTER)
WHOA!!
ふるふる
FURU (SHAKE)
FURU

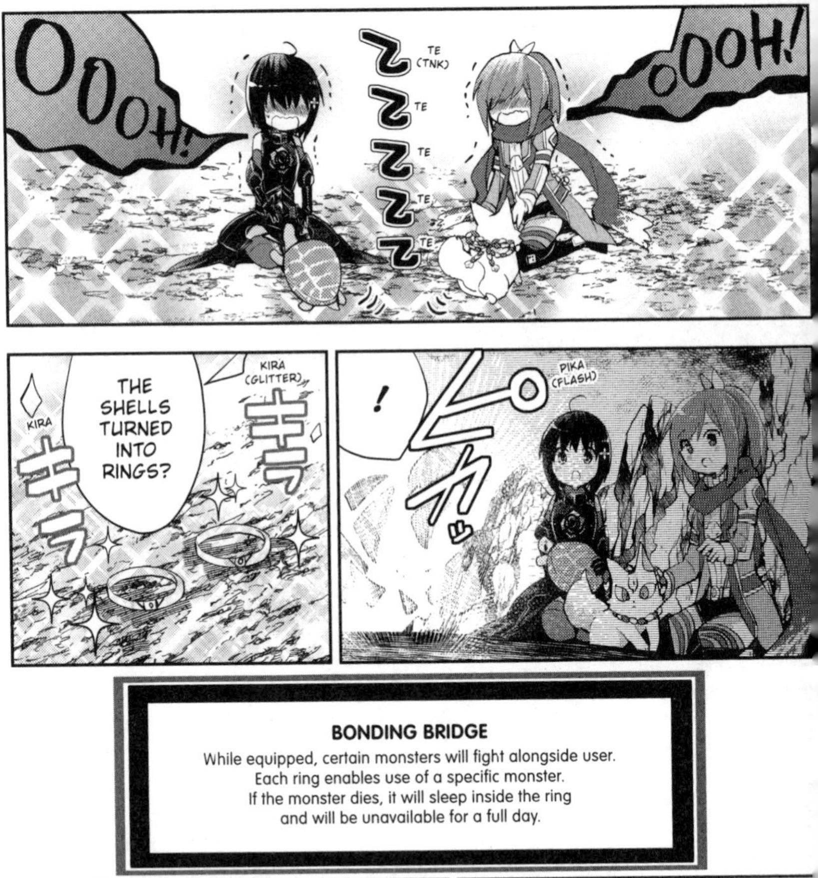
OOOH!
TE (TNK)
TE
TE
TE
TE
OOOH!
!
PIKA (FLASH)
KIRA (GLITTER)
THE SHELLS TURNED INTO RINGS?
KIRA

BONDING BRIDGE

While equipped, certain monsters will fight alongside user.
Each ring enables use of a specific monster.
If the monster dies, it will sleep inside the ring
and will be unavailable for a full day.

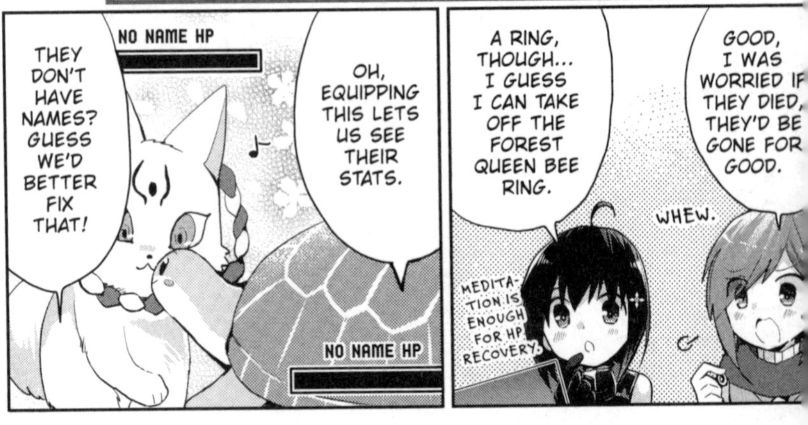
GOOD, I WAS WORRIED IF THEY DIED, THEY'D BE GONE FOR GOOD.
WHEW.
A RING, THOUGH... I GUESS I CAN TAKE OFF THE FOREST QUEEN BEE RING.
MEDITATION IS ENOUGH FOR HP RECOVERY.
OH, EQUIPPING THIS LETS US SEE THEIR STATS.
NO NAME HP
THEY DON'T HAVE NAMES? GUESS WE'D BETTER FIX THAT!
NO NAME HP

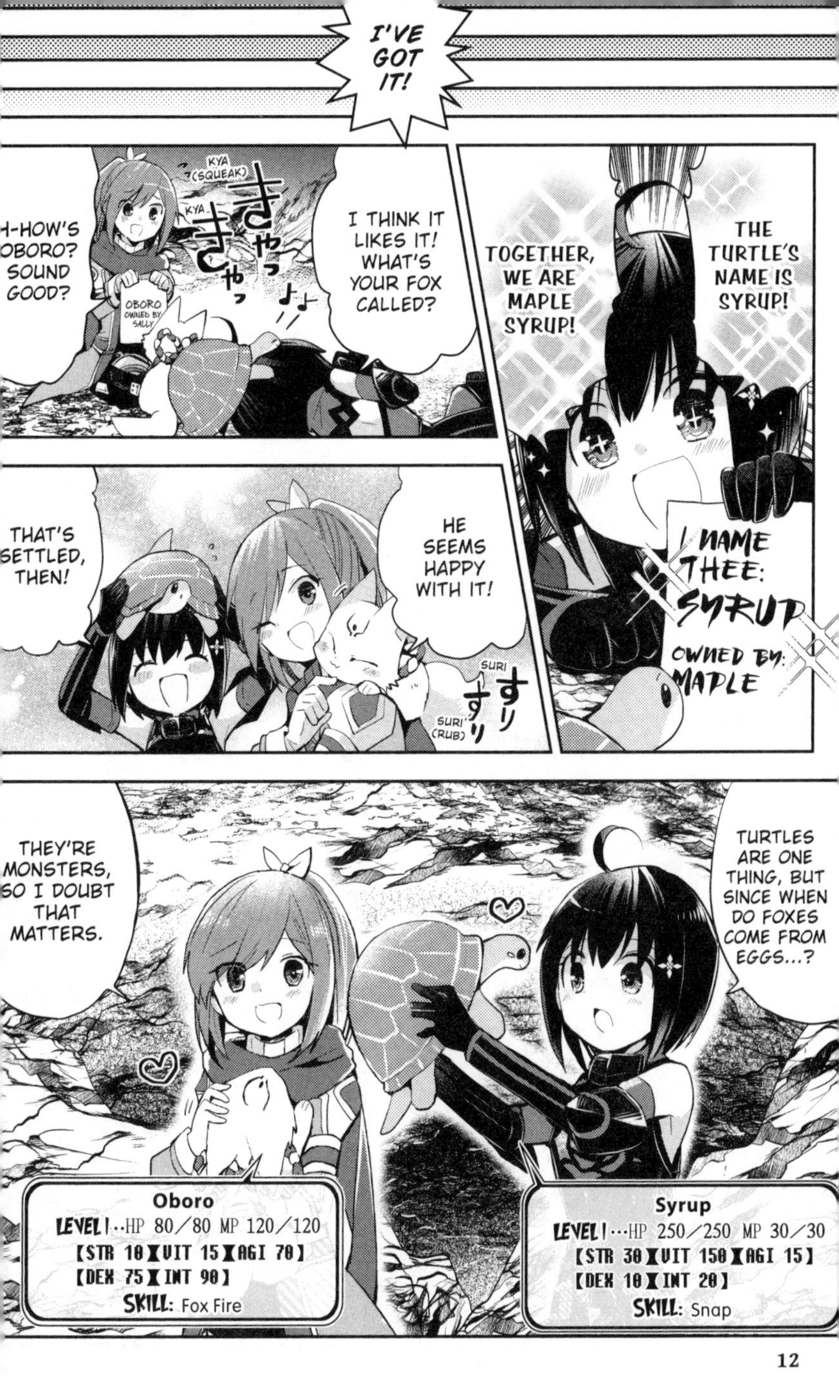
I'VE GOT IT!
THE TURTLE'S NAME IS SYRUP!
TOGETHER, WE ARE MAPLE SYRUP!
I NAME THEE: SYRUP
OWNED BY: MAPLE
I THINK IT LIKES IT! WHAT'S YOUR FOX CALLED?
KYA (SQUEAK) きゃっ
KYA きゃっ
H-HOW'S OBORO? SOUND GOOD?
OBORO OWNED BY: SALLY
HE SEEMS HAPPY WITH IT!
SURI すり
SURI (RUB) すり
THAT'S SETTLED, THEN!
TURTLES ARE ONE THING, BUT SINCE WHEN DO FOXES COME FROM EGGS...?
THEY'RE MONSTERS, SO I DOUBT THAT MATTERS.
Syrup
LEVEL 1 ··HP 250/250 MP 30/30
【STR 30】【VIT 150】【AGI 15】
【DEX 10】【INT 20】
SKILL: Snap
Oboro
LEVEL 1 ··HP 80/80 MP 120/120
【STR 10】【VIT 15】【AGI 70】
【DEX 75】【INT 90】
SKILL: Fox Fire

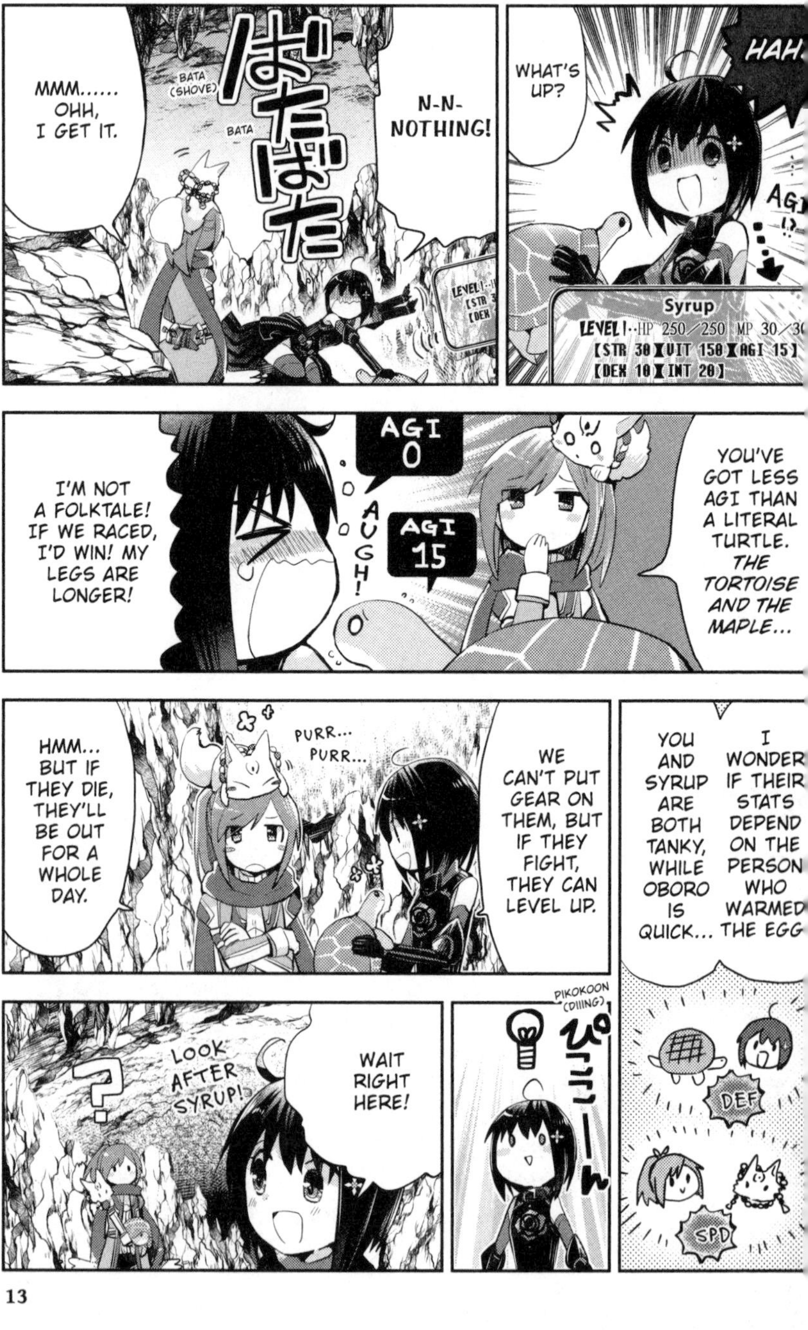
HAH!
WHAT'S UP?
AGI !?
Syrup
LEVEL 1 ·· HP 250/250 MP 30/3
[STR 30][VIT 150][AGI 15]
[DEX 10][INT 20]
N-N-NOTHING!
ばたばた
BATA (SHOVE)
BATA
MMM...... OHH, I GET IT.
YOU'VE GOT LESS AGI THAN A LITERAL TURTLE. THE TORTOISE AND THE MAPLE...
AGI 15
AGI 0
AUGH!
I'M NOT A FOLKTALE! IF WE RACED, I'D WIN! MY LEGS ARE LONGER!
I WONDER IF THEIR STATS DEPEND ON THE PERSON WHO WARMED THE EGG
YOU AND SYRUP ARE BOTH TANKY, WHILE OBORO IS QUICK...
DEF
SPD
WE CAN'T PUT GEAR ON THEM, BUT IF THEY FIGHT, THEY CAN LEVEL UP.
PURR... PURR...
HMM... BUT IF THEY DIE, THEY'LL BE OUT FOR A WHOLE DAY.
PIKOKOON (DIIING)
ぴこーん
WAIT RIGHT HERE!
LOOK AFTER SYRUP!
?

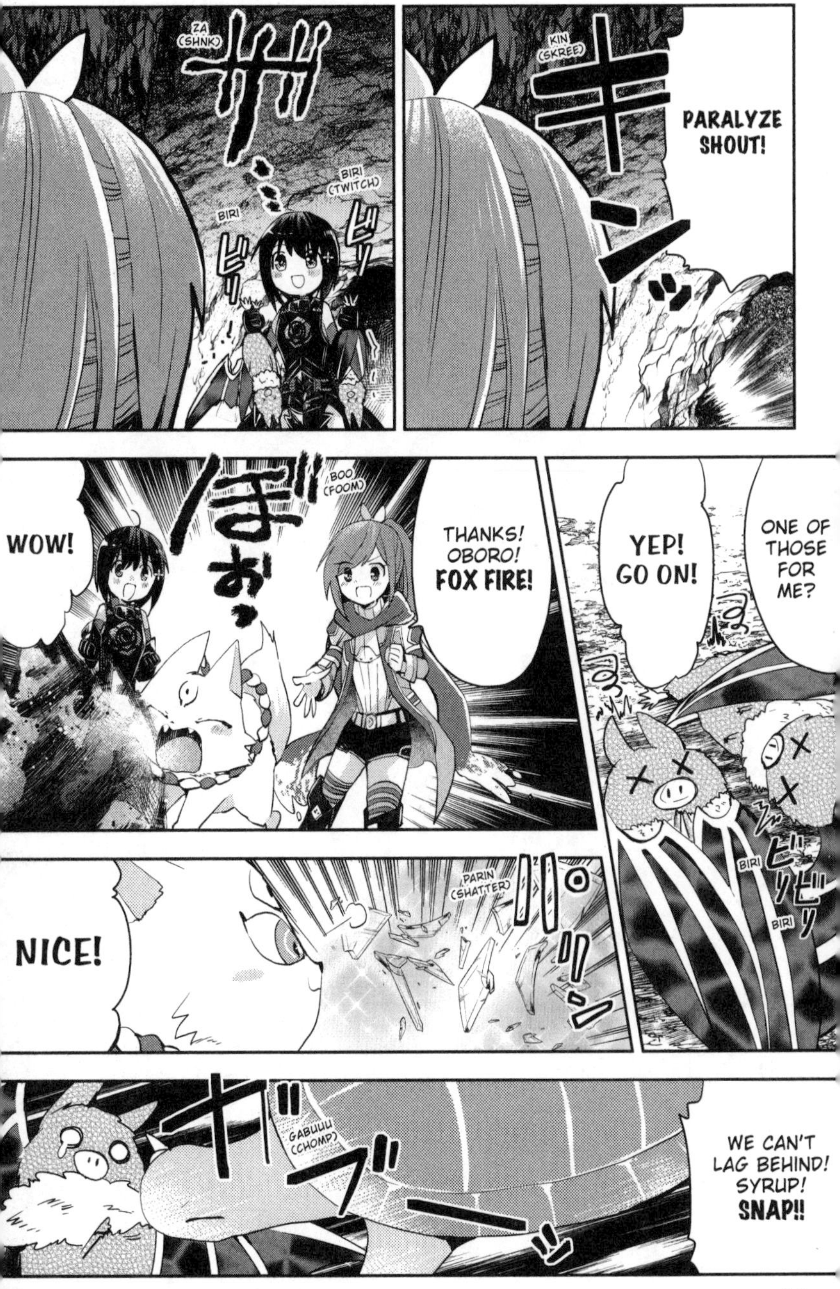
KIN (SKREE)
PARALYZE SHOUT!
ZA (SHNK)
BIRI (TWITCH)
BIRI
ONE OF THOSE FOR ME?
YEP! GO ON!
BIRI
BIRI
THANKS! OBORO! **FOX FIRE!**
BOO (FOOM)
WOW!
PARIN (SHATTER)
NICE!
WE CAN'T LAG BEHIND! SYRUP! **SNAP!!**
GABUUU (CHOMP)

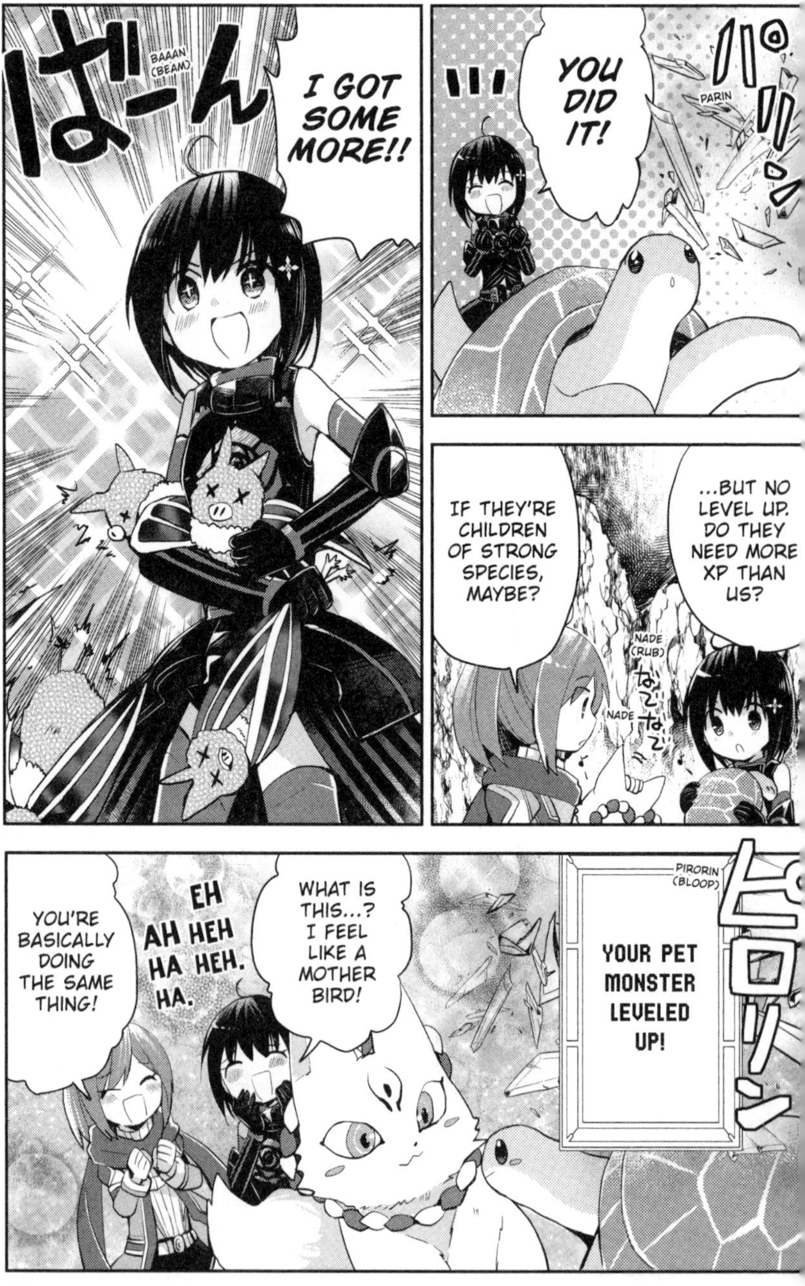
PARIN
YOU DID IT!
...BUT NO LEVEL UP. DO THEY NEED MORE XP THAN US?
IF THEY'RE CHILDREN OF STRONG SPECIES, MAYBE?
NADE (RUB)
なでなで
NADE
ばーん
BAAAN (BEAM)
I GOT SOME MORE!!
PIRORIN (BLOOP)
ピロリン
YOUR PET MONSTER LEVELED UP!
WHAT IS THIS...? I FEEL LIKE A MOTHER BIRD!
EH AH HEH HA HEH. HA.
YOU'RE BASICALLY DOING THE SAME THING!

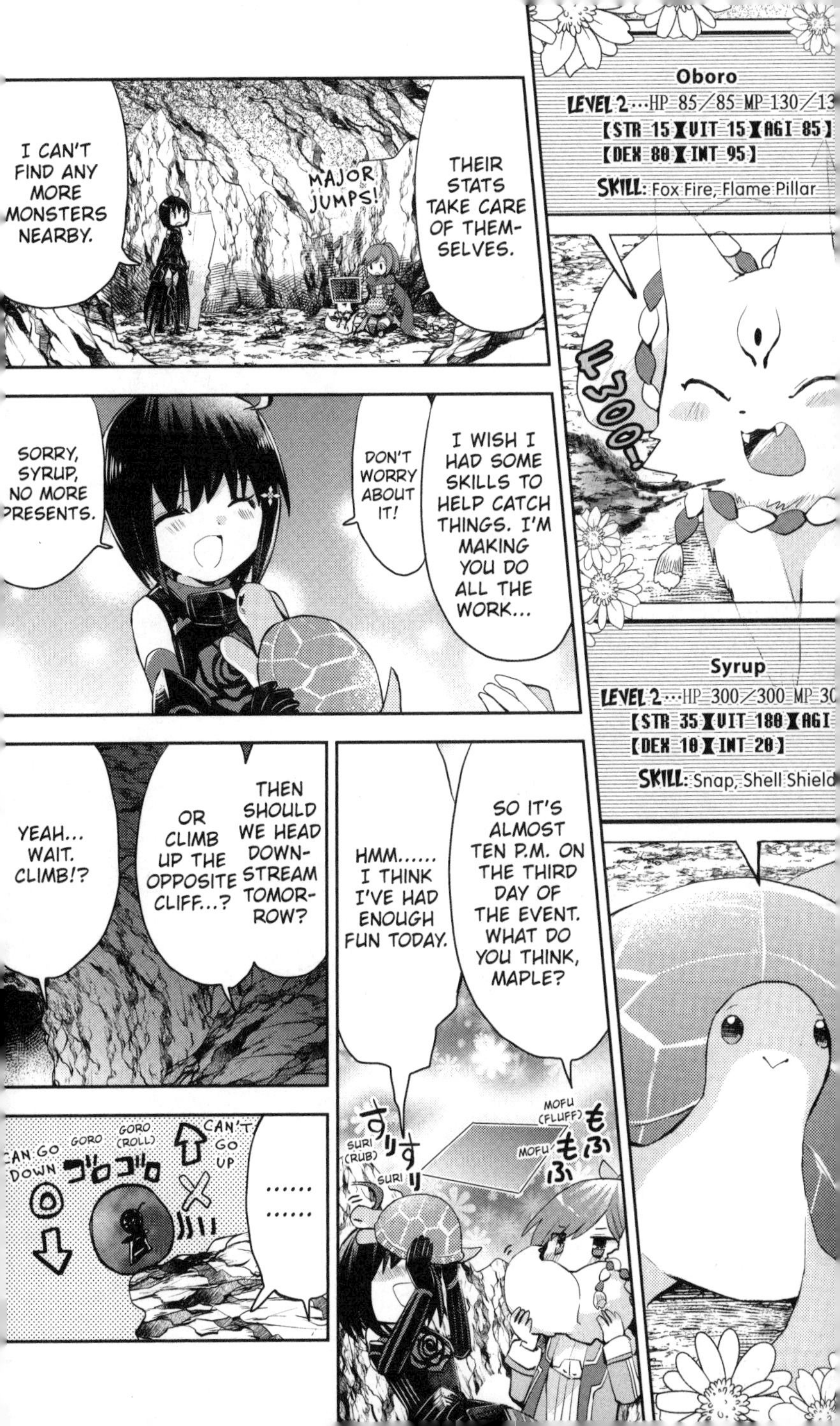
Oboro
LEVEL 2…HP 85/85 MP 130/13
【STR 15】【VIT 15】【AGI 85】
【DEX 80】【INT 95】
SKILL: Fox Fire, Flame Pillar
FWOO!
Syrup
LEVEL 2…HP 300/300 MP 30
【STR 35】【VIT 180】【AGI
【DEX 10】【INT 20】
SKILL: Snap, Shell Shield
THEIR STATS TAKE CARE OF THEMSELVES.
MAJOR JUMPS!
I CAN'T FIND ANY MORE MONSTERS NEARBY.
I WISH I HAD SOME SKILLS TO HELP CATCH THINGS. I'M MAKING YOU DO ALL THE WORK…
DON'T WORRY ABOUT IT!
SORRY, SYRUP, NO MORE PRESENTS.
SO IT'S ALMOST TEN P.M. ON THE THIRD DAY OF THE EVENT. WHAT DO YOU THINK, MAPLE?
HMM…… I THINK I'VE HAD ENOUGH FUN TODAY.
もふもふ MOFU (FLUFF) MOFU
すりすり SURI (RUB) SURI
THEN SHOULD WE HEAD DOWNSTREAM TOMORROW?
OR CLIMB UP THE OPPOSITE CLIFF…?
YEAH… WAIT. CLIMB!?
……
……
CAN'T GO UP
ゴロゴロ GORO GORO (ROLL)
CAN GO DOWN

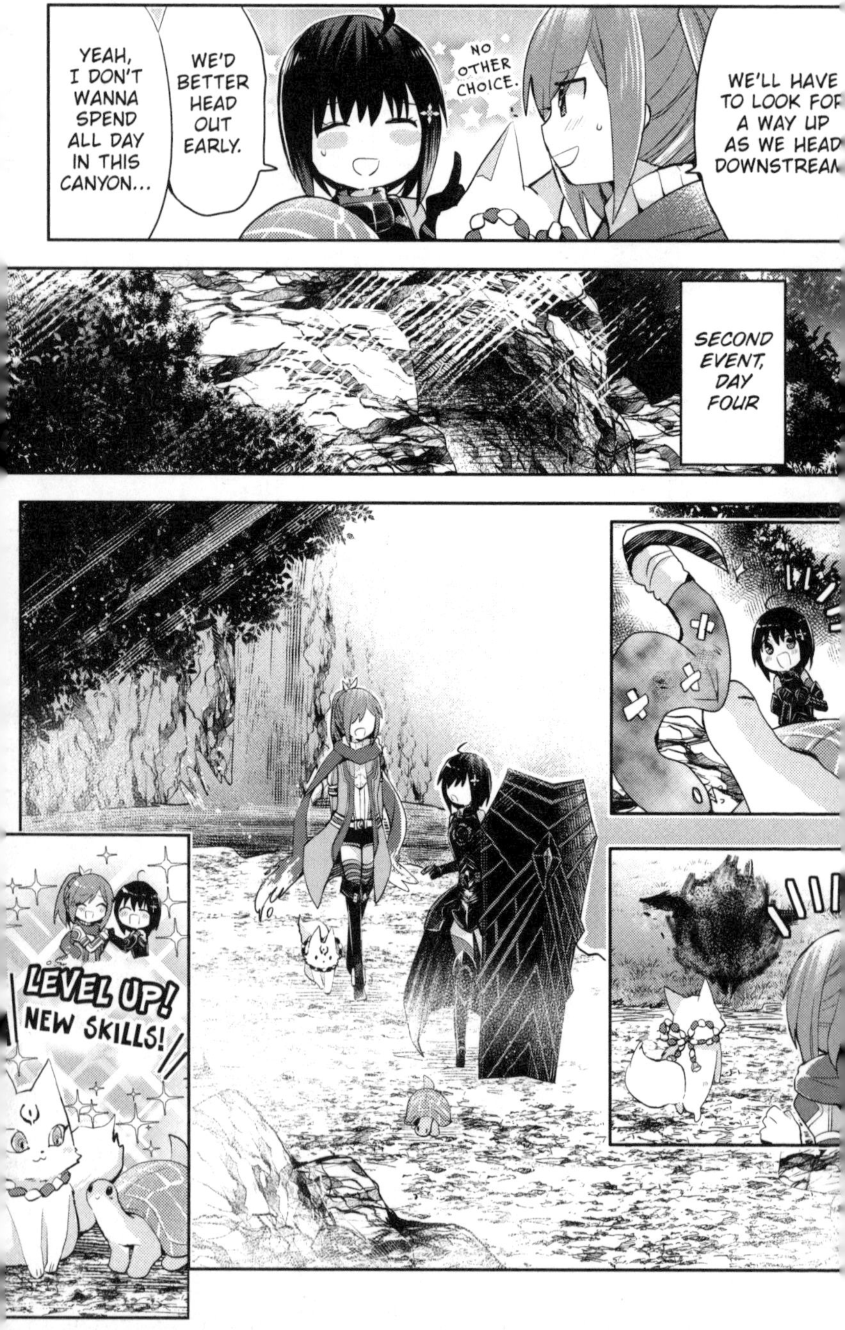
WE'LL HAVE TO LOOK FOR A WAY UP AS WE HEAD DOWNSTREAM
NO OTHER CHOICE.
WE'D BETTER HEAD OUT EARLY.
YEAH, I DON'T WANNA SPEND ALL DAY IN THIS CANYON...
SECOND EVENT, DAY FOUR
LEVEL UP! NEW SKILLS!

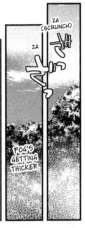

ZA (SCRUNCH)
ZA
FOG'S GETTING THICKER.
WAIT, SALLY ...?
THAT'S A ROCK, MAPLE.
THIS HAS TO BE THE SOURCE OF THE MIST.
YEAH, CLEARLY.
SHUGOOO (HISSSS)
SHOULD WE KEEP SYRUP AND OBORO IN THE RINGS?
GOOD IDEA. THIS IS TOO THICK FOR THEM.
I'M GLAD THEY BOTH LEARNED REST AND AWAKEN.
WE'D LOSE THEM INSTANTLY IN THIS.
ZAA (SCHAAA)
WIND!
!
IS THAT POT THE SOURCE OF THE FOG?
I THINK SO. I'LL CHECK IT OUT.
PAA (GLOW)
BASHA (SPLASH)
WHOA!
BUWA (FOOSH)

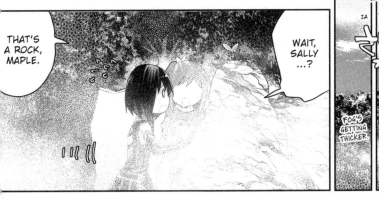

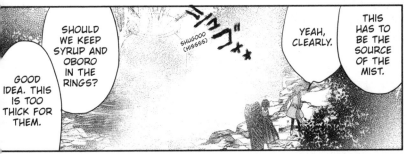

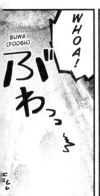

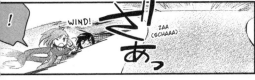

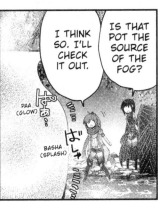

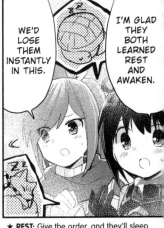

★ **REST:** Give the order, and they'll sleep inside the ring, safely recovering health.

AWAKEN: Give the order, and they'll emerge from the ring.

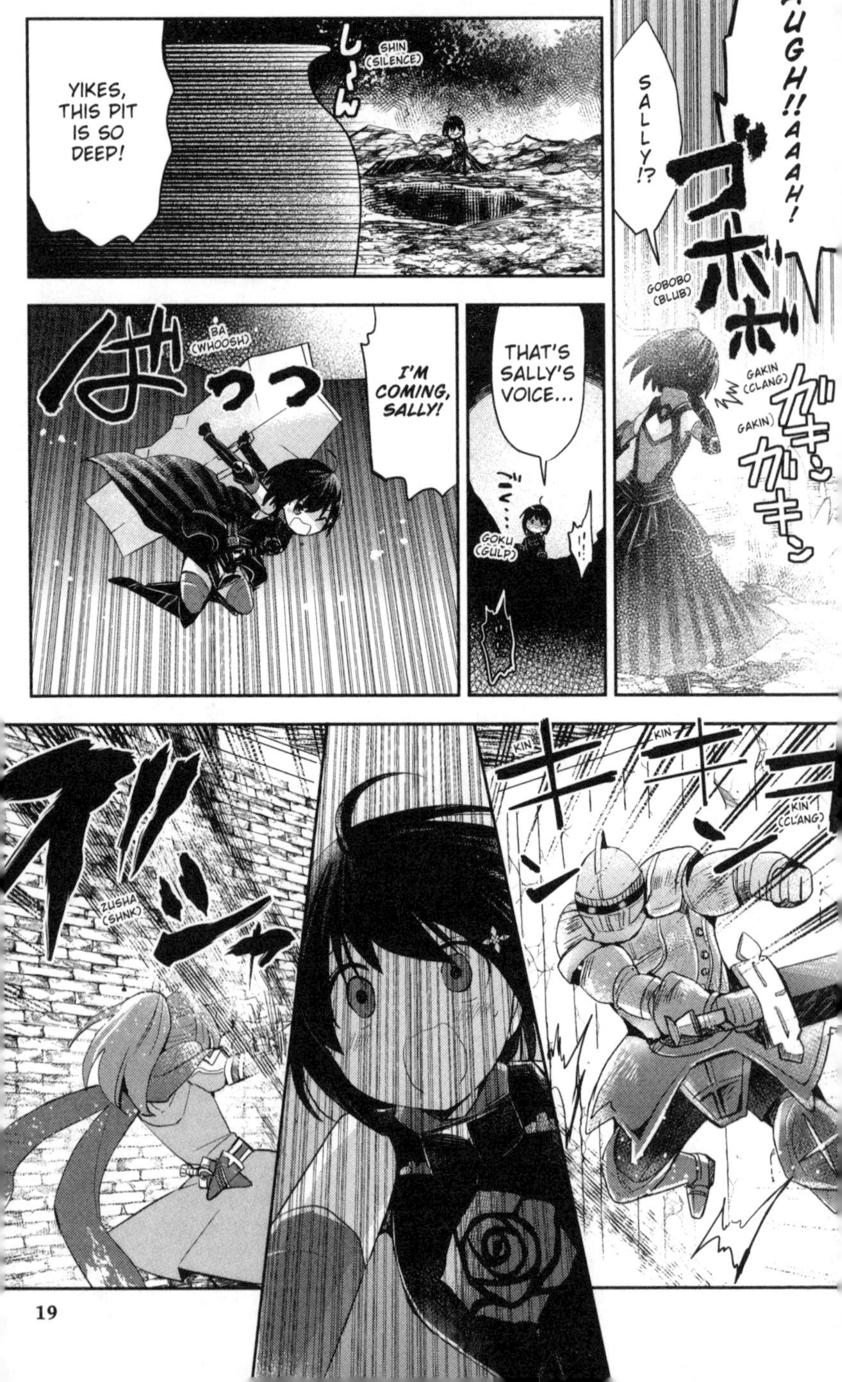
AUGH!! AAAAH!
SALLY!?
GOBOBO (BLUB)
GAKIN (CLANG) GAKIN)
YIKES, THIS PIT IS SO DEEP!
SHIN (SILENCE)
THAT'S SALLY'S VOICE...
GOKU (GULP)
I'M COMING, SALLY!
BA (WHOOSH)
KIN
KIN
KIN (CLANG)
ZUSHA (SHNK)

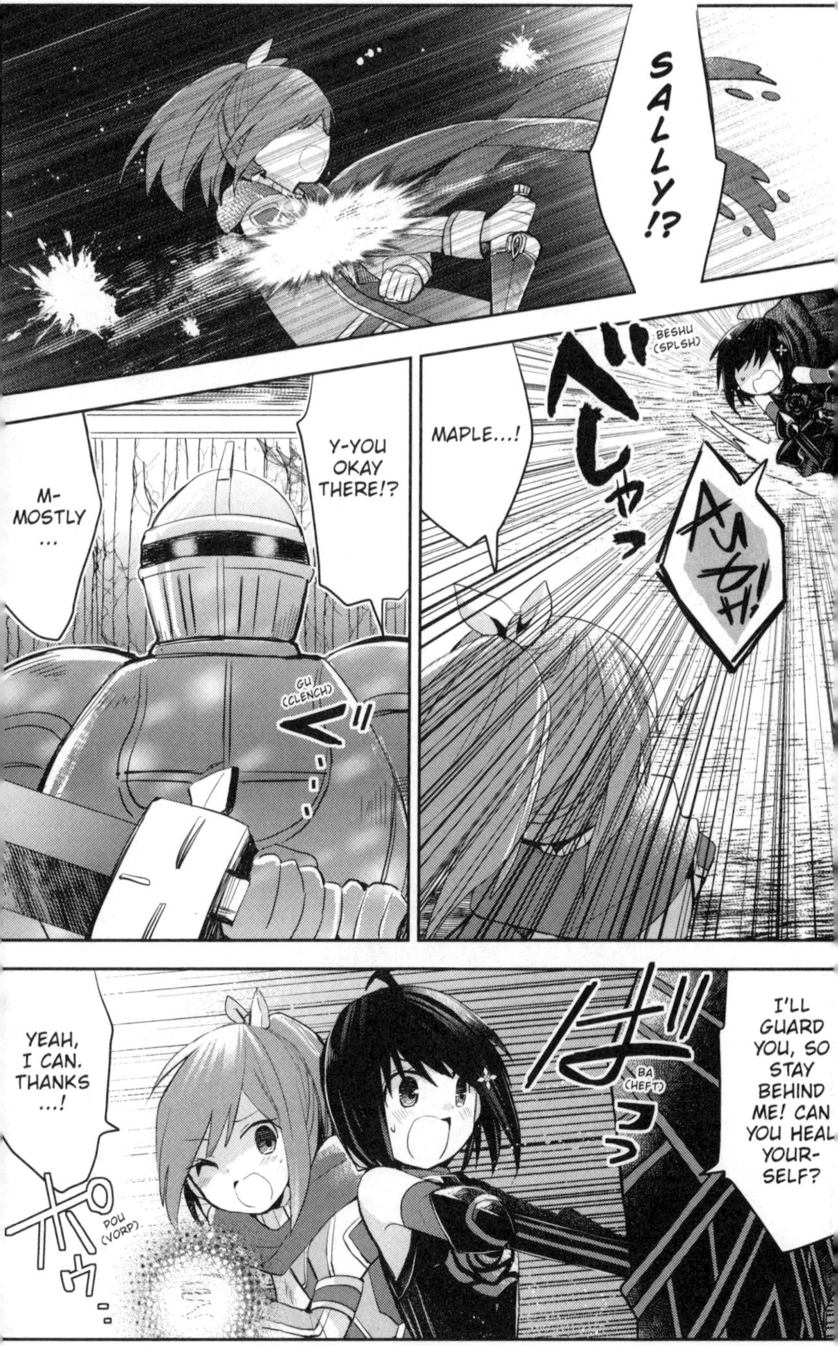
SALLY!?
べしゃっ
BESHU (SPLSH)
AUGH!
MAPLE...!
Y-YOU OKAY THERE!?
M-MOSTLY...
ぐ
GU (CLENCH)
I'LL GUARD YOU, SO STAY BEHIND ME! CAN YOU HEAL YOURSELF?
ばっ
BA (HEFT)
YEAH, I CAN. THANKS...!
ポゥ
POU (VORP)

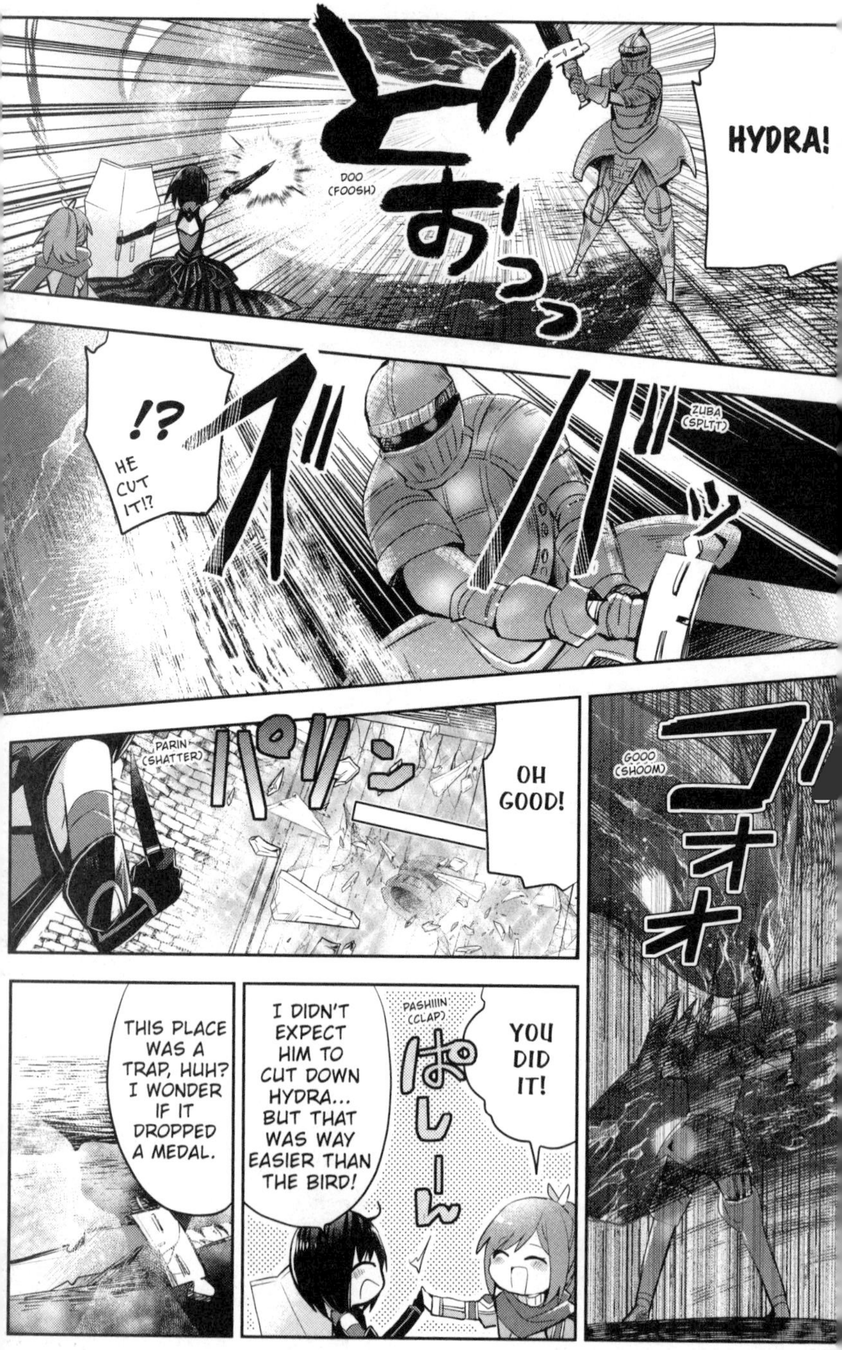
HYDRA!
DOO (FOOSH)
ZUBA (SPLTT)
!? HE CUT IT!?
GOOO (SHOOM)
PARIN (SHATTER)
OH GOOD!
YOU DID IT!
PASHIIIN (CLAP)
I DIDN'T EXPECT HIM TO CUT DOWN HYDRA... BUT THAT WAS WAY EASIER THAN THE BIRD!
THIS PLACE WAS A TRAP, HUH? I WONDER IF IT DROPPED A MEDAL.

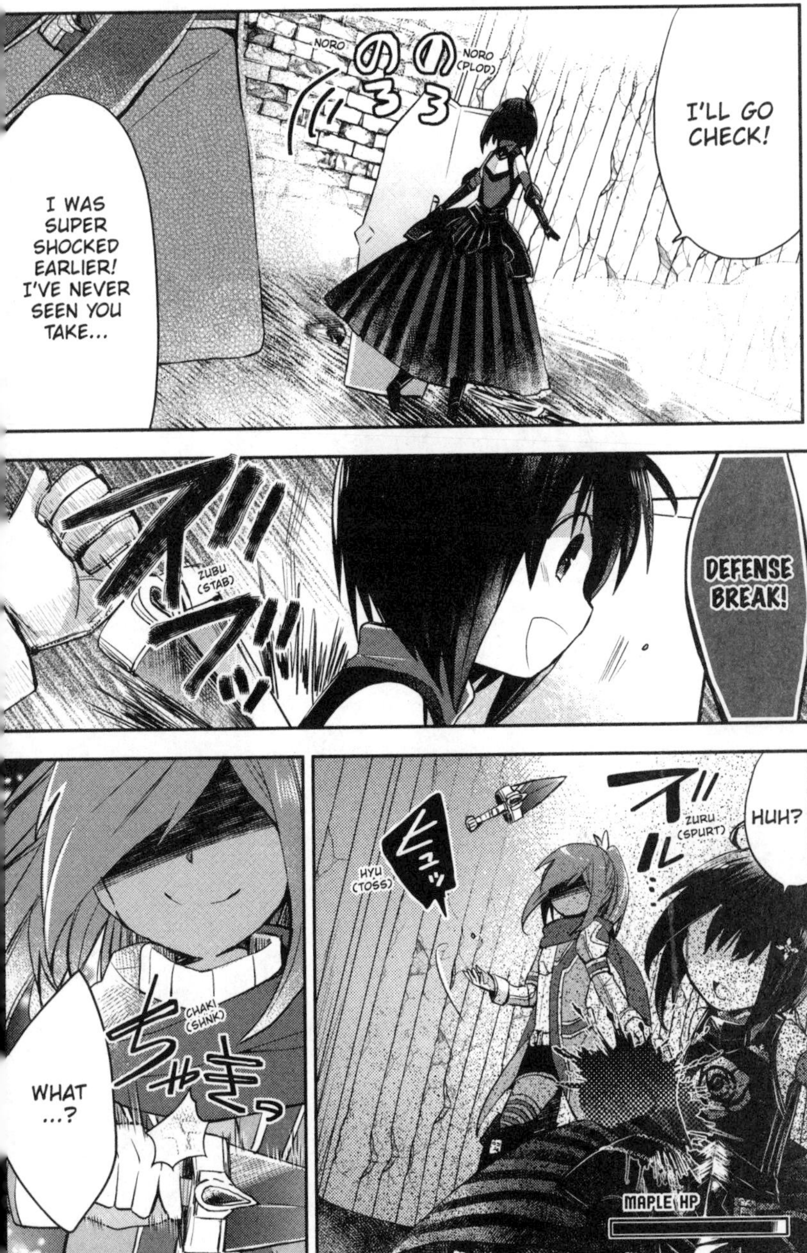
I'LL GO CHECK!
NORO (PLOD)
NORO
I WAS SUPER SHOCKED EARLIER! I'VE NEVER SEEN YOU TAKE...
...DAMAGE.
DEFENSE BREAK!
ZUBU (STAB)
HUH?
ZURU (SPURT)
HYU (TOSS)
MAPLE HP
CHAKI (SHNK)
WHAT ...?

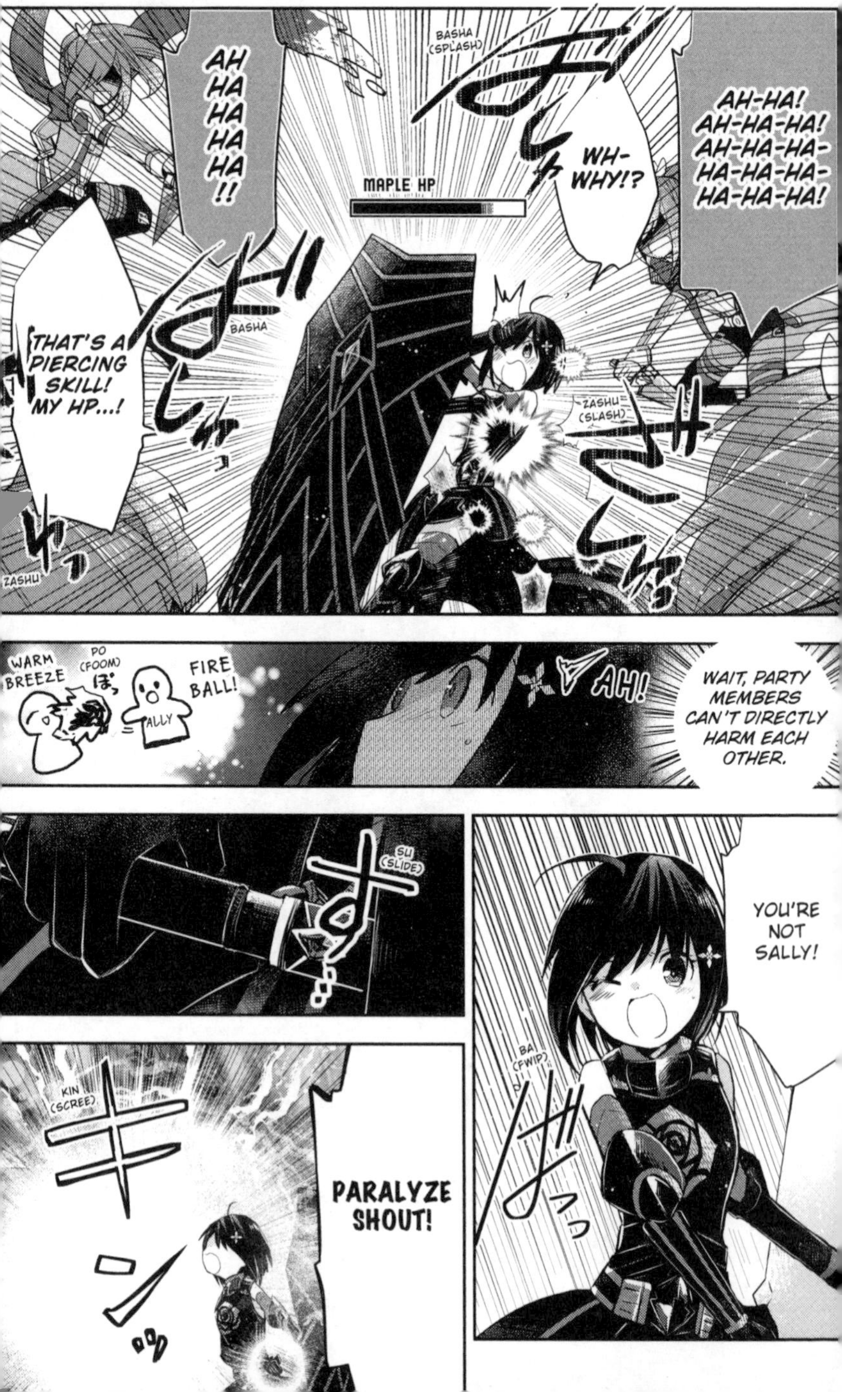
AH-HA! AH-HA-HA! AH-HA-HA-HA-HA-HA-HA-HA-HA!
BASHA (SPLASH)
AH HA HA HA HA!!
WH- WHY!?
MAPLE HP
ZASHU (SLASH)
BASHA
THAT'S A PIERCING SKILL! MY HP...!
ZASHU
WAIT, PARTY MEMBERS CAN'T DIRECTLY HARM EACH OTHER.
AH!
FIRE BALL!
PO (FOOM)
WARM BREEZE
ALLY
YOU'RE NOT SALLY!
BA (FWIP)
SU (SLIDE)
PARALYZE SHOUT!
KIN (SCREE)

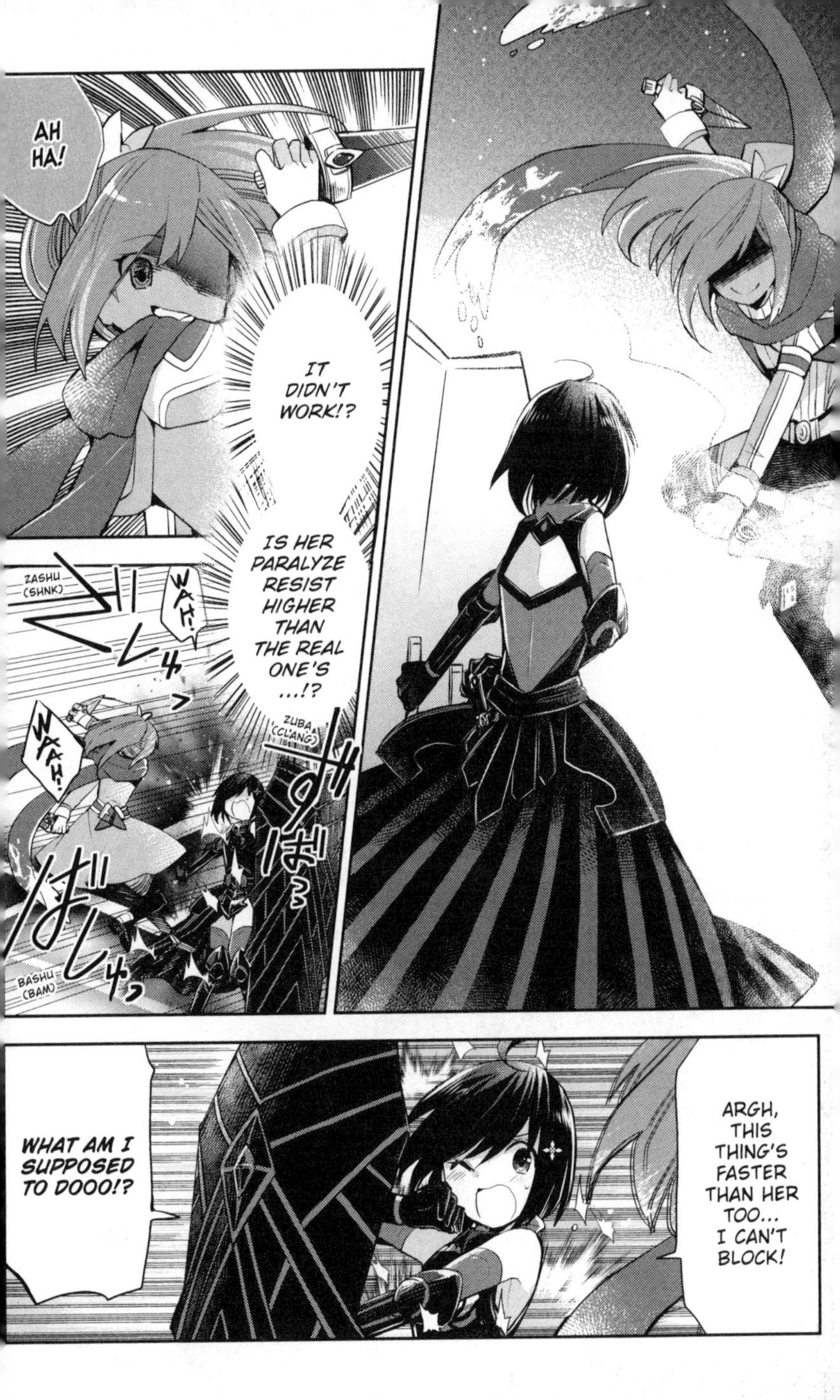
AH HA!
IT DIDN'T WORK!?
IS HER PARALYZE RESIST HIGHER THAN THE REAL ONE'S...!?
ZUBA (CLANG)
WAH!
ZASHU (SHNK)
WAAH!
BASHU (BAM)
ARGH, THIS THING'S FASTER THAN HER TOO... I CAN'T BLOCK!
WHAT AM I SUPPOSED TO DOOO!?

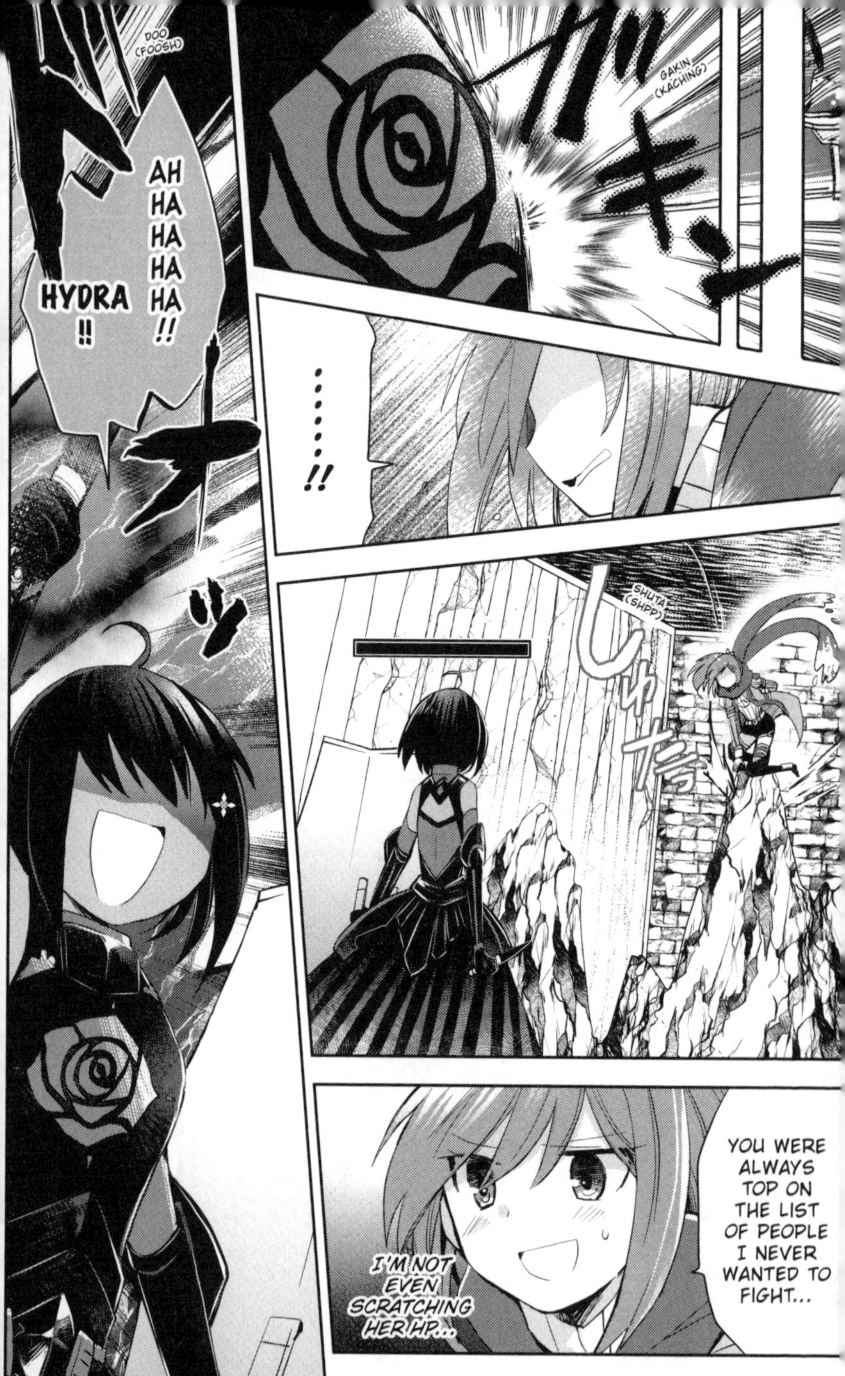
GAKIN (KACHING)
......!!
SHUTA (SHPP)
YOU WERE ALWAYS TOP ON THE LIST OF PEOPLE I NEVER WANTED TO FIGHT...
I'M NOT EVEN SCRATCHING HER HP...
DOO (FOOSH)
AH HA HA HA HA!!
HYDRA!!

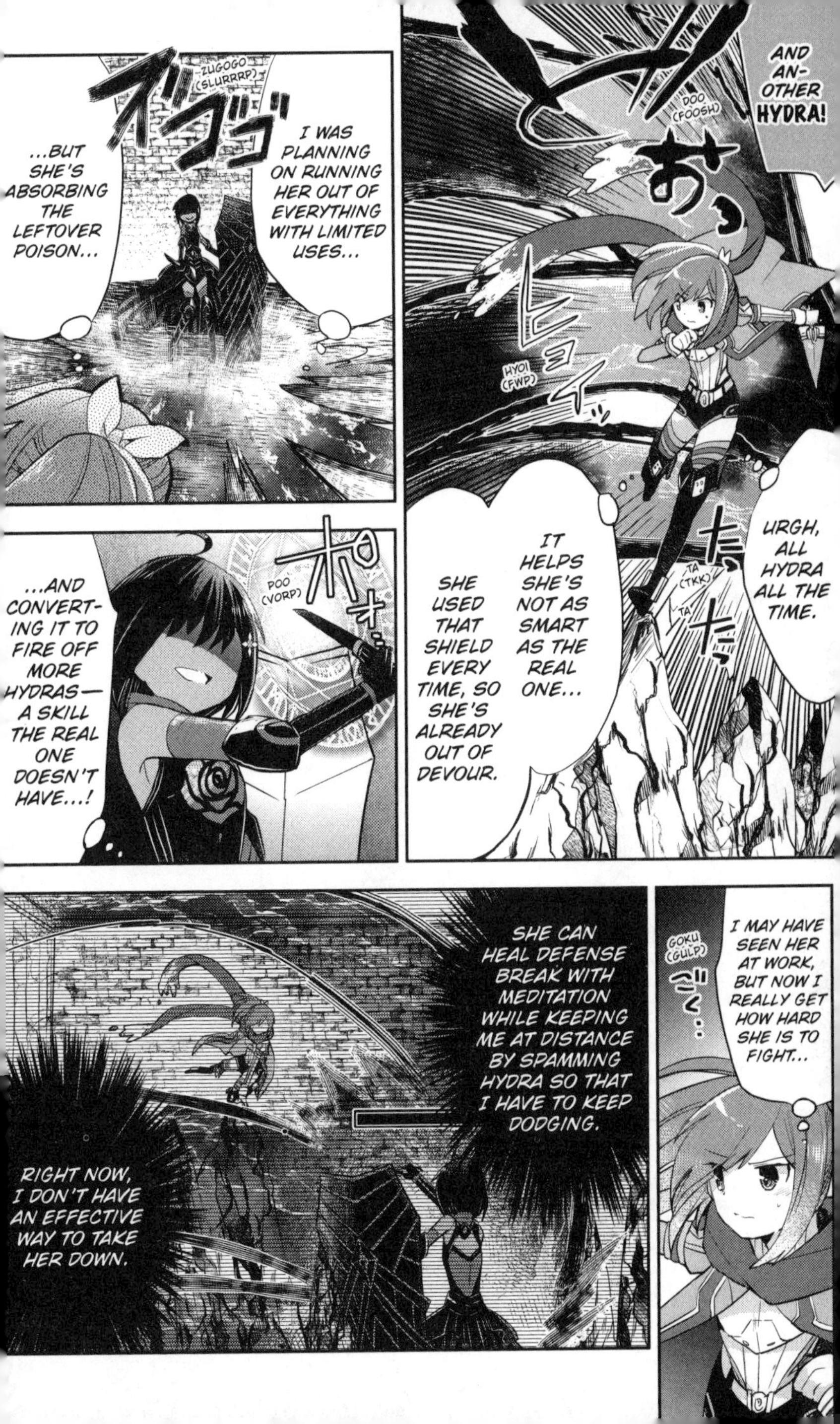
AND AN-OTHER HYDRA!
DOO (FOOSH)
HYOI (FWP)
URGH, ALL HYDRA ALL THE TIME.
TA (TKK) TA
IT HELPS SHE'S NOT AS SMART AS THE REAL ONE...
SHE USED THAT SHIELD EVERY TIME, SO SHE'S ALREADY OUT OF DEVOUR.
ZUGOGO (SLURRRP)
I WAS PLANNING ON RUNNING HER OUT OF EVERYTHING WITH LIMITED USES...
...BUT SHE'S ABSORBING THE LEFTOVER POISON...
POO (VORP)
...AND CONVERT-ING IT TO FIRE OFF MORE HYDRAS— A SKILL THE REAL ONE DOESN'T HAVE...!
GOKU (GULP)
I MAY HAVE SEEN HER AT WORK, BUT NOW I REALLY GET HOW HARD SHE IS TO FIGHT...
SHE CAN HEAL DEFENSE BREAK WITH MEDITATION WHILE KEEPING ME AT DISTANCE BY SPAMMING HYDRA SO THAT I HAVE TO KEEP DODGING.
RIGHT NOW, I DON'T HAVE AN EFFECTIVE WAY TO TAKE HER DOWN.

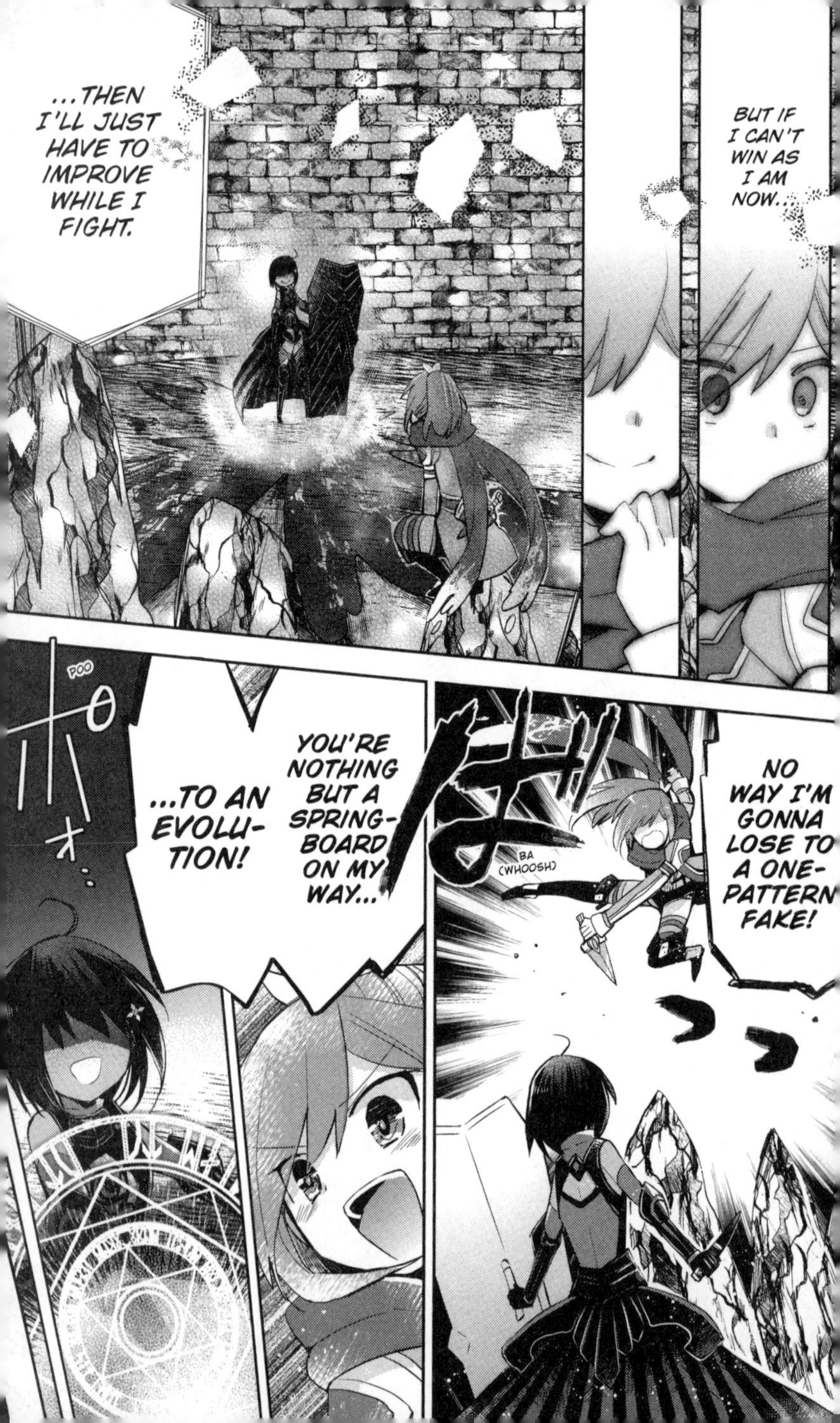
BUT IF I CAN'T WIN AS I AM NOW...
...THEN I'LL JUST HAVE TO IMPROVE WHILE I FIGHT.
NO WAY I'M GONNA LOSE TO A ONE-PATTERN FAKE!
BA (WHOOSH)
YOU'RE NOTHING BUT A SPRING-BOARD ON MY WAY...
...TO AN EVOLU-TION!
POO

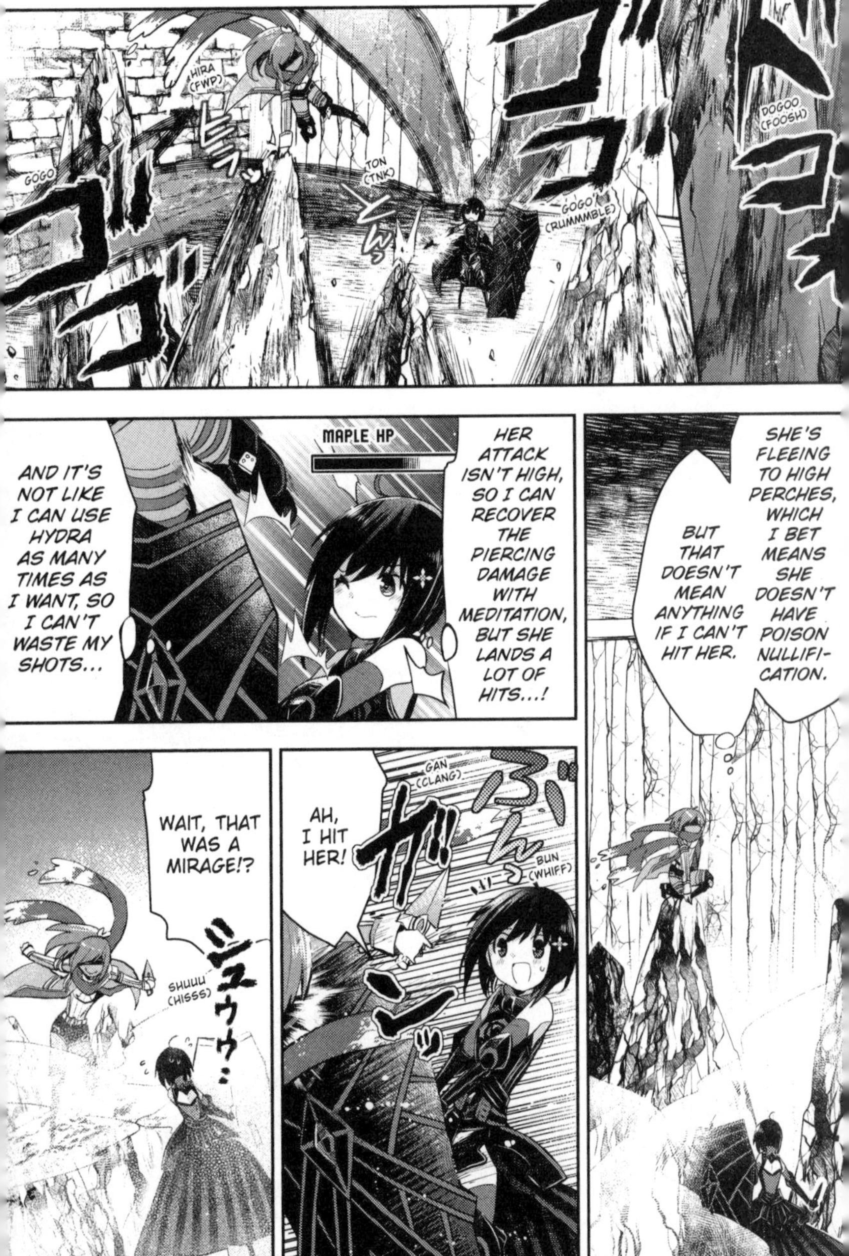
DOGOO (FOOSH)
GOGO (RUMMMBLE)
TON (TNK)
HIRA (FWP)
GOGO
SHE'S FLEEING TO HIGH PERCHES, WHICH I BET MEANS SHE DOESN'T HAVE POISON NULLIFICATION.
BUT THAT DOESN'T MEAN ANYTHING IF I CAN'T HIT HER.
MAPLE HP
HER ATTACK ISN'T HIGH, SO I CAN RECOVER THE PIERCING DAMAGE WITH MEDITATION, BUT SHE LANDS A LOT OF HITS...!
AND IT'S NOT LIKE I CAN USE HYDRA AS MANY TIMES AS I WANT, SO I CAN'T WASTE MY SHOTS...
GAN (CLANG)
BUN (WHIFF)
AH, I HIT HER!
WAIT, THAT WAS A MIRAGE!?
SHUUU (HISSS)

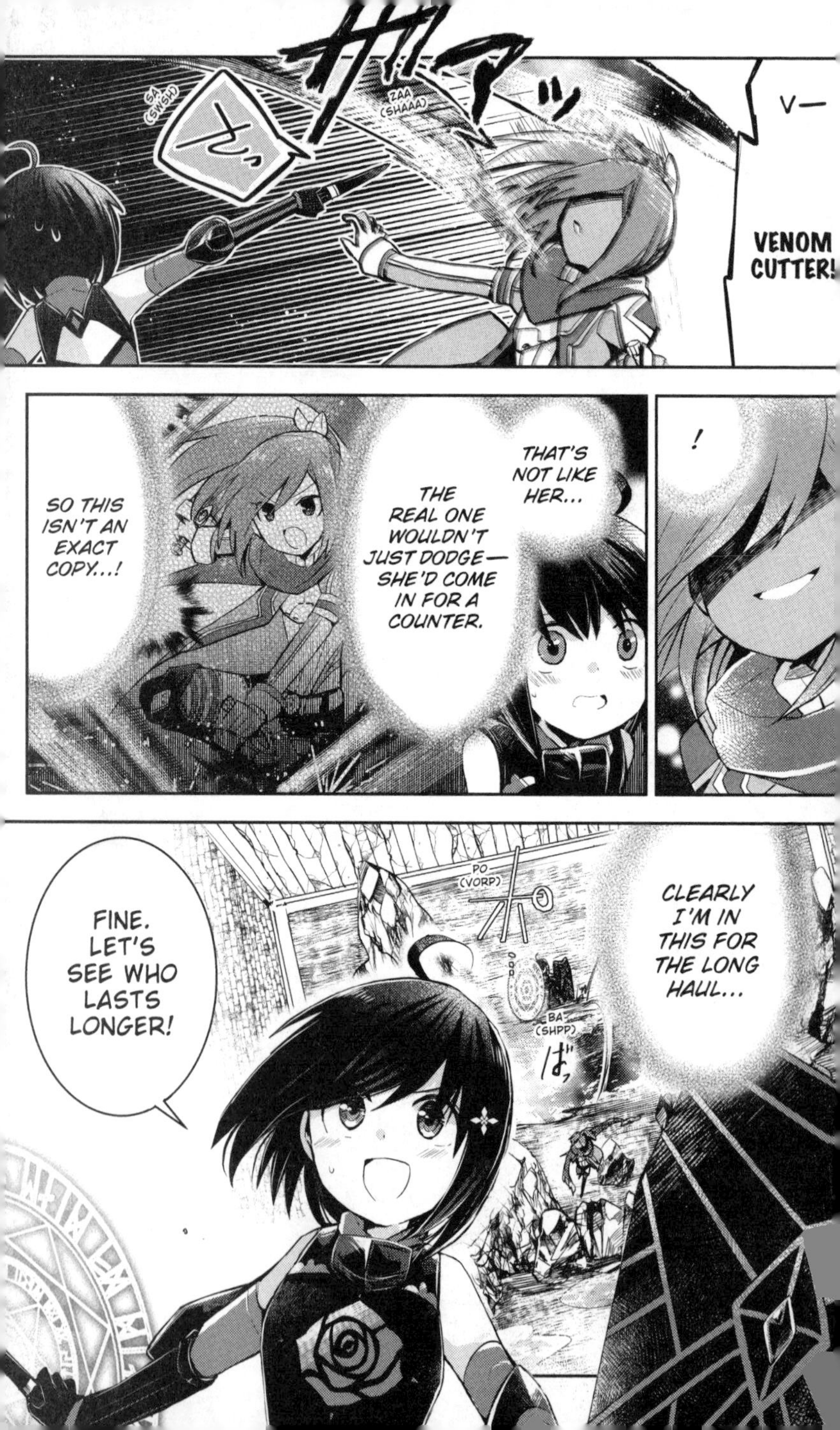

ZAA (SHAAA)
SA (SWSH)
さっ
VENOM CUTTER!
!
THAT'S NOT LIKE HER...
THE REAL ONE WOULDN'T JUST DODGE— SHE'D COME IN FOR A COUNTER.
SO THIS ISN'T AN EXACT COPY...!
CLEARLY I'M IN THIS FOR THE LONG HAUL...
PO (VORP)
BA (SHPP)
ばっ
FINE. LET'S SEE WHO LASTS LONGER!

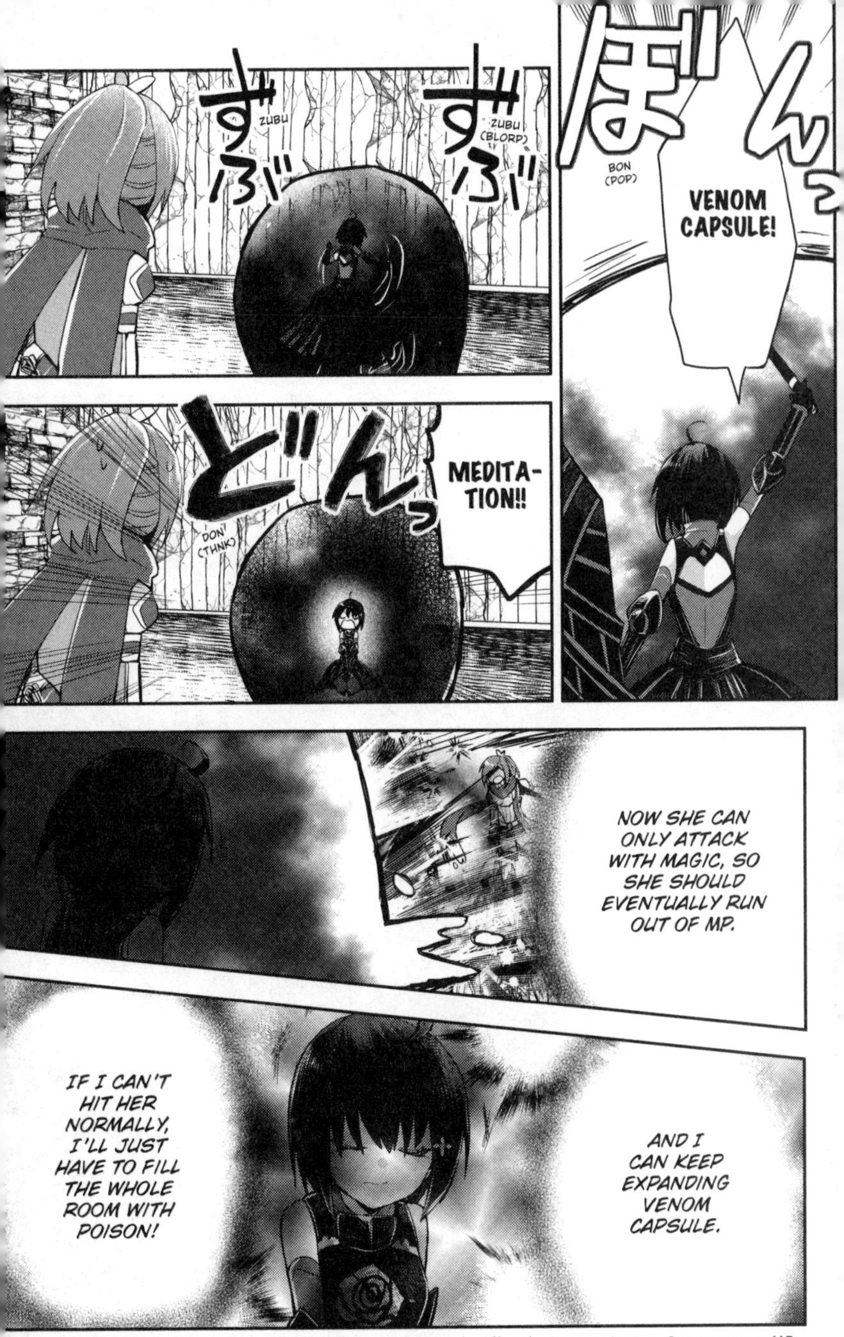
ぼんっ
BON (POP)
VENOM CAPSULE!
ずぶずぶ
ZUBU
ZUBU (BLORP)
どんっ
DON (THNK)
MEDITATION!!
NOW SHE CAN ONLY ATTACK WITH MAGIC, SO SHE SHOULD EVENTUALLY RUN OUT OF MP.
AND I CAN KEEP EXPANDING VENOM CAPSULE.
IF I CAN'T HIT HER NORMALLY, I'LL JUST HAVE TO FILL THE WHOLE ROOM WITH POISON!

★**MEDITATION:** Use to recover 1% of Max HP every ten seconds. Effect lasts ten minutes. Consumes no MP.

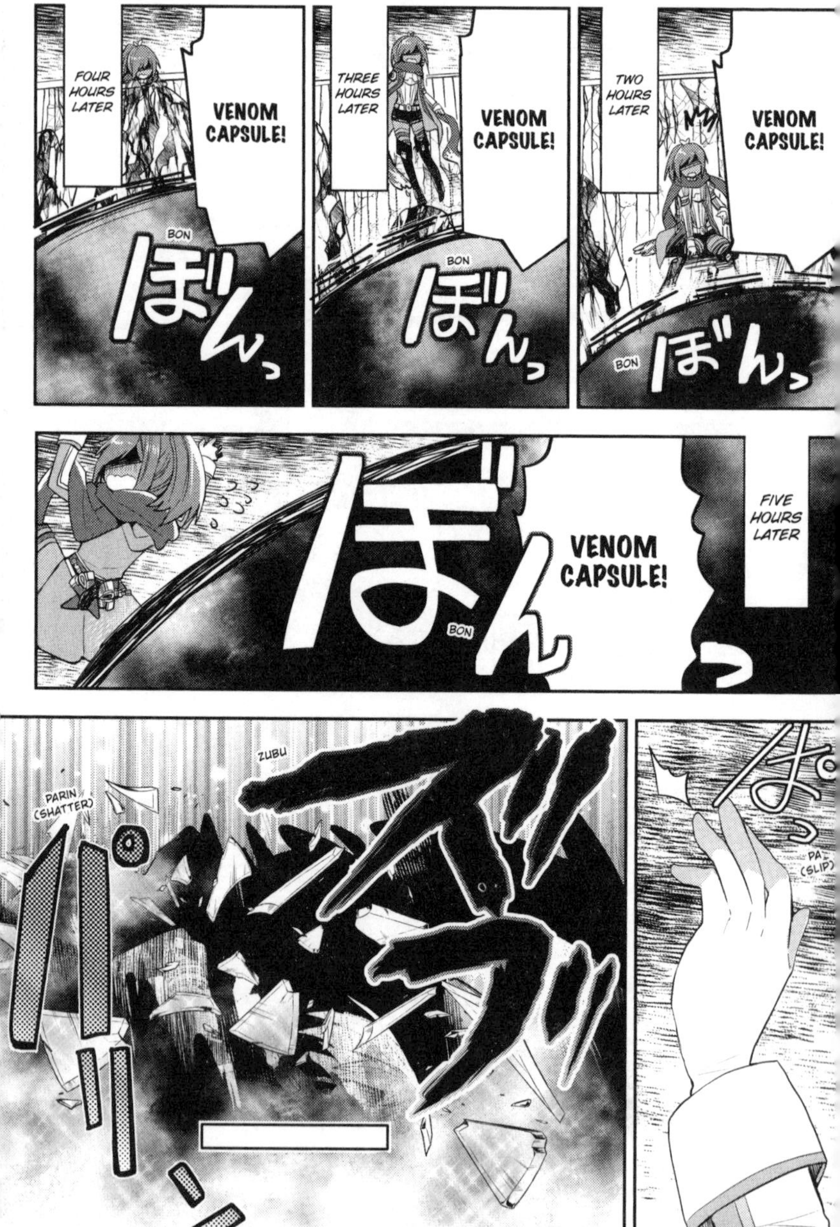
TWO HOURS LATER
VENOM CAPSULE!
BON
ぼんっ
THREE HOURS LATER
VENOM CAPSULE!
BON
ぼんっ
FOUR HOURS LATER
VENOM CAPSULE!
BON
ぼんっ
FIVE HOURS LATER
VENOM CAPSULE!
ぼんっ
BON
ぱっ
PA (SLIP)
ZUBU
ズブッ
PARIN (SHATTER)
パリーン

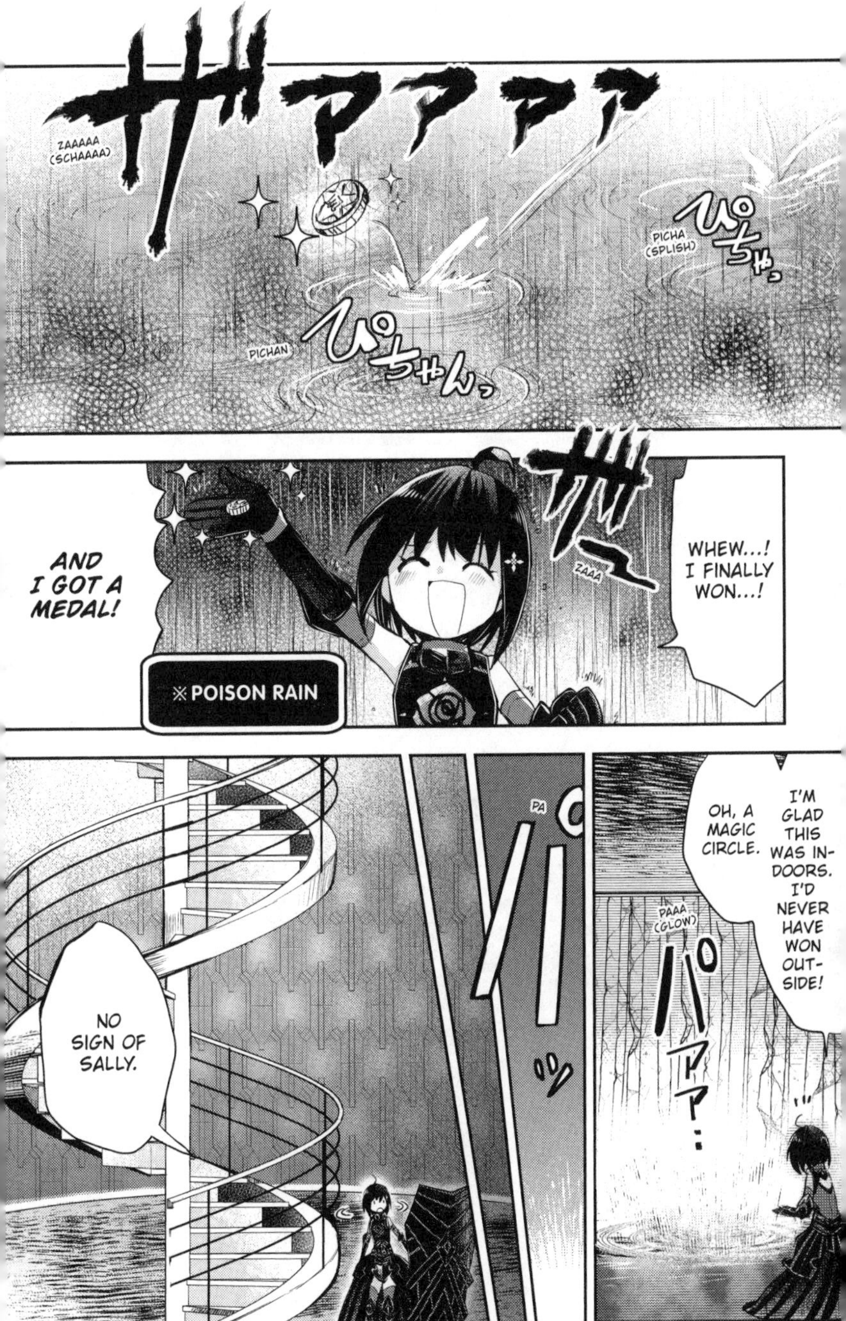
ザアアアア
ZAAAAA (SCHAAAA)
ぴちゅっ
PICHA (SPLISH)
ぴちゃんっ
PICHAN
WHEW...! I FINALLY WON...!
ZAAA
※POISON RAIN
AND I GOT A MEDAL!
I'M GLAD THIS WAS INDOORS. I'D NEVER HAVE WON OUTSIDE!
OH, A MAGIC CIRCLE.
PAAA (GLOW)
PA
NO SIGN OF SALLY.

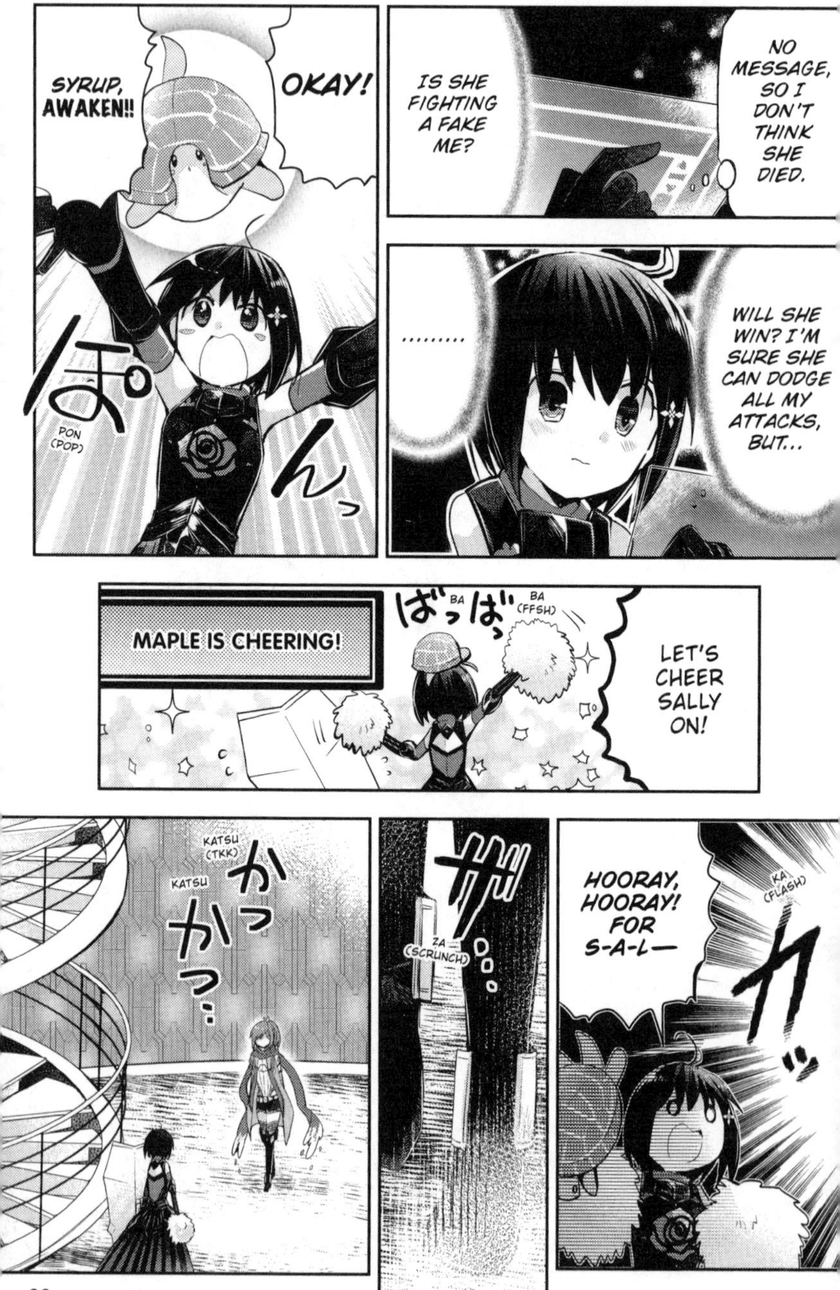
NO MESSAGE, SO I DON'T THINK SHE DIED.
IS SHE FIGHTING A FAKE ME?
WILL SHE WIN? I'M SURE SHE CAN DODGE ALL MY ATTACKS, BUT...
....
OKAY!
SYRUP, AWAKEN!!
ぽんっ
PON (POP)
LET'S CHEER SALLY ON!
ばっばっ
BA BA (FFSH)
MAPLE IS CHEERING!
HOORAY, HOORAY! FOR S-A-L—
カッ
KA (FLASH)
ザッ
ZA (SCRUNCH)
かっかっ
KATSU (TKK) KATSU

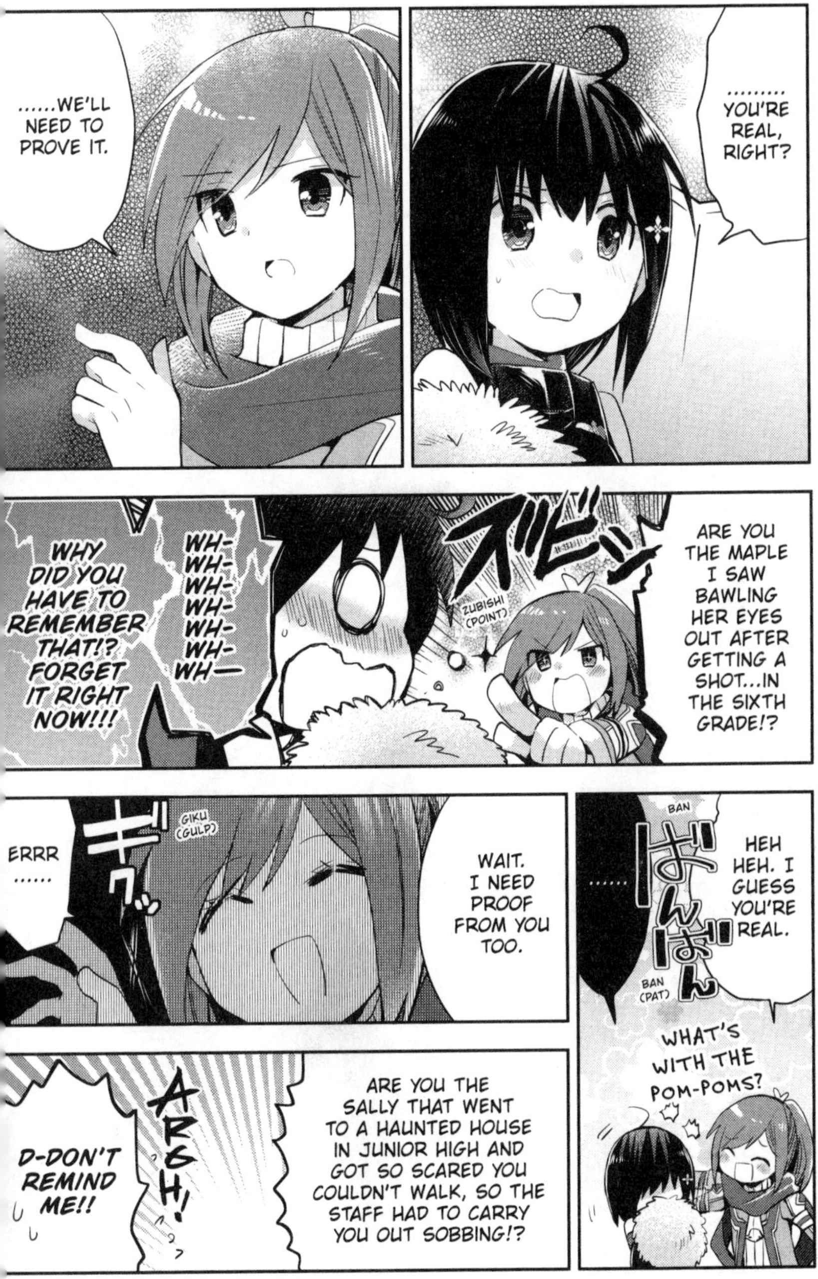
....
YOU'RE REAL, RIGHT?
......WE'LL NEED TO PROVE IT.
ARE YOU THE MAPLE I SAW BAWLING HER EYES OUT AFTER GETTING A SHOT...IN THE SIXTH GRADE!?
ZUBISHI (POINT)
WH-WH-WH-WH-WH-WH-WH—
WHY DID YOU HAVE TO REMEMBER THAT!? FORGET IT RIGHT NOW!!!
BAN
HEH HEH. I GUESS YOU'RE REAL.
......
BAN (PAT)
WHAT'S WITH THE POM-POMS?
WAIT. I NEED PROOF FROM YOU TOO.
GIKU (GULP)
ERRR ......
ARE YOU THE SALLY THAT WENT TO A HAUNTED HOUSE IN JUNIOR HIGH AND GOT SO SCARED YOU COULDN'T WALK, SO THE STAFF HAD TO CARRY YOU OUT SOBBING!?
ARGH!
D-DON'T REMIND ME!!

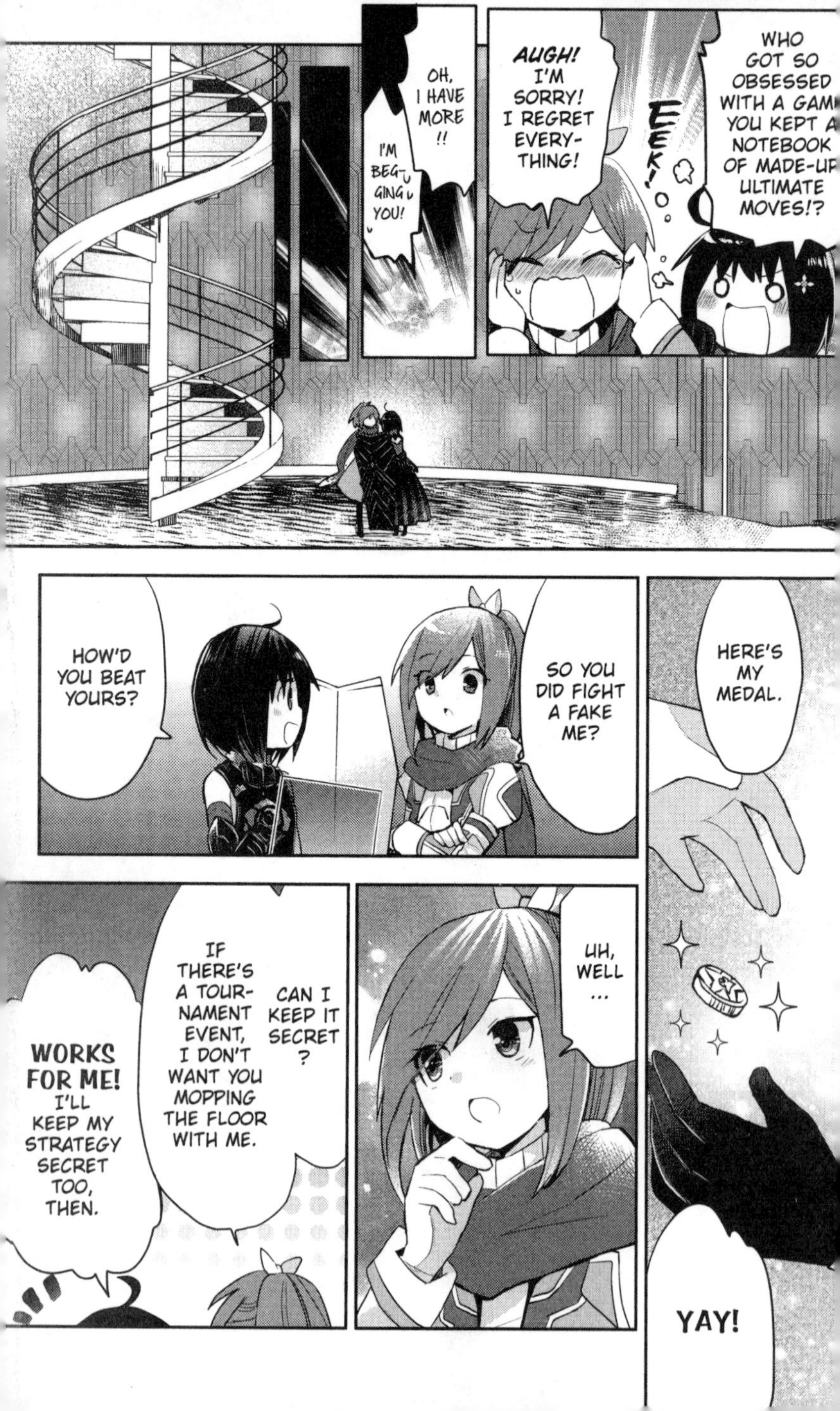
WHO GOT SO OBSESSED WITH A GAM YOU KEPT A NOTEBOOK OF MADE-UP ULTIMATE MOVES!?
EEEK!
AUGH! I'M SORRY! I REGRET EVERY-THING!
OH, I HAVE MORE !!
I'M BEG-GING YOU!
HERE'S MY MEDAL.
YAY!
SO YOU DID FIGHT A FAKE ME?
HOW'D YOU BEAT YOURS?
UH, WELL ...
CAN I KEEP IT SECRET ?
IF THERE'S A TOUR-NAMENT EVENT, I DON'T WANT YOU MOPPING THE FLOOR WITH ME.
WORKS FOR ME! I'LL KEEP MY STRATEGY SECRET TOO, THEN.

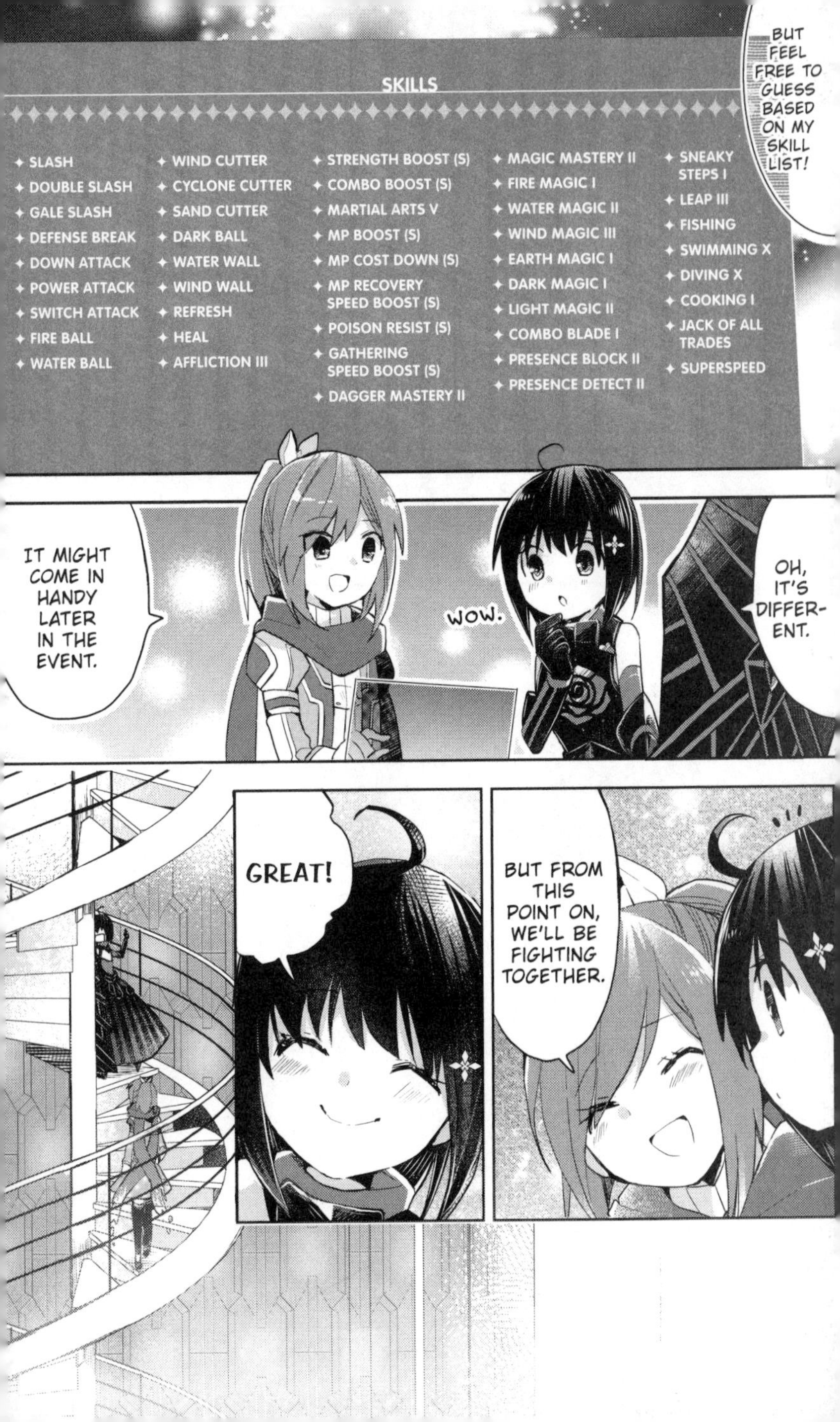
BUT FEEL FREE TO GUESS BASED ON MY SKILL LIST!
SKILLS
✦ SLASH
✦ DOUBLE SLASH
✦ GALE SLASH
✦ DEFENSE BREAK
✦ DOWN ATTACK
✦ POWER ATTACK
✦ SWITCH ATTACK
✦ FIRE BALL
✦ WATER BALL
✦ WIND CUTTER
✦ CYCLONE CUTTER
✦ SAND CUTTER
✦ DARK BALL
✦ WATER WALL
✦ WIND WALL
✦ REFRESH
✦ HEAL
✦ AFFLICTION III
✦ STRENGTH BOOST (S)
✦ COMBO BOOST (S)
✦ MARTIAL ARTS V
✦ MP BOOST (S)
✦ MP COST DOWN (S)
✦ MP RECOVERY SPEED BOOST (S)
✦ POISON RESIST (S)
✦ GATHERING SPEED BOOST (S)
✦ DAGGER MASTERY II
✦ MAGIC MASTERY II
✦ FIRE MAGIC I
✦ WATER MAGIC II
✦ WIND MAGIC III
✦ EARTH MAGIC I
✦ DARK MAGIC I
✦ LIGHT MAGIC II
✦ COMBO BLADE I
✦ PRESENCE BLOCK II
✦ PRESENCE DETECT II
✦ SNEAKY STEPS I
✦ LEAP III
✦ FISHING
✦ SWIMMING X
✦ DIVING X
✦ COOKING I
✦ JACK OF ALL TRADES
✦ SUPERSPEED
OH, IT'S DIFFERENT.
WOW.
IT MIGHT COME IN HANDY LATER IN THE EVENT.
!!
BUT FROM THIS POINT ON, WE'LL BE FIGHTING TOGETHER.
GREAT!

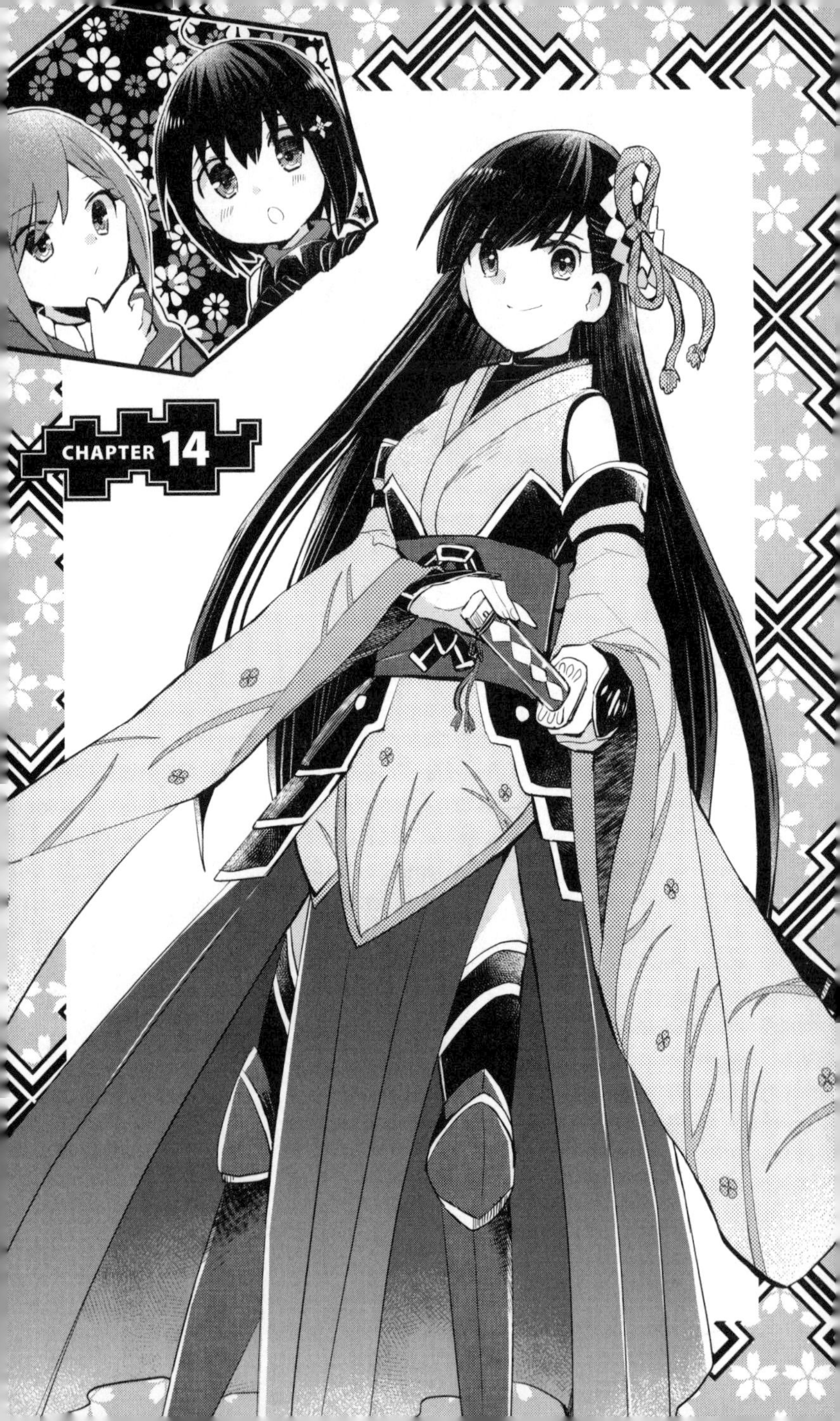
CHAPTER 14

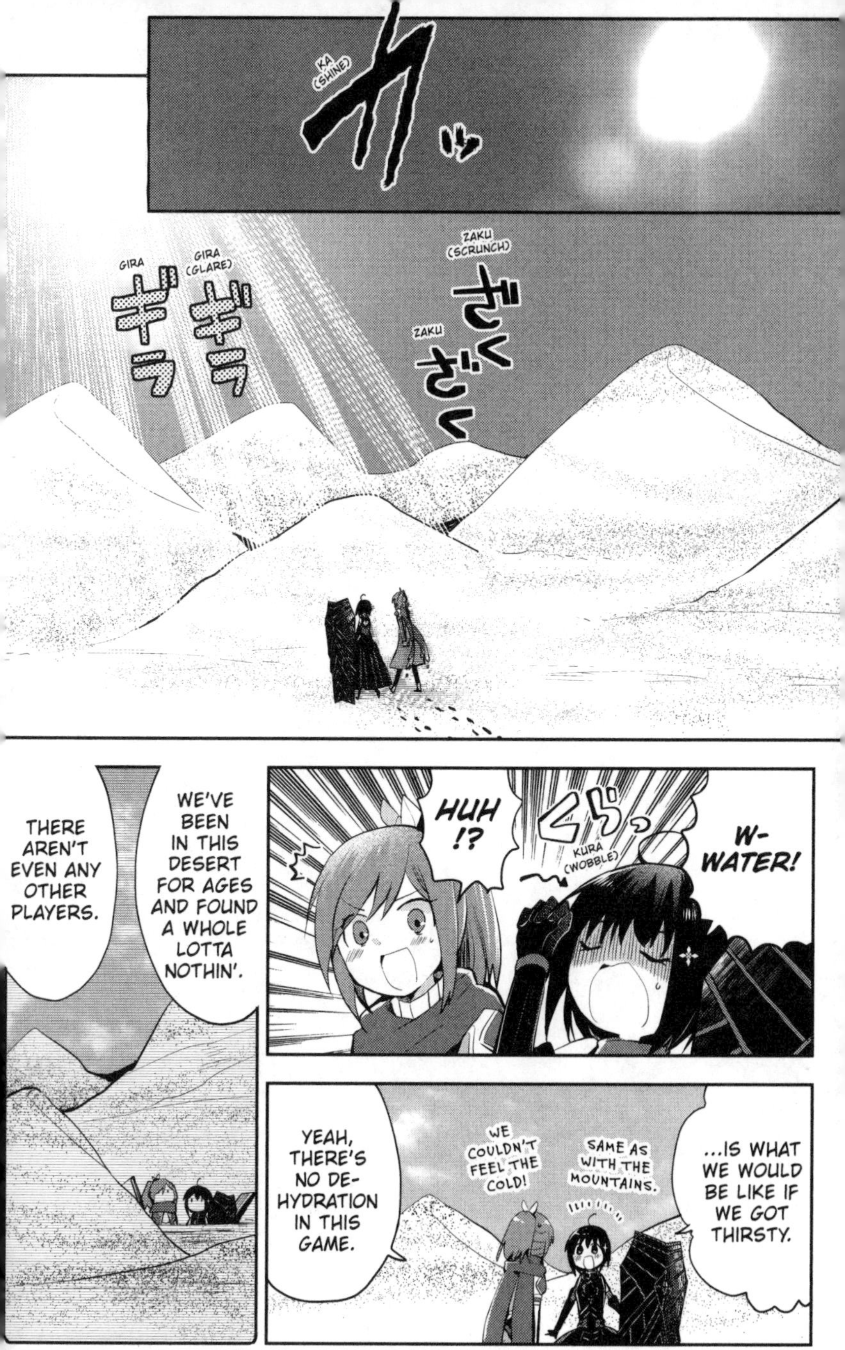
カッ
KA (SHINE)
ざくざく
ZAKU (SCRUNCH)
ZAKU
ギラギラ
GIRA (GLARE)
GIRA
W-WATER!
くらっ
KURA (WOBBLE)
HUH!?
...IS WHAT WE WOULD BE LIKE IF WE GOT THIRSTY.
SAME AS WITH THE MOUNTAINS.
WE COULDN'T FEEL THE COLD!
YEAH, THERE'S NO DE-HYDRATION IN THIS GAME.
WE'VE BEEN IN THIS DESERT FOR AGES AND FOUND A WHOLE LOTTA NOTHIN'.
THERE AREN'T EVEN ANY OTHER PLAYERS.

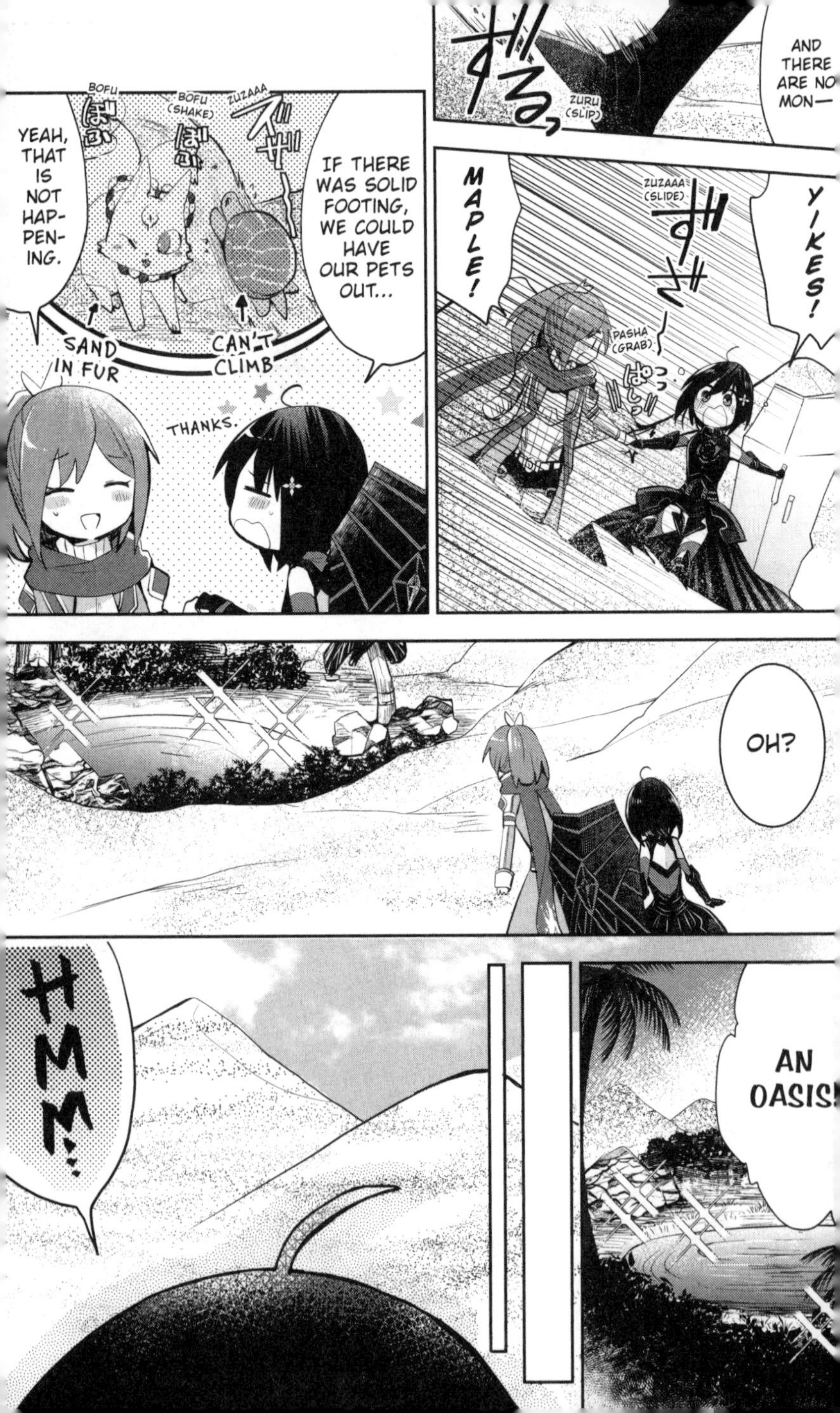
AND THERE ARE NO MON—
ZURU (SLIP)
YIKES!
ZUZAAA (SLIDE)
MAPLE!
PASHA (GRAB)
IF THERE WAS SOLID FOOTING, WE COULD HAVE OUR PETS OUT...
ZUZAAA
BOFU (SHAKE)
BOFU
YEAH, THAT IS NOT HAPPENING.
CAN'T CLIMB
SAND IN FUR
THANKS.
OH?
AN OASIS!
HMM...

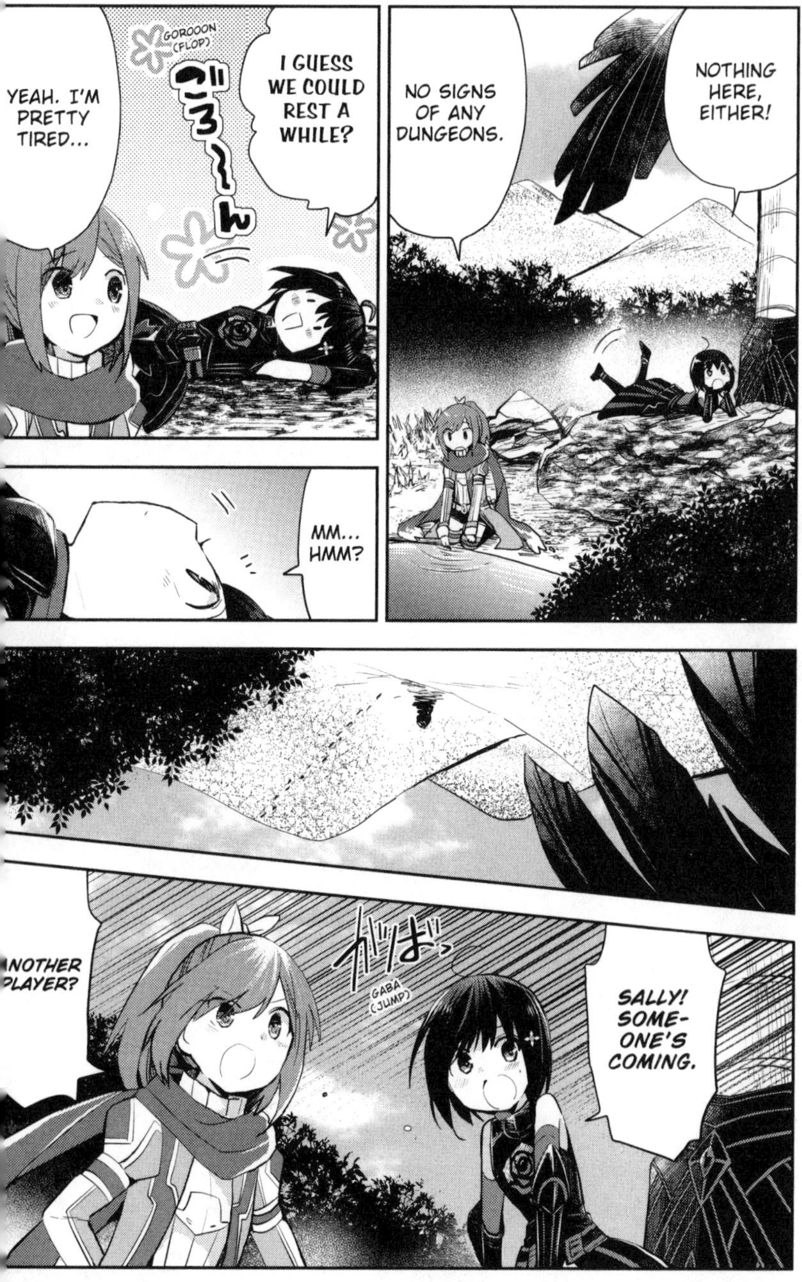
NOTHING HERE, EITHER!
NO SIGNS OF ANY DUNGEONS.
I GUESS WE COULD REST A WHILE?
ごろ〜ん
GOROOON (FLOP)
YEAH. I'M PRETTY TIRED...
MM... HMM?
SALLY! SOME-ONE'S COMING.
ガバっ
GABA (JUMP)
NOTHER PLAYER?

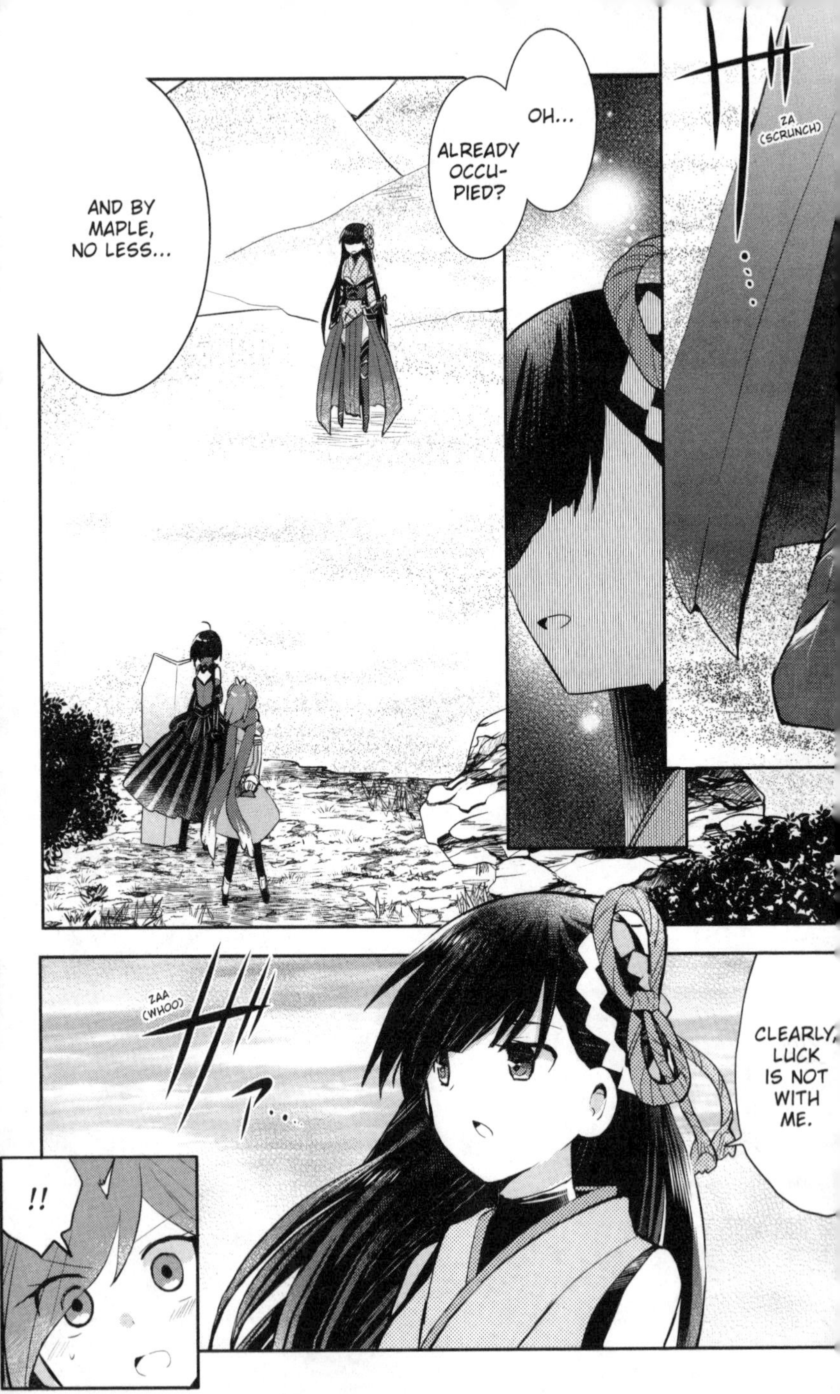
ZA (SCRUNCH)
OH... ALREADY OCCUPIED?
AND BY MAPLE, NO LESS...
CLEARLY, LUCK IS NOT WITH ME.
ZAA (WHOO)
!!

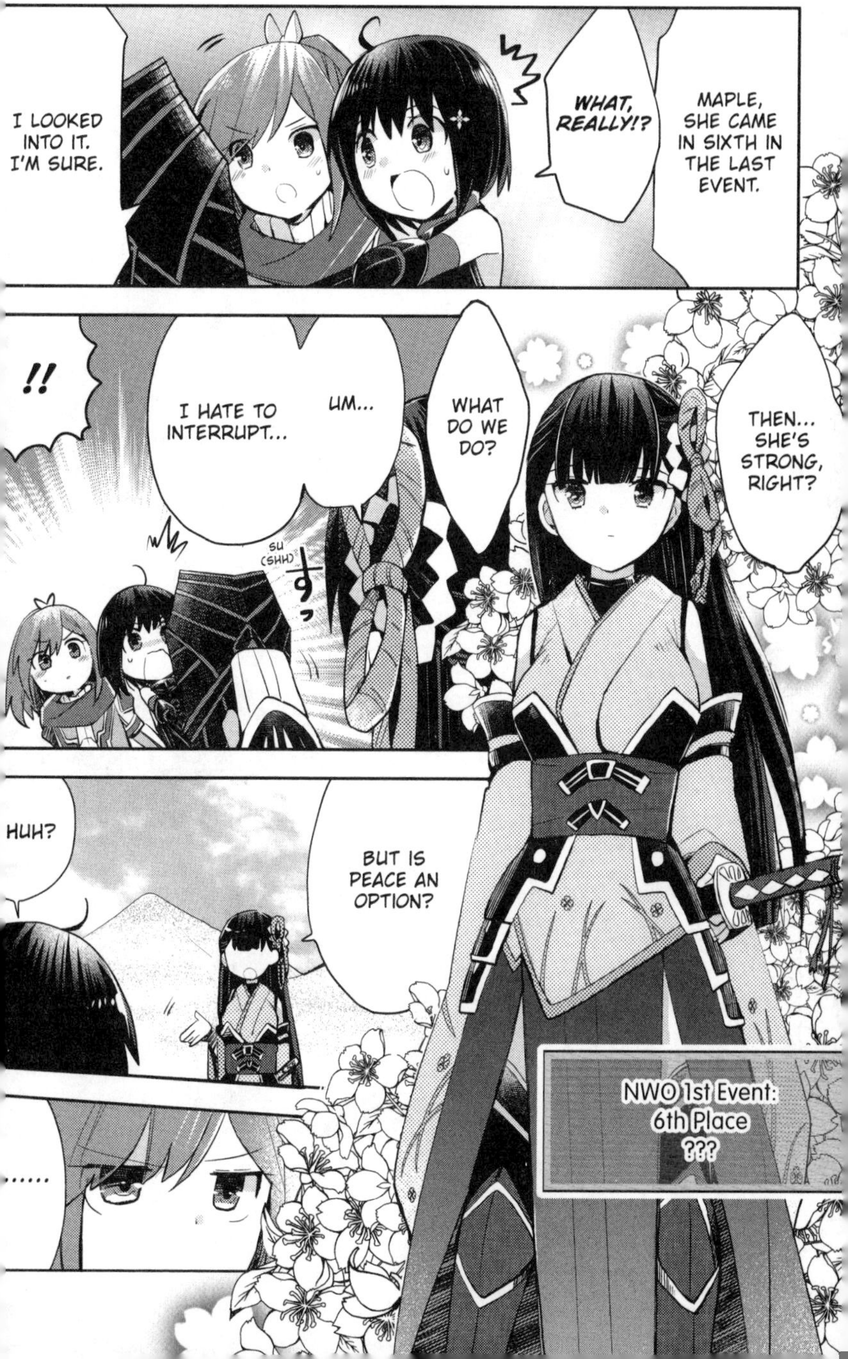
MAPLE, SHE CAME IN SIXTH IN THE LAST EVENT.
WHAT, REALLY!?
I LOOKED INTO IT. I'M SURE.
THEN... SHE'S STRONG, RIGHT?
WHAT DO WE DO?
UM...
I HATE TO INTERRUPT...
!!
SU (SHH)
すっ
NWO 1st Event: 6th Place ???
BUT IS PEACE AN OPTION?
HUH?
......

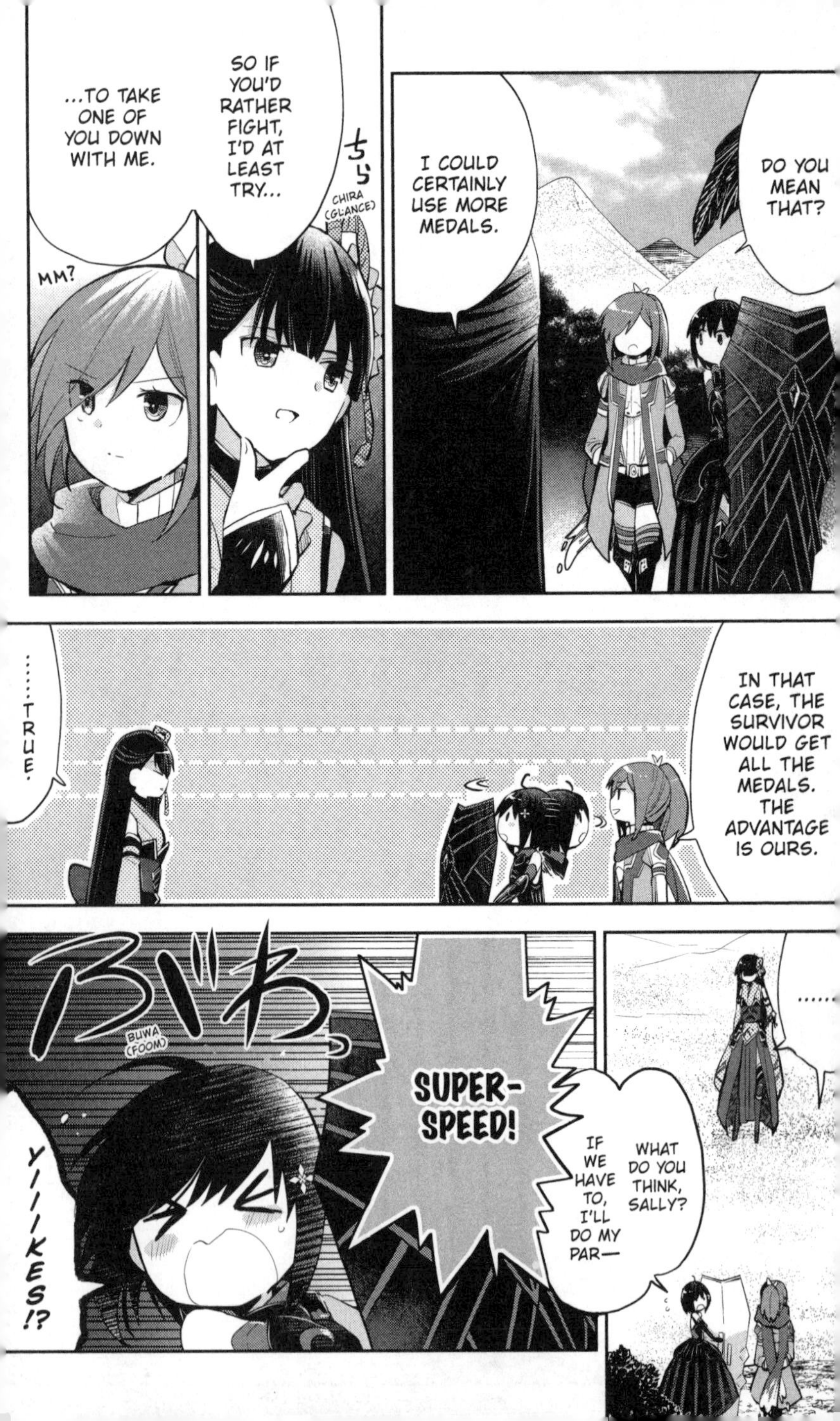
DO YOU MEAN THAT?
I COULD CERTAINLY USE MORE MEDALS.
SO IF YOU'D RATHER FIGHT, I'D AT LEAST TRY...
ちら
CHIRA (GLANCE)
...TO TAKE ONE OF YOU DOWN WITH ME.
MM?
IN THAT CASE, THE SURVIVOR WOULD GET ALL THE MEDALS. THE ADVANTAGE IS OURS.
......TRUE.
......
WHAT DO YOU THINK, SALLY?
IF WE HAVE TO, I'LL DO MY PAR—
SUPER-SPEED!
ぶわっ
BUWA (FOOM)
YIIIIKES!?

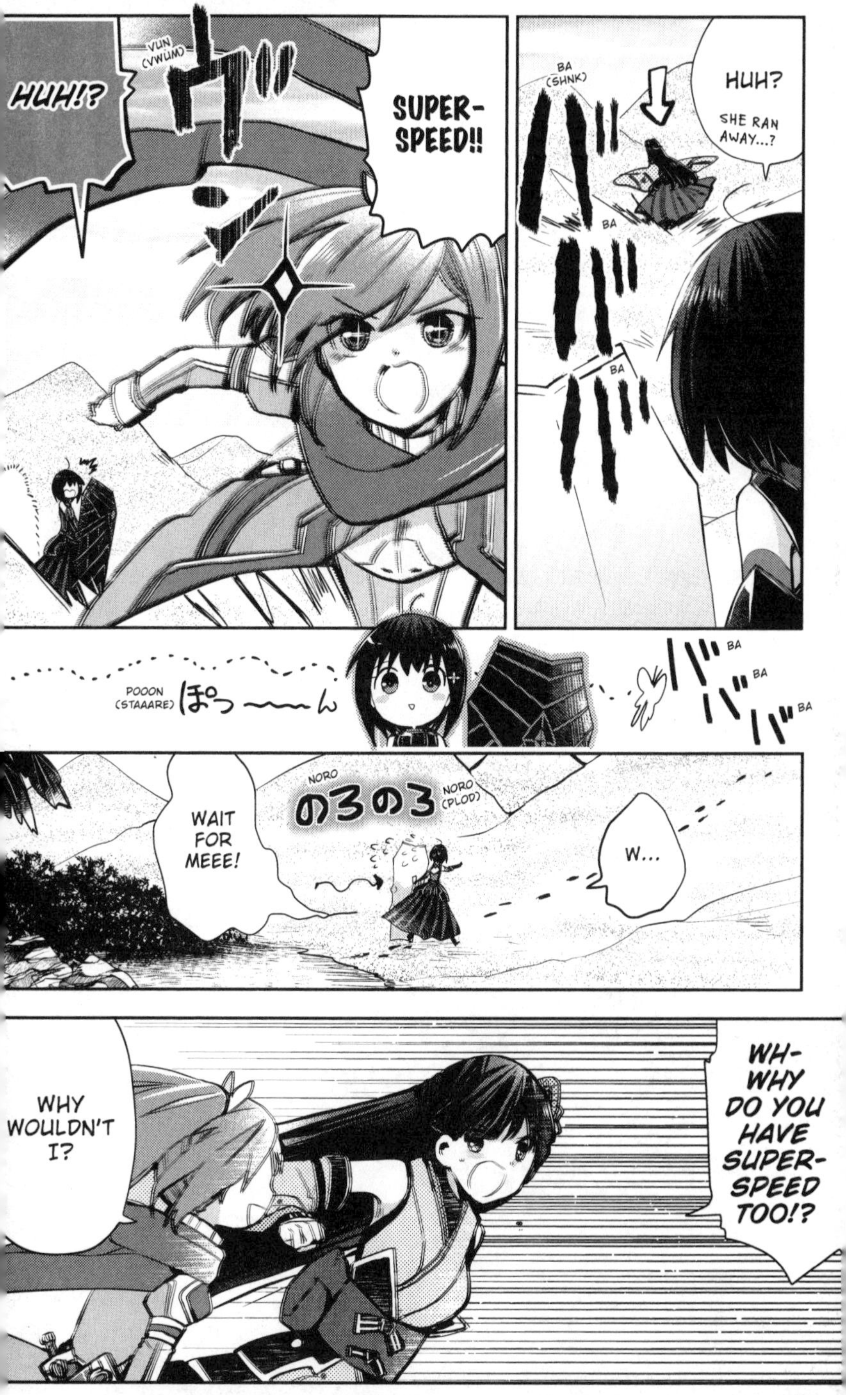
HUH?
SHE RAN AWAY...?
BA (SHNK)
BA
BA
VUN (VWUM)
SUPER-SPEED!!
HUH!?
BA
BA
BA
POOON (STAAARE)
W...
NORO NORO (PLOD)
のろのろ
WAIT FOR MEEE!
WH-WHY DO YOU HAVE SUPER-SPEED TOO!?
WHY WOULDN'T I?

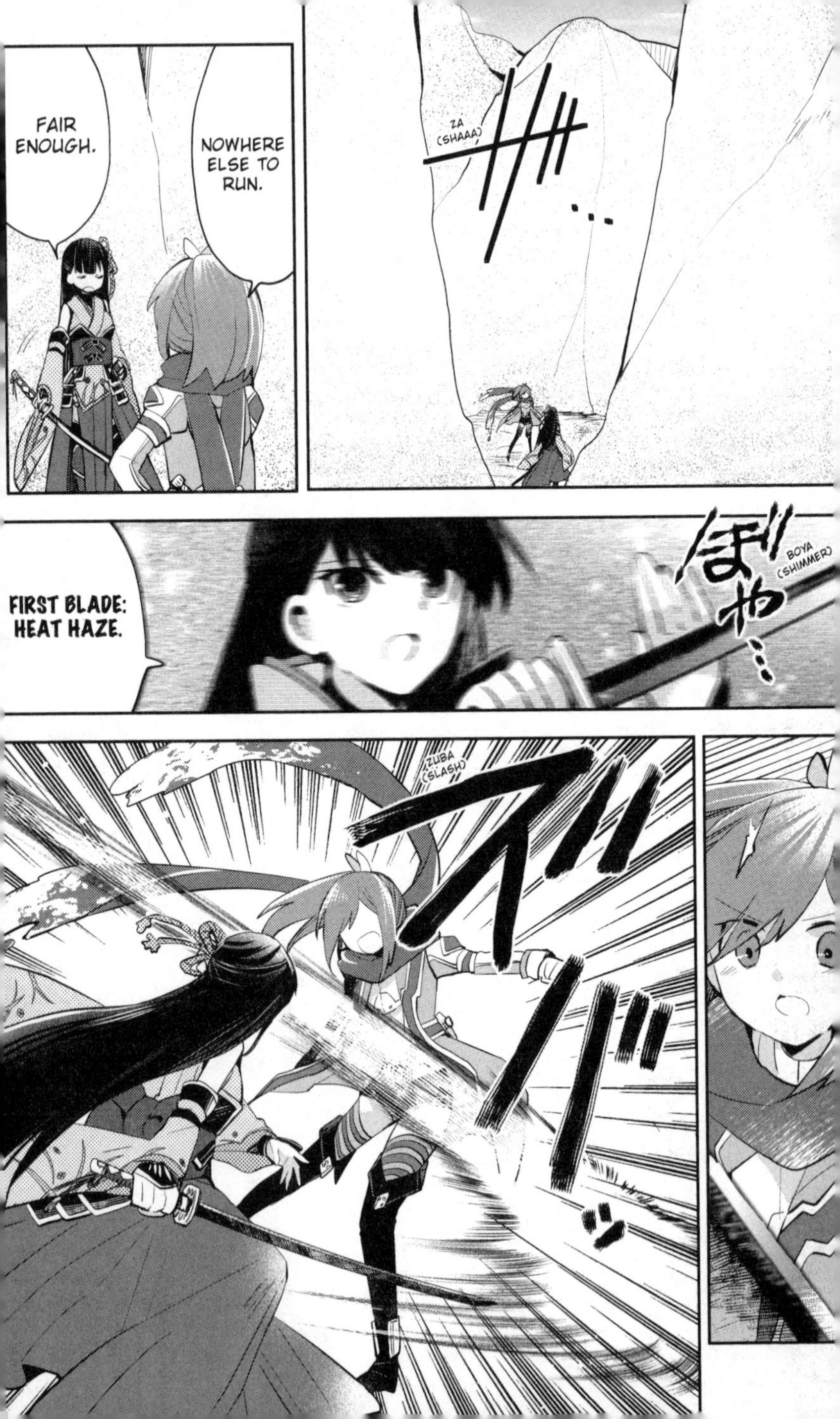
ZA (SHAAA)
...
NOWHERE ELSE TO RUN.
FAIR ENOUGH.
BOYA (SHIMMER)
FIRST BLADE: HEAT HAZE.
ZUBA (SLASH)

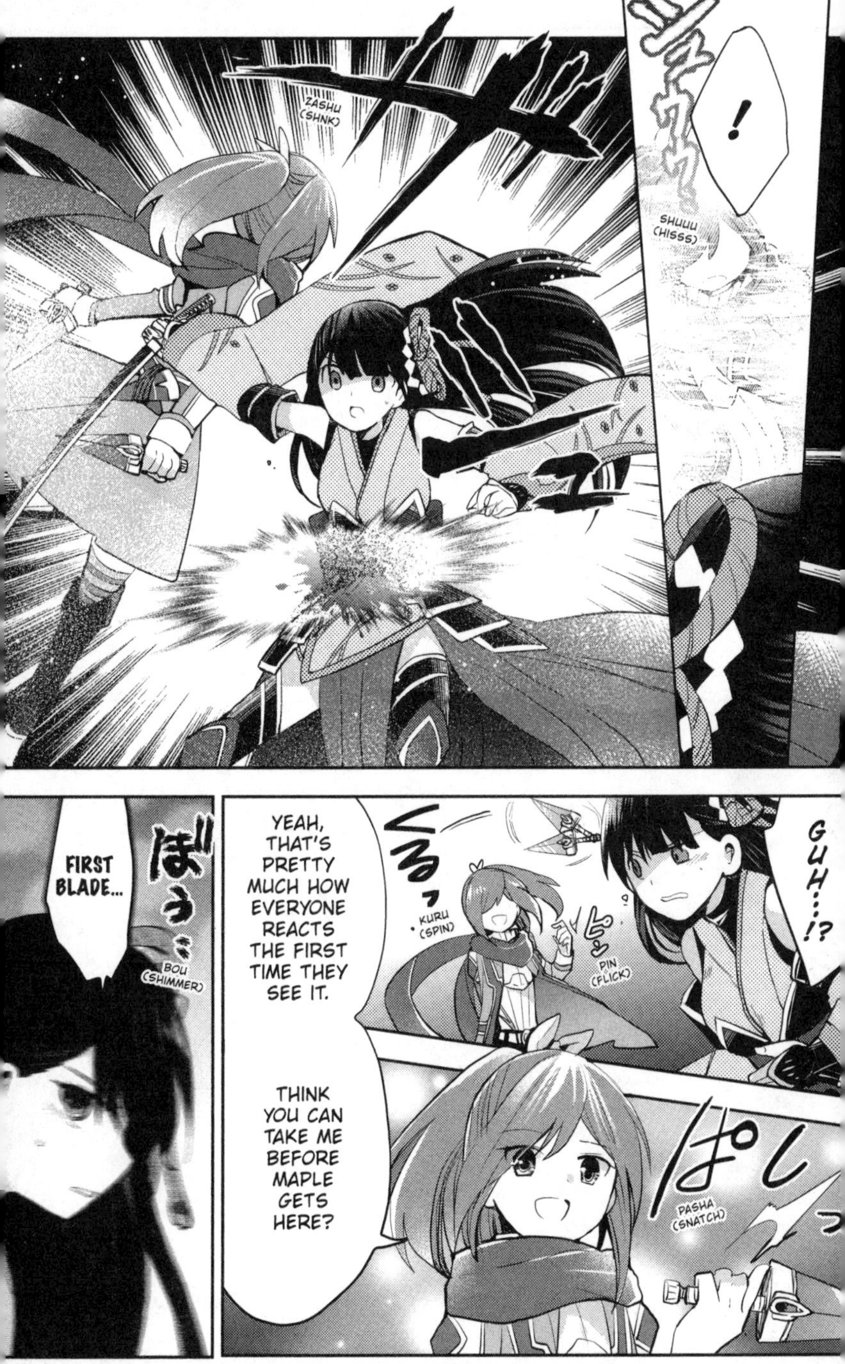
!
SHUUU (HISSS)
ZASHU (SHNK)
GUH...!?
PIN (FLICK)
KURU (SPIN)
YEAH, THAT'S PRETTY MUCH HOW EVERYONE REACTS THE FIRST TIME THEY SEE IT.
THINK YOU CAN TAKE ME BEFORE MAPLE GETS HERE?
PASHA (SNATCH)
FIRST BLADE...
BOU (SHIMMER)

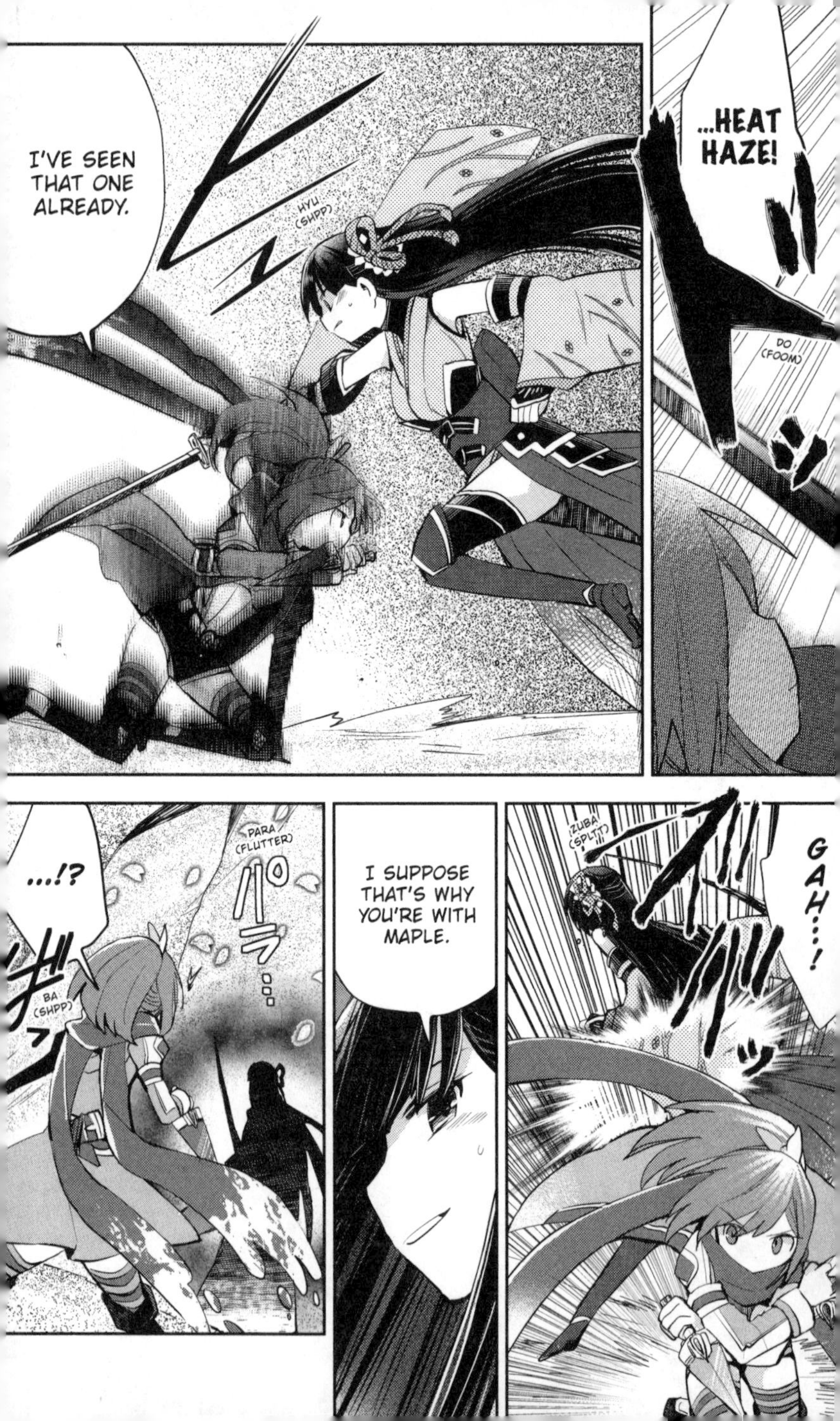

...HEAT HAZE!
DO (FOOM)
I'VE SEEN THAT ONE ALREADY.
HYU (SHPP)
GAH...!
ZUBA (SPLTT)
I SUPPOSE THAT'S WHY YOU'RE WITH MAPLE.
PARA (FLUTTER)
...!?
BA (SHPP)

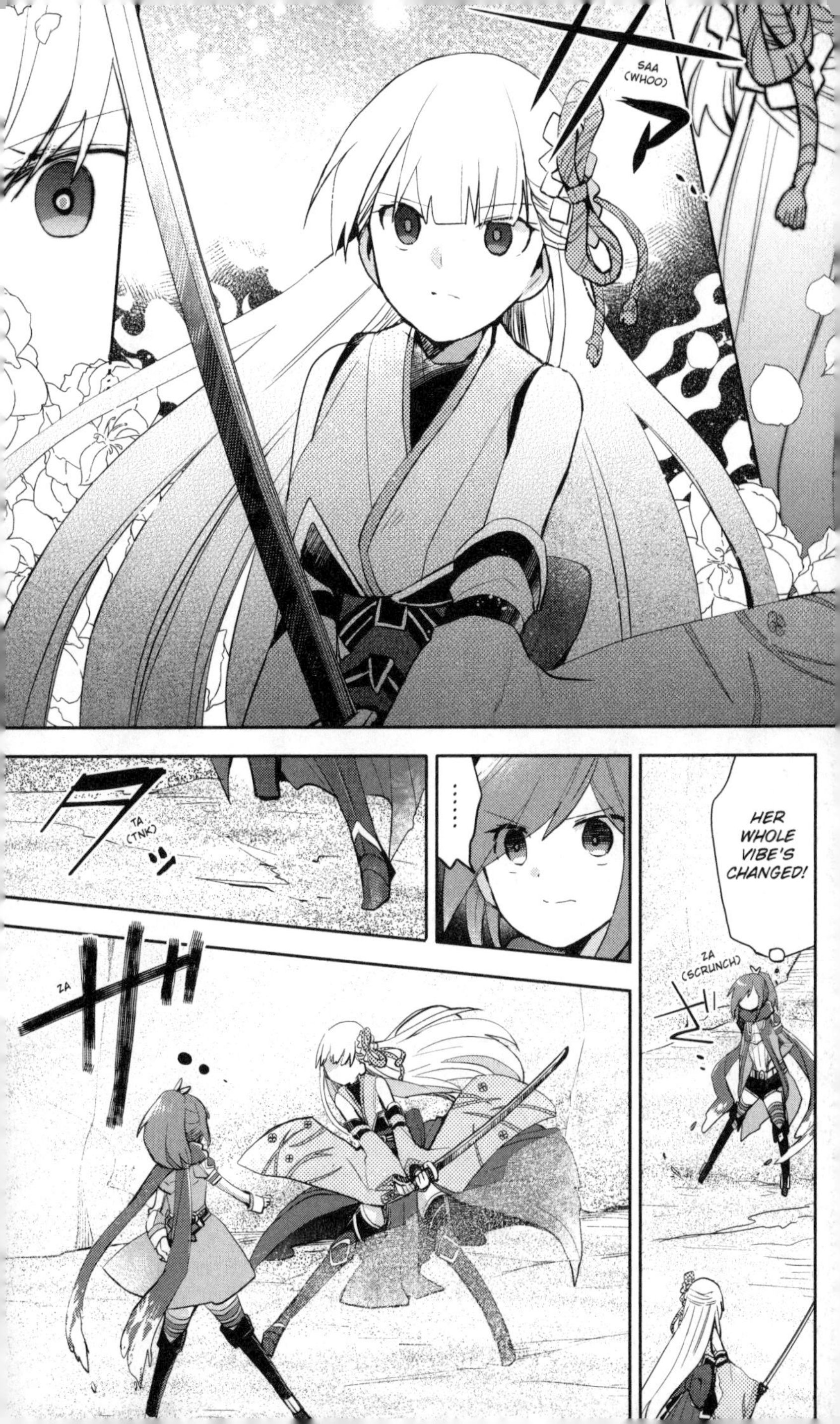
SAA (WHOO)
HER WHOLE VIBE'S CHANGED!
ZA (SCRUNCH)
......
TA (TNK)
ZA

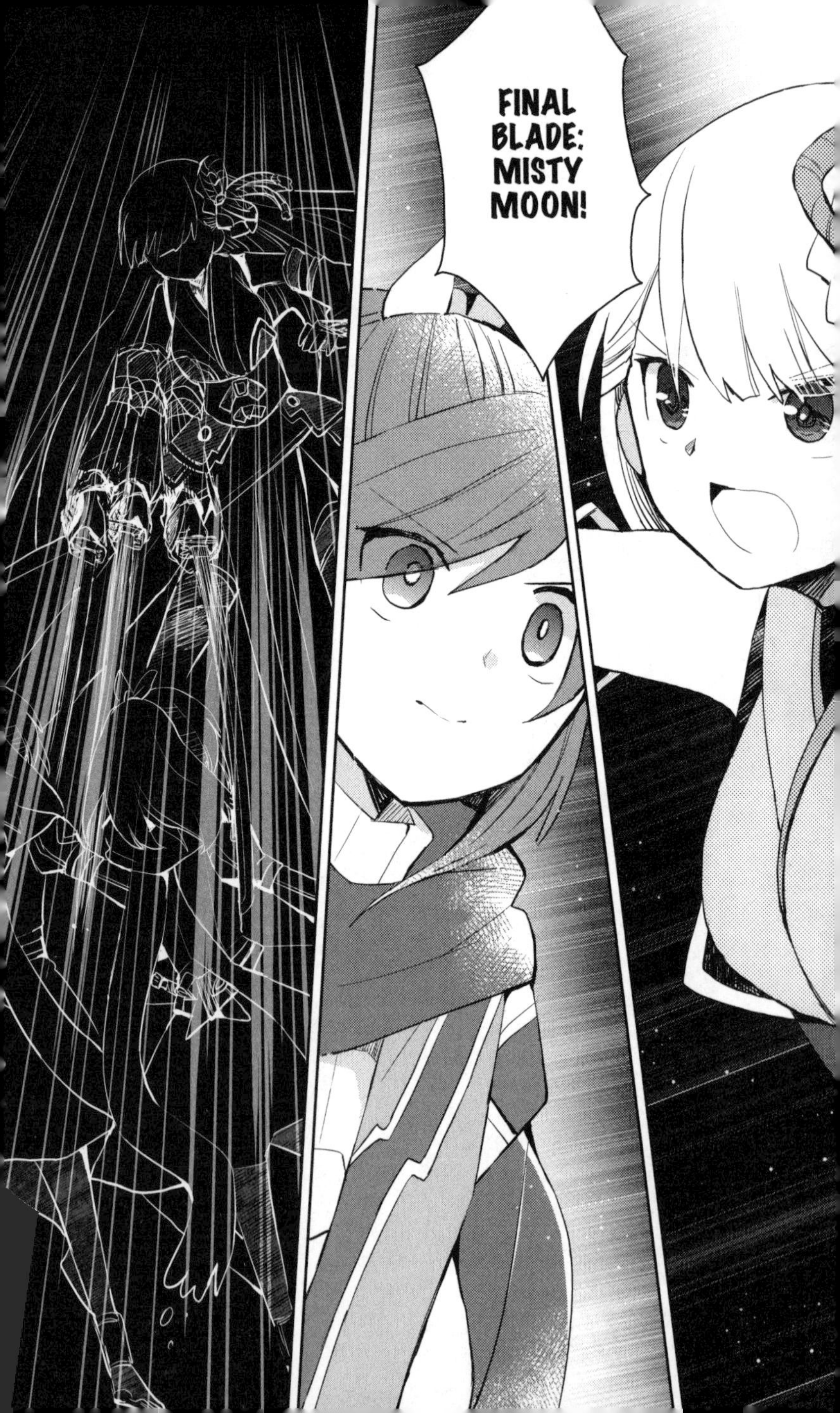
FINAL BLADE: MISTY MOON!

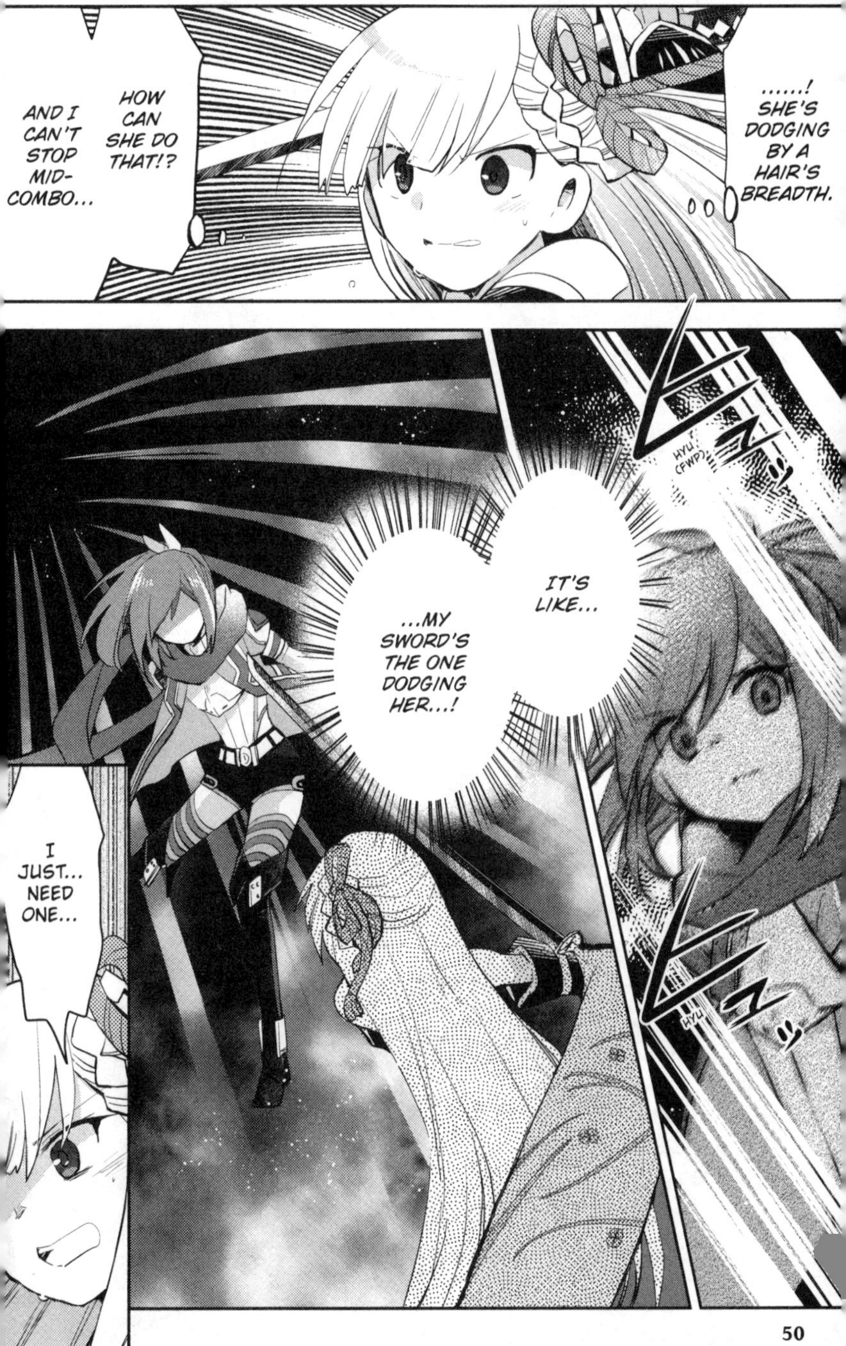
......! SHE'S DODGING BY A HAIR'S BREADTH.
HOW CAN SHE DO THAT!?
AND I CAN'T STOP MID-COMBO...
HYU (FWIP)
IT'S LIKE...
...MY SWORD'S THE ONE DODGING HER...!
HYU
I JUST... NEED ONE...

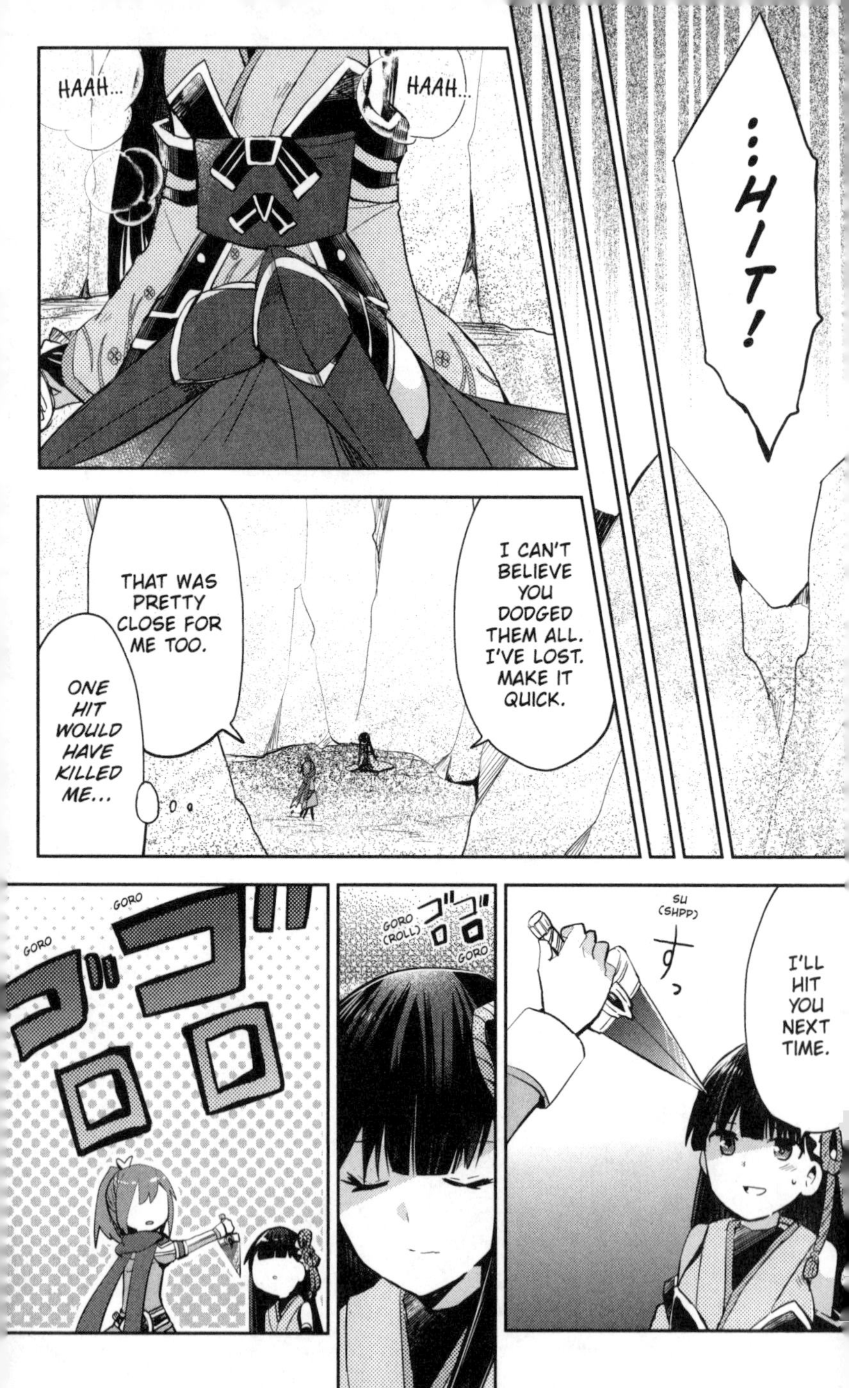

...HIT!
HAAH...
HAAH...
I CAN'T BELIEVE YOU DODGED THEM ALL. I'VE LOST. MAKE IT QUICK.
THAT WAS PRETTY CLOSE FOR ME TOO.
ONE HIT WOULD HAVE KILLED ME...
SU (SHPP)
I'LL HIT YOU NEXT TIME.
GORO (ROLL)
GORO
GORO
GORO

VENOM CAPSULE: Trap an enemy in a poison capsule.

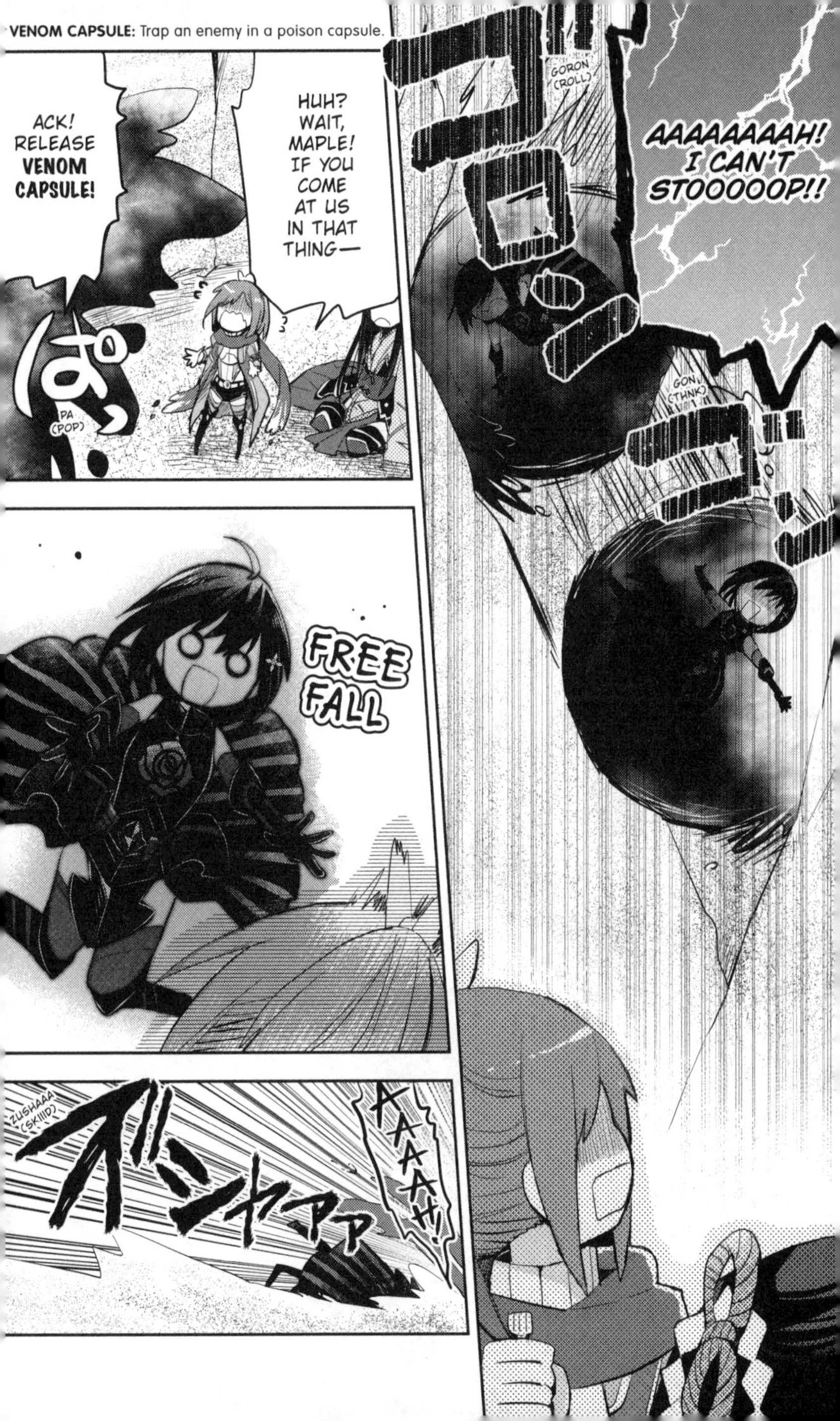
GORON (ROLL)
AAAAAAAAH! I CAN'T STOOOOOP!!
GON (THNK)
HUH? WAIT, MAPLE! IF YOU COME AT US IN THAT THING—
ACK! RELEASE VENOM CAPSULE!
PA (POP)
FREE FALL
AAAAAH!!
ZUSHAAA (SKIIID)

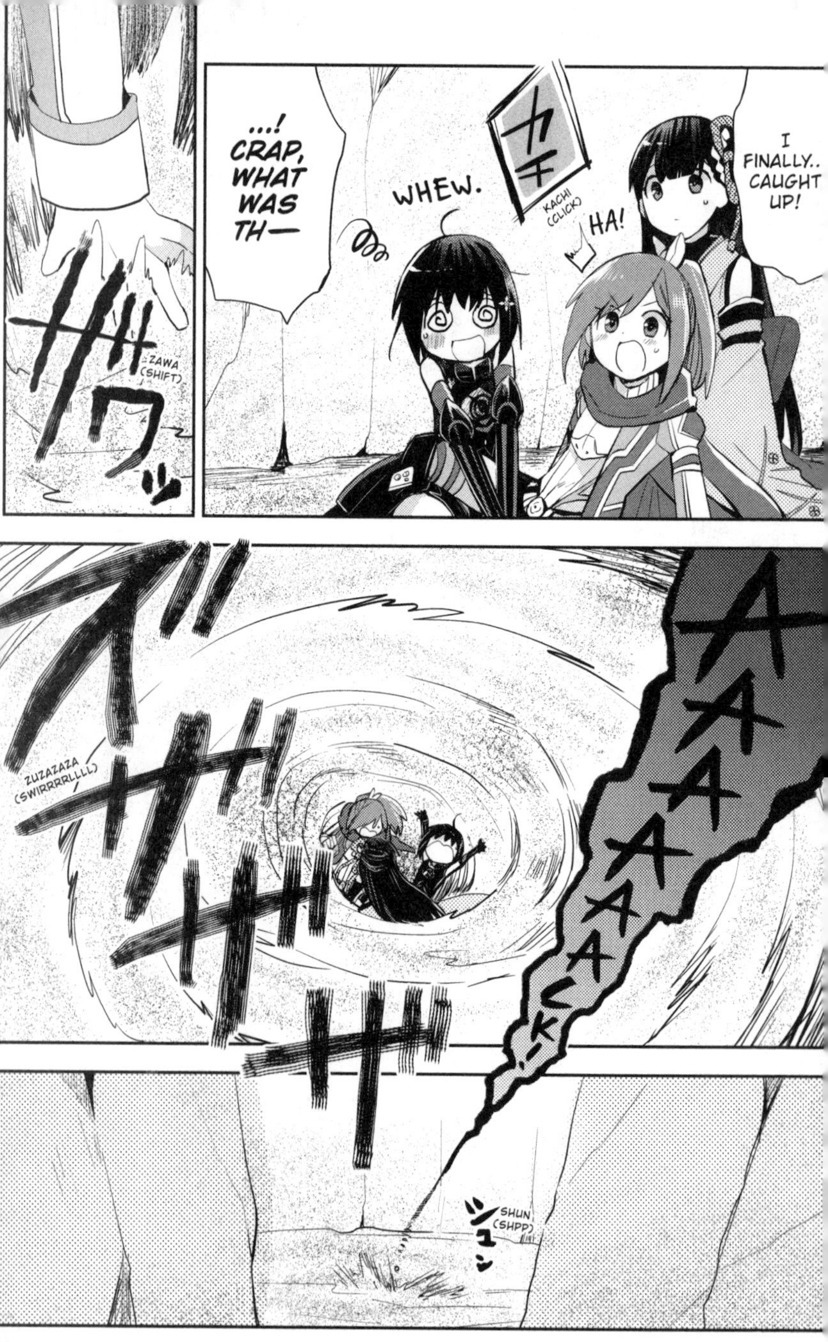
I FINALLY.. CAUGHT UP!
カチ
KACHI (CLICK)
HA!
WHEW.
...! CRAP, WHAT WAS TH—
ZAWA (SHIFT)
AAAAAACK—!
ZUZAZAZA (SWIRRRRLLLL)
SHUN (SHPP)

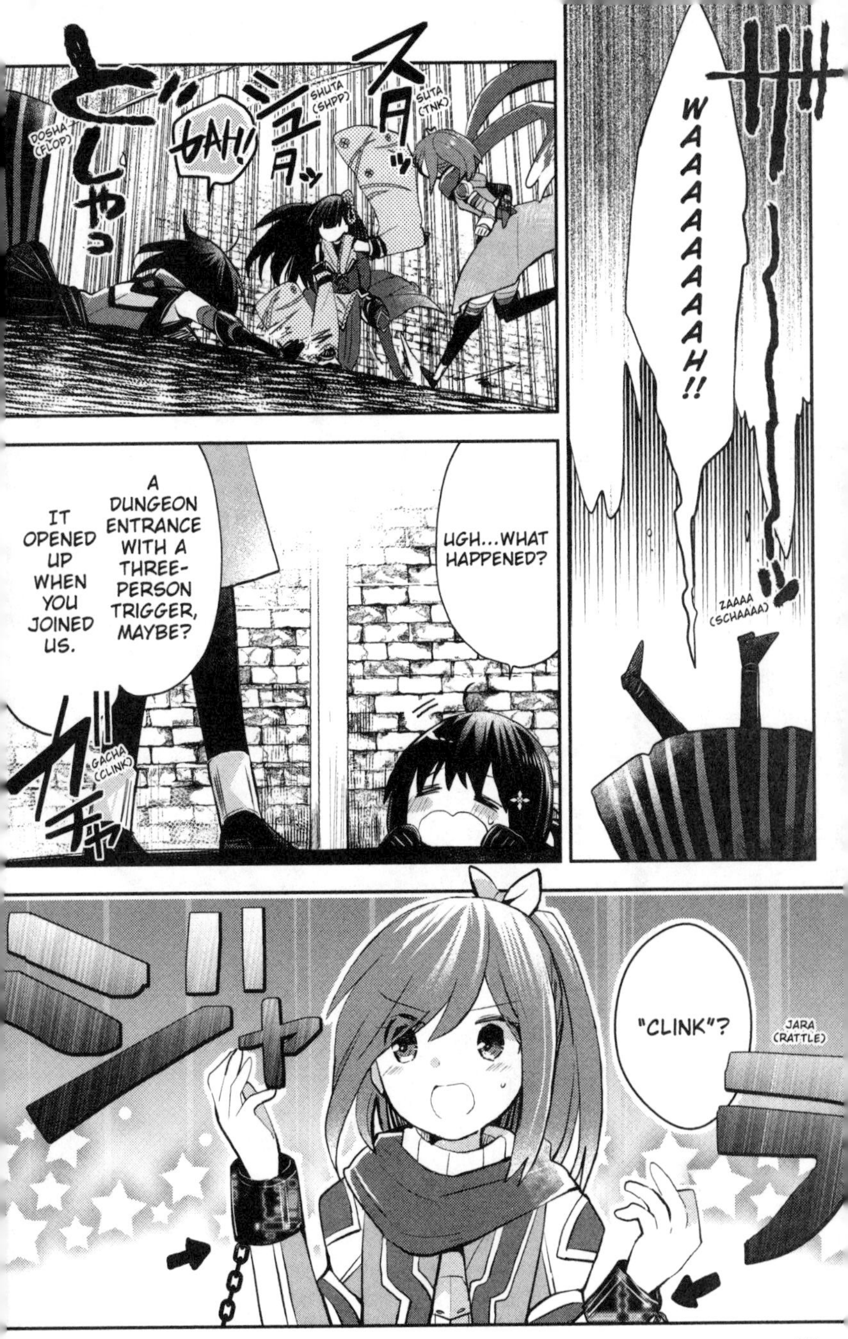
WAAAAAAAAAAH!!
ZAAAA (SCHAAAA)
SUTA (TNK)
SHUTA (SHPP)
GAH!!
DOSHA (FLOP)
UGH...WHAT HAPPENED?
A DUNGEON ENTRANCE WITH A THREE-PERSON TRIGGER, MAYBE?
IT OPENED UP WHEN YOU JOINED US.
GACHA (CLINK)
JARA (RATTLE)
"CLINK"?

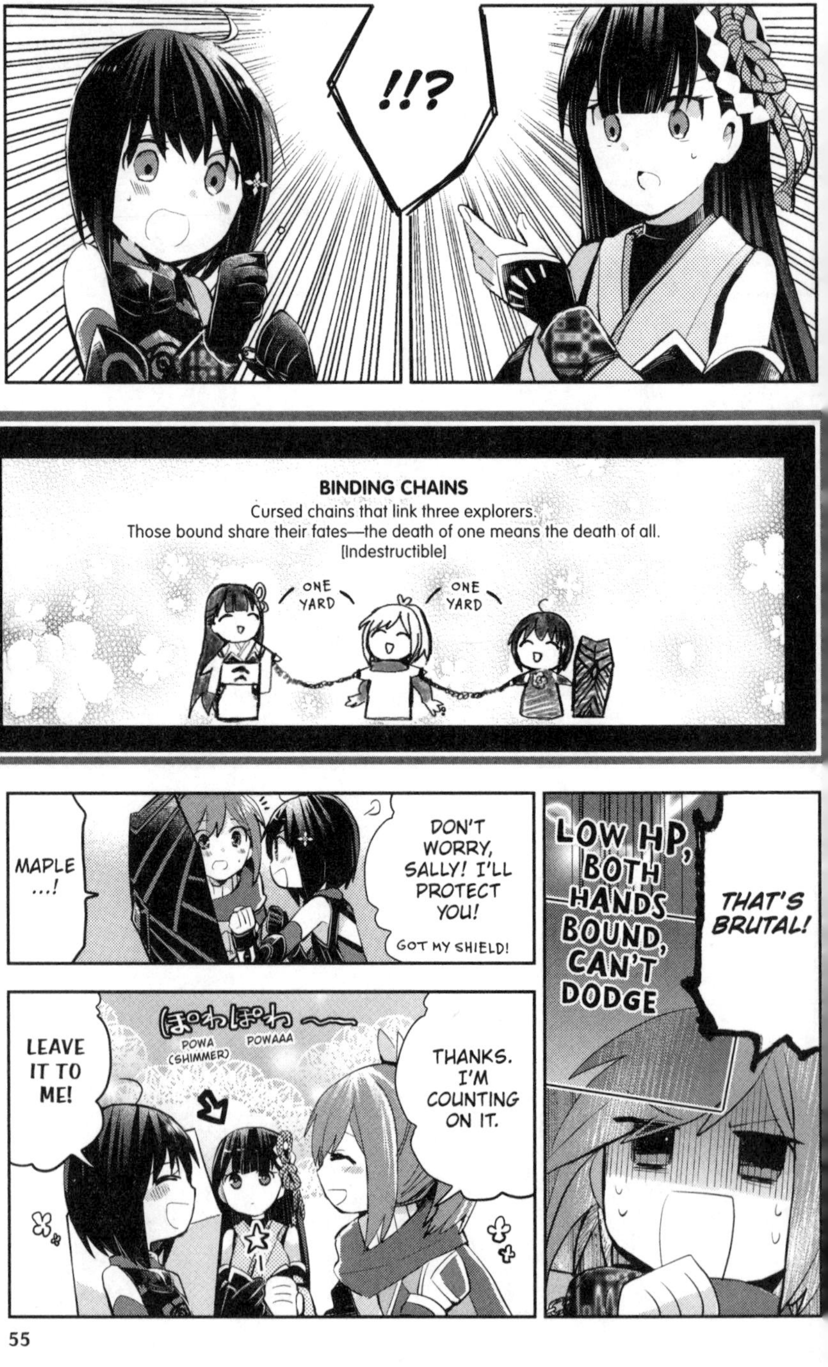
!!?
BINDING CHAINS
Cursed chains that link three explorers.
Those bound share their fates—the death of one means the death of all.
[Indestructible]
ONE YARD
ONE YARD
THAT'S BRUTAL!
LOW HP, BOTH HANDS BOUND, CAN'T DODGE
DON'T WORRY, SALLY! I'LL PROTECT YOU!
GOT MY SHIELD!
MAPLE ...!
ぽわぽわ〜〜
POWA (SHIMMER)
POWAAA
THANKS. I'M COUNTING ON IT.
LEAVE IT TO ME!

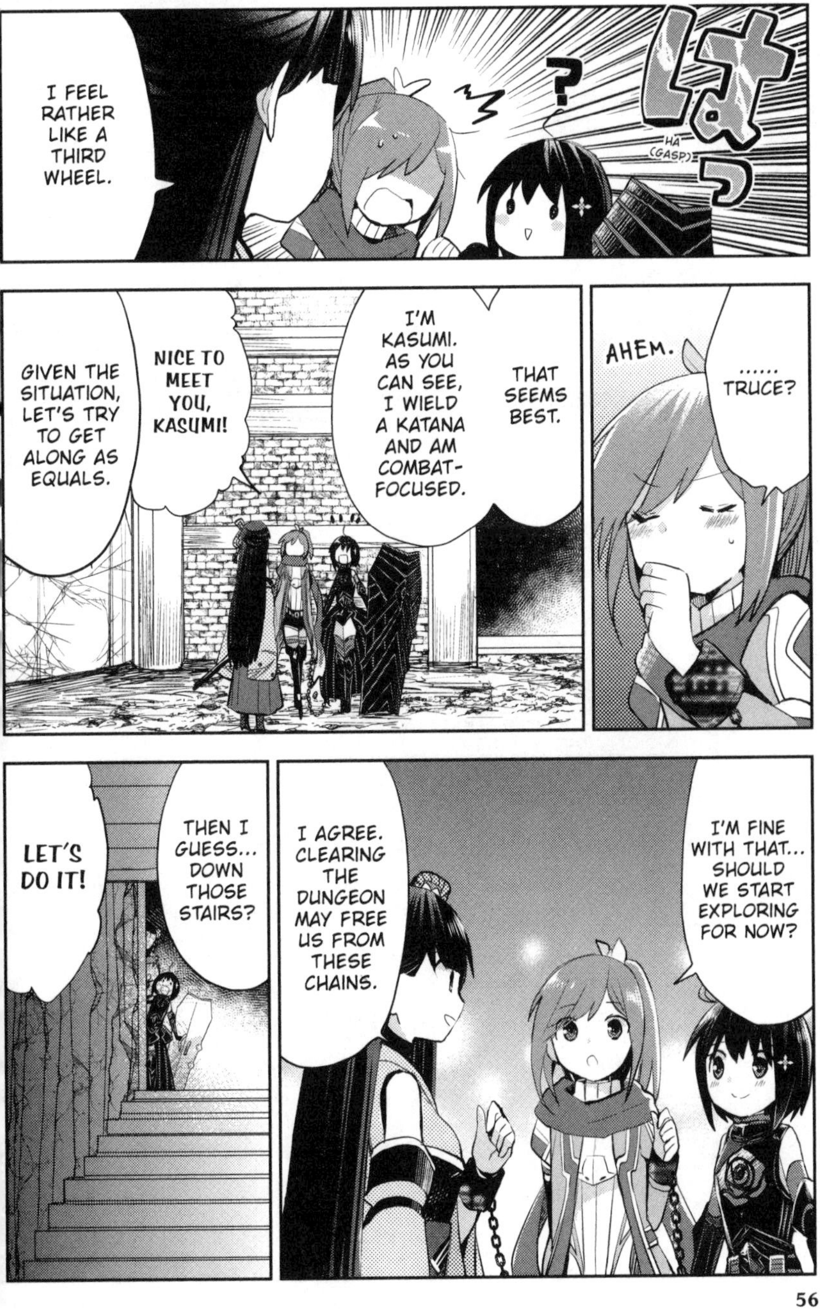
はっ
HA (GASP)
?
I FEEL RATHER LIKE A THIRD WHEEL.
AHEM.
......TRUCE?
THAT SEEMS BEST.
I'M KASUMI. AS YOU CAN SEE, I WIELD A KATANA AND AM COMBAT-FOCUSED.
NICE TO MEET YOU, KASUMI!
GIVEN THE SITUATION, LET'S TRY TO GET ALONG AS EQUALS.
I'M FINE WITH THAT... SHOULD WE START EXPLORING FOR NOW?
I AGREE. CLEARING THE DUNGEON MAY FREE US FROM THESE CHAINS.
THEN I GUESS... DOWN THOSE STAIRS?
LET'S DO IT!

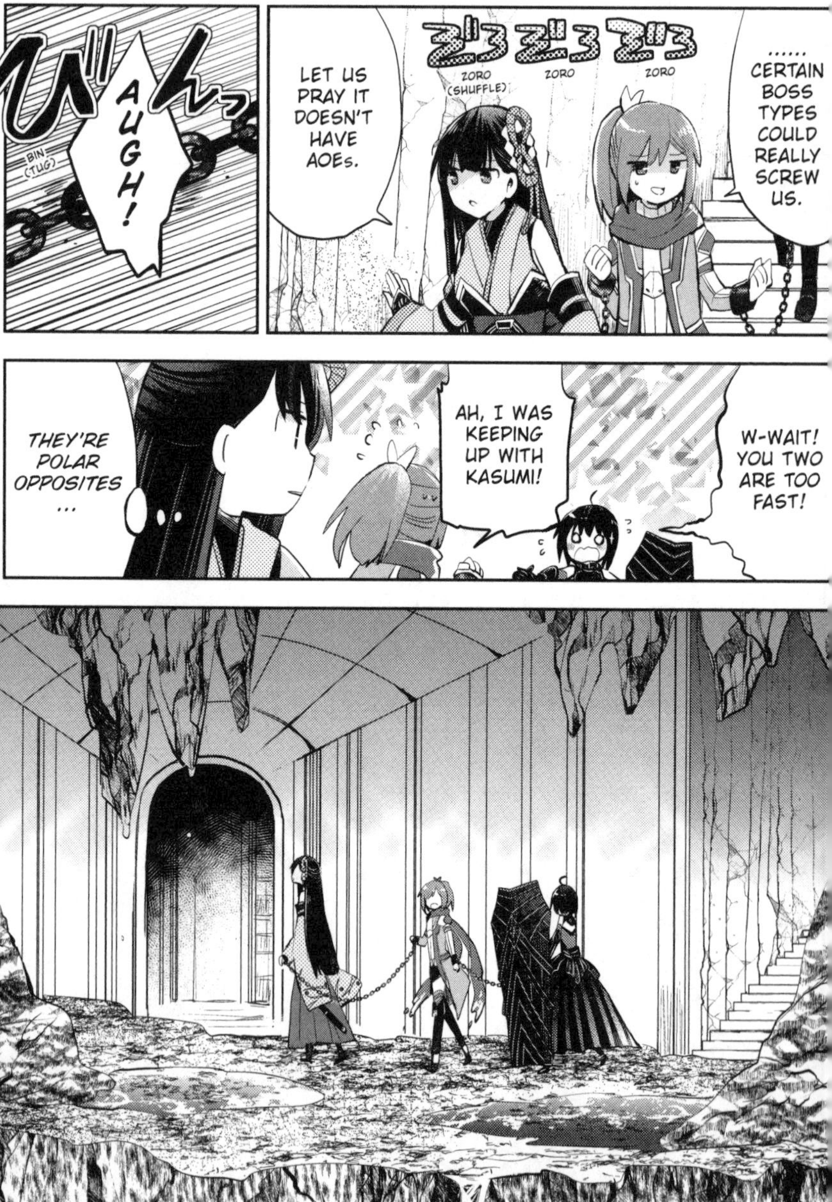
......CERTAIN BOSS TYPES COULD REALLY SCREW US.
ZORO ZORO ZORO (SHUFFLE)
LET US PRAY IT DOESN'T HAVE AOEs.
AUGH!
BIN (TUG)
W-WAIT! YOU TWO ARE TOO FAST!
AH, I WAS KEEPING UP WITH KASUMI!
THEY'RE POLAR OPPOSITES...

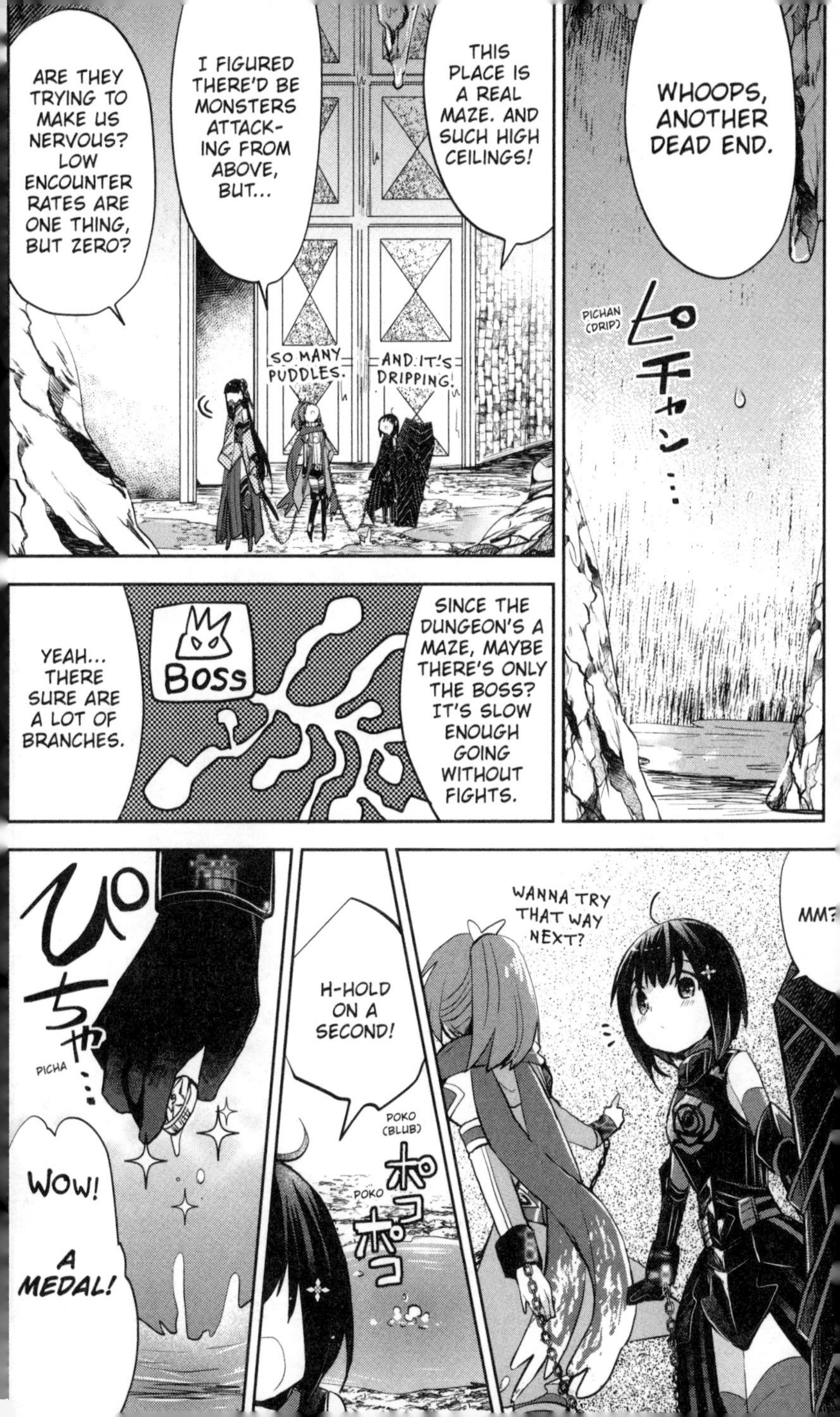
WHOOPS, ANOTHER DEAD END.
PICHAN (DRIP)
ピチャン…
THIS PLACE IS A REAL MAZE. AND SUCH HIGH CEILINGS!
I FIGURED THERE'D BE MONSTERS ATTACKING FROM ABOVE, BUT...
ARE THEY TRYING TO MAKE US NERVOUS? LOW ENCOUNTER RATES ARE ONE THING, BUT ZERO?
AND IT'S DRIPPING!
SO MANY PUDDLES.
SINCE THE DUNGEON'S A MAZE, MAYBE THERE'S ONLY THE BOSS? IT'S SLOW ENOUGH GOING WITHOUT FIGHTS.
BOSS
YEAH... THERE SURE ARE A LOT OF BRANCHES.
MM?
WANNA TRY THAT WAY NEXT?
H-HOLD ON A SECOND!
POKO (BLUB)
ポコ
POKO
ポコ
ぴちゃ…
PICHA
WOW!
A MEDAL!

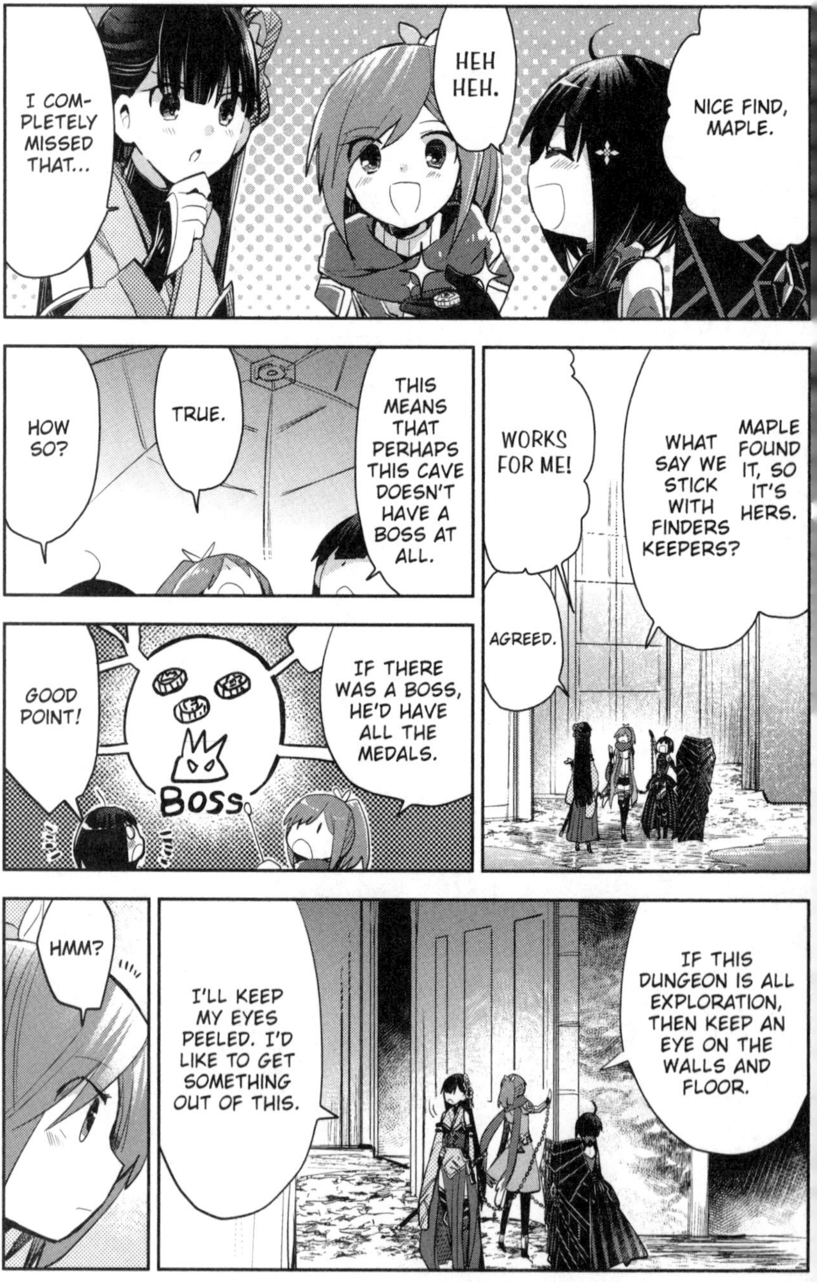
NICE FIND, MAPLE.
HEH HEH.
I COMPLETELY MISSED THAT...
MAPLE FOUND IT, SO IT'S HERS.
WHAT SAY WE STICK WITH FINDERS KEEPERS?
WORKS FOR ME!
AGREED.
THIS MEANS THAT PERHAPS THIS CAVE DOESN'T HAVE A BOSS AT ALL.
TRUE.
HOW SO?
IF THERE WAS A BOSS, HE'D HAVE ALL THE MEDALS.
BOSS
GOOD POINT!
IF THIS DUNGEON IS ALL EXPLORATION, THEN KEEP AN EYE ON THE WALLS AND FLOOR.
I'LL KEEP MY EYES PEELED. I'D LIKE TO GET SOMETHING OUT OF THIS.
HMM?

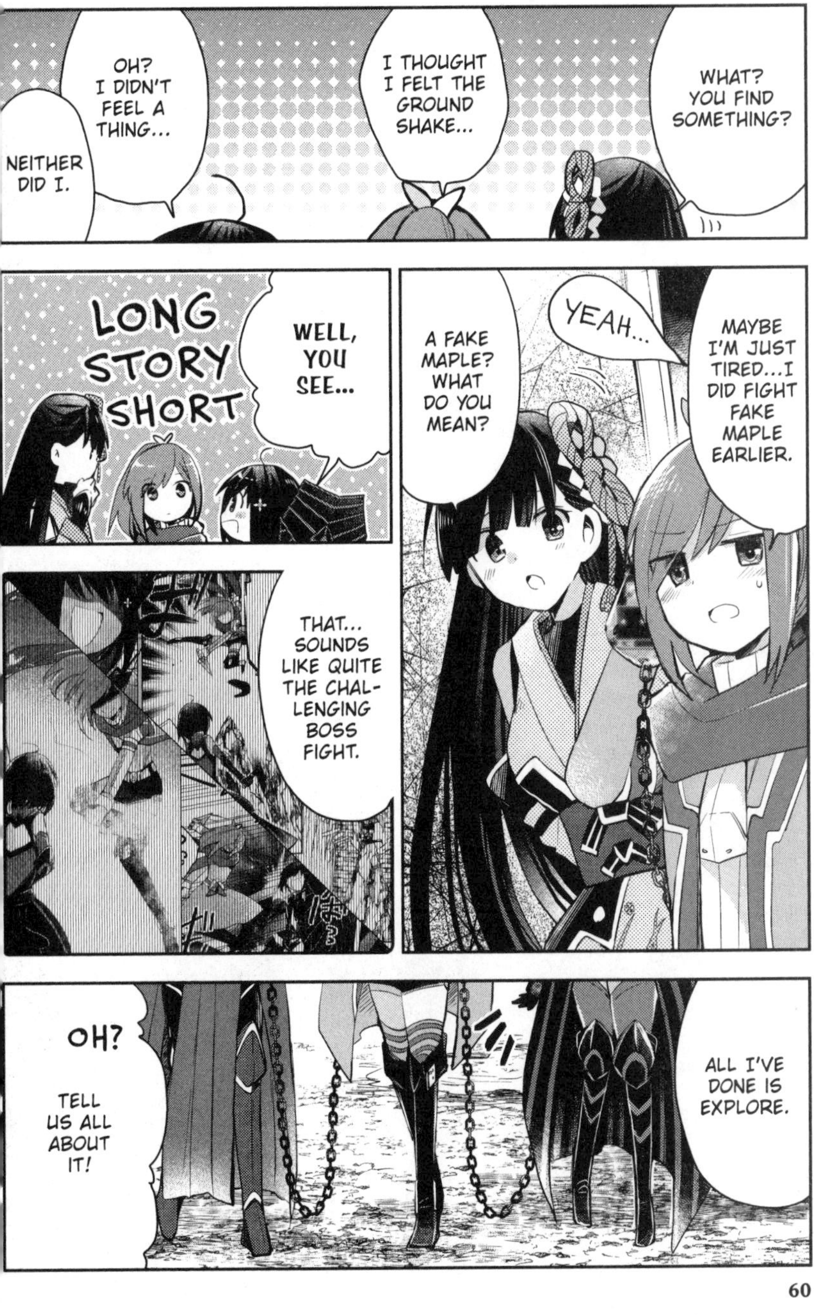
WHAT? YOU FIND SOMETHING?
I THOUGHT I FELT THE GROUND SHAKE...
OH? I DIDN'T FEEL A THING...
NEITHER DID I.
MAYBE I'M JUST TIRED...I DID FIGHT FAKE MAPLE EARLIER.
YEAH...
A FAKE MAPLE? WHAT DO YOU MEAN?
WELL, YOU SEE...
LONG STORY SHORT
THAT... SOUNDS LIKE QUITE THE CHAL-LENGING BOSS FIGHT.
ALL I'VE DONE IS EXPLORE.
OH?
TELL US ALL ABOUT IT!

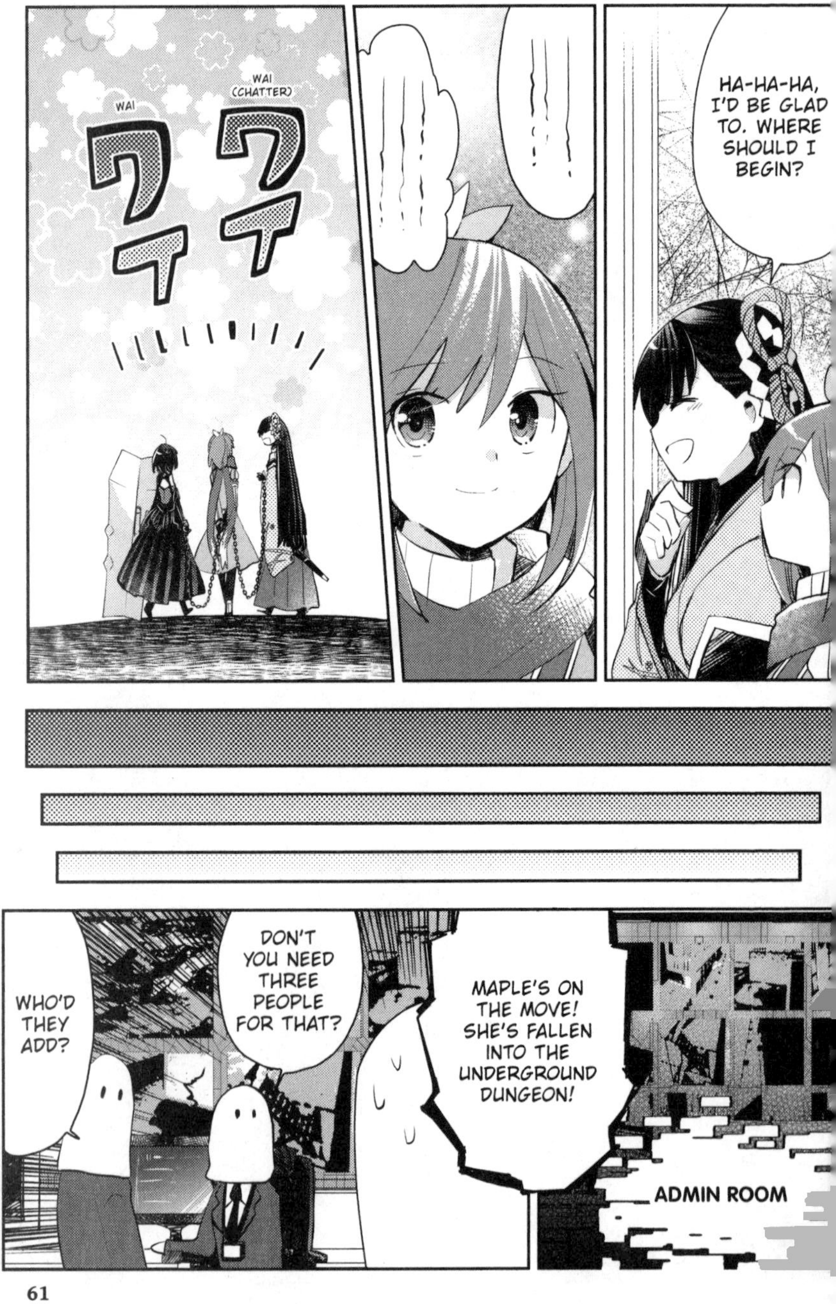
HA-HA-HA, I'D BE GLAD TO. WHERE SHOULD I BEGIN?
ワイ
WAI (CHATTER)
ワイ
WAI
ADMIN ROOM
MAPLE'S ON THE MOVE! SHE'S FALLEN INTO THE UNDERGROUND DUNGEON!
DON'T YOU NEED THREE PEOPLE FOR THAT?
WHO'D THEY ADD?

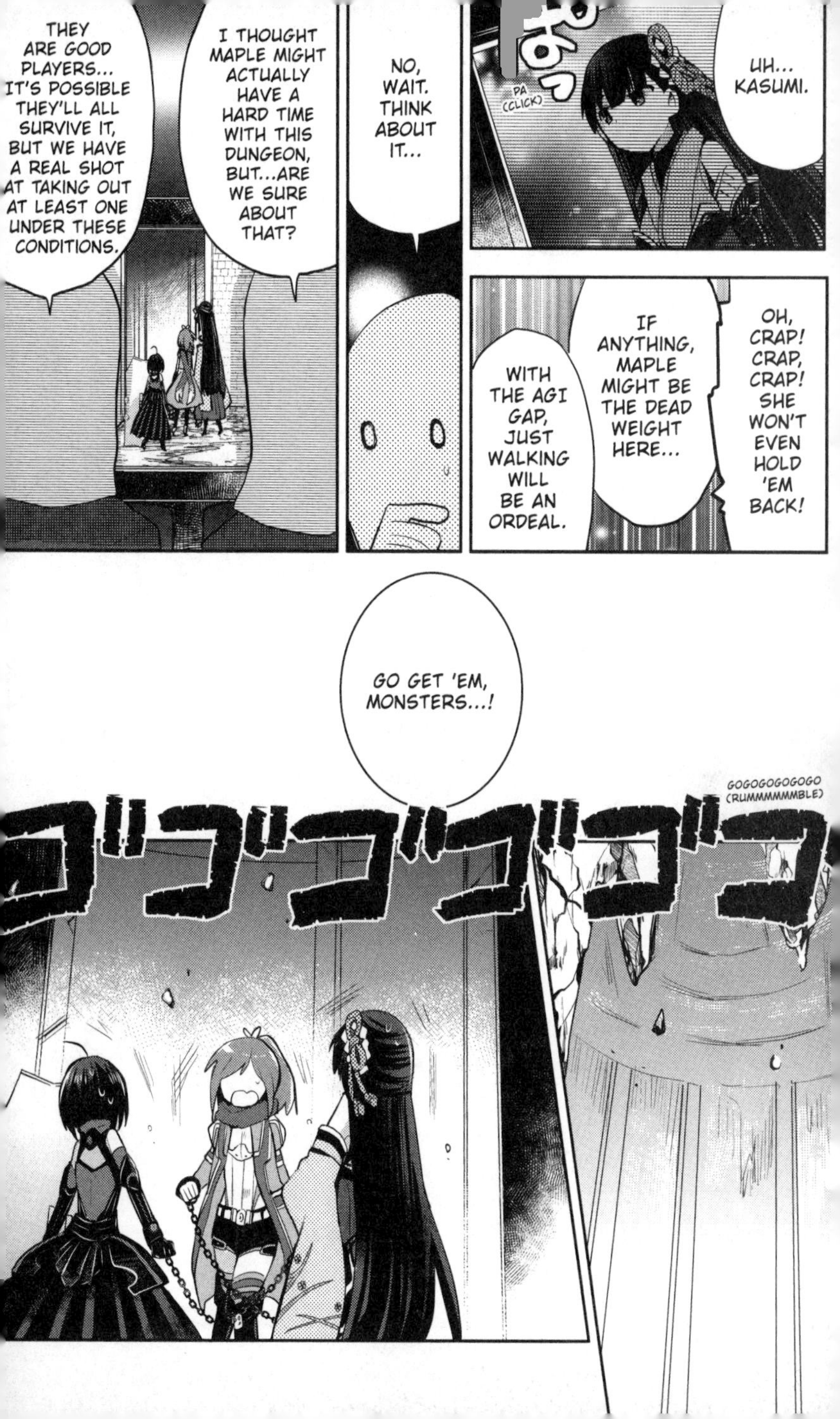
UH... KASUMI.
PA (CLICK)
OH, CRAP! CRAP, CRAP! SHE WON'T EVEN HOLD 'EM BACK!
IF ANYTHING, MAPLE MIGHT BE THE DEAD WEIGHT HERE...
WITH THE AGI GAP, JUST WALKING WILL BE AN ORDEAL.
NO, WAIT. THINK ABOUT IT...
I THOUGHT MAPLE MIGHT ACTUALLY HAVE A HARD TIME WITH THIS DUNGEON, BUT...ARE WE SURE ABOUT THAT?
THEY ARE GOOD PLAYERS... IT'S POSSIBLE THEY'LL ALL SURVIVE IT, BUT WE HAVE A REAL SHOT AT TAKING OUT AT LEAST ONE UNDER THESE CONDITIONS.
GO GET 'EM, MONSTERS...!
GOGOGOGOGOGO (RUMMMMMMBLE)

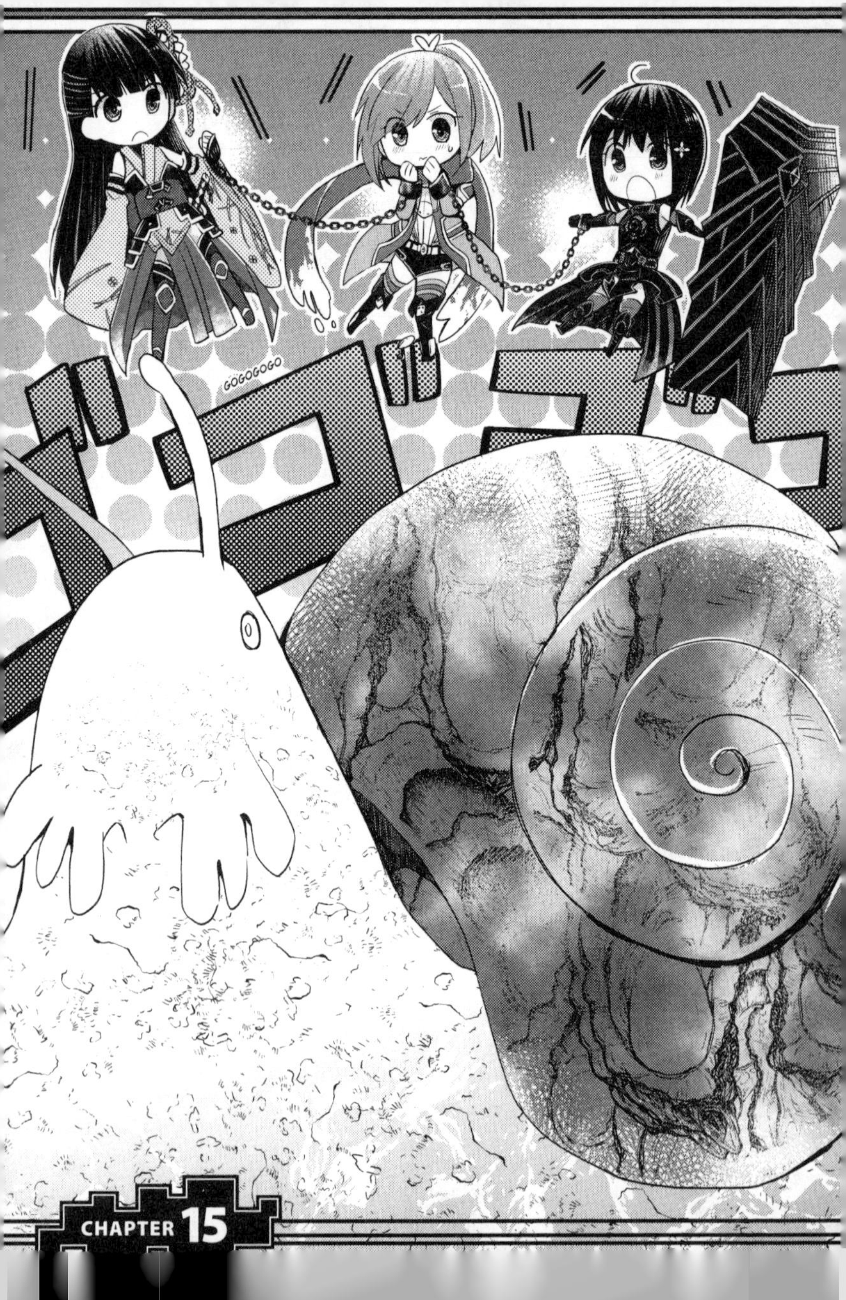
GOGOGOGO
CHAPTER 15

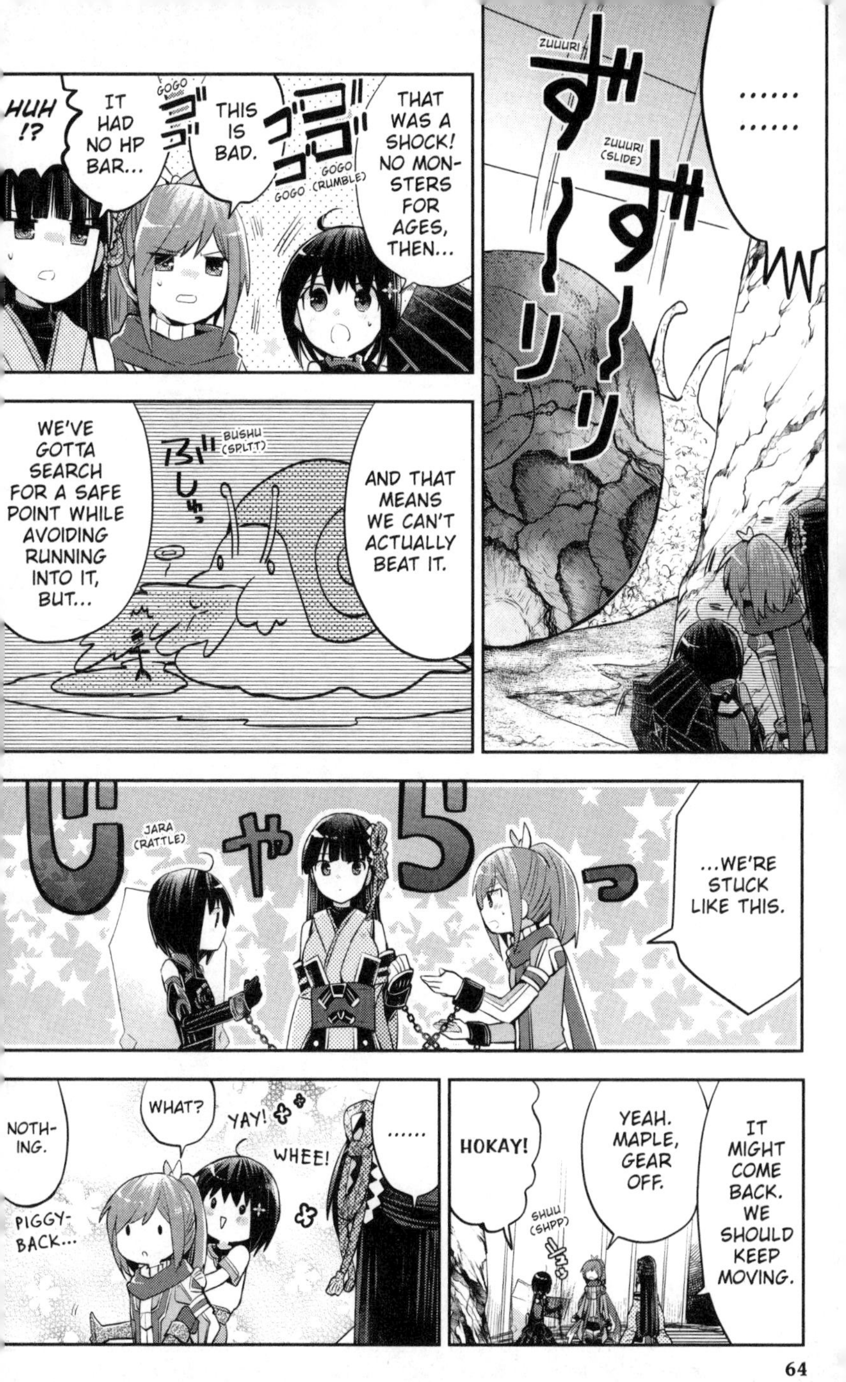
......
......
ZUUURI
ZUUURI (SLIDE)
THAT WAS A SHOCK! NO MONSTERS FOR AGES, THEN...
GOGO (RUMBLE)
GOGO
THIS IS BAD.
GOGO
IT HAD NO HP BAR...
HUH!?
AND THAT MEANS WE CAN'T ACTUALLY BEAT IT.
BUSHU (SPLTT)
WE'VE GOTTA SEARCH FOR A SAFE POINT WHILE AVOIDING RUNNING INTO IT, BUT...
...WE'RE STUCK LIKE THIS.
JARA (RATTLE)
IT MIGHT COME BACK. WE SHOULD KEEP MOVING.
YEAH. MAPLE, GEAR OFF.
SHUU (SHPP)
HOKAY!
......
WHEE!
YAY!
WHAT?
NOTHING.
PIGGYBACK...

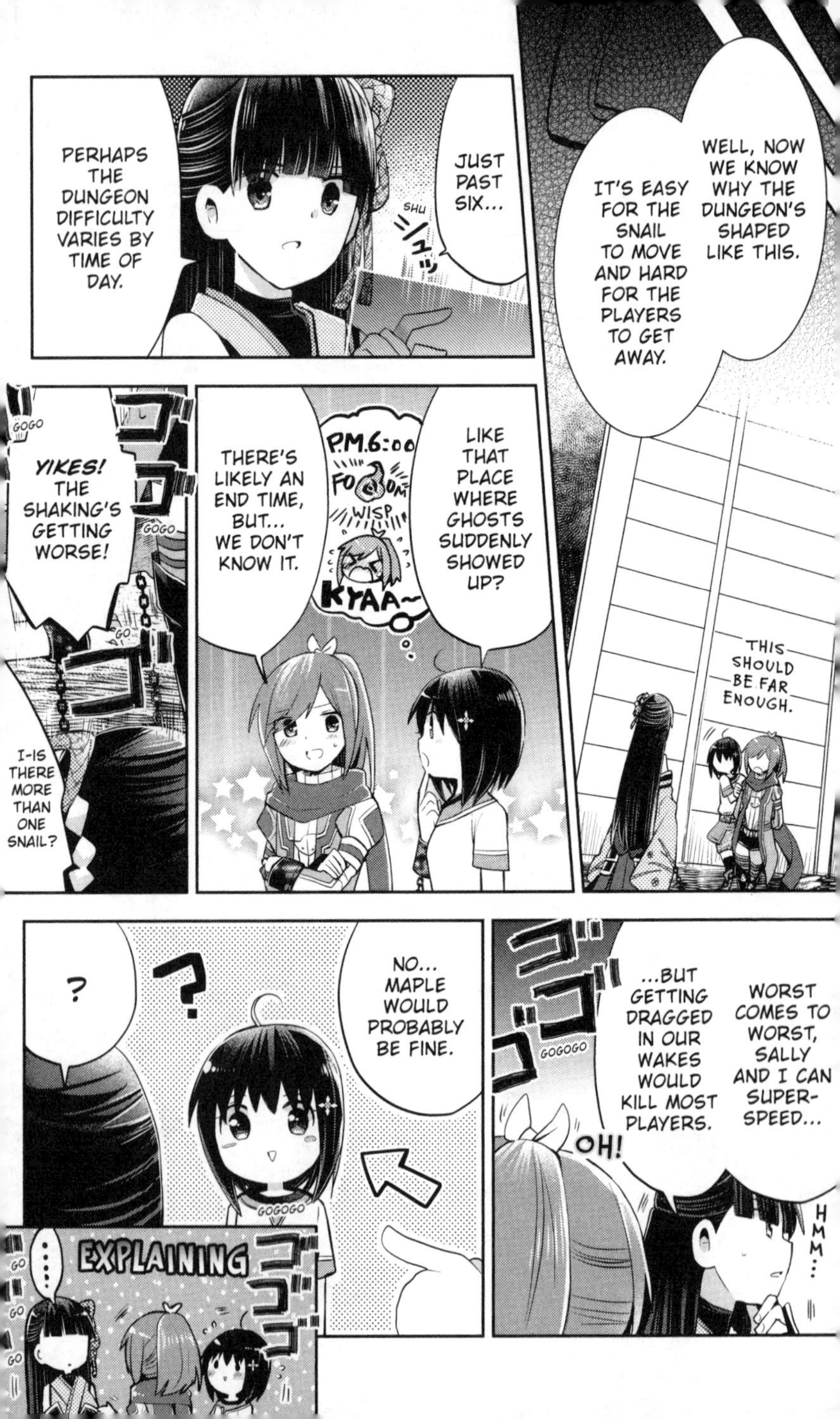

WELL, NOW WE KNOW WHY THE DUNGEON'S SHAPED LIKE THIS.
IT'S EASY FOR THE SNAIL TO MOVE AND HARD FOR THE PLAYERS TO GET AWAY.
THIS SHOULD BE FAR ENOUGH.
JUST PAST SIX...
SHU
PERHAPS THE DUNGEON DIFFICULTY VARIES BY TIME OF DAY.
LIKE THAT PLACE WHERE GHOSTS SUDDENLY SHOWED UP?
P.M.6:00
FOOM
WISP
KYAA~
THERE'S LIKELY AN END TIME, BUT... WE DON'T KNOW IT.
GOGO
YIKES! THE SHAKING'S GETTING WORSE!
GOGO
GO
I-IS THERE MORE THAN ONE SNAIL?
HMM...
WORST COMES TO WORST, SALLY AND I CAN SUPER-SPEED...
...BUT GETTING DRAGGED IN OUR WAKES WOULD KILL MOST PLAYERS.
GOGOGO
OH!
NO... MAPLE WOULD PROBABLY BE FINE.
?
?
GOGOGO
EXPLAINING
...
GO
GO
GO

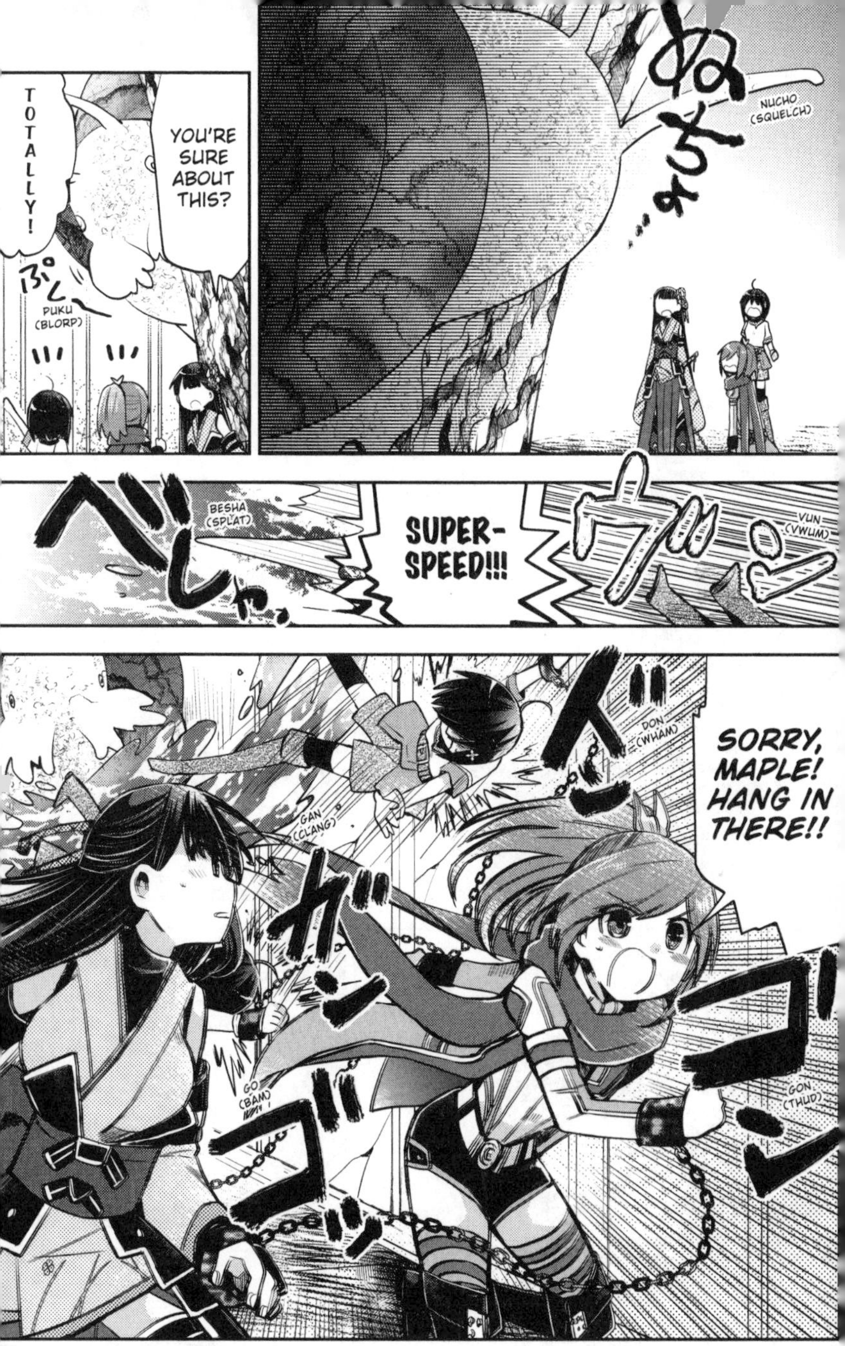
NUCHO (SQUELCH)
YOU'RE SURE ABOUT THIS?
TOTALLY!
PUKU (BLORP)
VUN (VWUM)
SUPER-SPEED!!!
BESHA (SPLAT)
SORRY, MAPLE! HANG IN THERE!!
DON (WHAM)
GAN (CLANG)
GON (THUD)
GO (BAM)

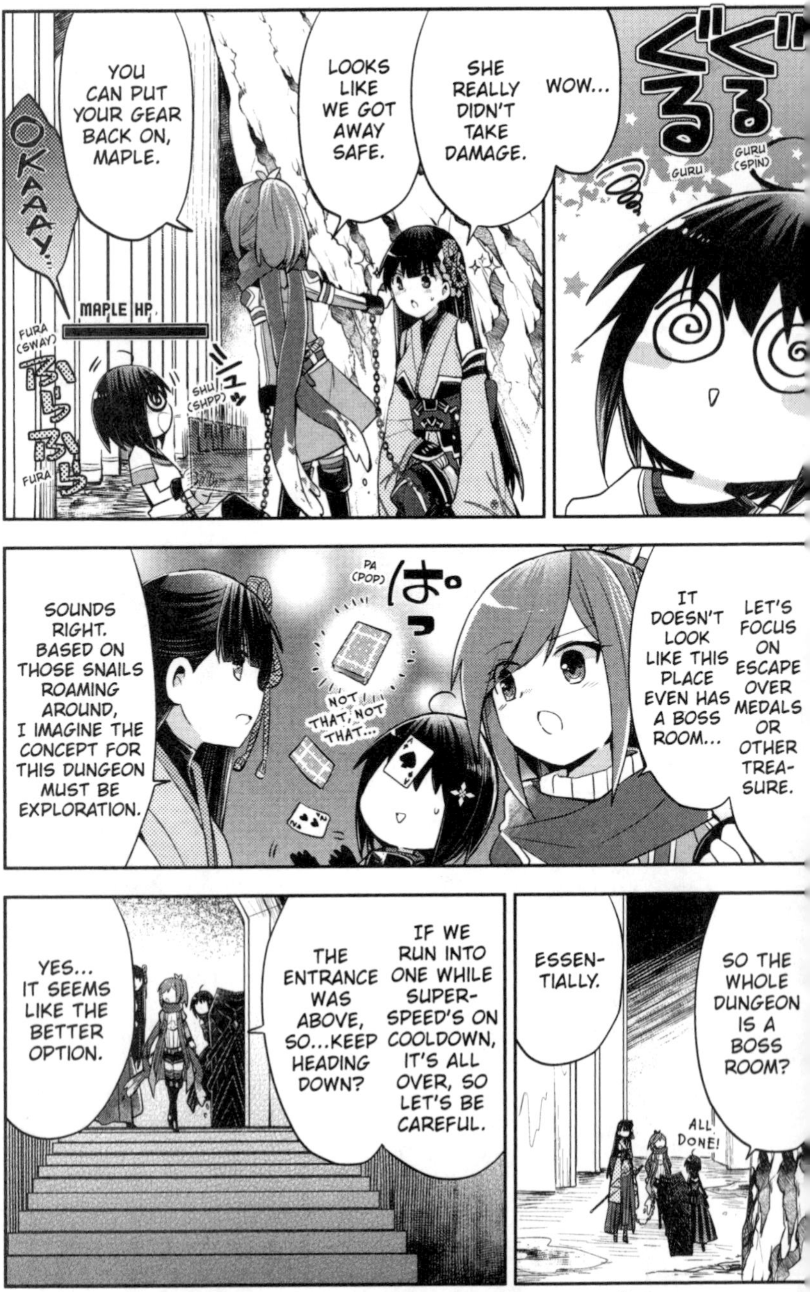
GURU
GURU (SPIN)
WOW...
SHE REALLY DIDN'T TAKE DAMAGE.
LOOKS LIKE WE GOT AWAY SAFE.
YOU CAN PUT YOUR GEAR BACK ON, MAPLE.
OKAAAY...
MAPLE HP
SHU (SHPP)
FURA (SWAY)
FURA
LET'S FOCUS ON ESCAPE OVER MEDALS OR OTHER TREASURE.
IT DOESN'T LOOK LIKE THIS PLACE EVEN HAS A BOSS ROOM...
PA (POP)
NOT THAT, NOT THAT...
SOUNDS RIGHT. BASED ON THOSE SNAILS ROAMING AROUND, I IMAGINE THE CONCEPT FOR THIS DUNGEON MUST BE EXPLORATION.
SO THE WHOLE DUNGEON IS A BOSS ROOM?
ESSEN-TIALLY.
ALL DONE!
IF WE RUN INTO ONE WHILE SUPER-SPEED'S ON COOLDOWN, IT'S ALL OVER, SO LET'S BE CAREFUL.
THE ENTRANCE WAS ABOVE, SO...KEEP HEADING DOWN?
YES... IT SEEMS LIKE THE BETTER OPTION.

★ **SUPERSPEED:** 50% AGI boost. Lasts one minute. Thirty-minute cooldown.

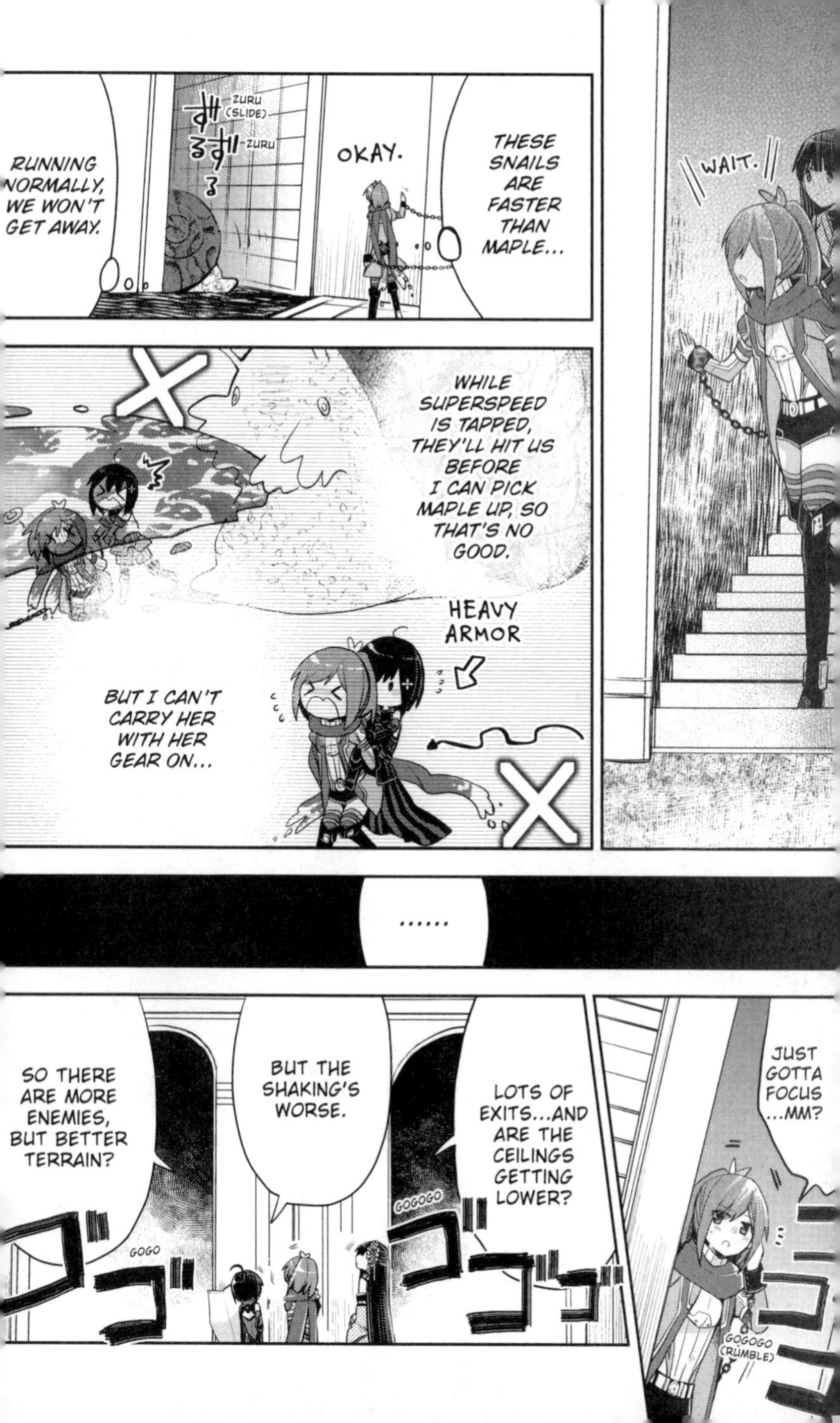
WAIT.
THESE SNAILS ARE FASTER THAN MAPLE...
OKAY.
ZURU (SLIDE)
ZURU
RUNNING NORMALLY, WE WON'T GET AWAY.
WHILE SUPERSPEED IS TAPPED, THEY'LL HIT US BEFORE I CAN PICK MAPLE UP, SO THAT'S NO GOOD.
HEAVY ARMOR
BUT I CAN'T CARRY HER WITH HER GEAR ON...
......
JUST GOTTA FOCUS ...MM?
GOGOGO (RUMBLE)
LOTS OF EXITS...AND ARE THE CEILINGS GETTING LOWER?
GOGOGO
BUT THE SHAKING'S WORSE.
SO THERE ARE MORE ENEMIES, BUT BETTER TERRAIN?
GOGO

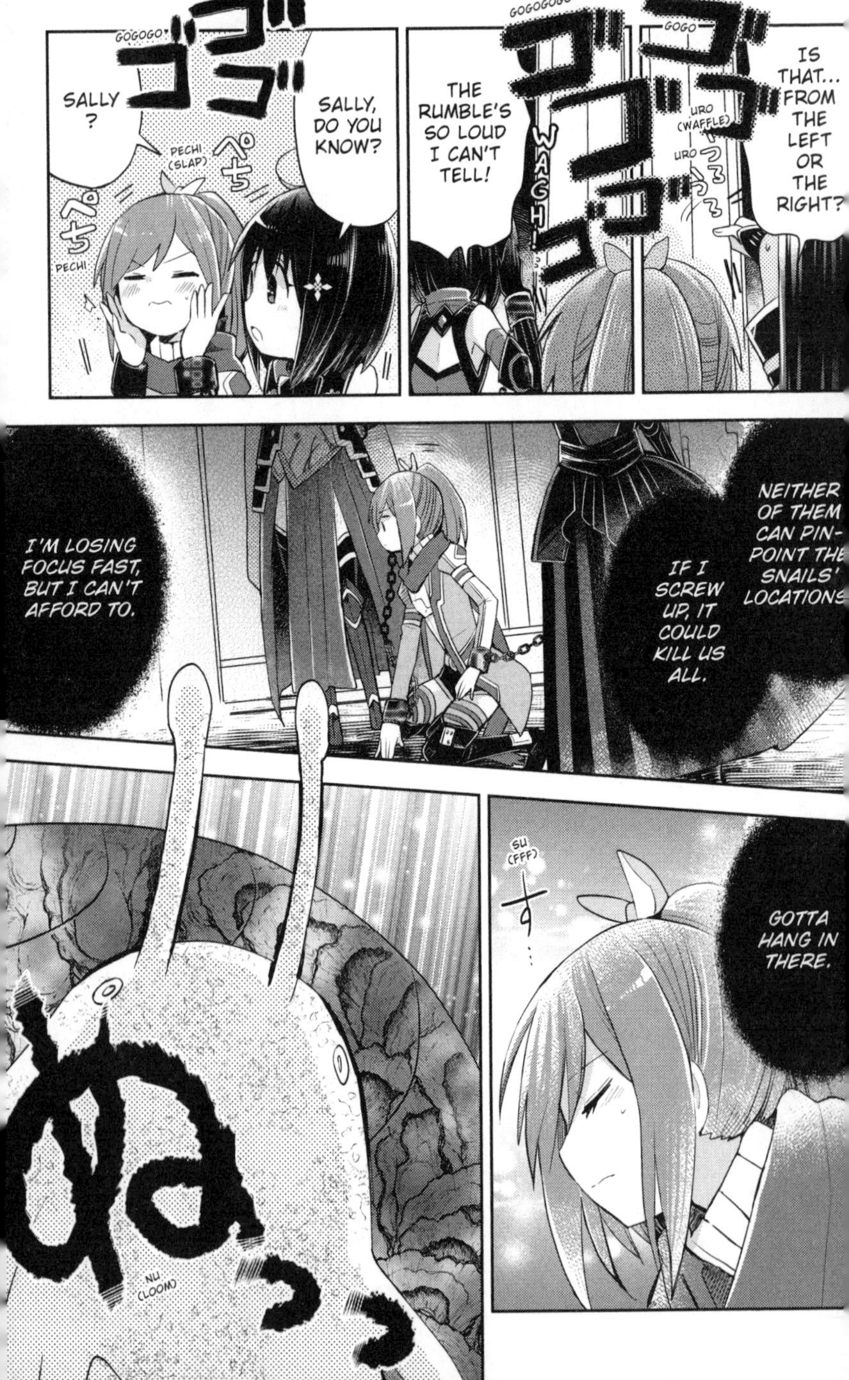
GOGO
IS THAT... FROM THE LEFT OR THE RIGHT?
URO (WAFFLE)
URO
GOGOGOGO
THE RUMBLE'S SO LOUD I CAN'T TELL!
WAGH!!
GOGOGO
SALLY, DO YOU KNOW?
SALLY?
PECHI (SLAP)
PECHI
NEITHER OF THEM CAN PIN-POINT THE SNAILS' LOCATIONS
IF I SCREW UP, IT COULD KILL US ALL.
I'M LOSING FOCUS FAST, BUT I CAN'T AFFORD TO.
SU (FFF)
GOTTA HANG IN THERE.
NU (LOOM)

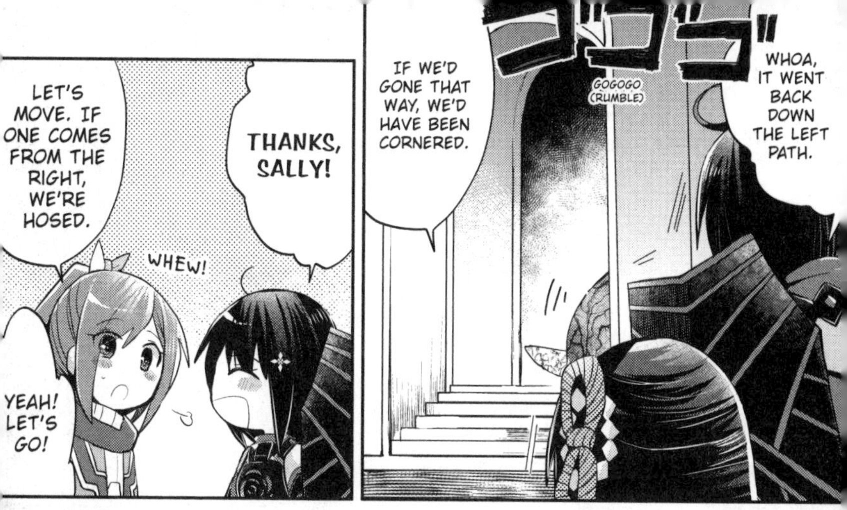
WHOA, IT WENT BACK DOWN THE LEFT PATH.
GOGOGO (RUMBLE)
IF WE'D GONE THAT WAY, WE'D HAVE BEEN CORNERED.
THANKS, SALLY!
LET'S MOVE. IF ONE COMES FROM THE RIGHT, WE'RE HOSED.
WHEW!
YEAH! LET'S GO!

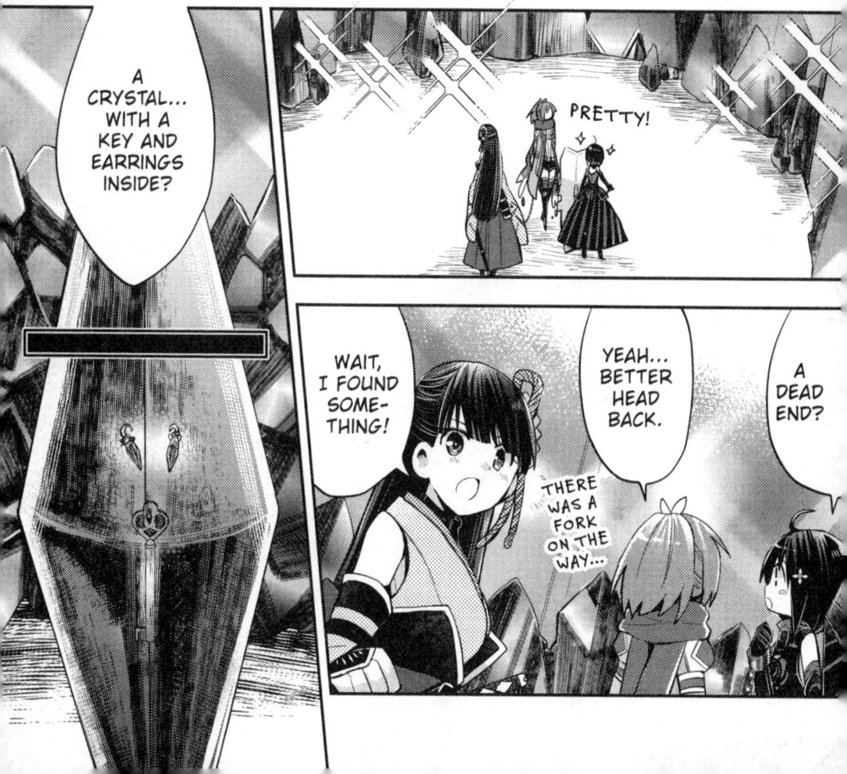
PRETTY!
A DEAD END?
YEAH... BETTER HEAD BACK.
THERE WAS A FORK ON THE WAY...
WAIT, I FOUND SOME-THING!
A CRYSTAL... WITH A KEY AND EARRINGS INSIDE?

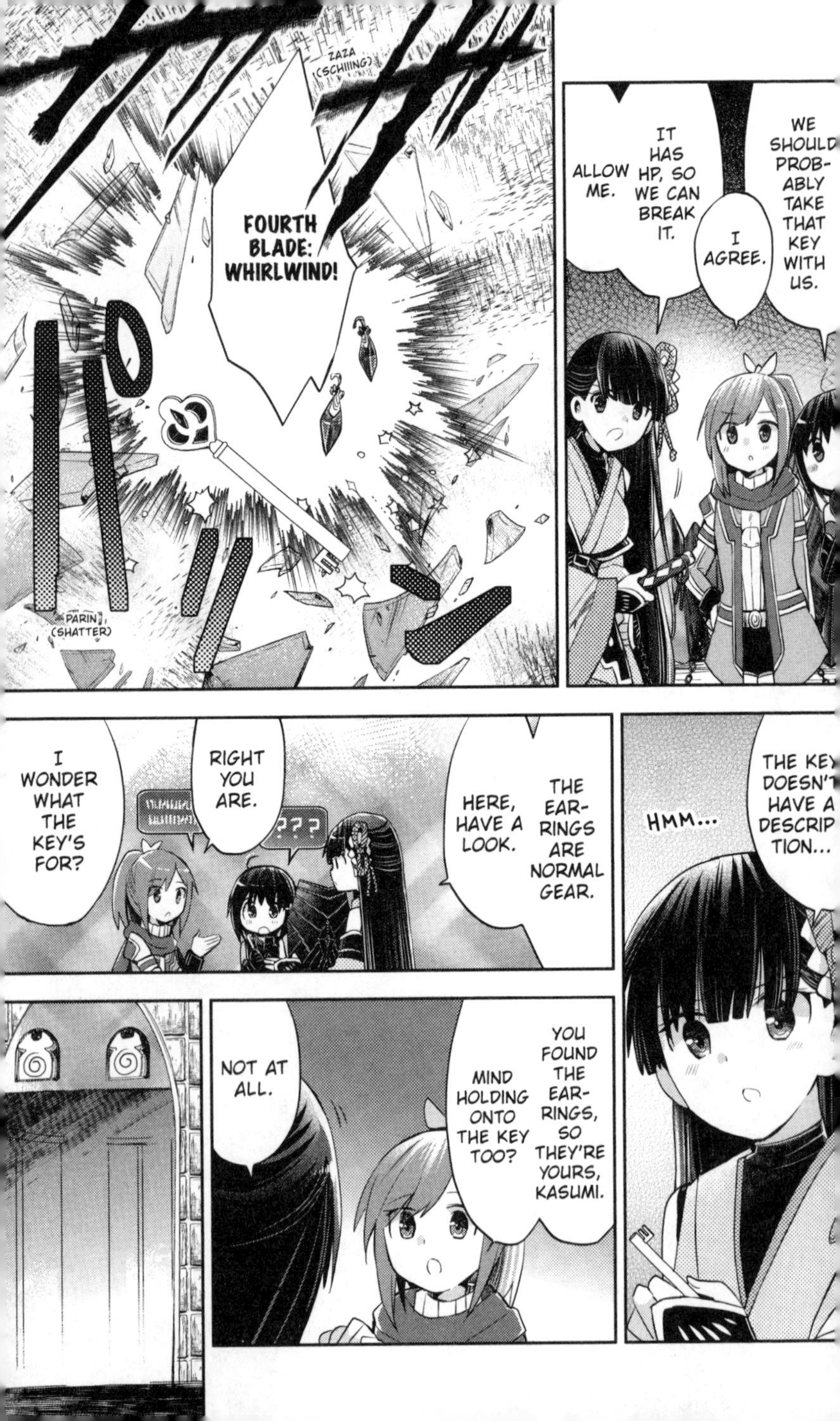
WE SHOULD PROB-ABLY TAKE THAT KEY WITH US.
I AGREE.
IT HAS HP, SO WE CAN BREAK IT.
ALLOW ME.
ZAZA (SCHIIING)
FOURTH BLADE: WHIRLWIND!
PARIN (SHATTER)
THE KEY DOESN'T HAVE A DESCRIP TION...
HMM...
THE EAR-RINGS ARE NORMAL GEAR.
HERE, HAVE A LOOK.
RIGHT YOU ARE.
???
I WONDER WHAT THE KEY'S FOR?
YOU FOUND THE EAR-RINGS, SO THEY'RE YOURS, KASUMI.
MIND HOLDING ONTO THE KEY TOO?
NOT AT ALL.

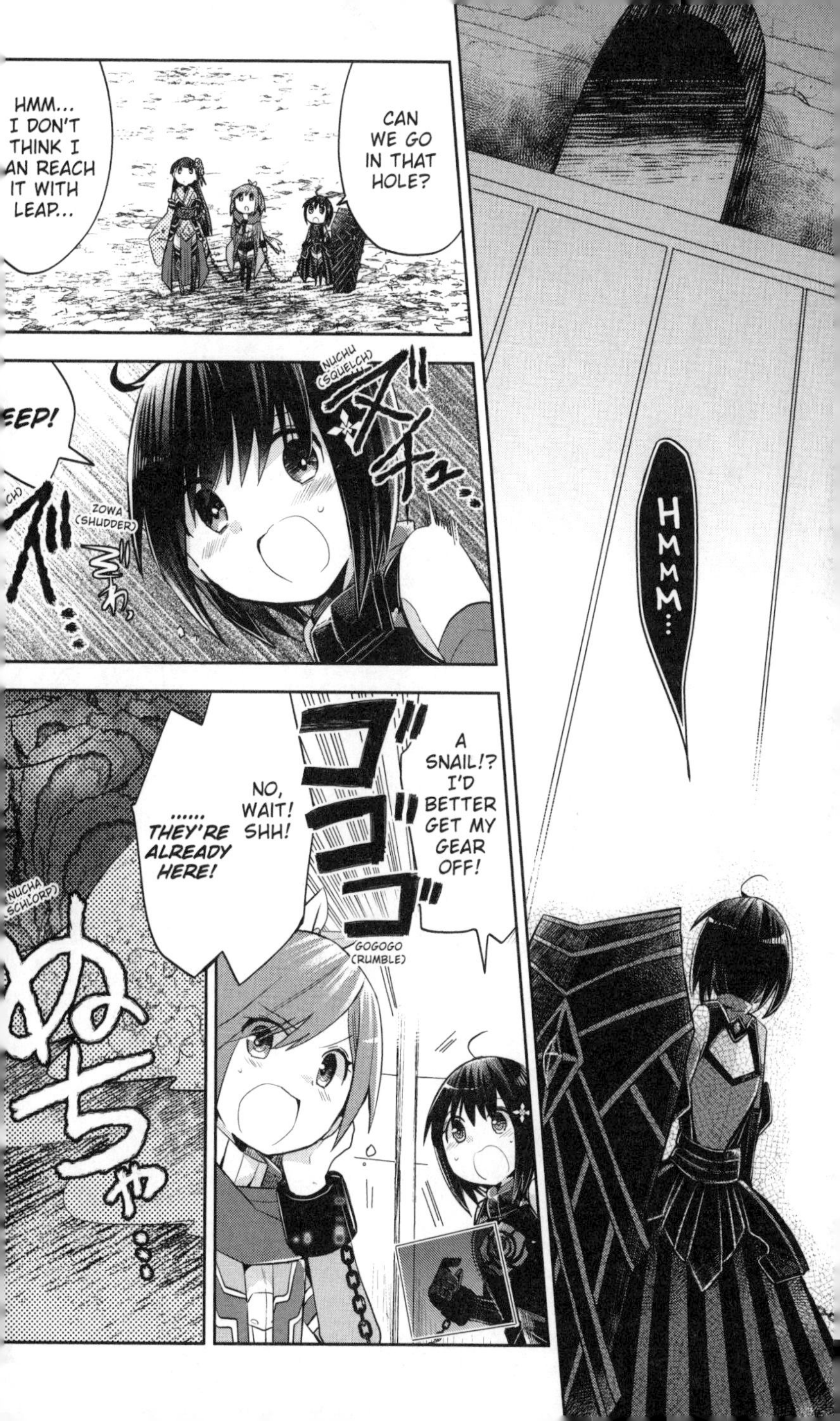
HMMM...
CAN WE GO IN THAT HOLE?
HMM... I DON'T THINK I AN REACH IT WITH LEAP...
NUCHU (SQUELCH)
EEP!
ZOWA (SHUDDER)
A SNAIL!? I'D BETTER GET MY GEAR OFF!
GOGOGO (RUMBLE)
NO, WAIT! SHH!
NUCHA SCHLORP
......THEY'RE ALREADY HERE!

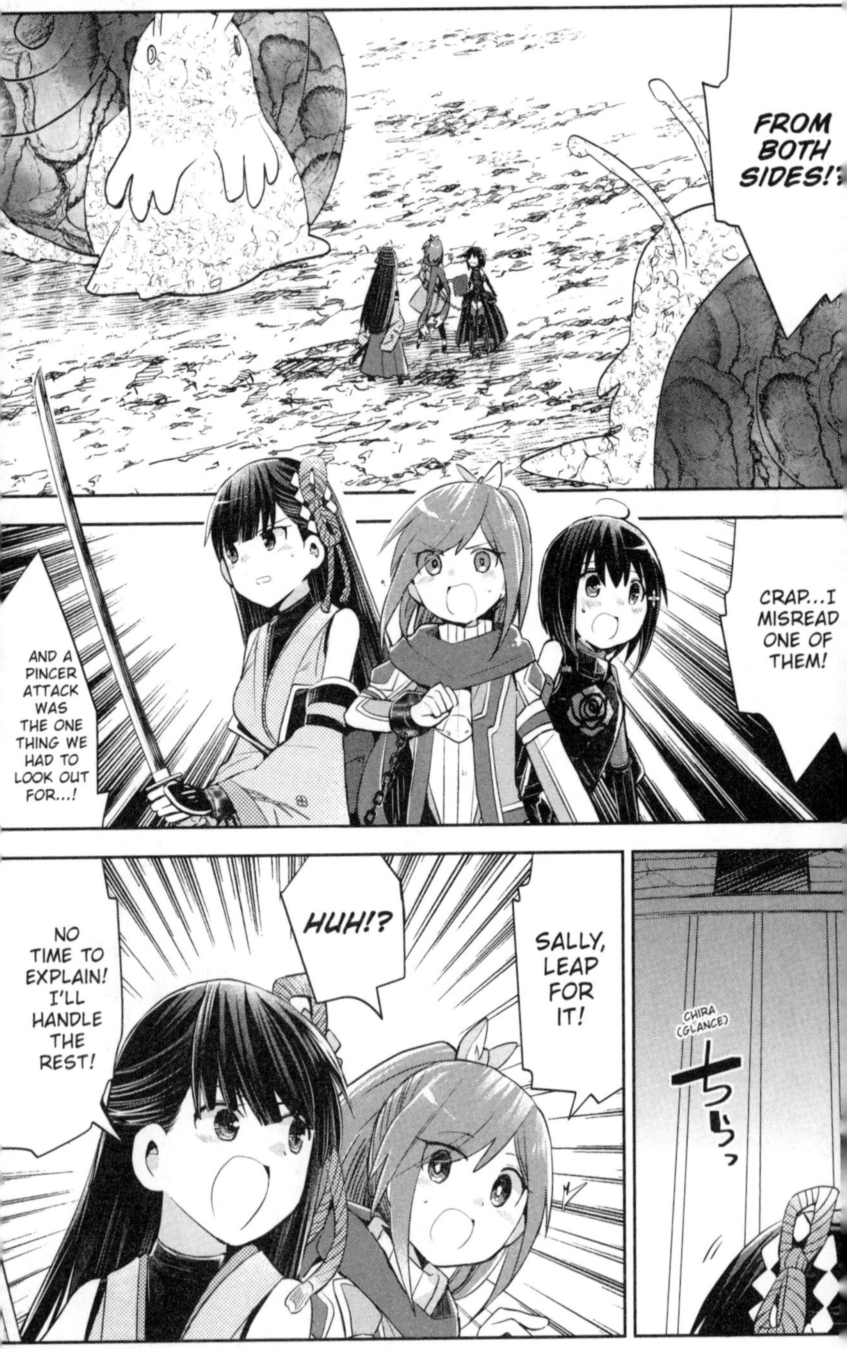
FROM BOTH SIDES!?
CRAP...I MISREAD ONE OF THEM!
AND A PINCER ATTACK WAS THE ONE THING WE HAD TO LOOK OUT FOR...!
CHIRA (GLANCE)
ちらっ
SALLY, LEAP FOR IT!
HUH!?
NO TIME TO EXPLAIN! I'LL HANDLE THE REST!

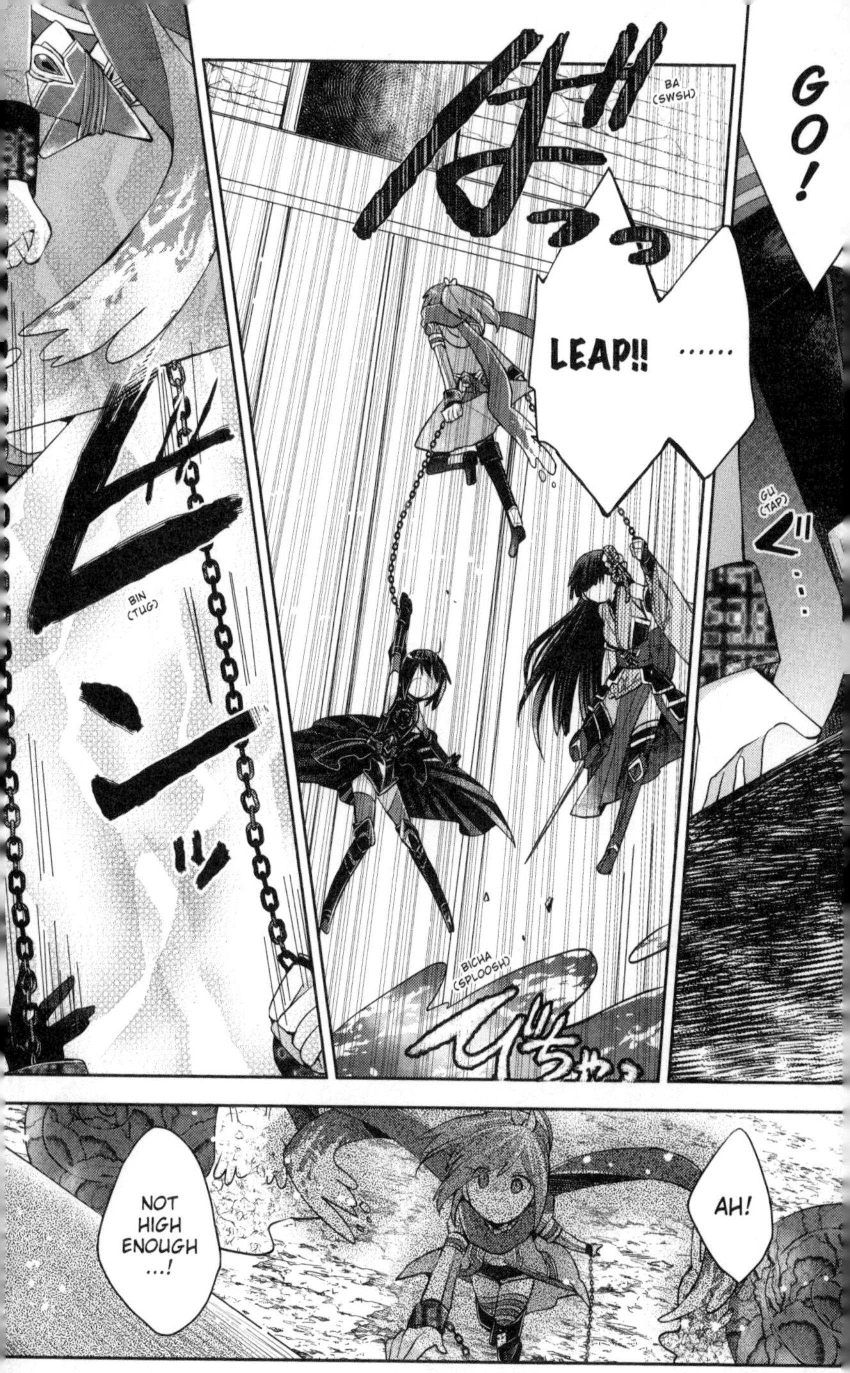
GO!
GU (TAP)
BA (SWSH)
LEAP!! ......
BICHA (SPLOOSH)
BIN (TUG)
AH!
NOT HIGH ENOUGH ...!

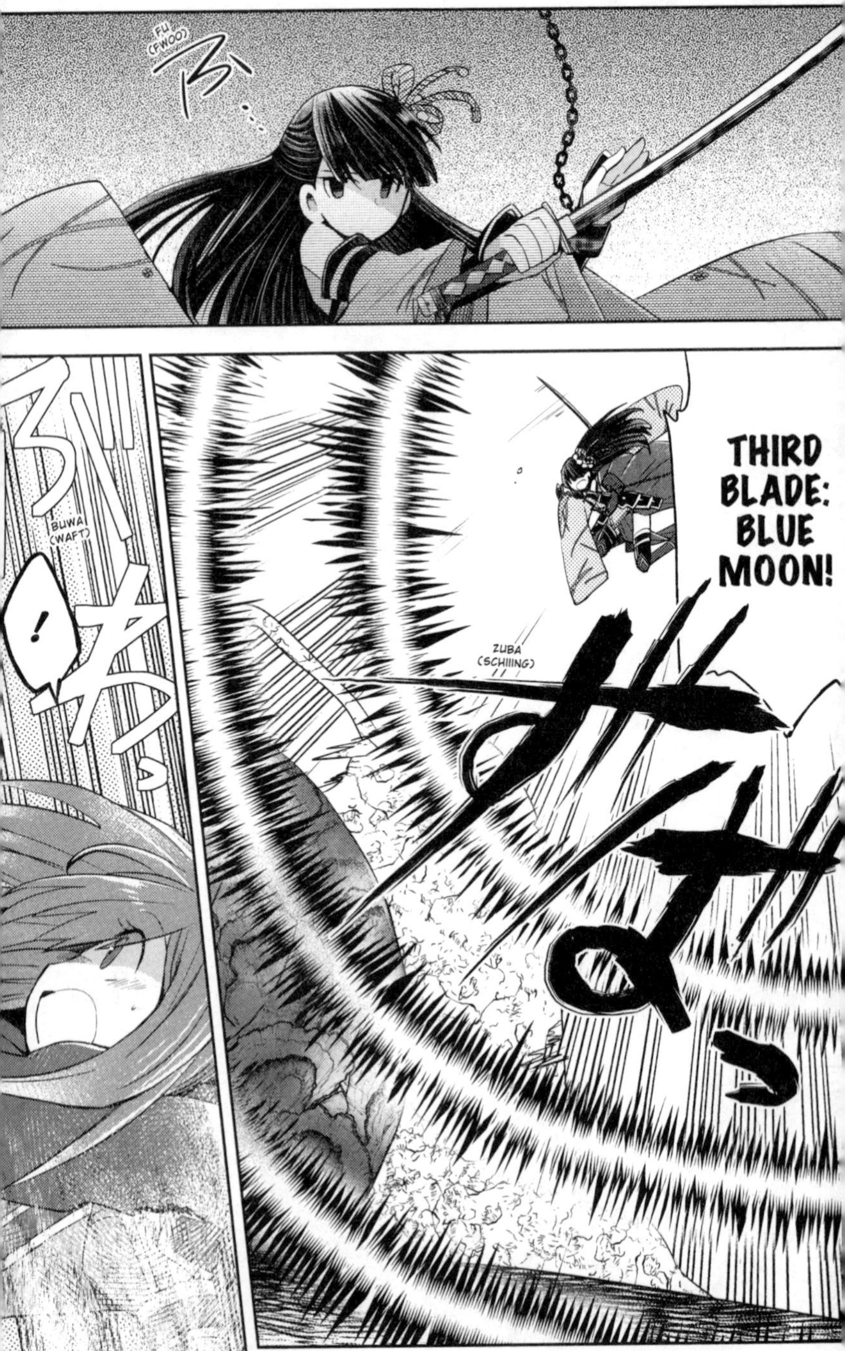
FU (FWOO)
THIRD BLADE: BLUE MOON!
ZUBA (SCHIIING)
BUWA (WAFT)
!

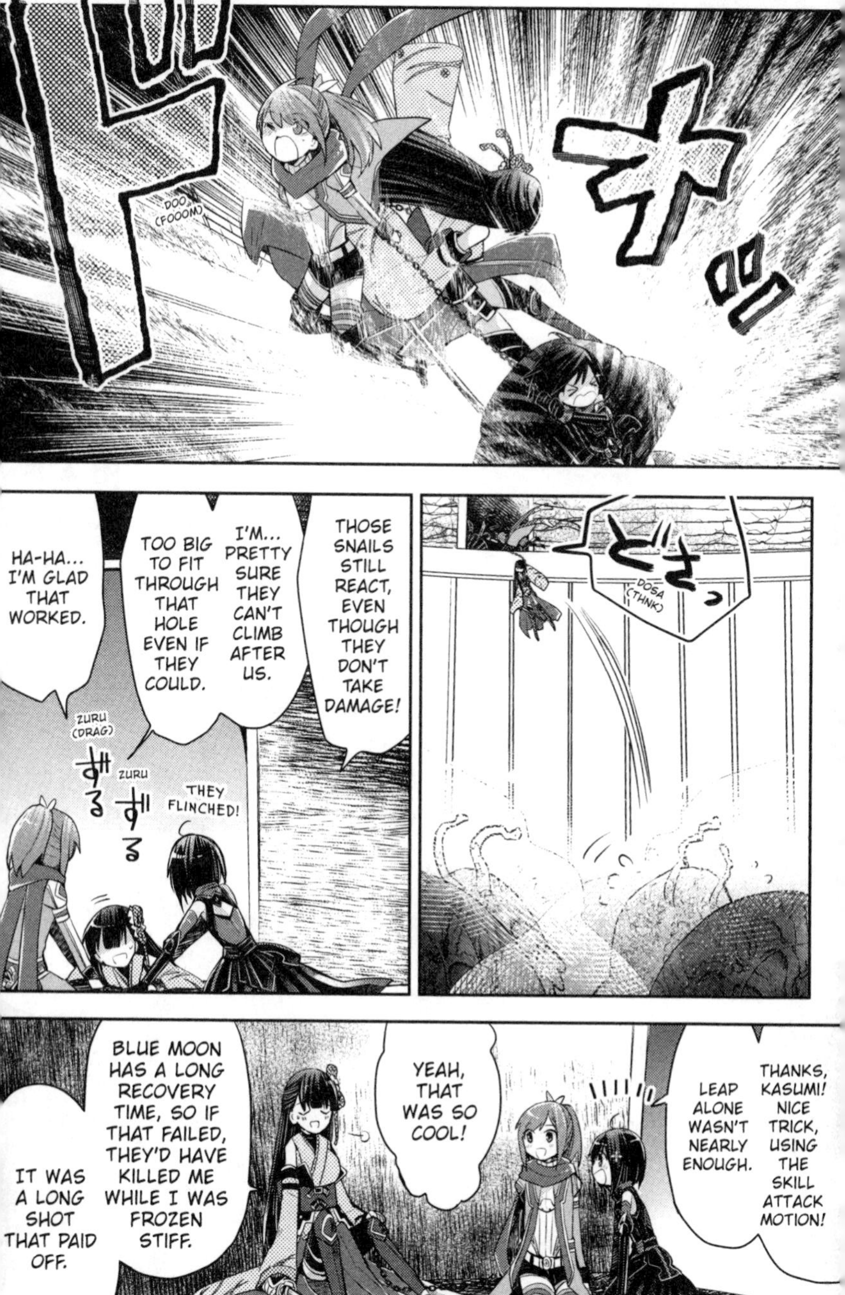

ドオッ
DOO (FOOOM)
どさっ
DOSA (THNK)
THOSE SNAILS STILL REACT, EVEN THOUGH THEY DON'T TAKE DAMAGE!
I'M... PRETTY SURE THEY CAN'T CLIMB AFTER US.
TOO BIG TO FIT THROUGH THAT HOLE EVEN IF THEY COULD.
HA-HA... I'M GLAD THAT WORKED.
ZURU (DRAG)
ずる
ZURU
ずる
THEY FLINCHED!
THANKS, KASUMI! NICE TRICK, USING THE SKILL ATTACK MOTION!
LEAP ALONE WASN'T NEARLY ENOUGH.
YEAH, THAT WAS SO COOL!
BLUE MOON HAS A LONG RECOVERY TIME, SO IF THAT FAILED, THEY'D HAVE KILLED ME WHILE I WAS FROZEN STIFF.
IT WAS A LONG SHOT THAT PAID OFF.

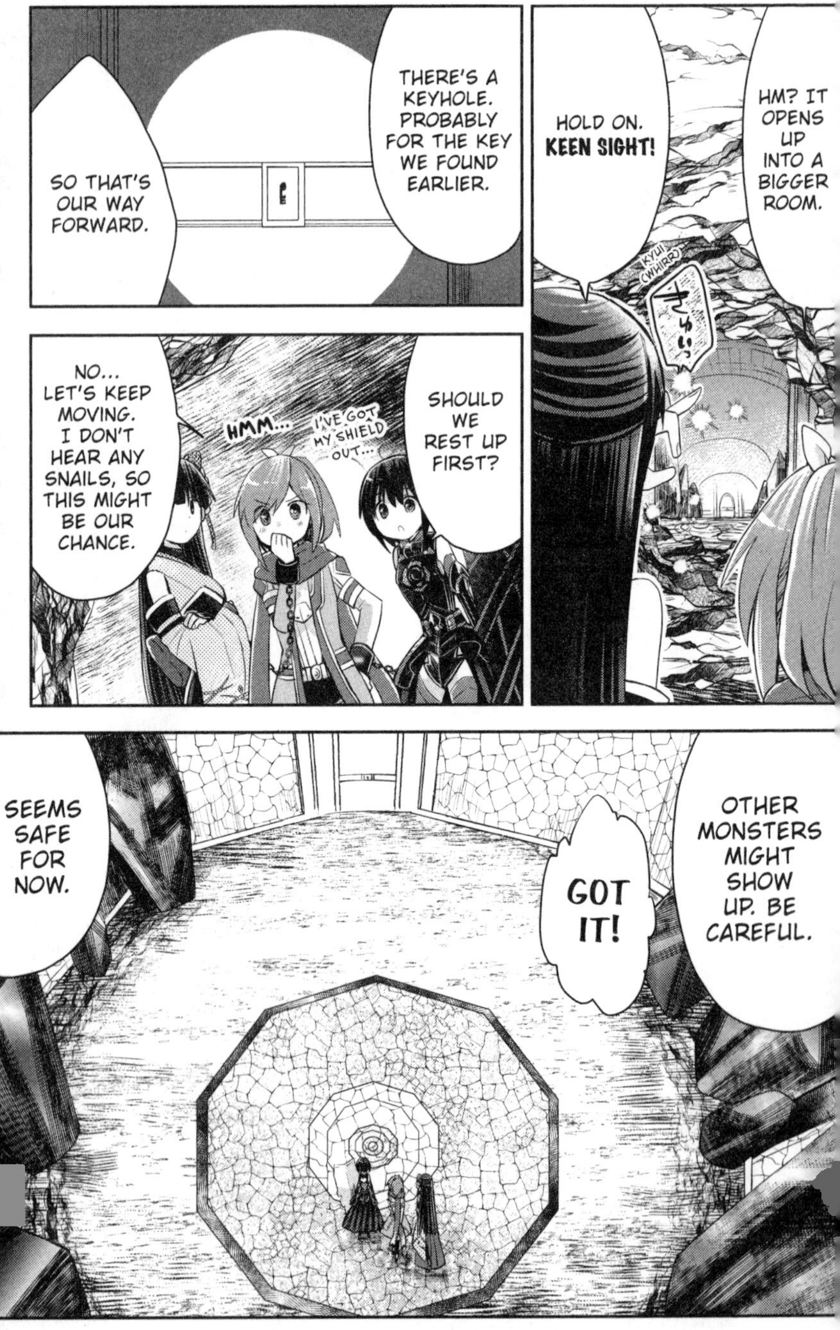
HM? IT OPENS UP INTO A BIGGER ROOM.
HOLD ON. KEEN SIGHT!
KYUI (WHIRR)
THERE'S A KEYHOLE. PROBABLY FOR THE KEY WE FOUND EARLIER.
SO THAT'S OUR WAY FORWARD.
SHOULD WE REST UP FIRST?
I'VE GOT MY SHIELD OUT...
HMM...
NO... LET'S KEEP MOVING. I DON'T HEAR ANY SNAILS, SO THIS MIGHT BE OUR CHANCE.
OTHER MONSTERS MIGHT SHOW UP. BE CAREFUL.
GOT IT!
SEEMS SAFE FOR NOW.

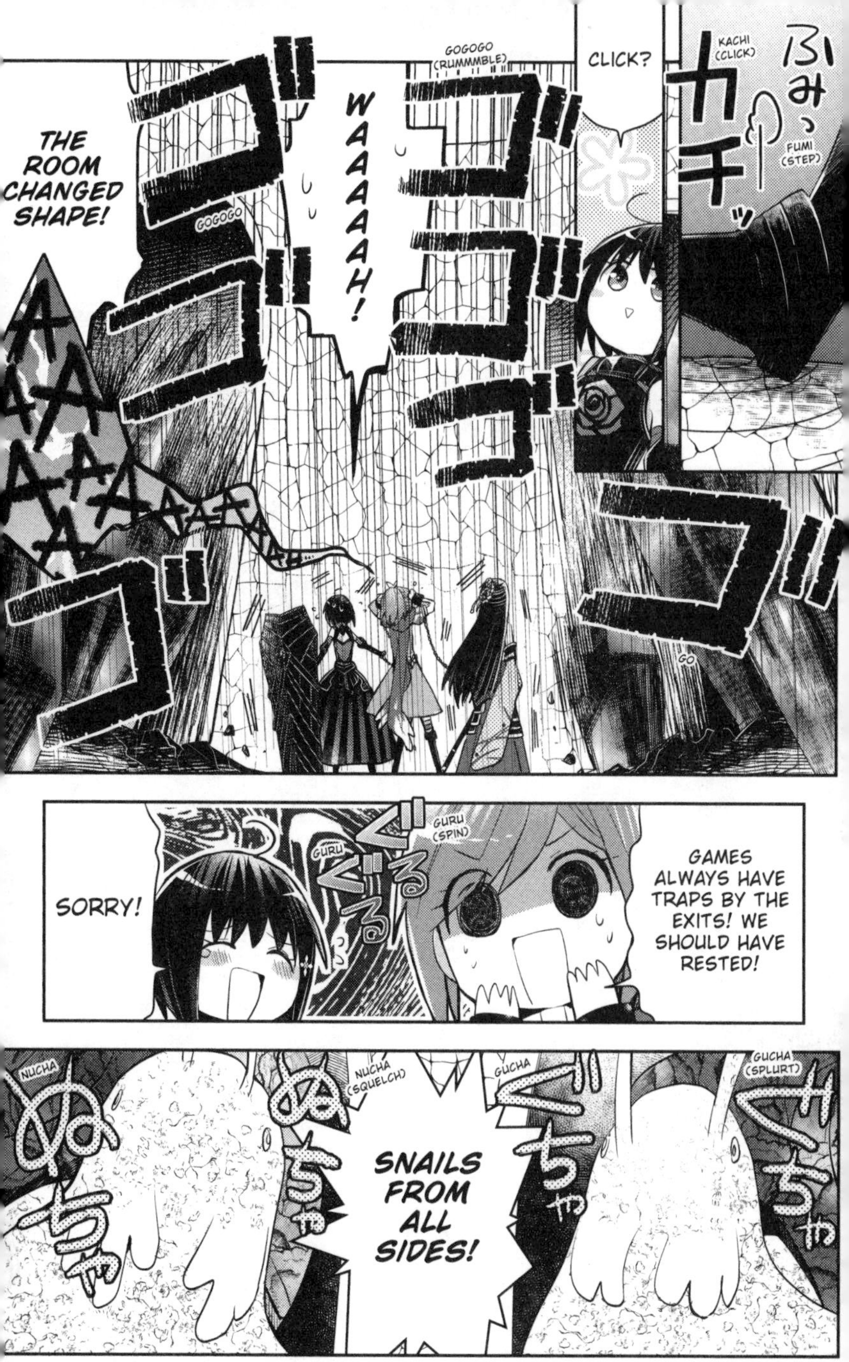
KACHI (CLICK)
FUMI (STEP)
CLICK?
GOGOGO (RUMMMBLE)
WAAAAAAAH!
GO
GOGOGO
THE ROOM CHANGED SHAPE!
GAMES ALWAYS HAVE TRAPS BY THE EXITS! WE SHOULD HAVE RESTED!
GURU (SPIN)
GURU
SORRY!
GUCHA (SPLURT)
GUCHA
NUCHA (SQUELCH)
SNAILS FROM ALL SIDES!
NUCHA

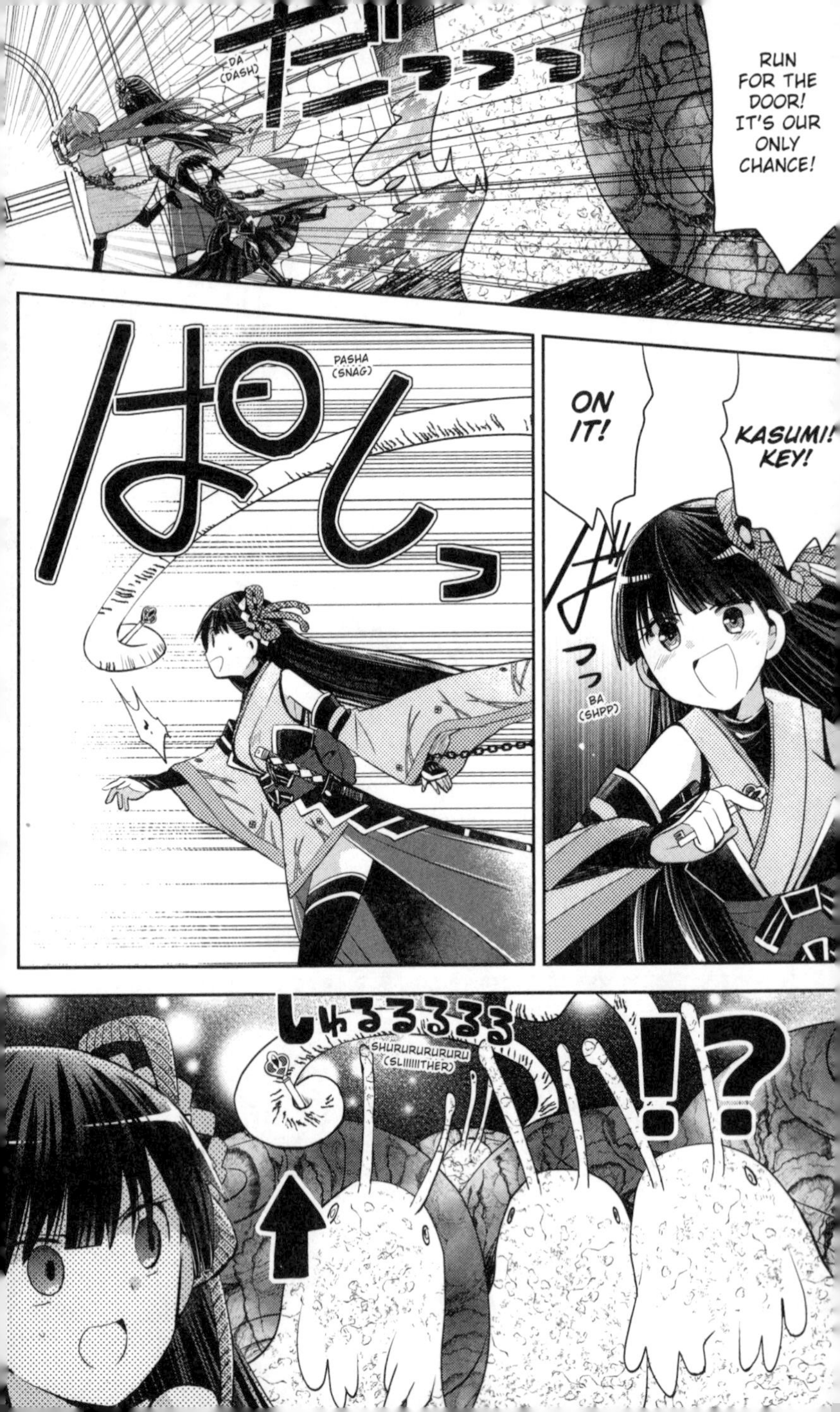
RUN FOR THE DOOR! IT'S OUR ONLY CHANCE!
だっっっっ
DA (DASH)
KASUMI! KEY!
ON IT!
ばっ
BA (SHPP)
ぱしっ
PASHA (SNAG)
しゅるるるるる
SHURURURURURU (SLIIIIIITHER)
!?

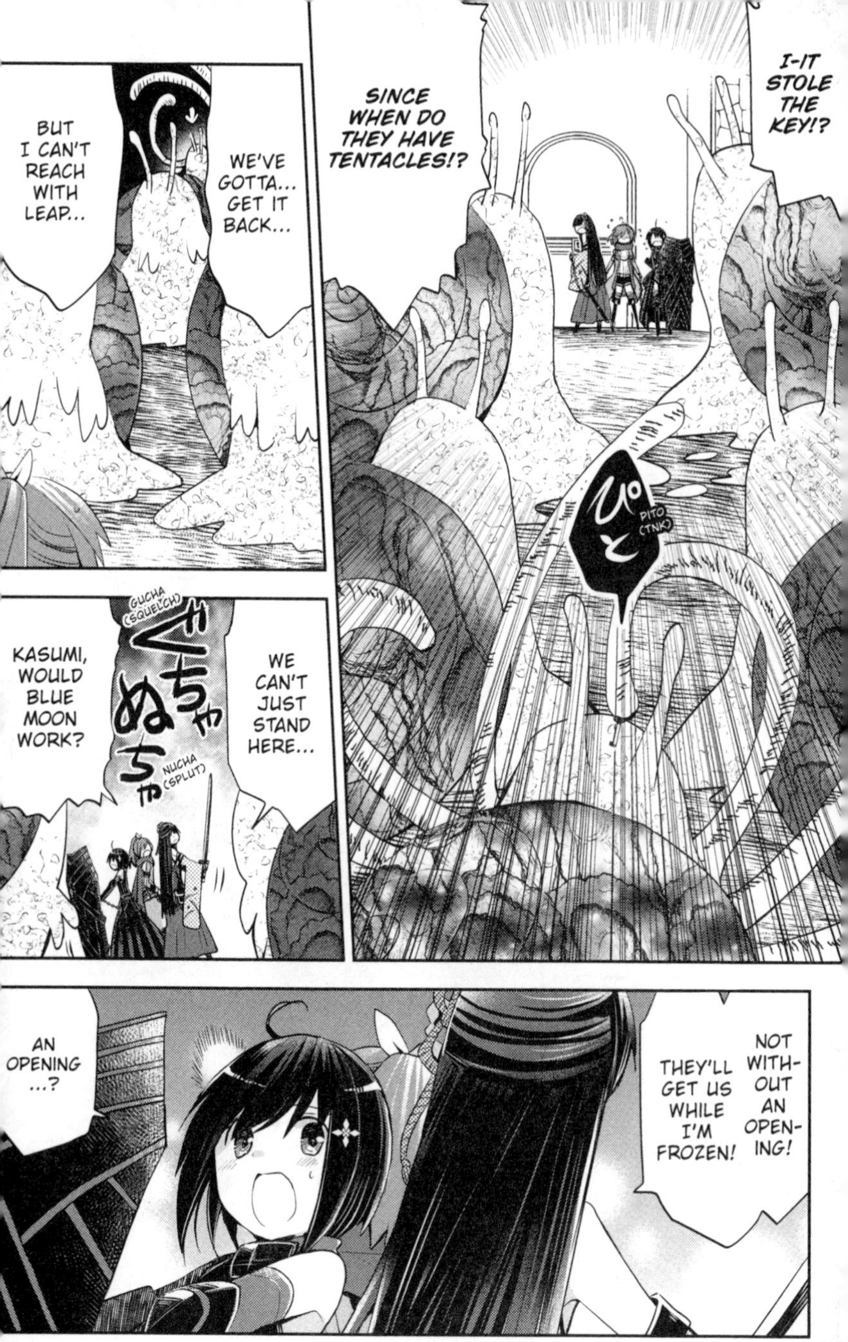
I-IT STOLE THE KEY!?
SINCE WHEN DO THEY HAVE TENTACLES!?
ぴと
PITO (TNK)
WE'VE GOTTA... GET IT BACK...
BUT I CAN'T REACH WITH LEAP...
ぐちゃ
GUCHA (SQUELCH)
WE CAN'T JUST STAND HERE...
ぬちゃ
NUCHA (SPLUT)
KASUMI, WOULD BLUE MOON WORK?
NOT WITH-OUT AN OPEN-ING!
THEY'LL GET US WHILE I'M FROZEN!
AN OPENING...?

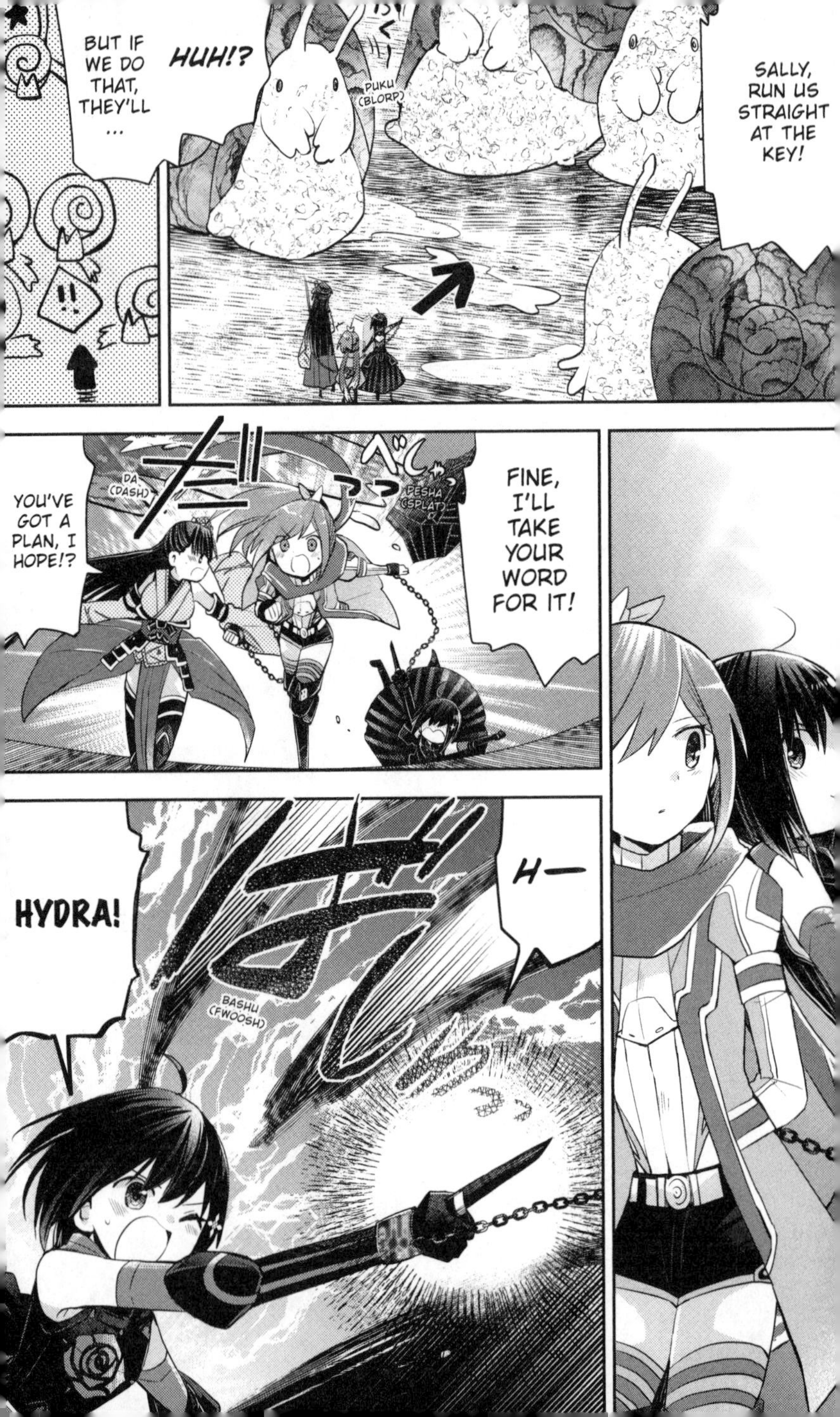

SALLY, RUN US STRAIGHT AT THE KEY!
PUKU (BLORP)
HUH!?
BUT IF WE DO THAT, THEY'LL ...
!!
FINE, I'LL TAKE YOUR WORD FOR IT!
PESHA (SPLAT)
DA (DASH)
YOU'VE GOT A PLAN, I HOPE!?
H—
BASHU (FWOOSH)
HYDRA!

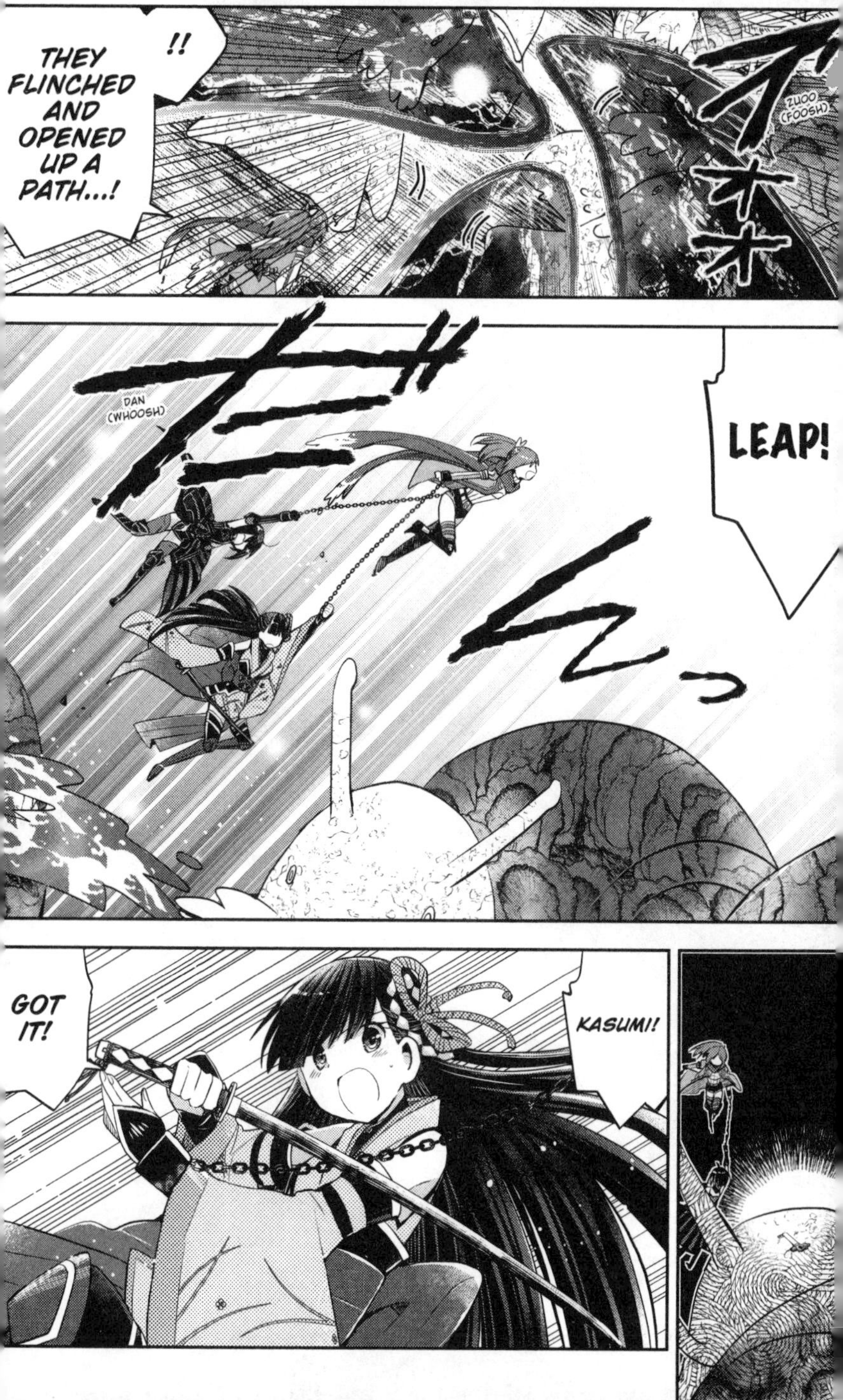
ZUOO (FOOSH)
!!
THEY FLINCHED AND OPENED UP A PATH...!
LEAP!
DAN (WHOOSH)
KASUMI!
GOT IT!

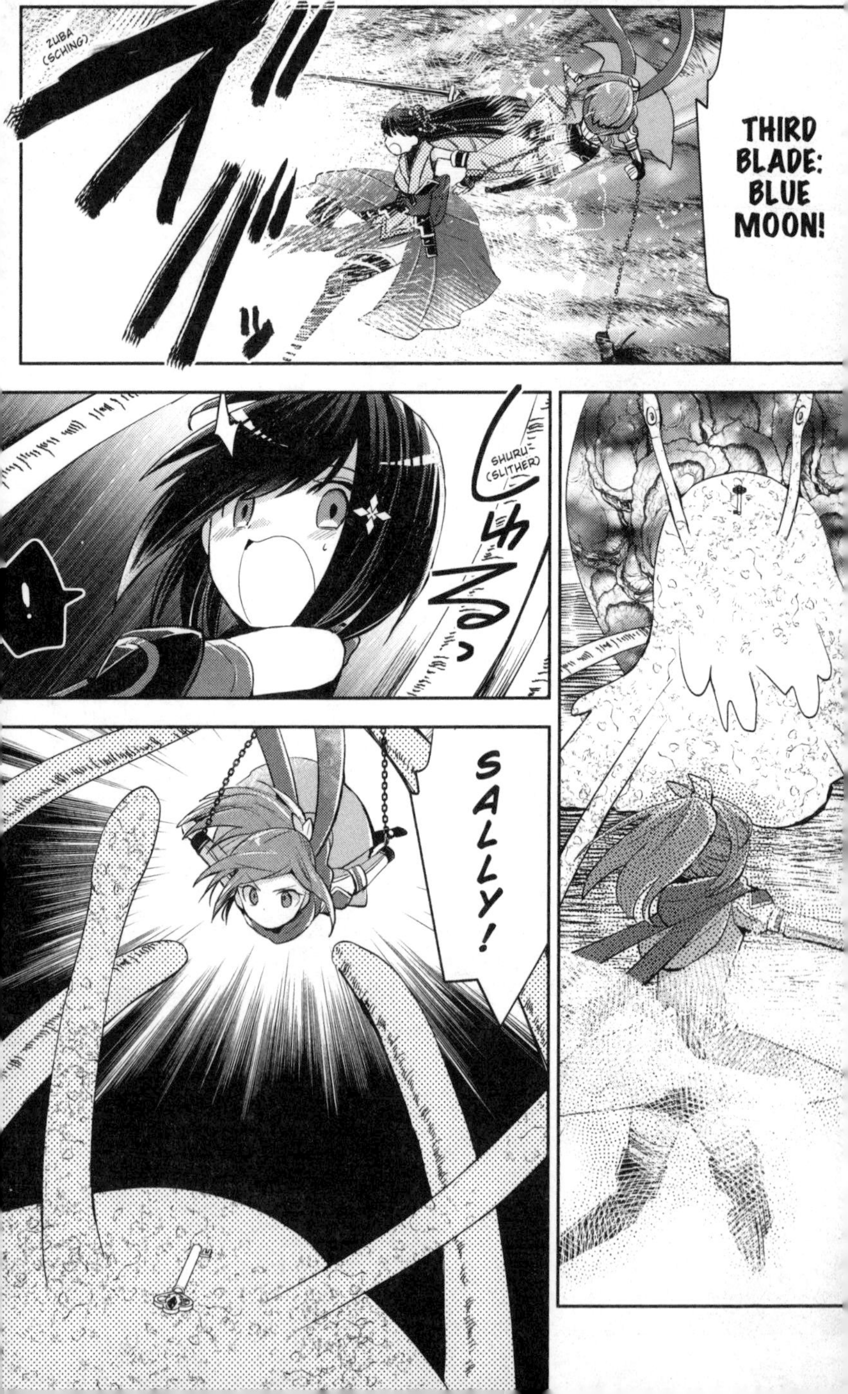
THIRD BLADE: BLUE MOON!
ZUBA (SCHING)
ズバッ
SHURU (SLITHER)
しゅるっ
!
SALLY!

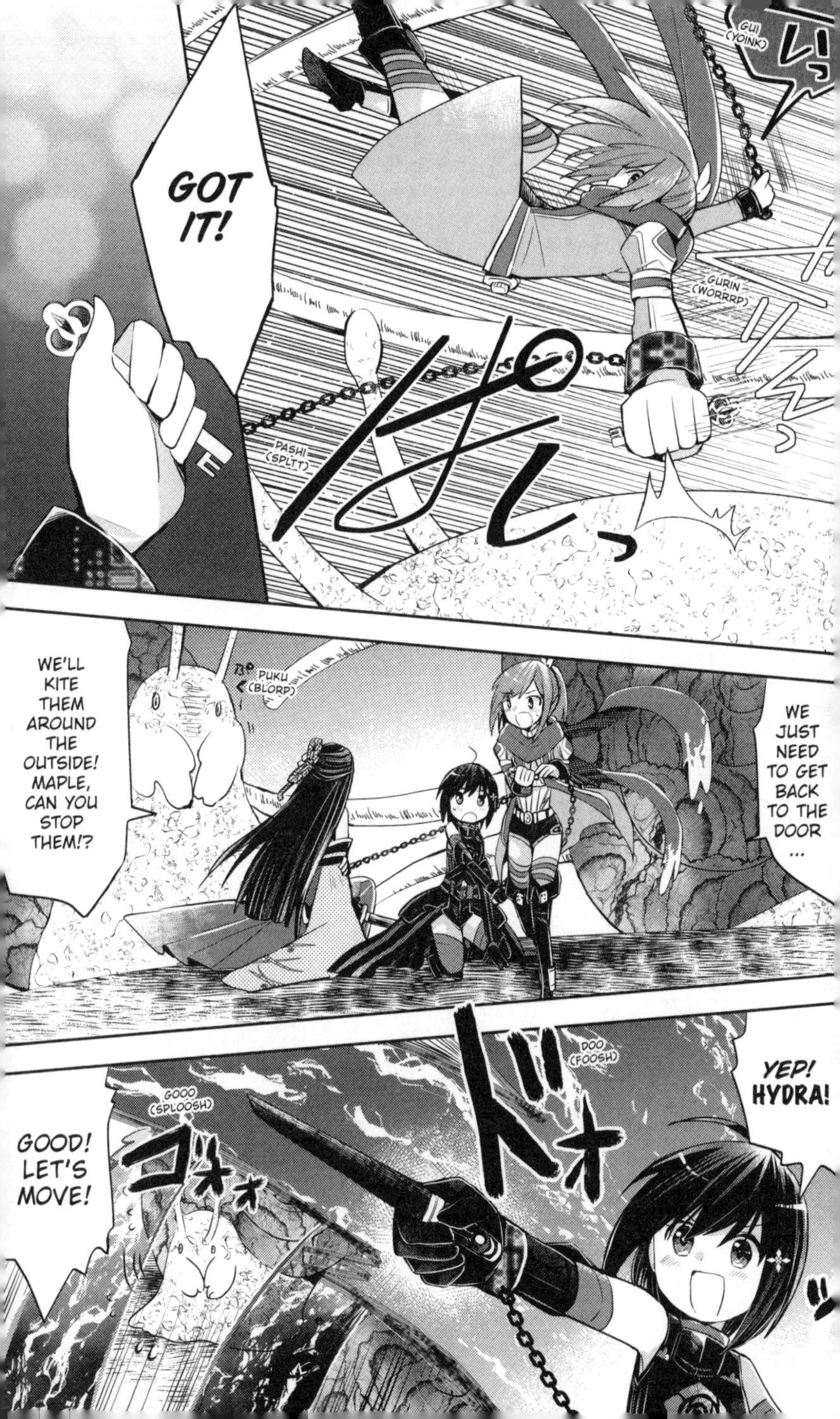
GUI (YOINK)
GURIN (WORRRP)
GOT IT!
PASHI (SPLTT)
WE JUST NEED TO GET BACK TO THE DOOR...
PUKU (BLORP)
WE'LL KITE THEM AROUND THE OUTSIDE! MAPLE, CAN YOU STOP THEM!?
YEP! HYDRA!
DOO (FOOSH)
GOOO (SPLOOSH)
GOOD! LET'S MOVE!

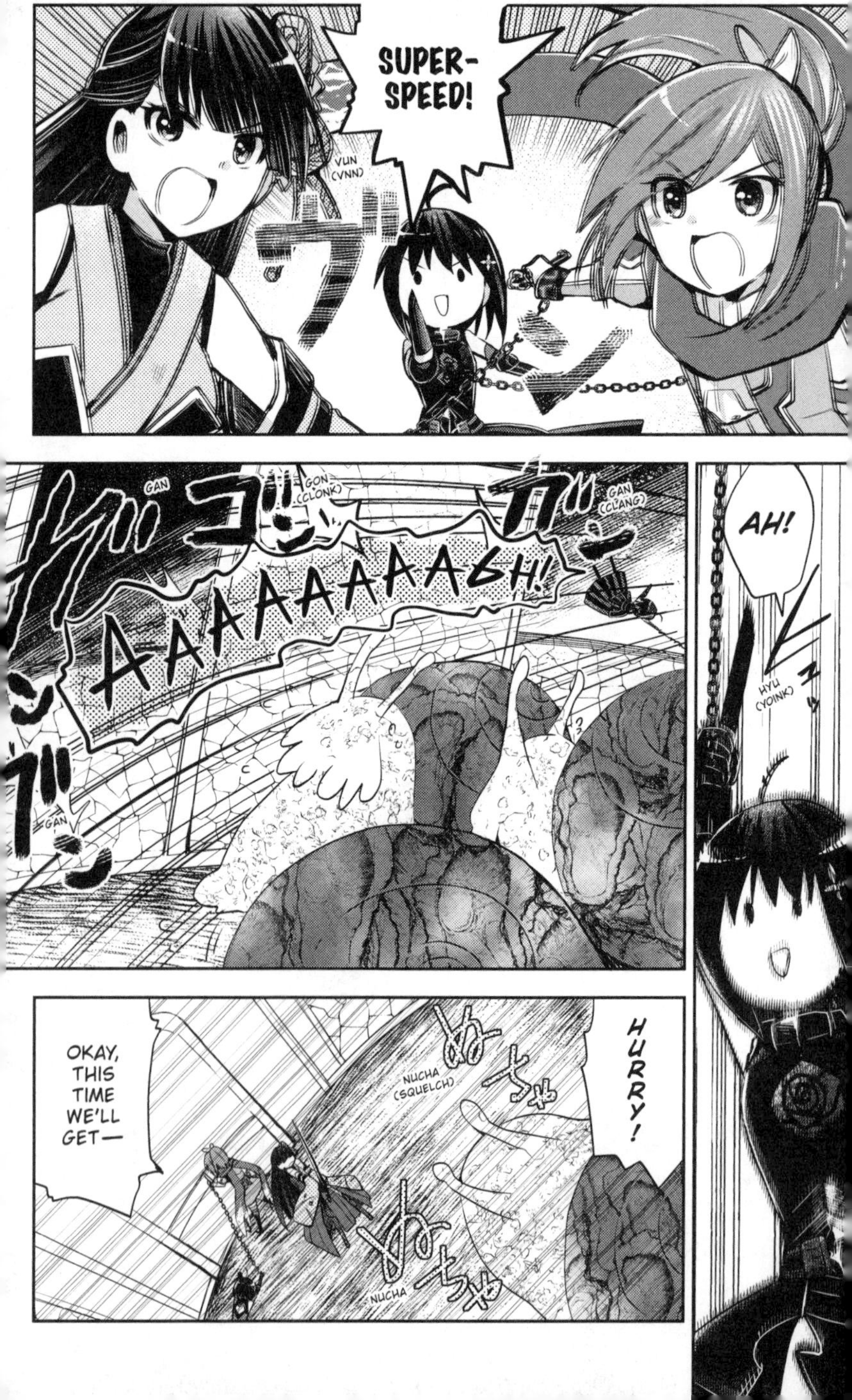
SUPER-SPEED!
VUN (VNN)
AH!
HYU (YOINK)
GAN (CLANG)
GON (CLONK)
GAN
AAAAAAAAGH!
GAN
HURRY!
NUCHA (SQUELCH)
NUCHA
OKAY, THIS TIME WE'LL GET—

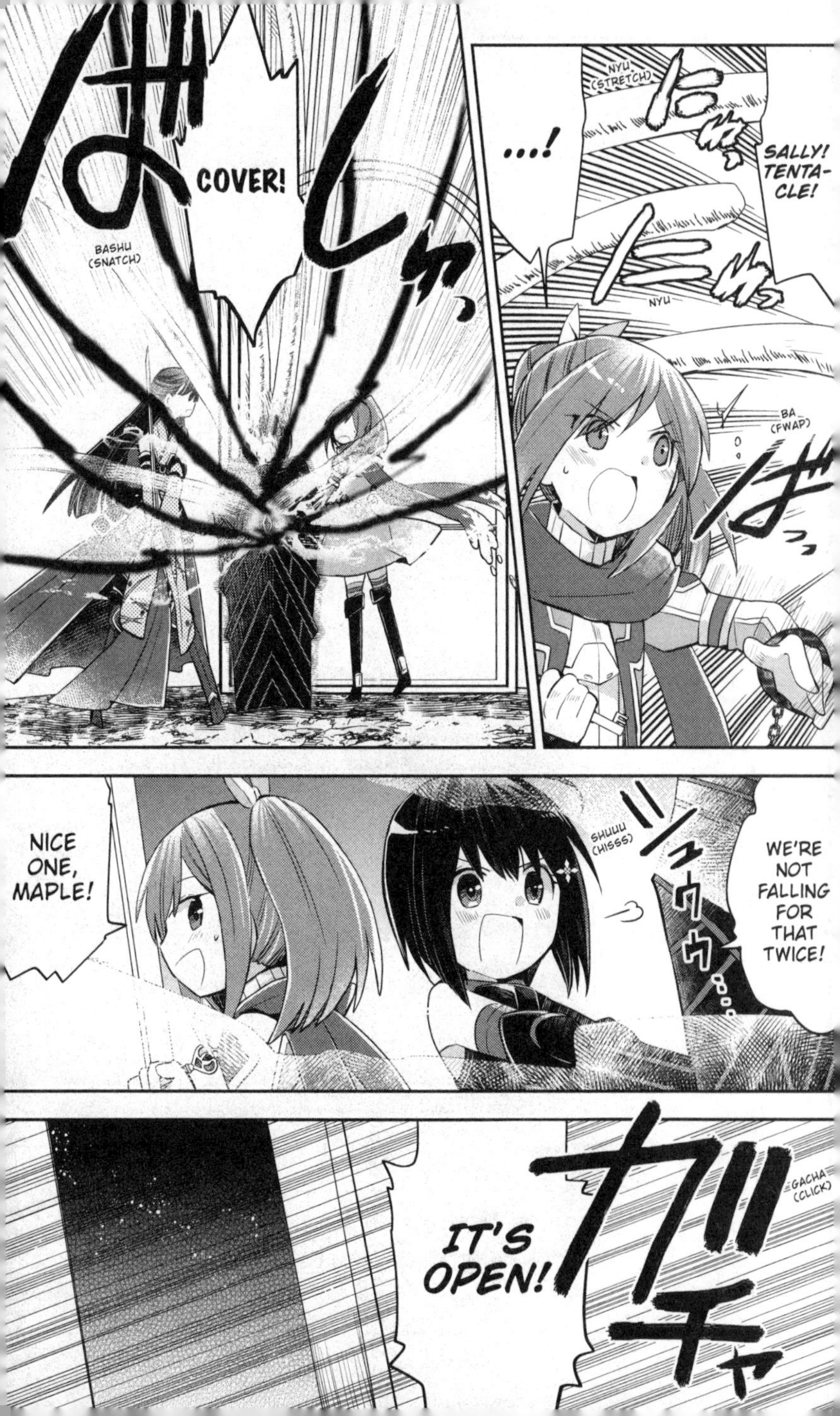
NYU (STRETCH)
SALLY! TENTA-CLE!
...!
NYU
BA (FWAP)
COVER!
BASHU (SNATCH)
WE'RE NOT FALLING FOR THAT TWICE!
SHUUU (HISSS)
NICE ONE, MAPLE!
GACHA (CLICK)
IT'S OPEN!

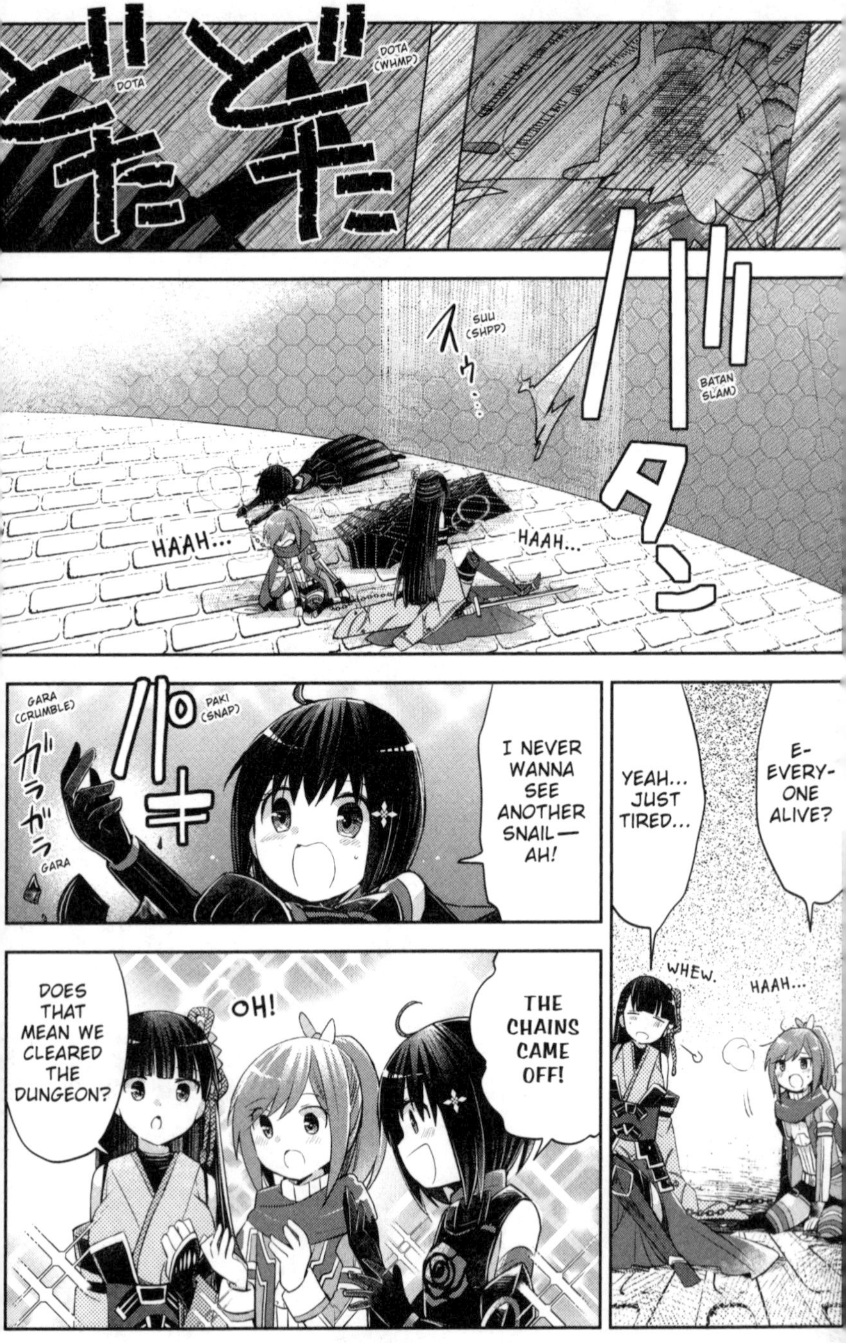
どた
DOTA (WHMP)
どた
DOTA
バタン
BATAN SLAM
スゥ…
SUU (SHPP)
HAAH...
HAAH...
E-EVERY-ONE ALIVE?
YEAH... JUST TIRED...
WHEW.
HAAH...
I NEVER WANNA SEE ANOTHER SNAIL—AH!
パキ
PAKI (SNAP)
GARA (CRUMBLE)
ガラガラ
GARA
THE CHAINS CAME OFF!
OH!
DOES THAT MEAN WE CLEARED THE DUNGEON?

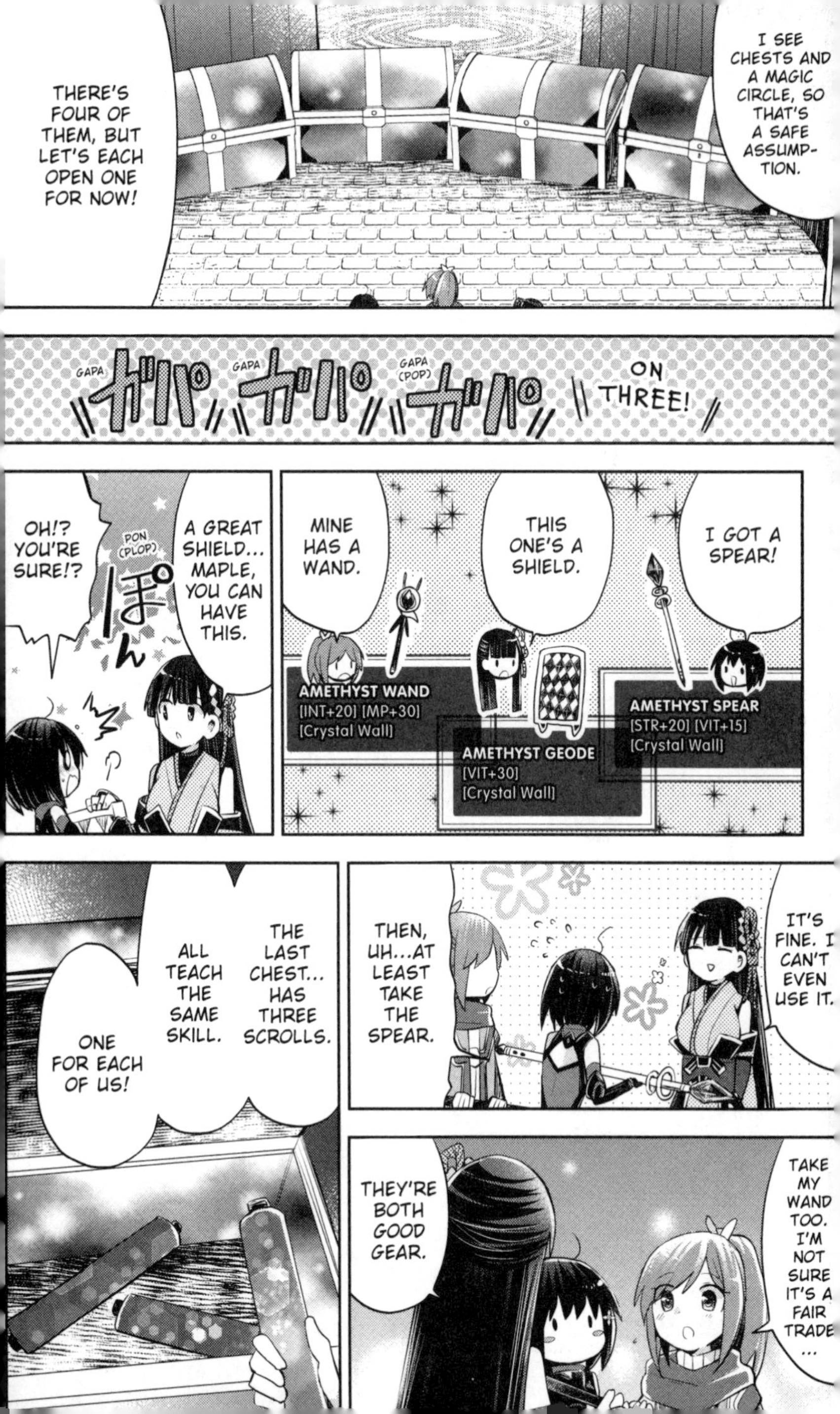

I SEE CHESTS AND A MAGIC CIRCLE, SO THAT'S A SAFE ASSUMPTION.
THERE'S FOUR OF THEM, BUT LET'S EACH OPEN ONE FOR NOW!
ON THREE!
GAPA (POP)
ガパ
GAPA
ガパ
GAPA
ガパ
I GOT A SPEAR!
AMETHYST SPEAR
[STR+20] [VIT+15]
[Crystal Wall]
THIS ONE'S A SHIELD.
AMETHYST GEODE
[VIT+30]
[Crystal Wall]
MINE HAS A WAND.
AMETHYST WAND
[INT+20] [MP+30]
[Crystal Wall]
A GREAT SHIELD... MAPLE, YOU CAN HAVE THIS.
PON (PLOP)
ぽん
OH!? YOU'RE SURE!?
IT'S FINE. I CAN'T EVEN USE IT.
THEN, UH...AT LEAST TAKE THE SPEAR.
TAKE MY WAND TOO. I'M NOT SURE IT'S A FAIR TRADE...
THEY'RE BOTH GOOD GEAR.
THE LAST CHEST... HAS THREE SCROLLS.
ALL TEACH THE SAME SKILL.
ONE FOR EACH OF US!

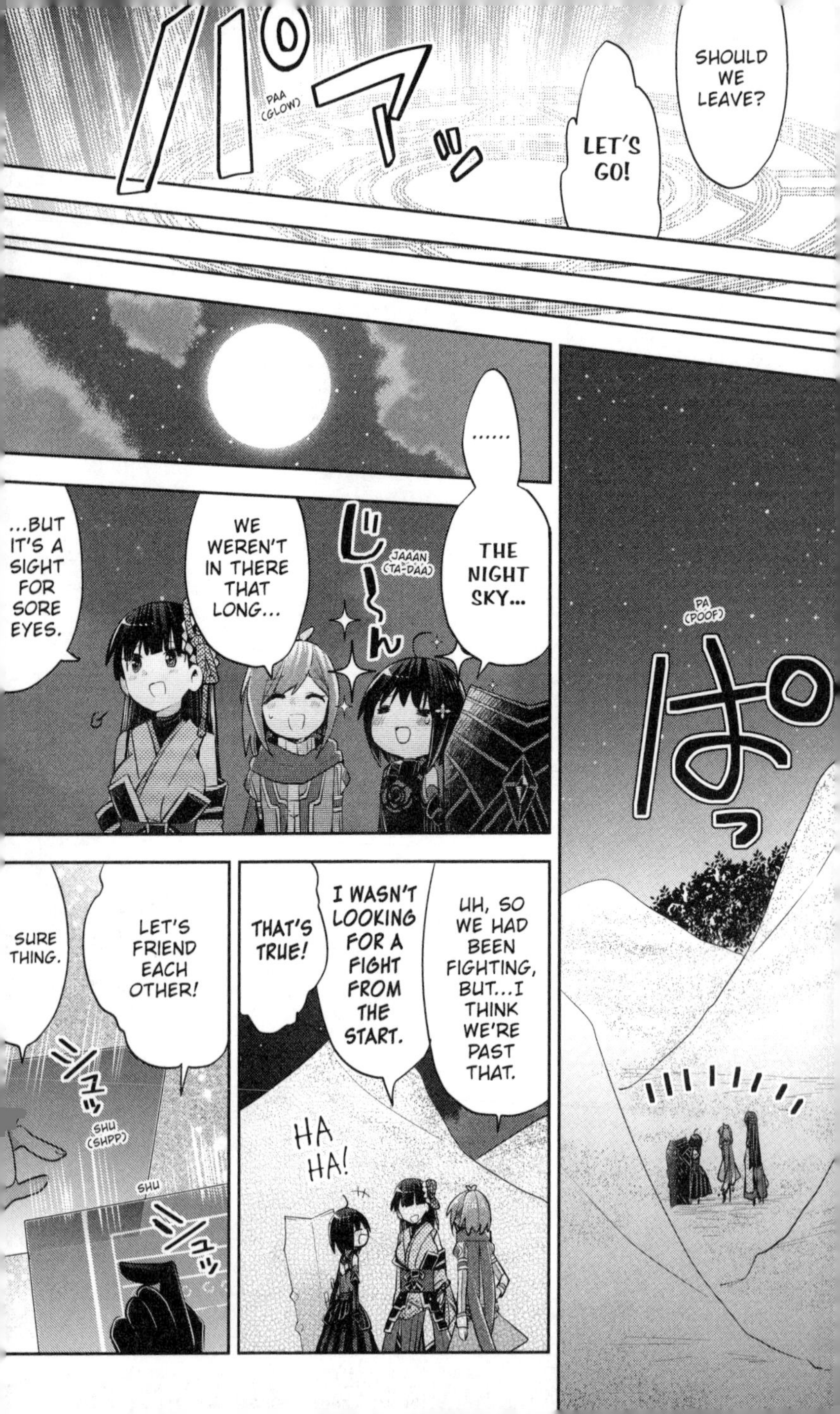
SHOULD WE LEAVE?
LET'S GO!
PAA (GLOW)
PA (POOF)
......
THE NIGHT SKY...
JAAAN (TA-DAA)
WE WEREN'T IN THERE THAT LONG...
...BUT IT'S A SIGHT FOR SORE EYES.
UH, SO WE HAD BEEN FIGHTING, BUT...I THINK WE'RE PAST THAT.
I WASN'T LOOKING FOR A FIGHT FROM THE START.
THAT'S TRUE!
HA HA!
LET'S FRIEND EACH OTHER!
SURE THING.
SHU (SHPP)
SHU

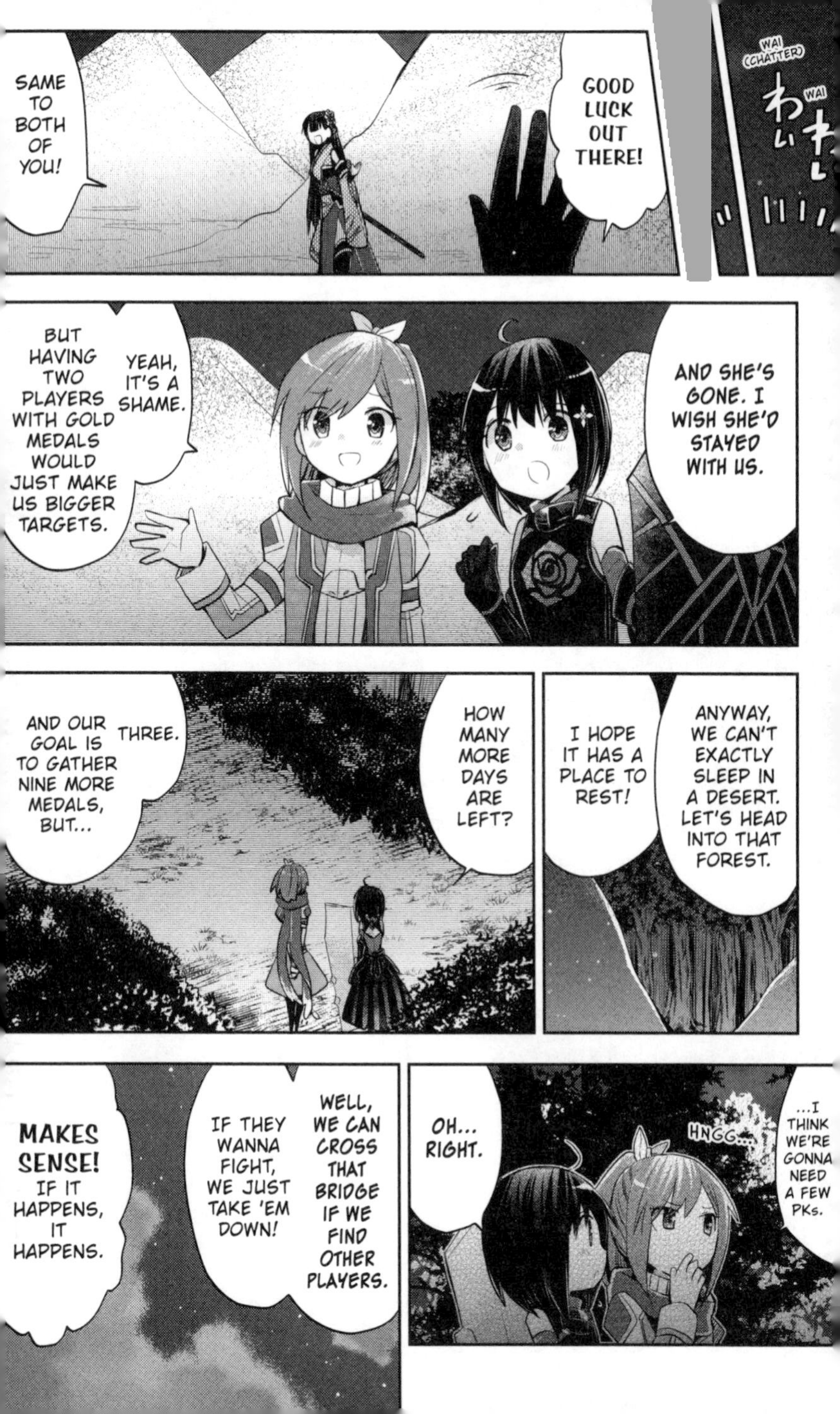
WAI (CHATTER)
わいわい
WAI
GOOD LUCK OUT THERE!
SAME TO BOTH OF YOU!
AND SHE'S GONE. I WISH SHE'D STAYED WITH US.
YEAH, IT'S A SHAME.
BUT HAVING TWO PLAYERS WITH GOLD MEDALS WOULD JUST MAKE US BIGGER TARGETS.
ANYWAY, WE CAN'T EXACTLY SLEEP IN A DESERT. LET'S HEAD INTO THAT FOREST.
I HOPE IT HAS A PLACE TO REST!
HOW MANY MORE DAYS ARE LEFT?
THREE.
AND OUR GOAL IS TO GATHER NINE MORE MEDALS, BUT...
...I THINK WE'RE GONNA NEED A FEW PKs.
HNGG...
OH... RIGHT.
WELL, WE CAN CROSS THAT BRIDGE IF WE FIND OTHER PLAYERS.
IF THEY WANNA FIGHT, WE JUST TAKE 'EM DOWN!
MAKES SENSE! IF IT HAPPENS, IT HAPPENS.

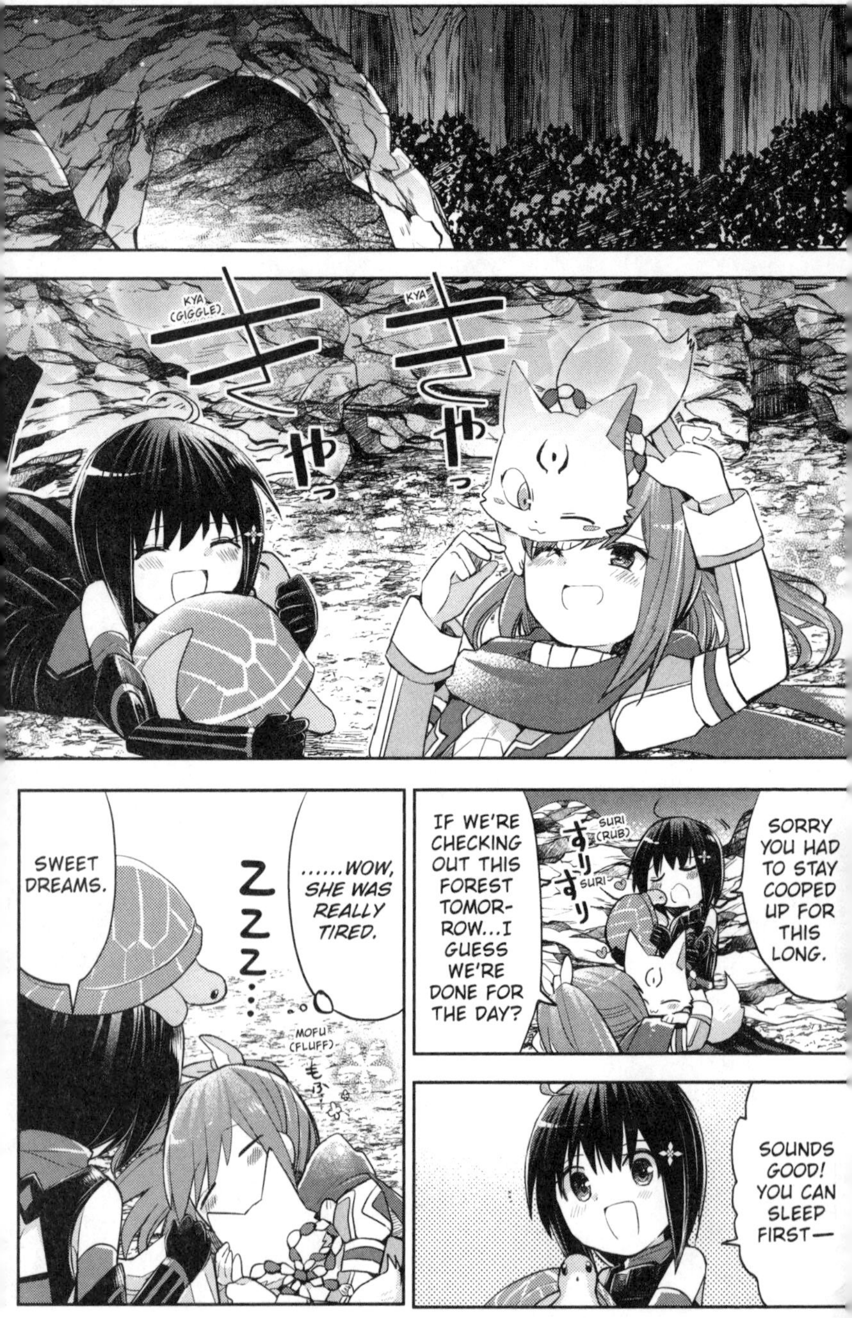
KYA
KYA (GIGGLE)
SORRY YOU HAD TO STAY COOPED UP FOR THIS LONG.
SURI (RUB) SURI
IF WE'RE CHECKING OUT THIS FOREST TOMORROW...I GUESS WE'RE DONE FOR THE DAY?
SOUNDS GOOD! YOU CAN SLEEP FIRST—
......WOW, SHE WAS REALLY TIRED.
ZZZ...
MOFU (FLUFF)
SWEET DREAMS.

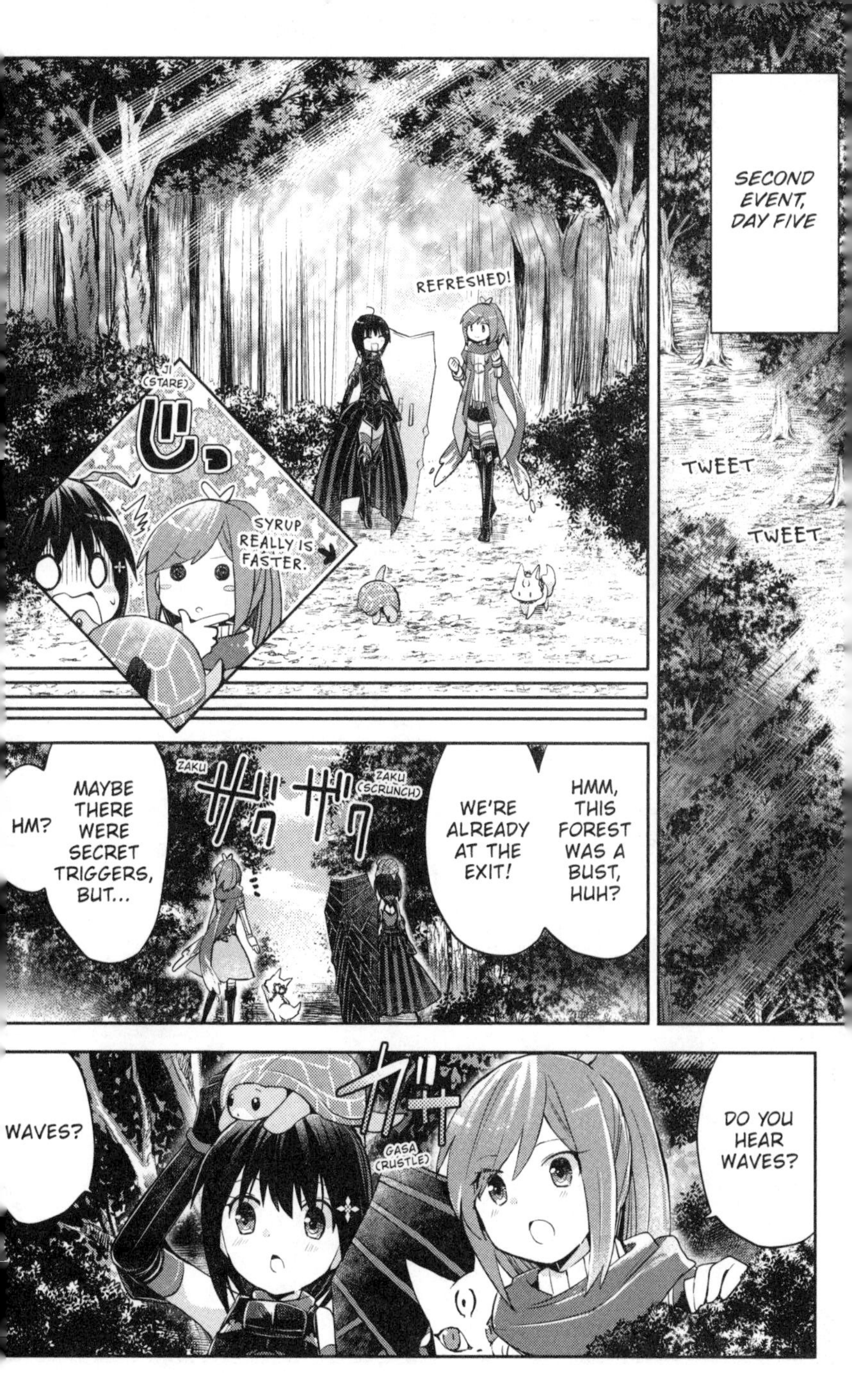
SECOND EVENT, DAY FIVE
TWEET
TWEET
REFRESHED!
JI (STARE)
SYRUP REALLY IS FASTER.
HMM, THIS FOREST WAS A BUST, HUH?
WE'RE ALREADY AT THE EXIT!
ZAKU (SCRUNCH)
ZAKU
MAYBE THERE WERE SECRET TRIGGERS, BUT...
HM?
DO YOU HEAR WAVES?
GASA (RUSTLE)
WAVES?

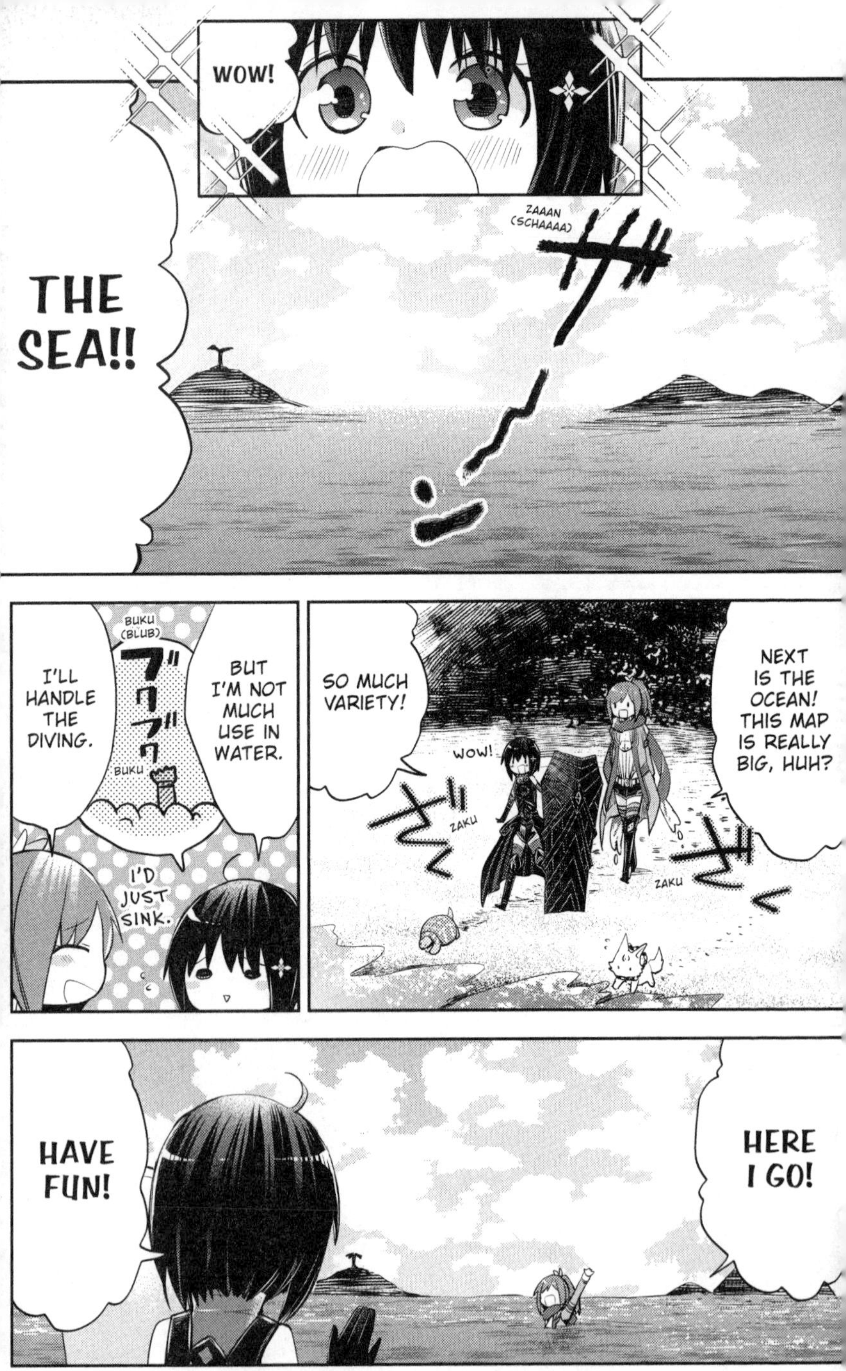
WOW!
ZAAAN (SCHAAAA)
THE SEA!!
NEXT IS THE OCEAN! THIS MAP IS REALLY BIG, HUH?
SO MUCH VARIETY!
WOW!
ZAKU
ZAKU
BUT I'M NOT MUCH USE IN WATER.
BUKU (BLUB)
BUKU
I'LL HANDLE THE DIVING.
I'D JUST SINK.
HERE I GO!
HAVE FUN!

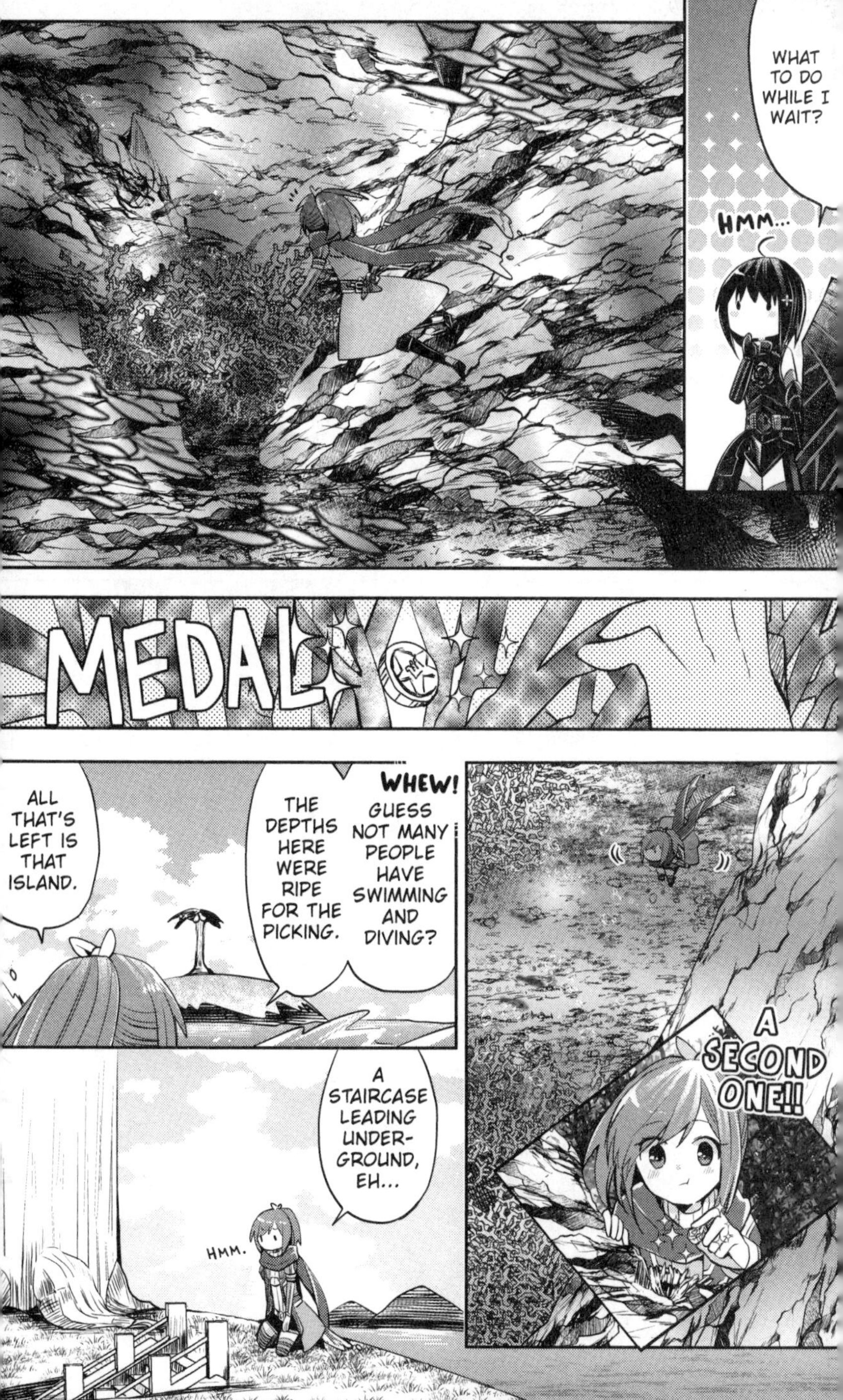
WHAT TO DO WHILE I WAIT?
HMM...
MEDAL
A SECOND ONE!!
WHEW!
GUESS NOT MANY PEOPLE HAVE SWIMMING AND DIVING?
THE DEPTHS HERE WERE RIPE FOR THE PICKING.
ALL THAT'S LEFT IS THAT ISLAND.
A STAIRCASE LEADING UNDER-GROUND, EH...
HMM.

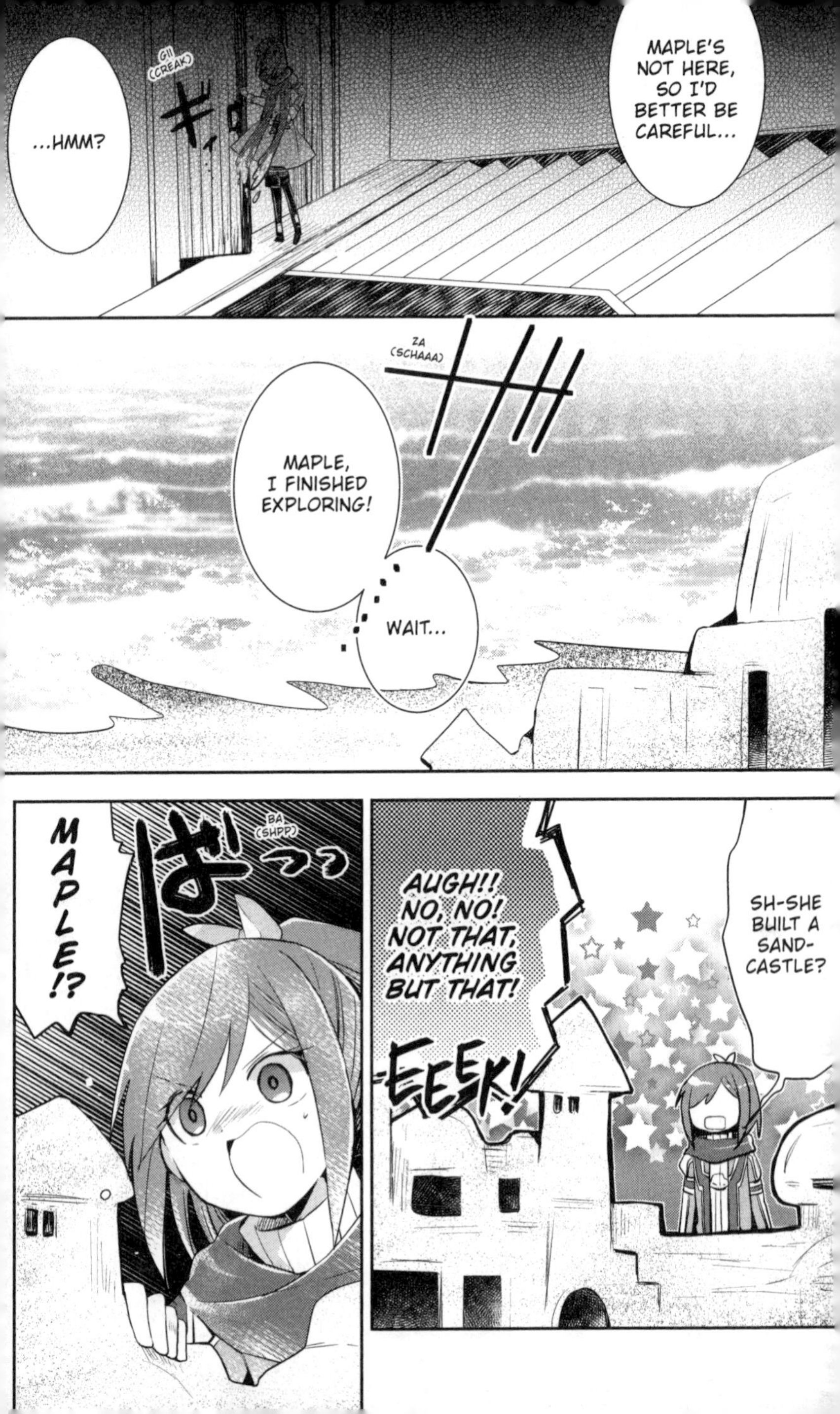
MAPLE'S NOT HERE, SO I'D BETTER BE CAREFUL...
GII (CREAK)
...HMM?
ZA (SCHAAA)
MAPLE, I FINISHED EXPLORING!
WAIT...
SH-SHE BUILT A SAND-CASTLE?
AUGH!! NO, NO! NOT THAT, ANYTHING BUT THAT!
EEEK!
BA (SHPP)
MAPLE!?

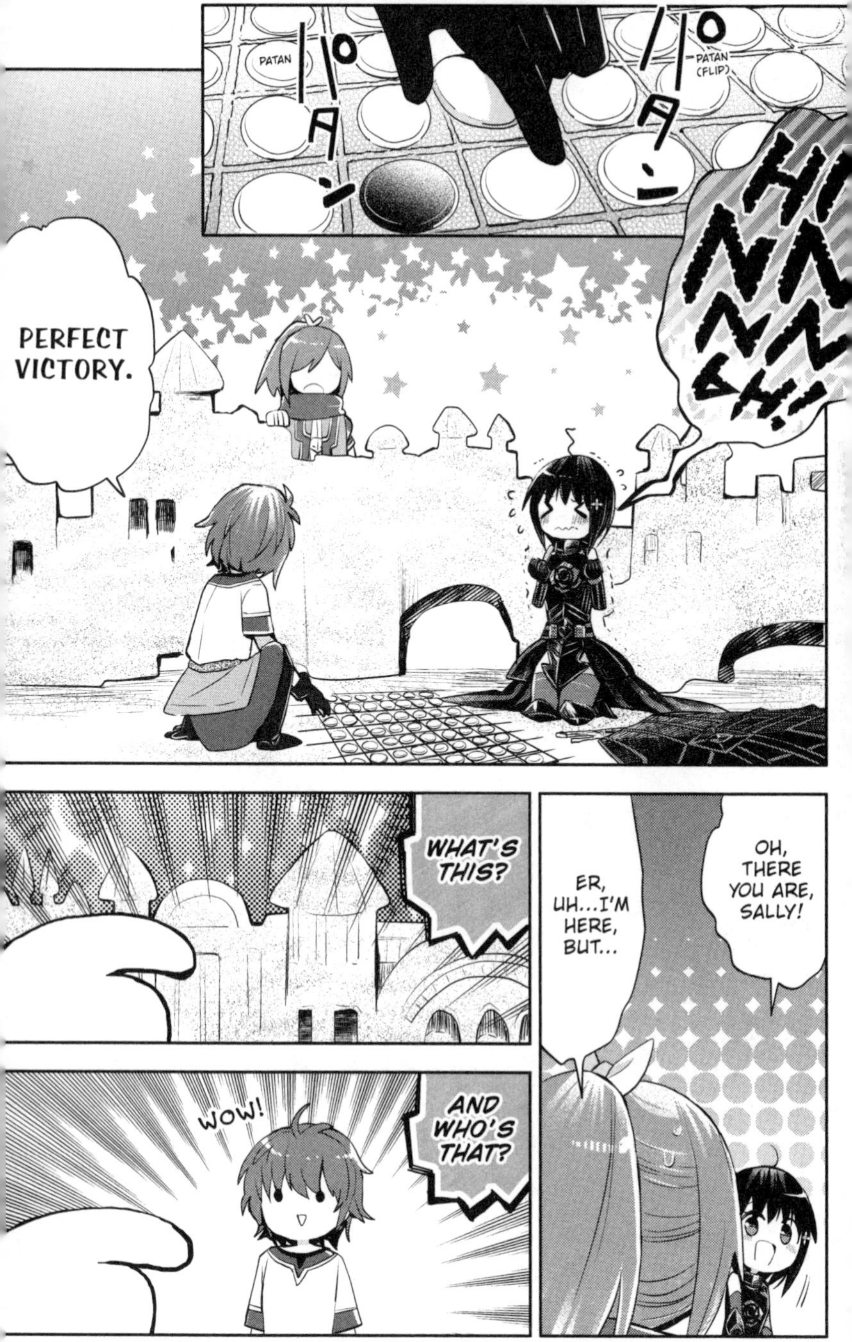
PATAN (FLIP)
PATAN
PERFECT VICTORY.
OH, THERE YOU ARE, SALLY!
ER, UH...I'M HERE, BUT...
WHAT'S THIS?
AND WHO'S THAT?
WOW!

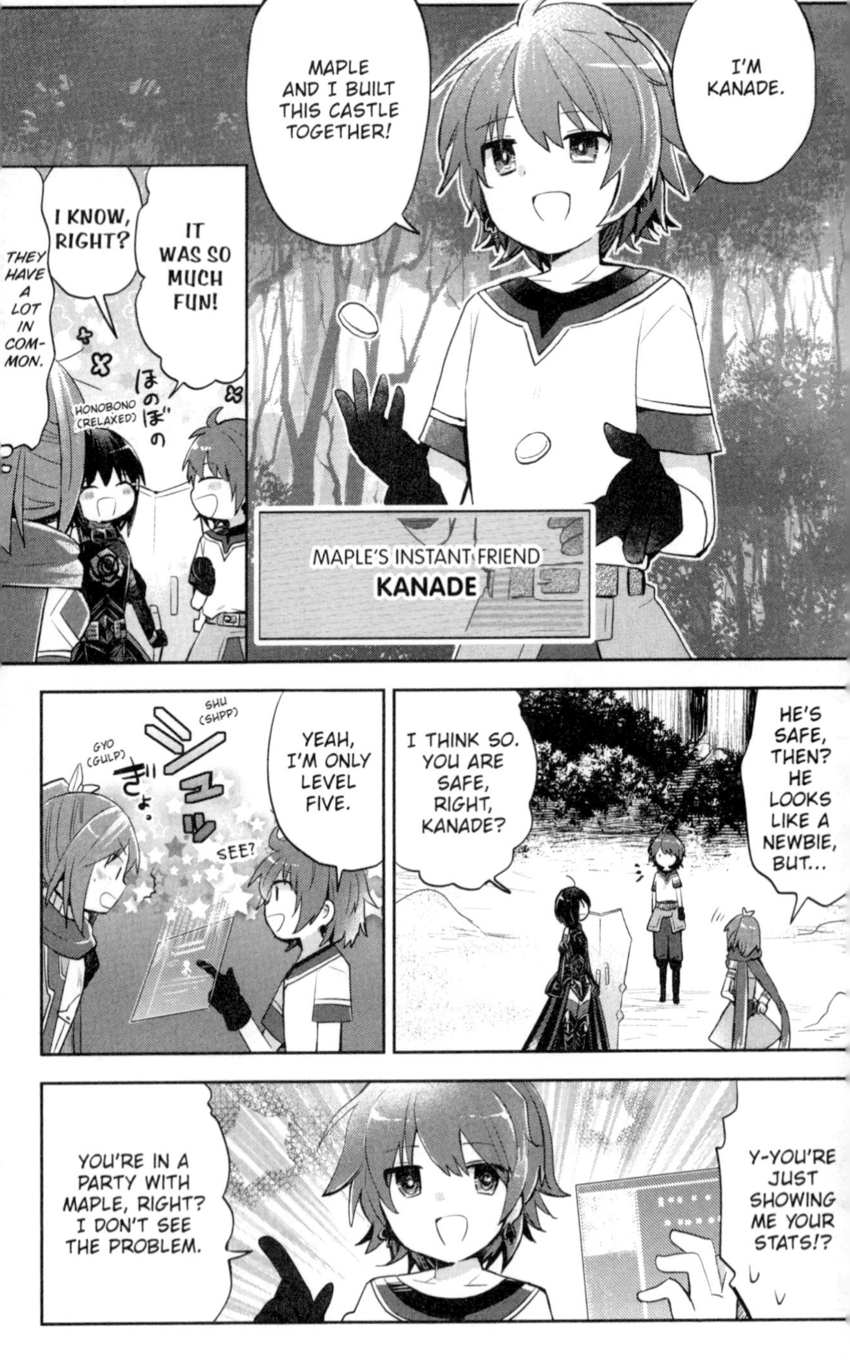
I'M KANADE.
MAPLE AND I BUILT THIS CASTLE TOGETHER!
MAPLE'S INSTANT FRIEND
KANADE
IT WAS SO MUCH FUN!
I KNOW, RIGHT?
THEY HAVE A LOT IN COM-MON.
ほのぼの
HONOBONO (RELAXED)
HE'S SAFE, THEN? HE LOOKS LIKE A NEWBIE, BUT...
I THINK SO. YOU ARE SAFE, RIGHT, KANADE?
YEAH, I'M ONLY LEVEL FIVE.
SEE?
シュッ
SHU (SHPP)
ぎょ。
GYO (GULP)
Y-YOU'RE JUST SHOWING ME YOUR STATS!?
YOU'RE IN A PARTY WITH MAPLE, RIGHT? I DON'T SEE THE PROBLEM.

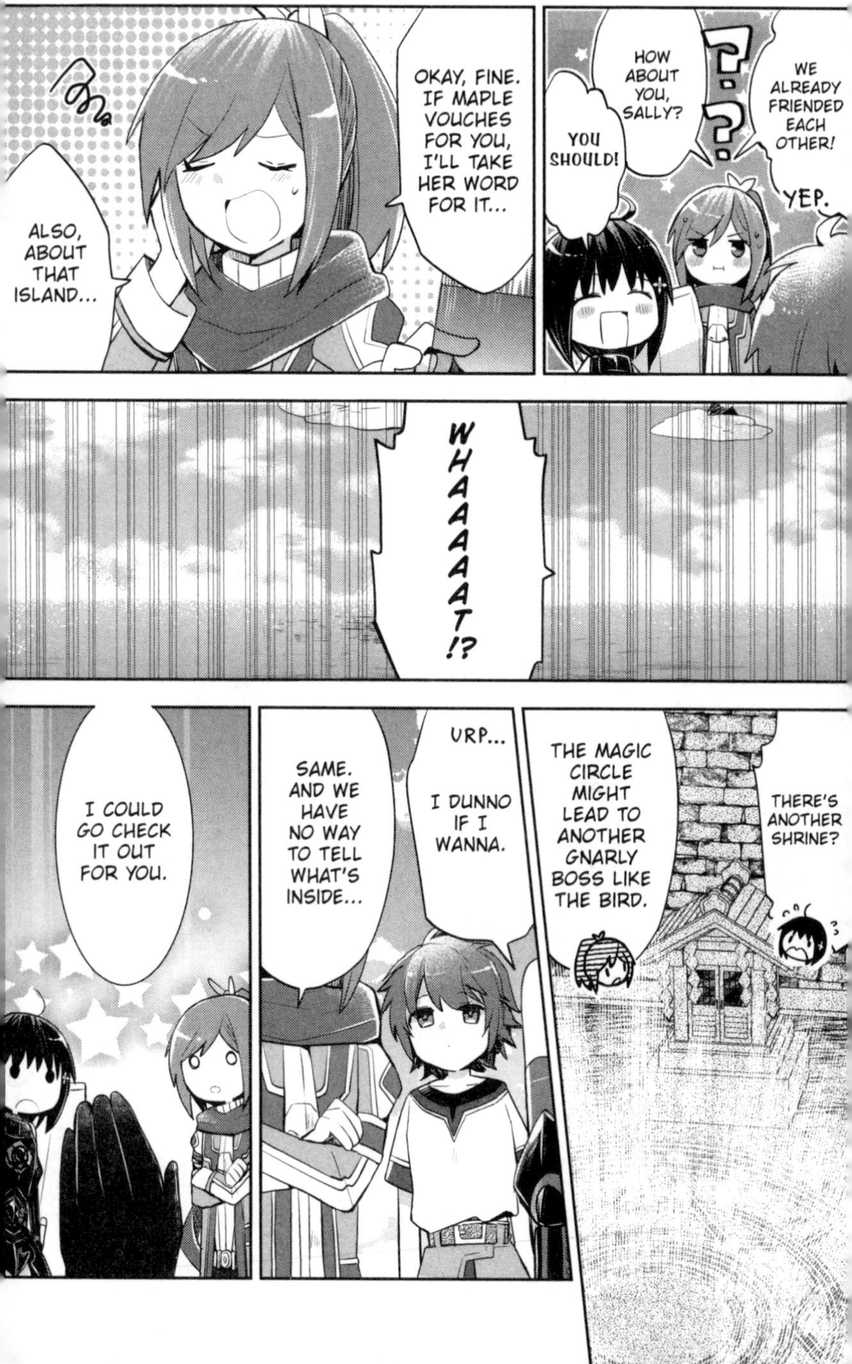
WE ALREADY FRIENDED EACH OTHER!
HOW ABOUT YOU, SALLY?
YOU SHOULD!
YEP.
OKAY, FINE. IF MAPLE VOUCHES FOR YOU, I'LL TAKE HER WORD FOR IT...
ALSO, ABOUT THAT ISLAND...
WHAAAAAT!?
THERE'S ANOTHER SHRINE?
THE MAGIC CIRCLE MIGHT LEAD TO ANOTHER GNARLY BOSS LIKE THE BIRD.
URP...
I DUNNO IF I WANNA.
SAME. AND WE HAVE NO WAY TO TELL WHAT'S INSIDE...
I COULD GO CHECK IT OUT FOR YOU.

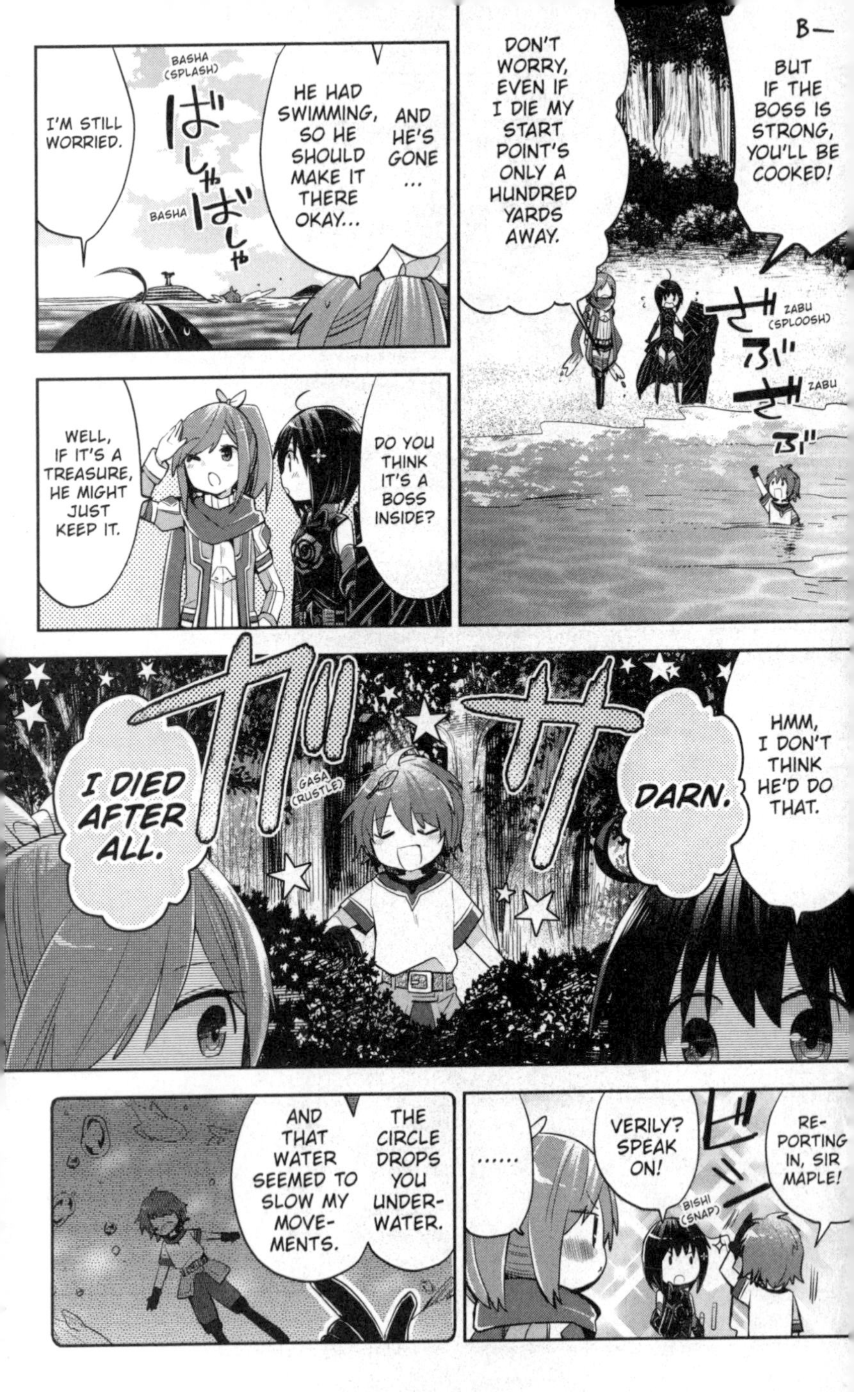
B—
BUT IF THE BOSS IS STRONG, YOU'LL BE COOKED!
DON'T WORRY, EVEN IF I DIE MY START POINT'S ONLY A HUNDRED YARDS AWAY.
ざぶざぶ
ZABU (SPLOOSH)
ZABU
AND HE'S GONE ...
HE HAD SWIMMING, SO HE SHOULD MAKE IT THERE OKAY...
ばしゃばしゃ
BASHA (SPLASH)
BASHA
I'M STILL WORRIED.
DO YOU THINK IT'S A BOSS INSIDE?
WELL, IF IT'S A TREASURE, HE MIGHT JUST KEEP IT.
HMM, I DON'T THINK HE'D DO THAT.
DARN.
ガサ
GASA (RUSTLE)
I DIED AFTER ALL.
RE-PORTING IN, SIR MAPLE!
ビシ
BISHI (SNAP)
VERILY? SPEAK ON!
......
THE CIRCLE DROPS YOU UNDER-WATER.
AND THAT WATER SEEMED TO SLOW MY MOVE-MENTS.

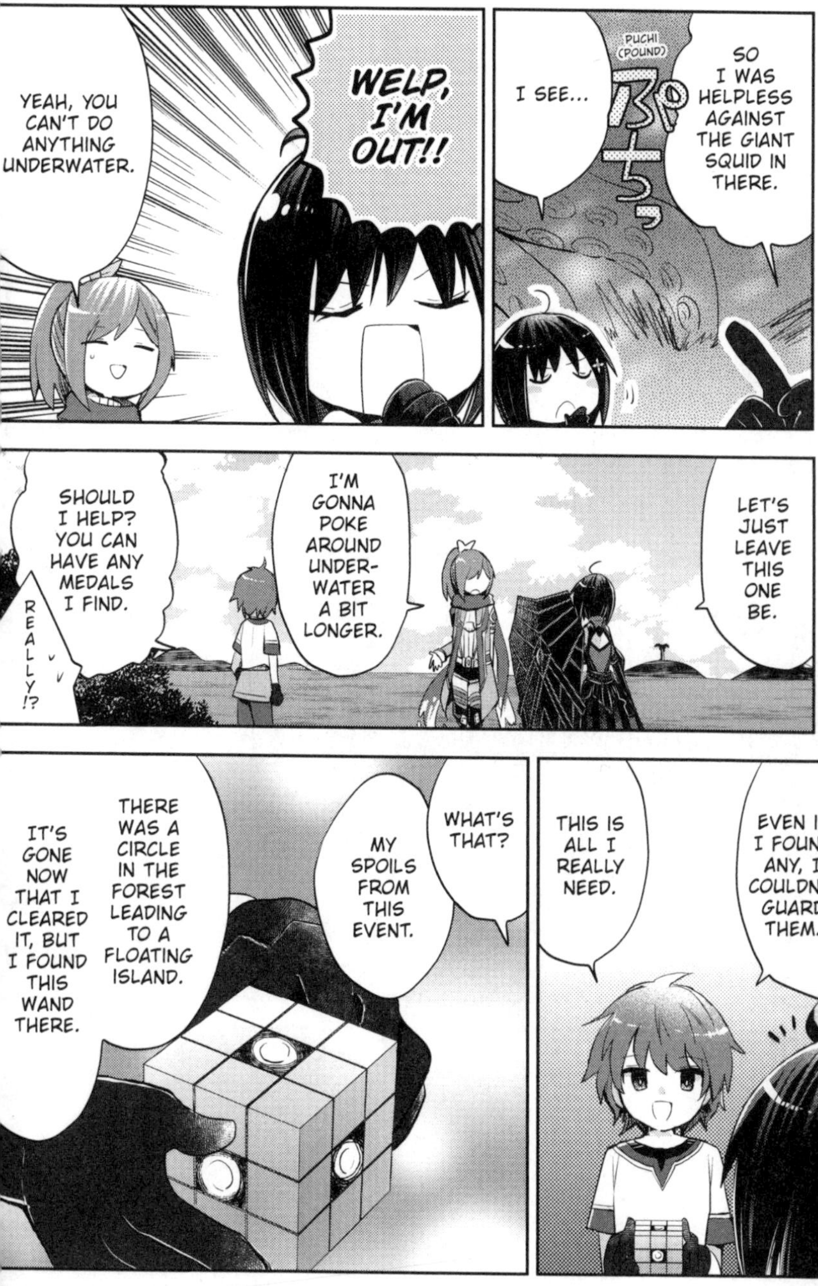
SO I WAS HELPLESS AGAINST THE GIANT SQUID IN THERE.
PUCHI (POUND)
I SEE...
WELP, I'M OUT!!
YEAH, YOU CAN'T DO ANYTHING UNDERWATER.
LET'S JUST LEAVE THIS ONE BE.
I'M GONNA POKE AROUND UNDER-WATER A BIT LONGER.
SHOULD I HELP? YOU CAN HAVE ANY MEDALS I FIND.
REALLY!?
EVEN IF I FOUND ANY, I COULDN'T GUARD THEM.
THIS IS ALL I REALLY NEED.
WHAT'S THAT?
MY SPOILS FROM THIS EVENT.
THERE WAS A CIRCLE IN THE FOREST LEADING TO A FLOATING ISLAND.
IT'S GONE NOW THAT I CLEARED IT, BUT I FOUND THIS WAND THERE.

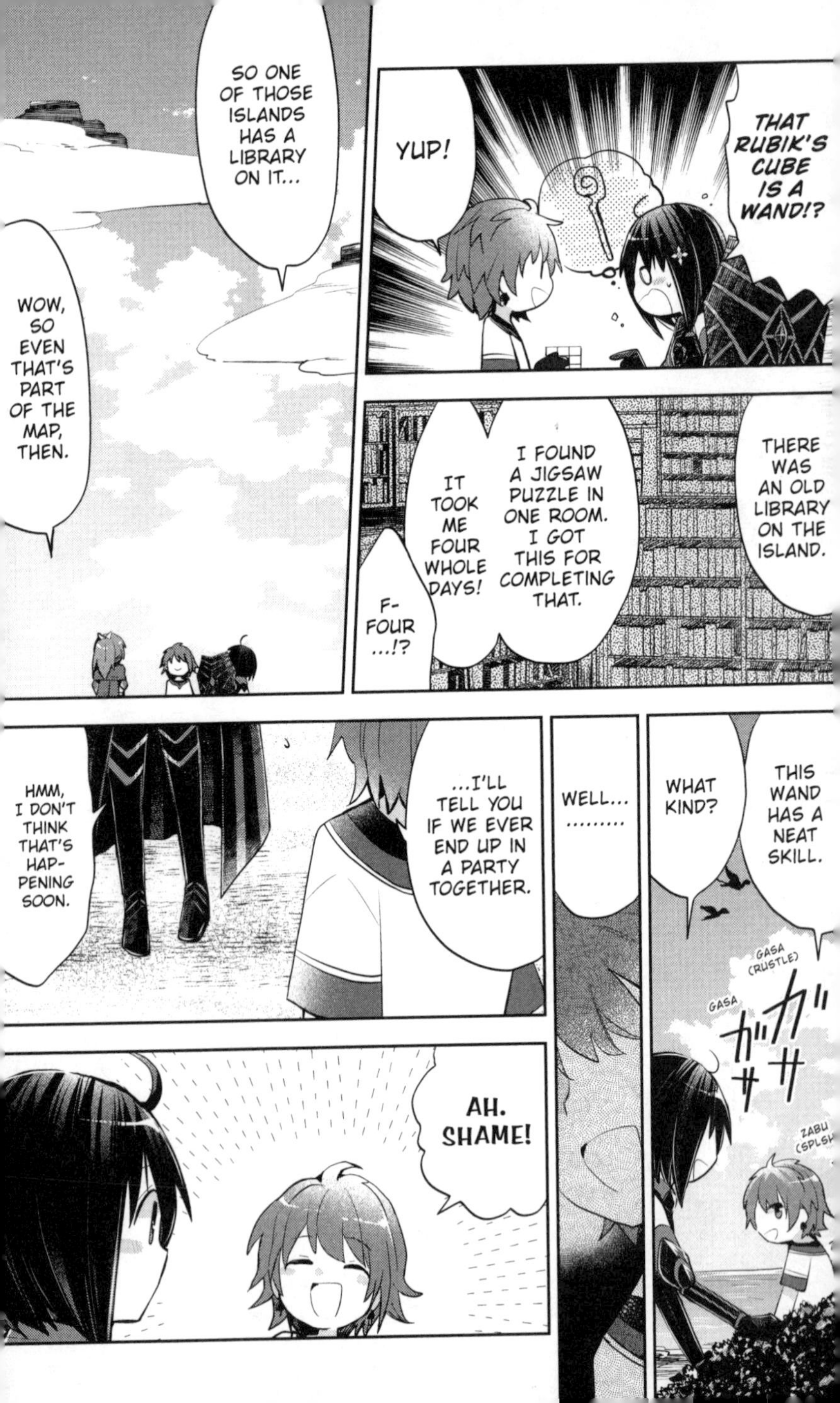
THAT RUBIK'S CUBE IS A WAND!?
YUP!
THERE WAS AN OLD LIBRARY ON THE ISLAND.
I FOUND A JIGSAW PUZZLE IN ONE ROOM. I GOT THIS FOR COMPLETING THAT.
IT TOOK ME FOUR WHOLE DAYS!
F-FOUR...!?
SO ONE OF THOSE ISLANDS HAS A LIBRARY ON IT...
WOW, SO EVEN THAT'S PART OF THE MAP, THEN.
THIS WAND HAS A NEAT SKILL.
WHAT KIND?
GASA (RUSTLE)
GASA
ZABU (SPLSH)
WELL... ....
...I'LL TELL YOU IF WE EVER END UP IN A PARTY TOGETHER.
HMM, I DON'T THINK THAT'S HAPPENING SOON.
AH. SHAME!

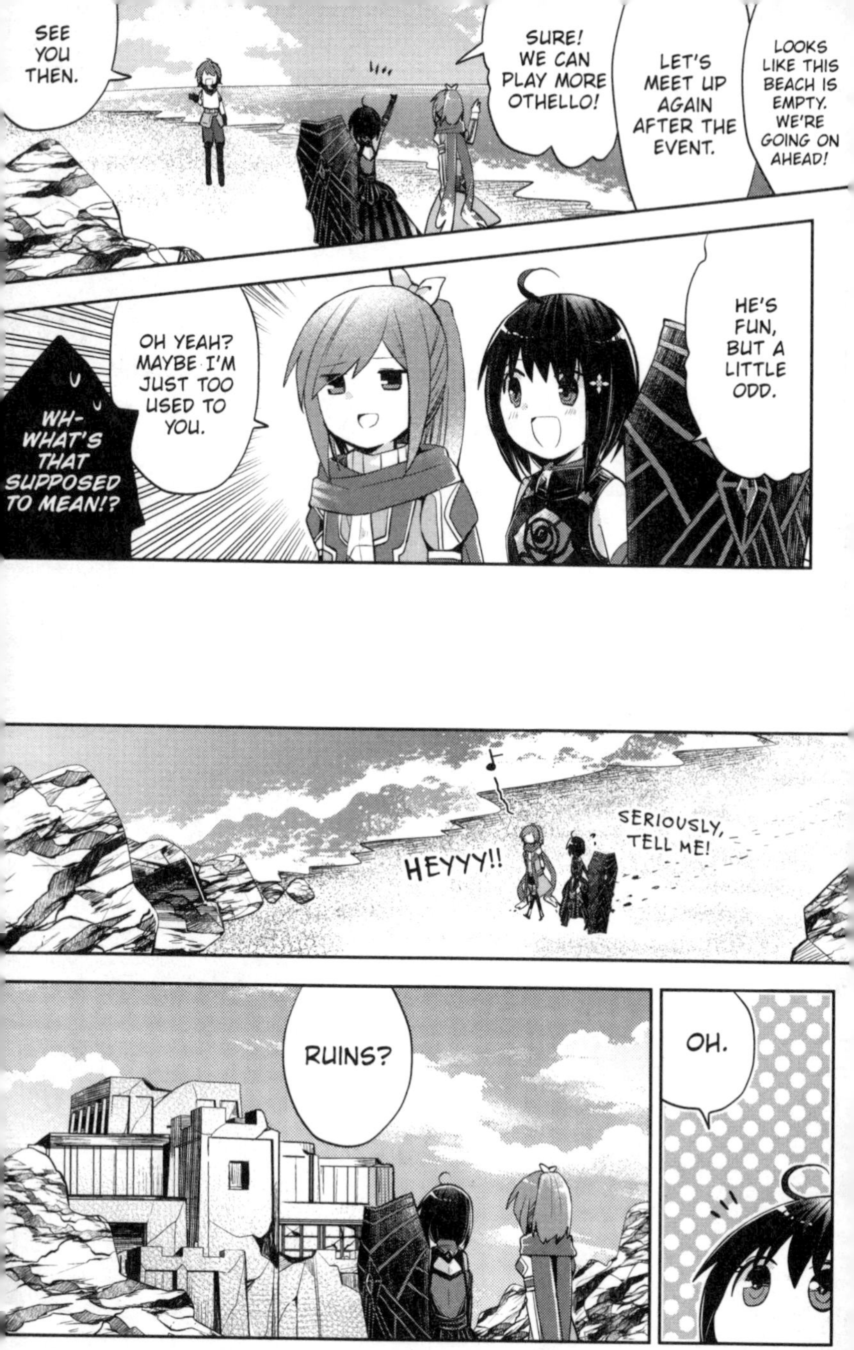

LOOKS LIKE THIS BEACH IS EMPTY. WE'RE GOING ON AHEAD!
LET'S MEET UP AGAIN AFTER THE EVENT.
SURE! WE CAN PLAY MORE OTHELLO!
SEE YOU THEN.
HE'S FUN, BUT A LITTLE ODD.
OH YEAH? MAYBE I'M JUST TOO USED TO YOU.
WH-WHAT'S THAT SUPPOSED TO MEAN!?
SERIOUSLY, TELL ME!
HEYYY!!
OH.
RUINS?

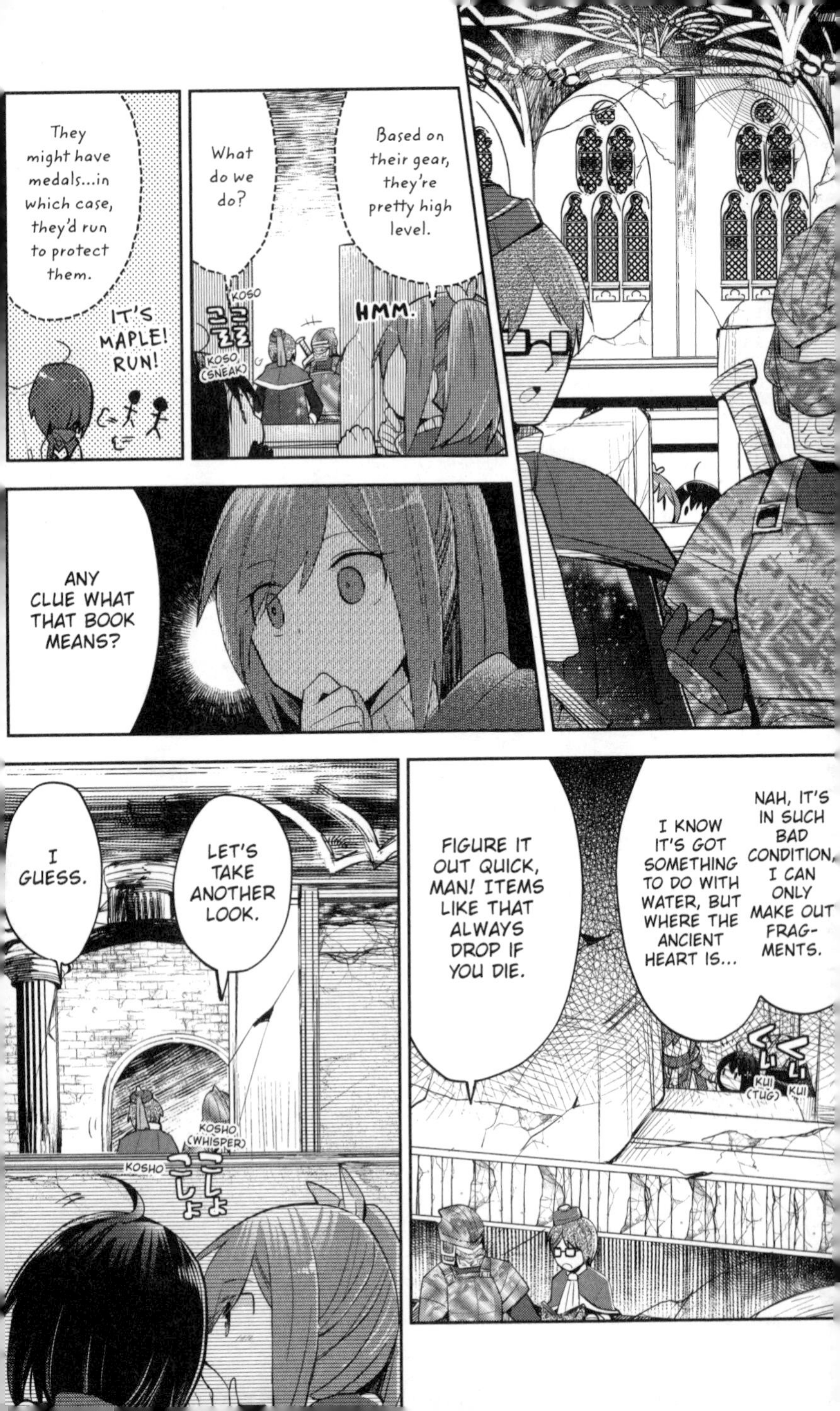

Based on their gear, they're pretty high level.
HMM.
What do we do?
KOSO
KOSO (SNEAK)
They might have medals...in which case, they'd run to protect them.
IT'S MAPLE! RUN!
ANY CLUE WHAT THAT BOOK MEANS?
NAH, IT'S IN SUCH BAD CONDITION, I CAN ONLY MAKE OUT FRAG-MENTS.
I KNOW IT'S GOT SOMETHING TO DO WITH WATER, BUT WHERE THE ANCIENT HEART IS...
FIGURE IT OUT QUICK, MAN! ITEMS LIKE THAT ALWAYS DROP IF YOU DIE.
KUI (TUG) KUI
LET'S TAKE ANOTHER LOOK.
I GUESS.
KOSHO
KOSHO (WHISPER)

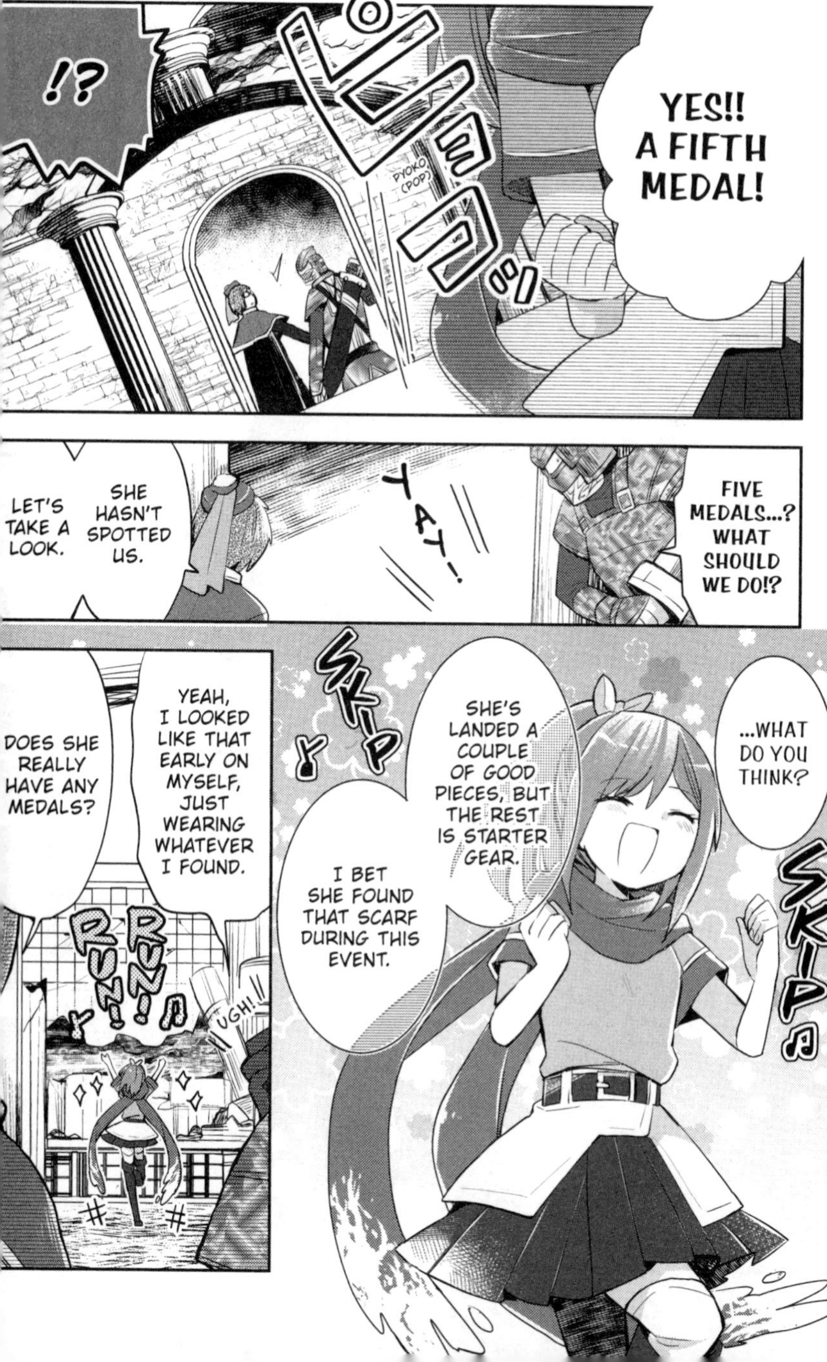
YES!! A FIFTH MEDAL!
PYOKO (POP)
!?
FIVE MEDALS...? WHAT SHOULD WE DO!?
YAY!
SHE HASN'T SPOTTED US.
LET'S TAKE A LOOK.
SKIP♪
...WHAT DO YOU THINK?
SHE'S LANDED A COUPLE OF GOOD PIECES, BUT THE REST IS STARTER GEAR.
SKIP♪
I BET SHE FOUND THAT SCARF DURING THIS EVENT.
YEAH, I LOOKED LIKE THAT EARLY ON MYSELF, JUST WEARING WHATEVER I FOUND.
DOES SHE REALLY HAVE ANY MEDALS?
RUN! RUN!♪
UGH!

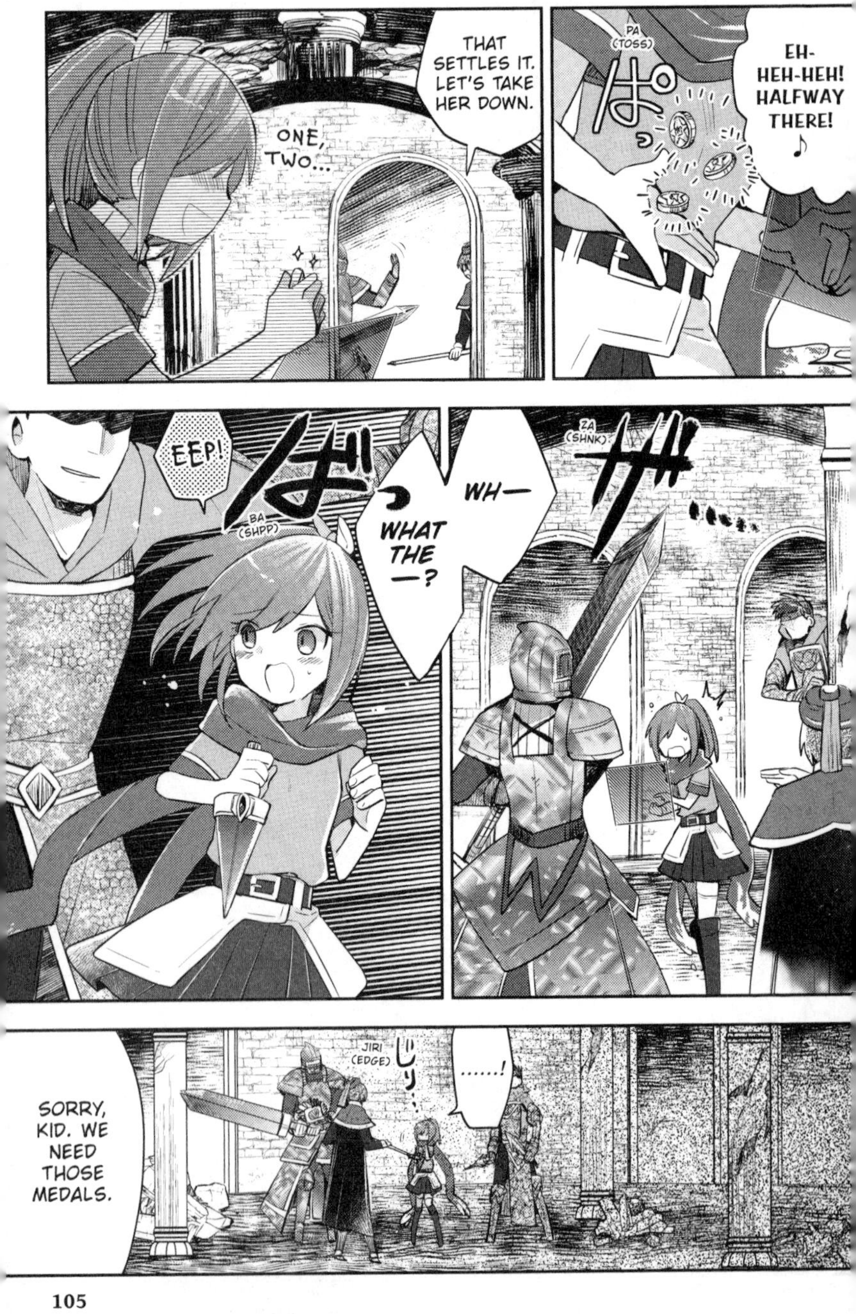

PA (TOSS)
ぱっ
EH-HEH-HEH! HALFWAY THERE! ♪
THAT SETTLES IT. LET'S TAKE HER DOWN.
ONE, TWO...
ZA (SHNK)
ザッ
WH— WHAT THE—?
ばっ
BA (SHPP)
EEP!
......!
JIRI (EDGE)
じり
SORRY, KID. WE NEED THOSE MEDALS.

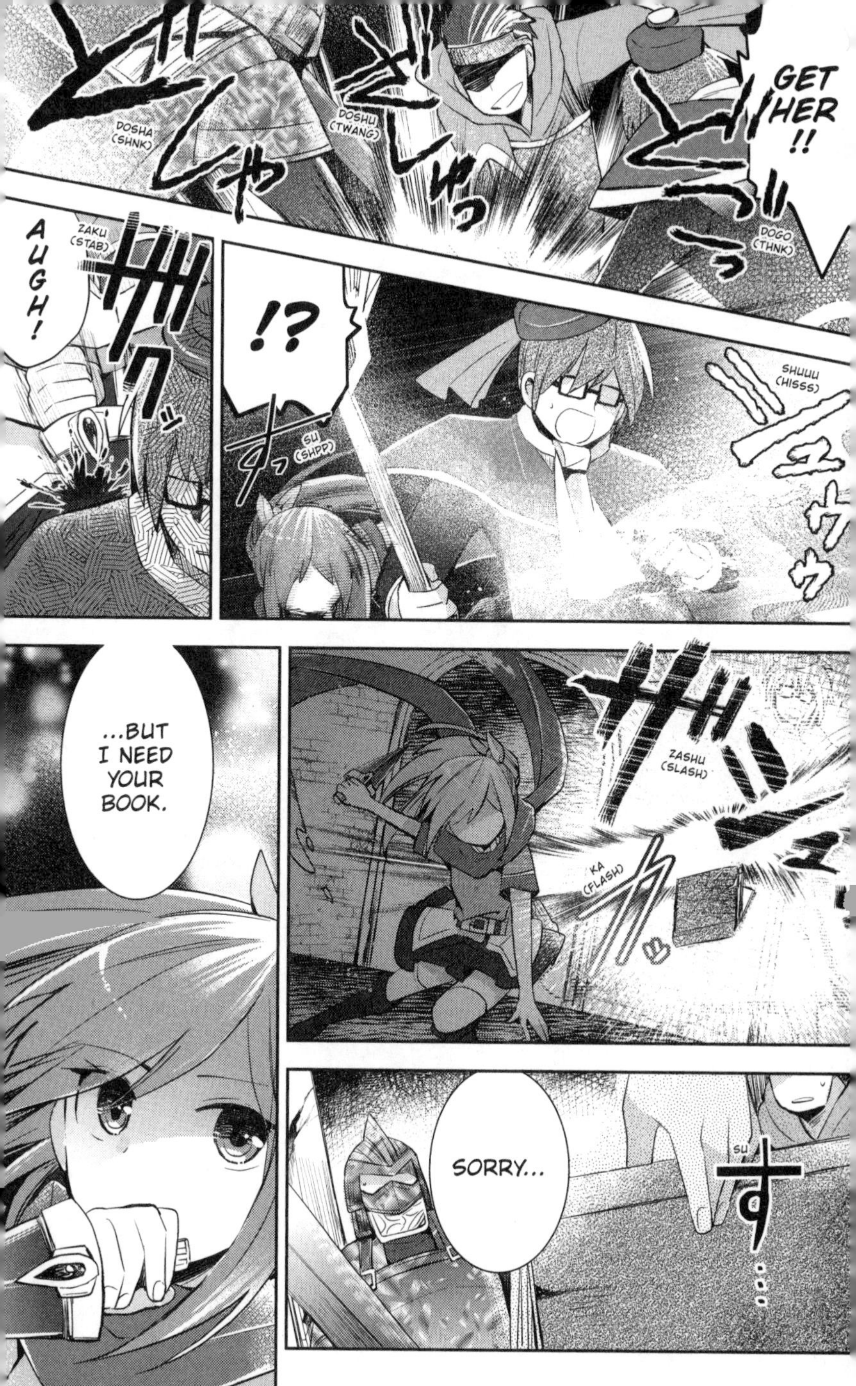
GET HER!!
DOGO (THNK)
DOSHU (TWANG)
DOSHA (SHNK)
SHUUU (HISSS)
!?
SU (SHPP)
ZAKU (STAB)
AUGH!
ZASHU (SLASH)
KA (FLASH)
SU
SORRY...
...BUT I NEED YOUR BOOK.

Bofuri

I Don't Want to Get Hurt, so I'll Max Out My Defense.

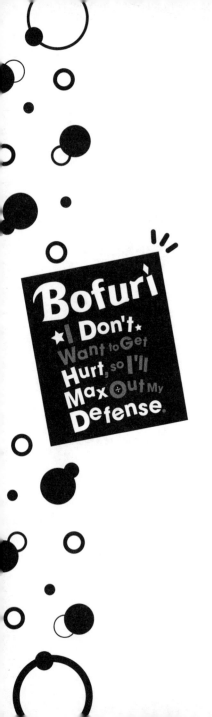

Welcome to *NewWorld Online*.

I Don't Want to Get Hurt,

so I'll Max Out My Defense.

presented by: **JIROU OIMOTO & YUUMIKAN**

CHAPTER 16

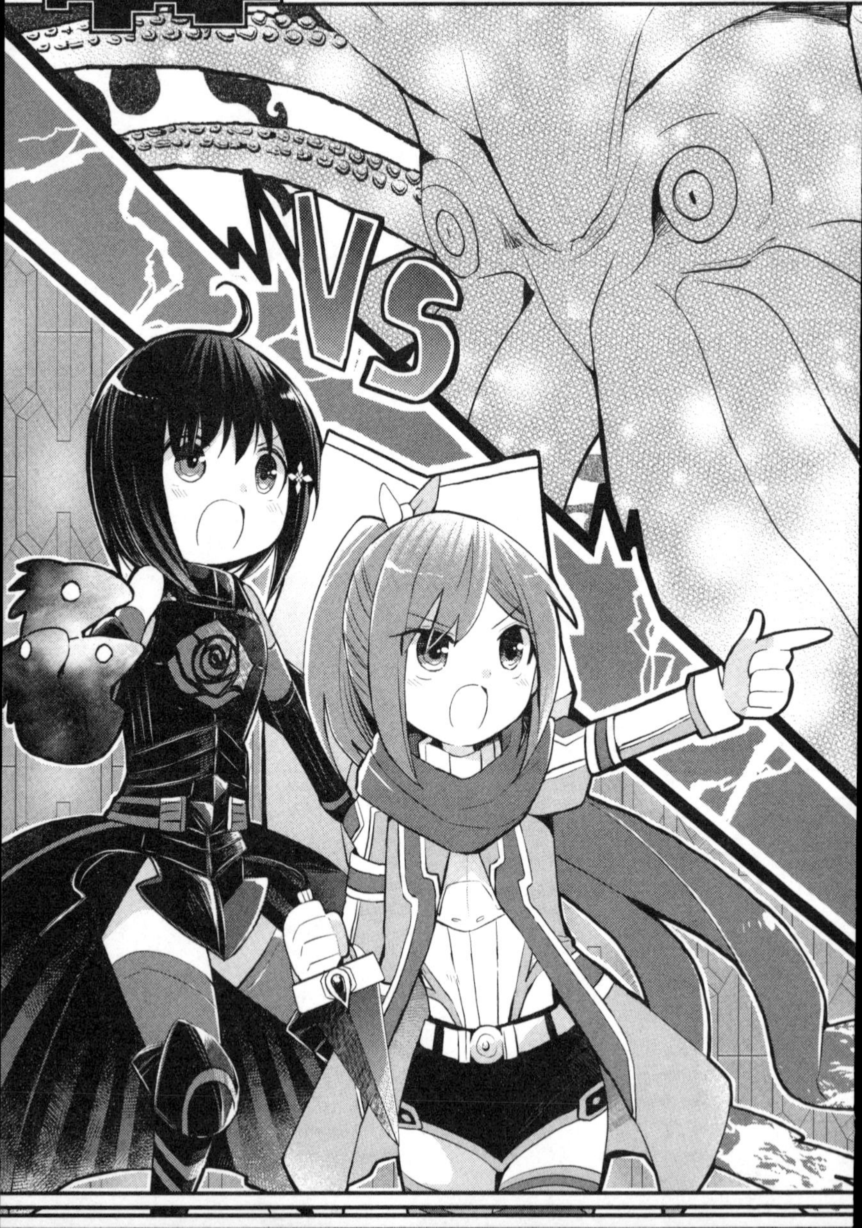
VS

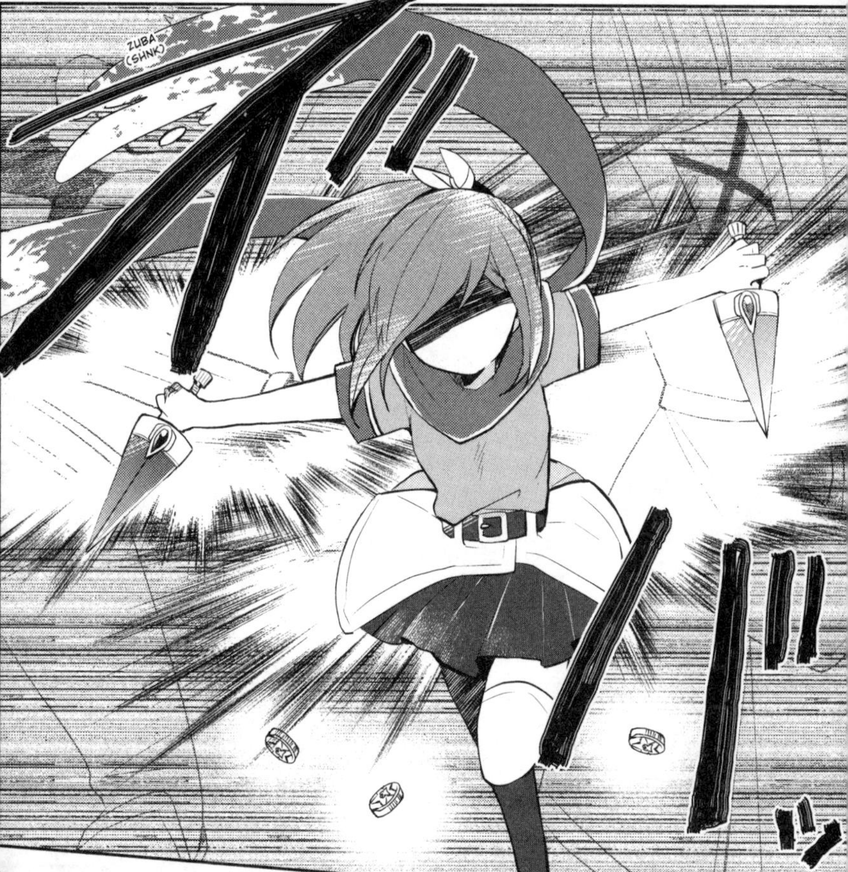
ズバッ
ZUBA (SHNK)

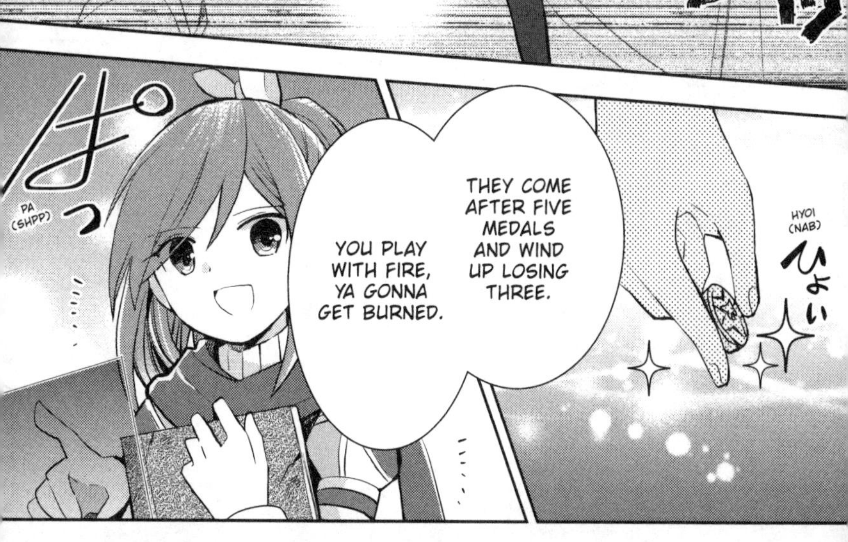
ひょい
HYOI (NAB)
THEY COME AFTER FIVE MEDALS AND WIND UP LOSING THREE.
YOU PLAY WITH FIRE, YA GONNA GET BURNED.
ぱっ
PA (SHPP)

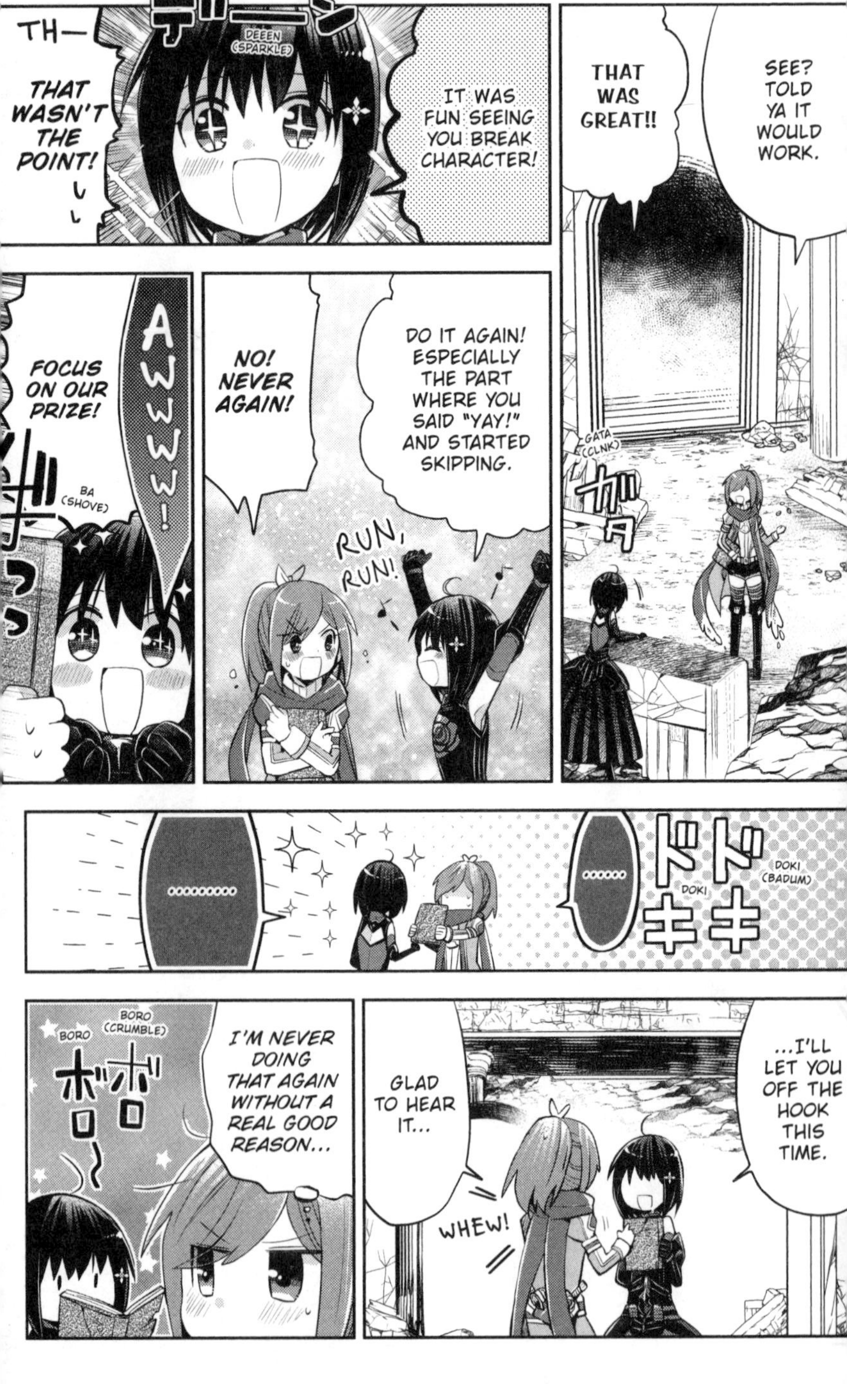
SEE? TOLD YA IT WOULD WORK.
THAT WAS GREAT!!
GATA (CLNK)
IT WAS FUN SEEING YOU BREAK CHARACTER!
DEEEN (SPARKLE)
TH— THAT WASN'T THE POINT!
DO IT AGAIN! ESPECIALLY THE PART WHERE YOU SAID "YAY!" AND STARTED SKIPPING.
NO! NEVER AGAIN!
RUN, RUN!
AWWWWW!
FOCUS ON OUR PRIZE!
BA (SHOVE)
DOKI (BADUM)
DOKI
......
....
...I'LL LET YOU OFF THE HOOK THIS TIME.
GLAD TO HEAR IT...
WHEW!
I'M NEVER DOING THAT AGAIN WITHOUT A REAL GOOD REASON...
BORO (CRUMBLE)
BORO

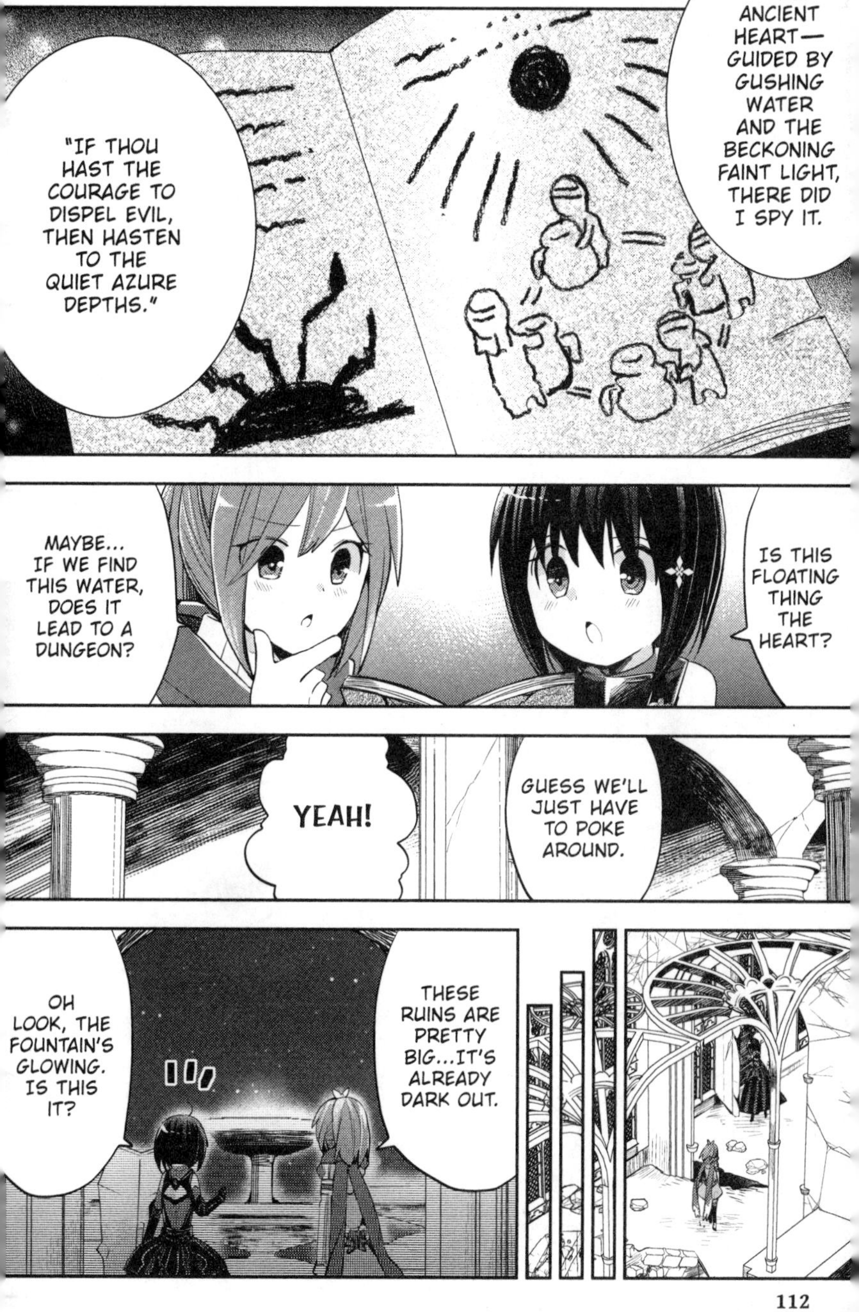
"THE ANCIENT HEART—GUIDED BY GUSHING WATER AND THE BECKONING FAINT LIGHT, THERE DID I SPY IT.
"IF THOU HAST THE COURAGE TO DISPEL EVIL, THEN HASTEN TO THE QUIET AZURE DEPTHS."
IS THIS FLOATING THING THE HEART?
MAYBE... IF WE FIND THIS WATER, DOES IT LEAD TO A DUNGEON?
GUESS WE'LL JUST HAVE TO POKE AROUND.
YEAH!
THESE RUINS ARE PRETTY BIG...IT'S ALREADY DARK OUT.
OH LOOK, THE FOUNTAIN'S GLOWING. IS THIS IT?

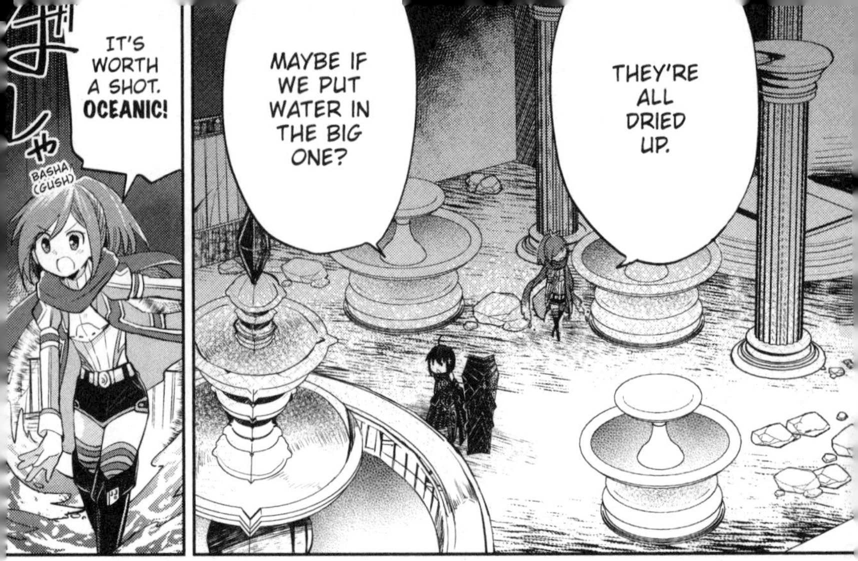
THEY'RE ALL DRIED UP.
MAYBE IF WE PUT WATER IN THE BIG ONE?
IT'S WORTH A SHOT. **OCEANIC!**
BASHA (GUSH)

★ **OCEANIC:** Emits a horizonal circle of water centered on user that reduces monster/player AGI by 20% on contact. Cannot be used in the air. Fixed radius of ten yards. Only the user is immune. Use limit is three times per day. Effect lasts ten seconds.

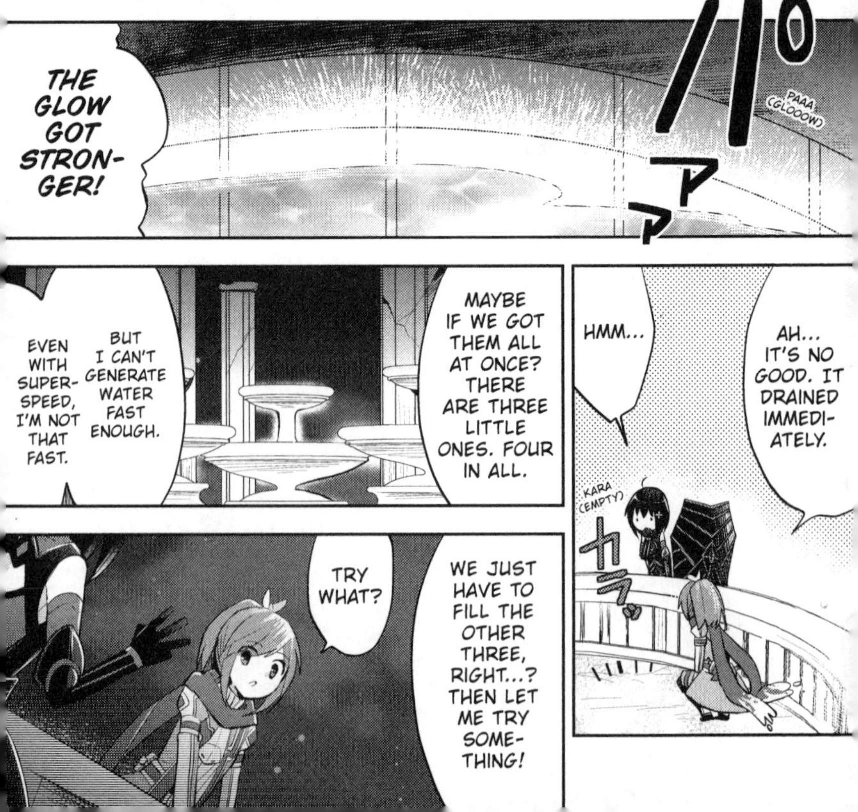
PAAA (GLOOOW)
THE GLOW GOT STRONGER!
AH... IT'S NO GOOD. IT DRAINED IMMEDIATELY.
HMM...
KARA (EMPTY)
MAYBE IF WE GOT THEM ALL AT ONCE? THERE ARE THREE LITTLE ONES. FOUR IN ALL.
BUT I CAN'T GENERATE WATER FAST ENOUGH.
EVEN WITH SUPER-SPEED, I'M NOT THAT FAST.
WE JUST HAVE TO FILL THE OTHER THREE, RIGHT...? THEN LET ME TRY SOMETHING!
TRY WHAT?

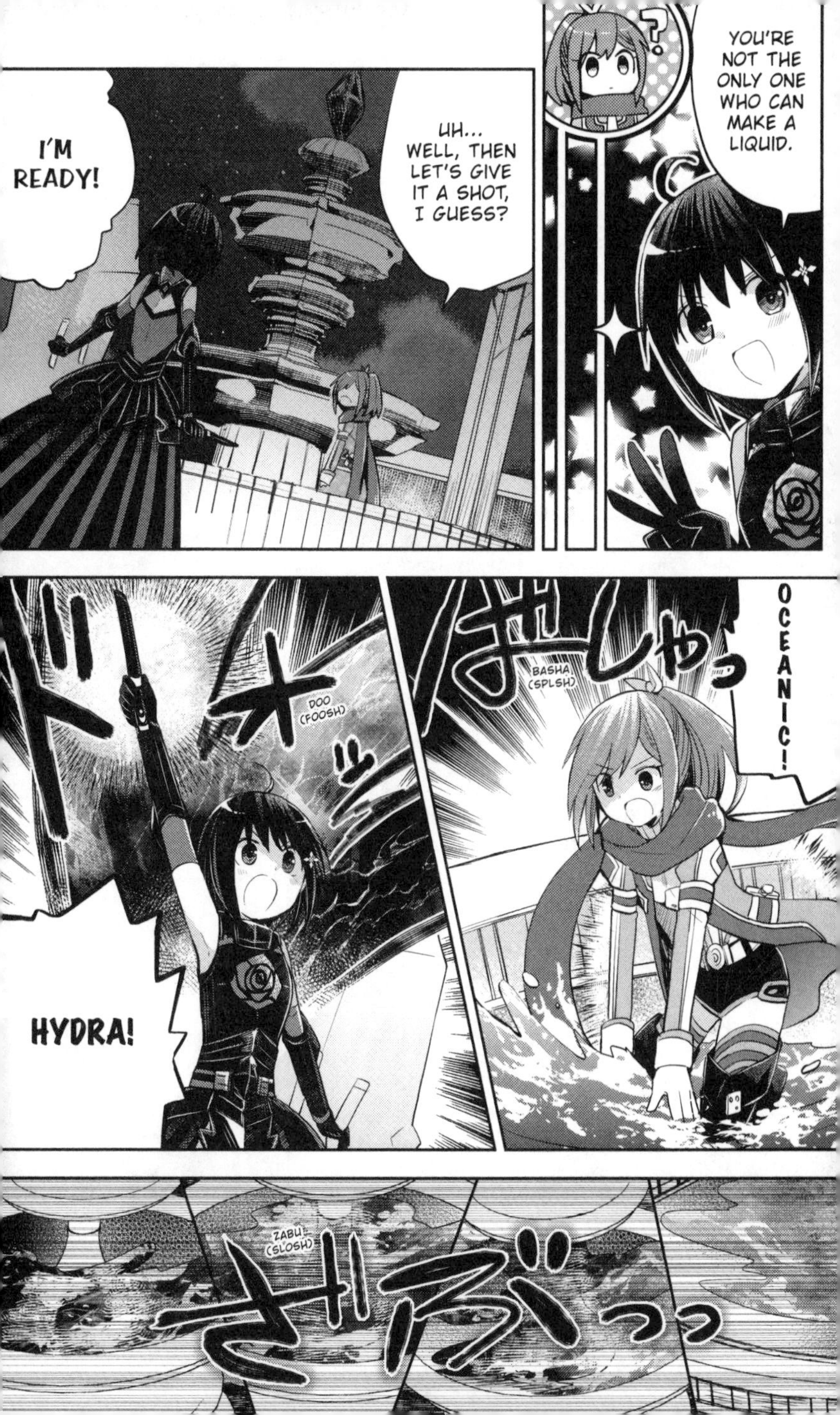
?
YOU'RE NOT THE ONLY ONE WHO CAN MAKE A LIQUID.
UH... WELL, THEN LET'S GIVE IT A SHOT, I GUESS?
I'M READY!
OCEANIC!
BASHA (SPLSH)
DOO (FOOSH)
HYDRA!
ZABU (SLOSH)

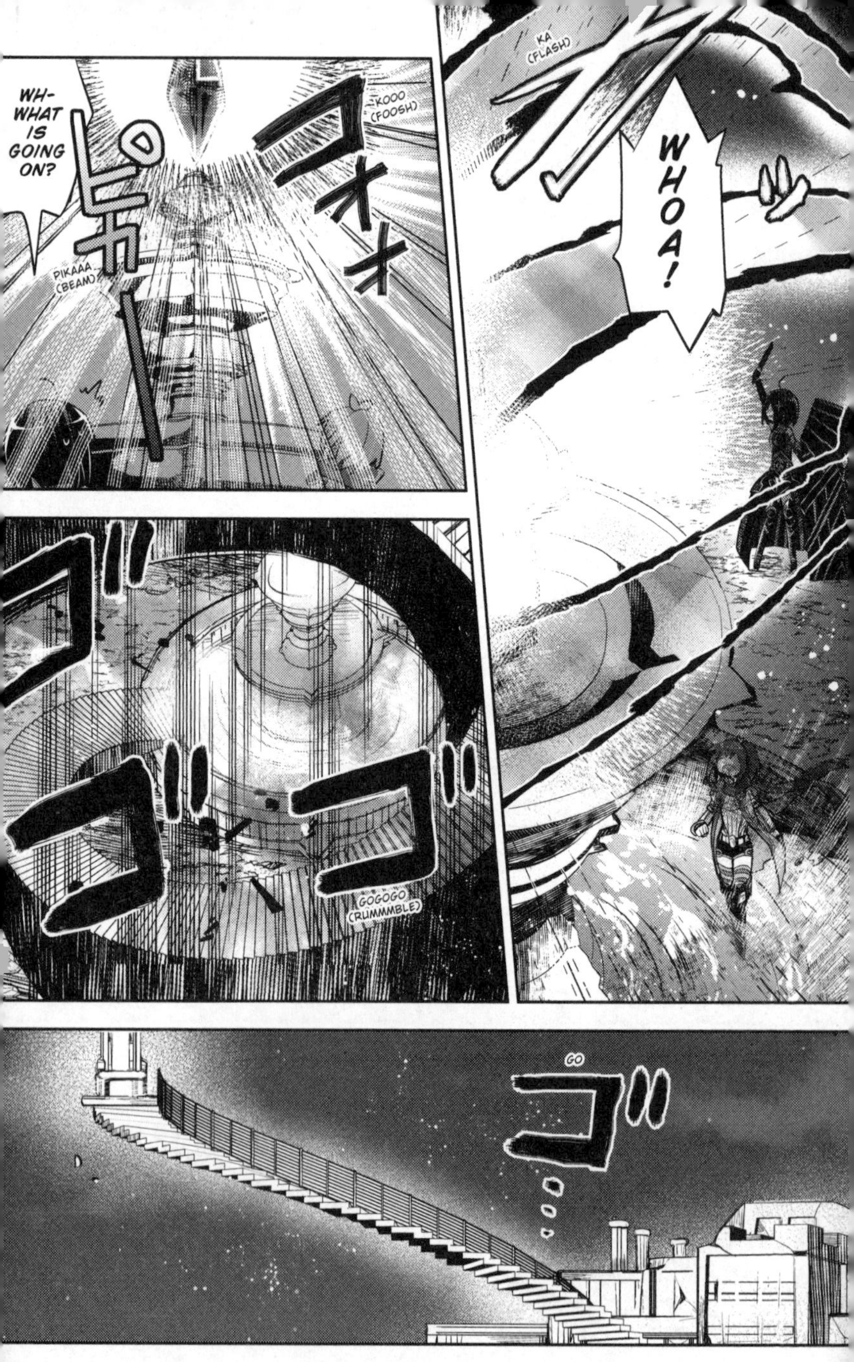
KA (FLASH)
WHOA!
KOOO (FOOSH)
WH- WHAT IS GOING ON?
PIKAAA (BEAM)
GOGOGO (RUMMMBLE)
GO

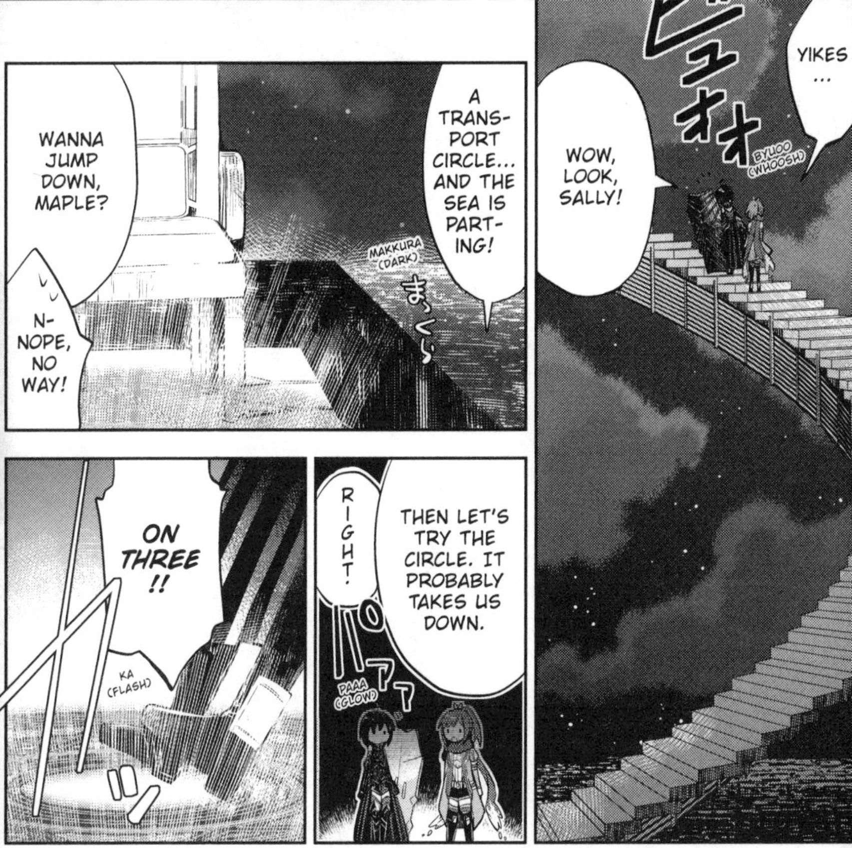
YIKES ...
BYUOO (WHOOSH)
WOW, LOOK, SALLY!
A TRANSPORT CIRCLE... AND THE SEA IS PARTING!
MAKKURA (DARK)
WANNA JUMP DOWN, MAPLE?
N-NOPE, NO WAY!
THEN LET'S TRY THE CIRCLE. IT PROBABLY TAKES US DOWN.
RIGHT!
PAAA (GLOW)
ON THREE!!
KA (FLASH)

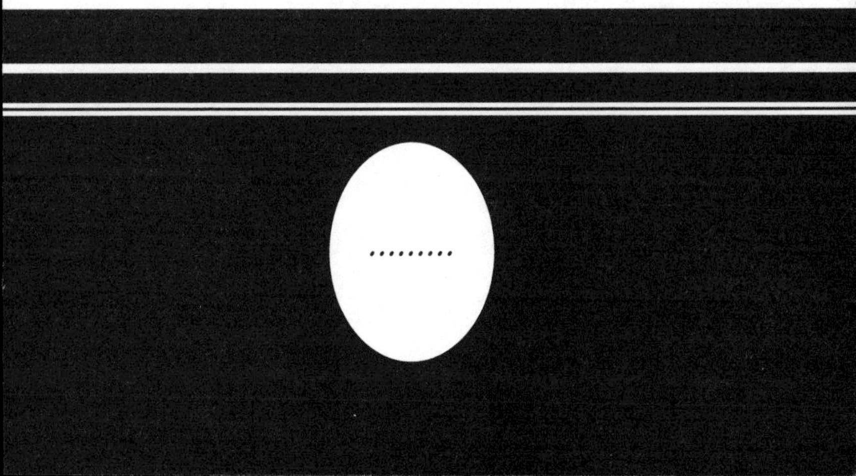
....

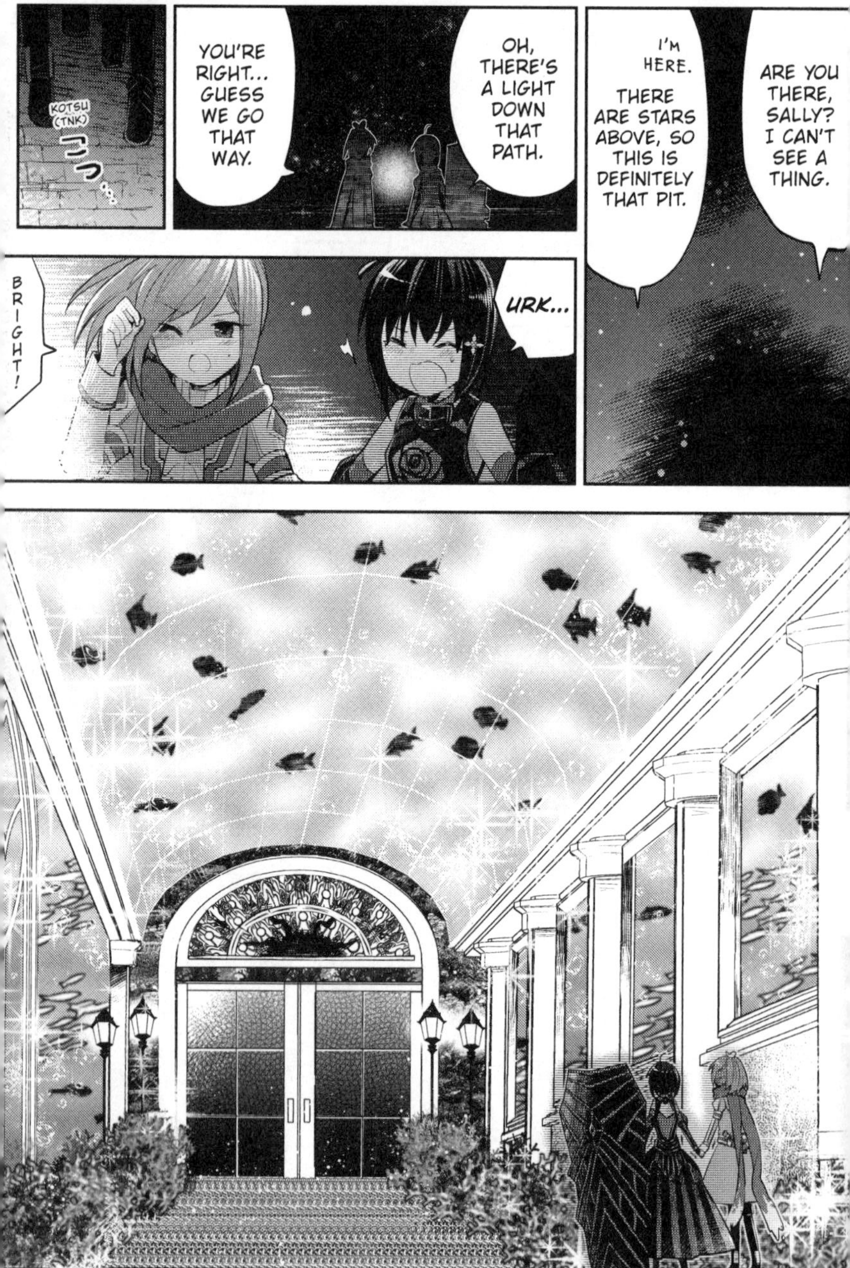
ARE YOU THERE, SALLY? I CAN'T SEE A THING.
I'M HERE.
THERE ARE STARS ABOVE, SO THIS IS DEFINITELY THAT PIT.
OH, THERE'S A LIGHT DOWN THAT PATH.
YOU'RE RIGHT... GUESS WE GO THAT WAY.
KOTSU (TNK)
コツ…
URK...
BRIGHT!

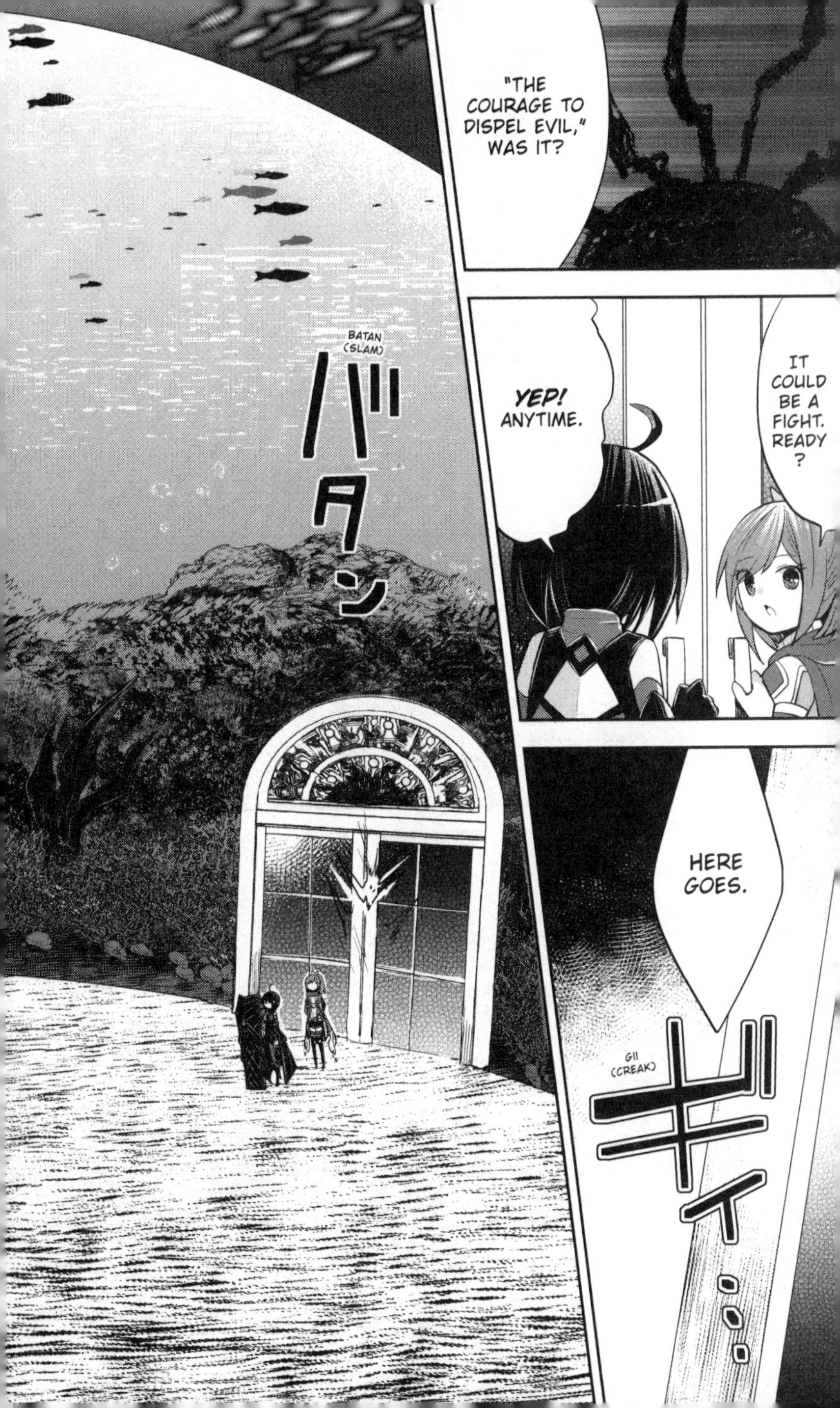
"THE COURAGE TO DISPEL EVIL," WAS IT?
IT COULD BE A FIGHT. READY?
YEP! ANYTIME.
HERE GOES.
GII (CREAK)
ギィ…
BATAN (SLAM)
バタン

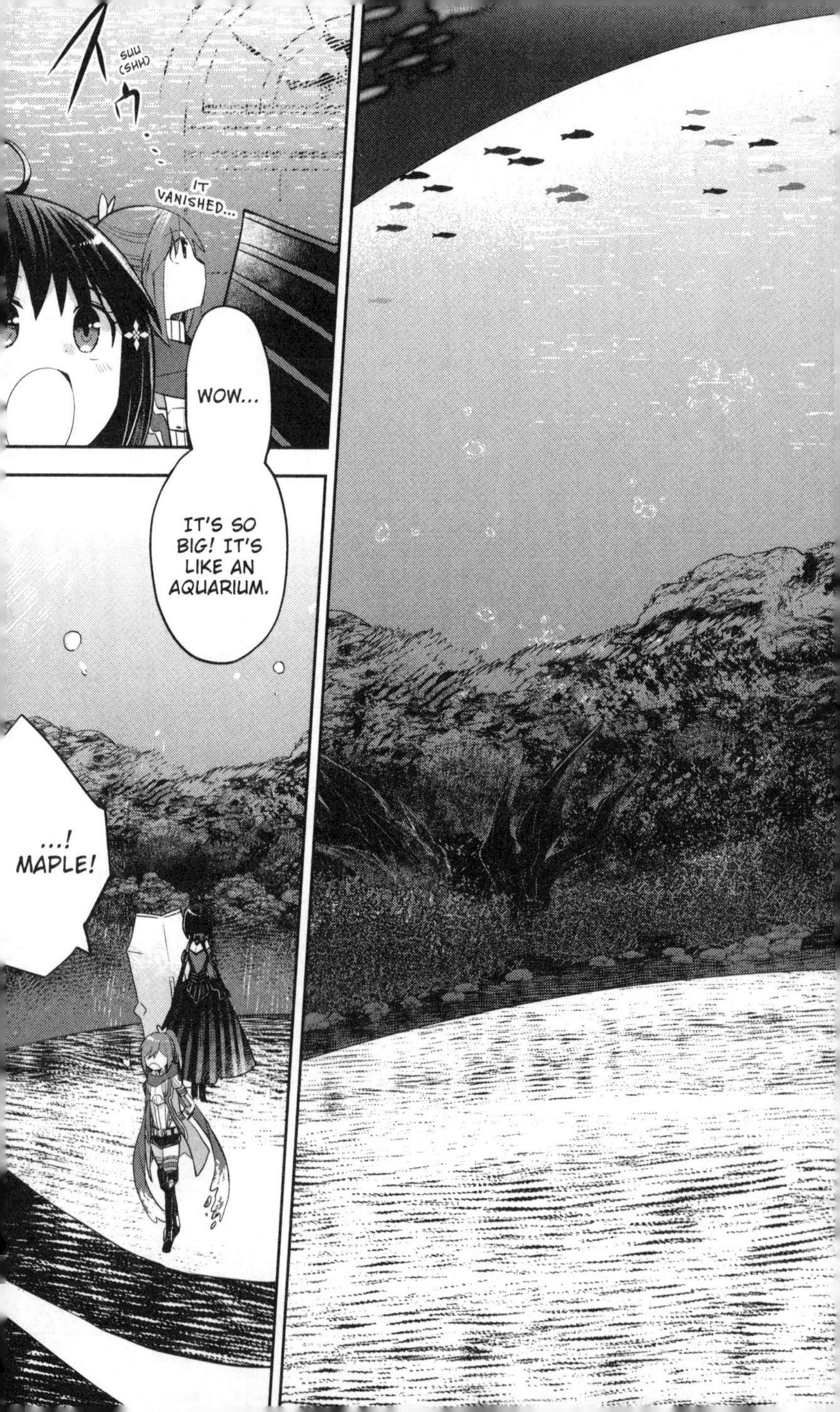
SUU (SHH)
IT VANISHED...
WOW...
IT'S SO BIG! IT'S LIKE AN AQUARIUM.
...! MAPLE!

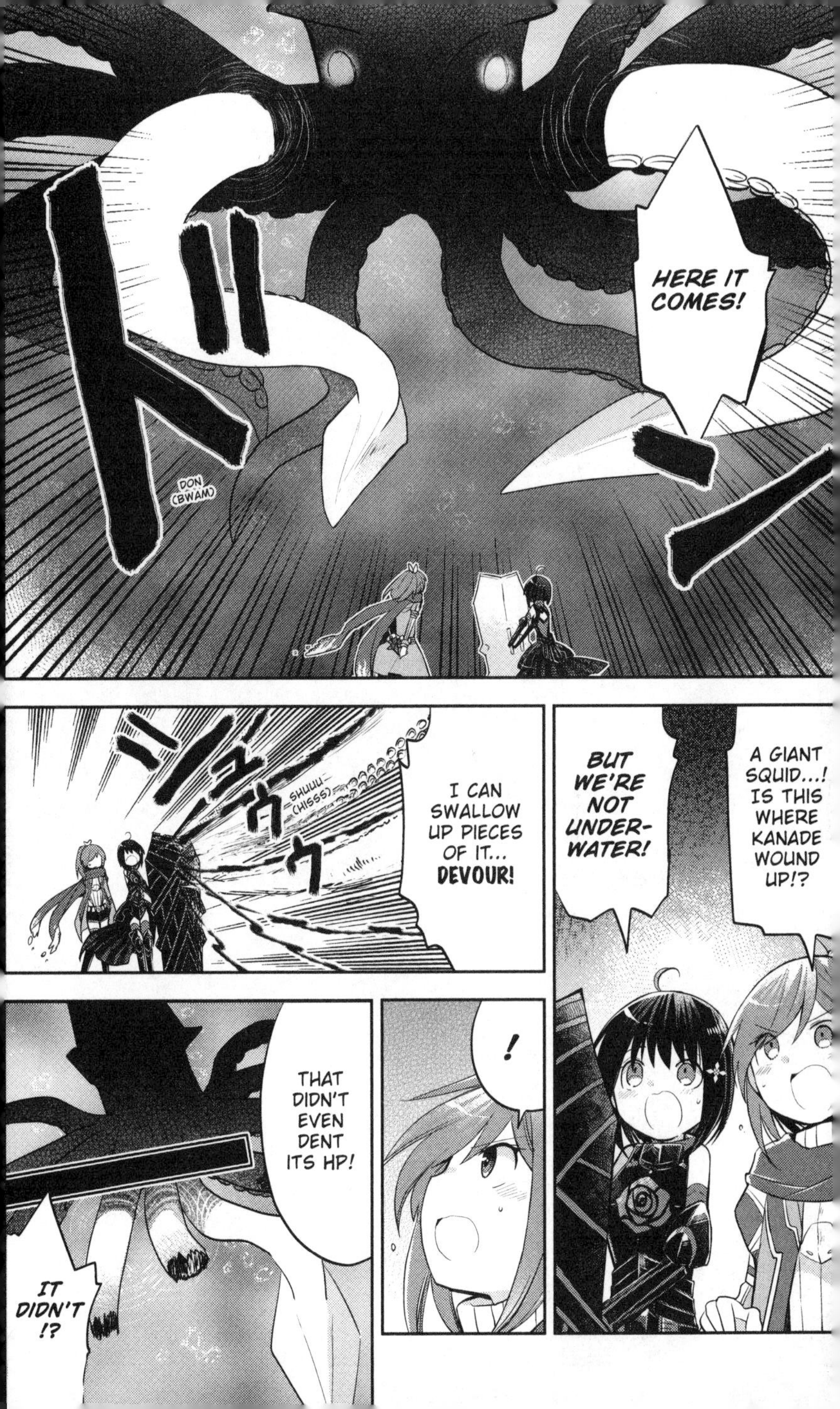
HERE IT COMES!
DON (BWAM)
A GIANT SQUID...! IS THIS WHERE KANADE WOUND UP!?
BUT WE'RE NOT UNDER-WATER!
I CAN SWALLOW UP PIECES OF IT... **DEVOUR!**
SHUUU (HISSS)
!
THAT DIDN'T EVEN DENT ITS HP!
IT DIDN'T !?

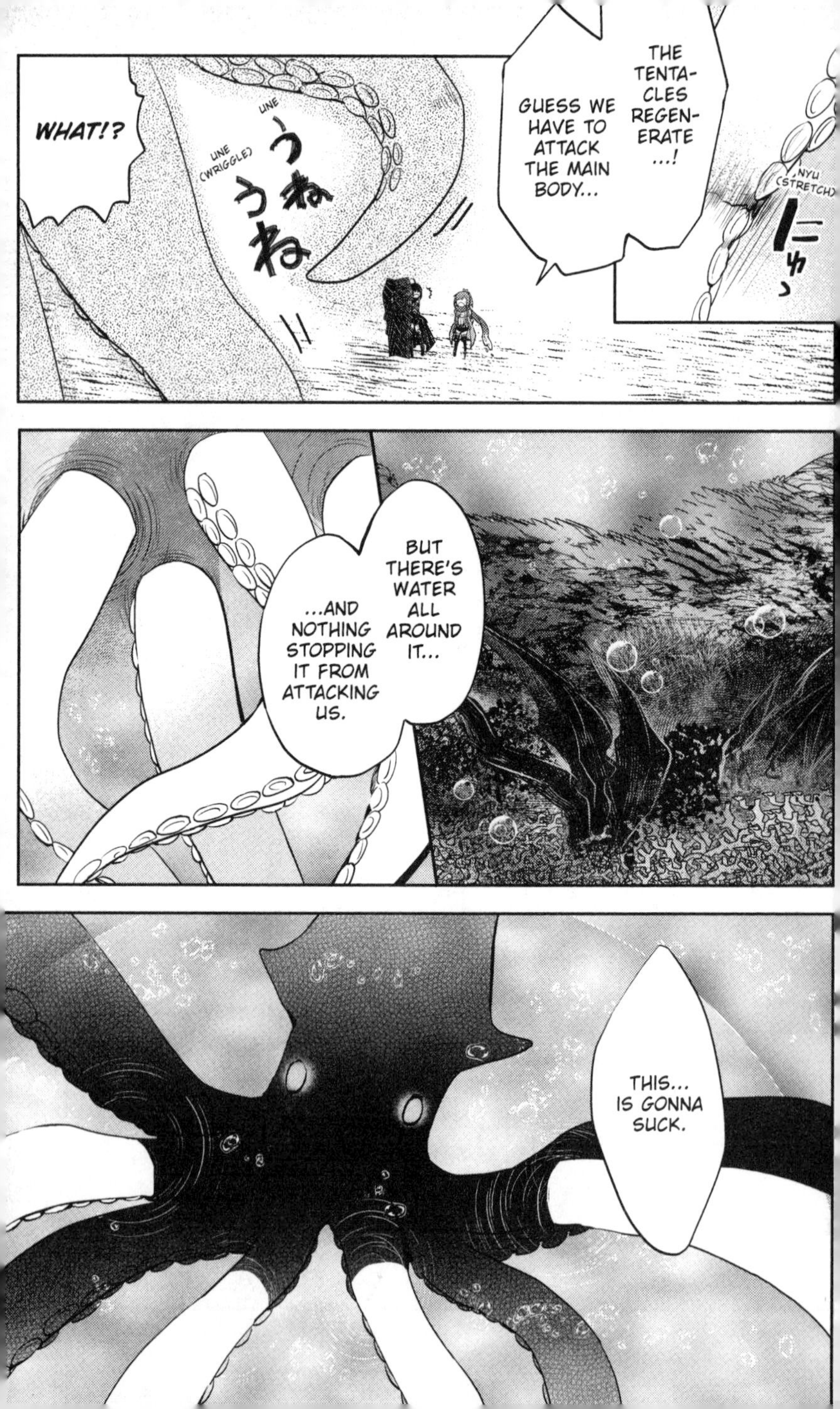
NYU (STRETCH)
にゅっ
THE TENTACLES REGENERATE...!
GUESS WE HAVE TO ATTACK THE MAIN BODY...
WHAT!?
UNE
UNE (WRIGGLE)
うねうね
BUT THERE'S WATER ALL AROUND IT...
...AND NOTHING STOPPING IT FROM ATTACKING US.
THIS... IS GONNA SUCK.

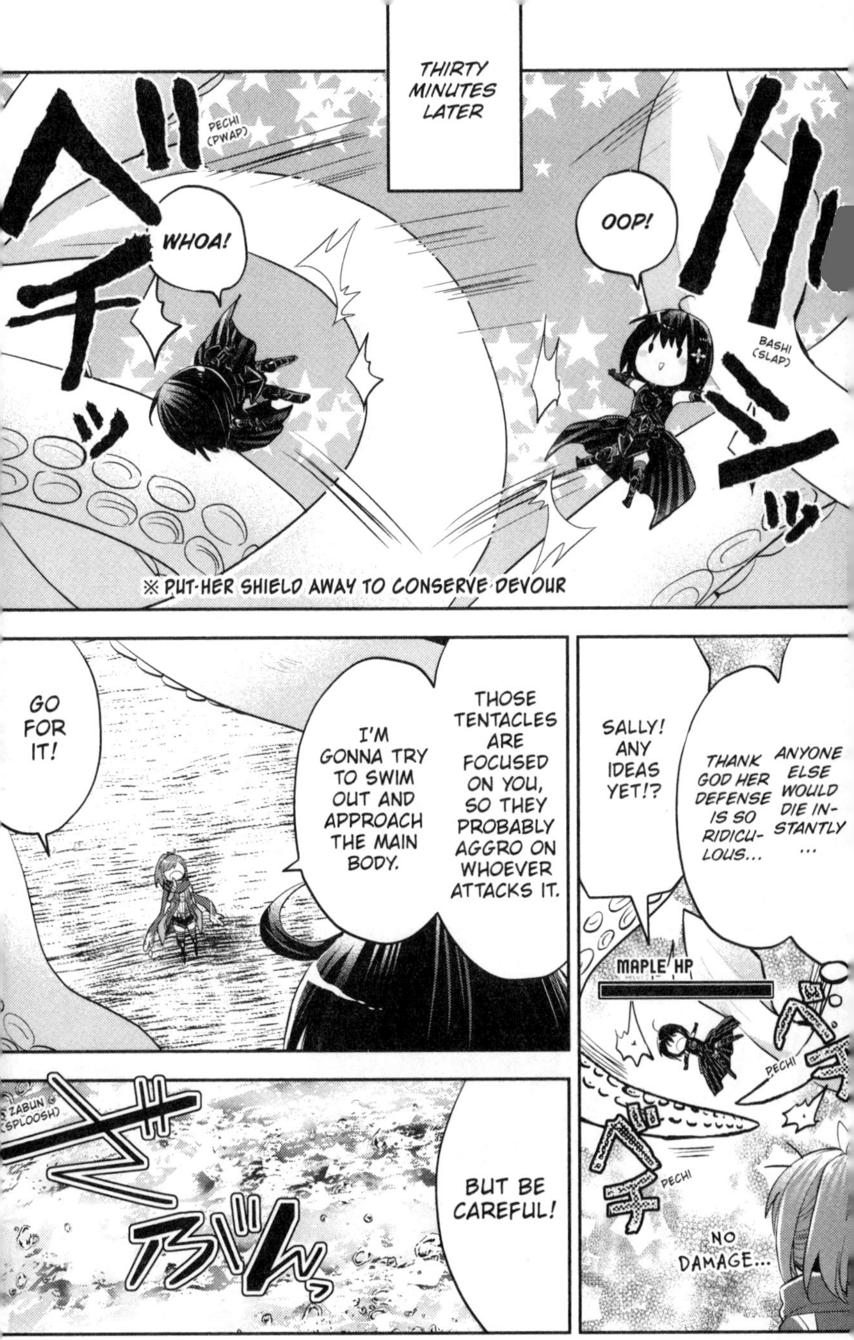

THIRTY MINUTES LATER
OOP!
BASHI (SLAP)
PECHI (PWAP)
WHOA!
※ PUT HER SHIELD AWAY TO CONSERVE DEVOUR
ANYONE ELSE WOULD DIE IN-STANTLY...
THANK GOD HER DEFENSE IS SO RIDICU-LOUS...
SALLY! ANY IDEAS YET!?
MAPLE HP
PECHI
PECHI
NO DAMAGE...
THOSE TENTACLES ARE FOCUSED ON YOU, SO THEY PROBABLY AGGRO ON WHOEVER ATTACKS IT.
I'M GONNA TRY TO SWIM OUT AND APPROACH THE MAIN BODY.
GO FOR IT!
BUT BE CAREFUL!
ZABUN (SPLOOSH)

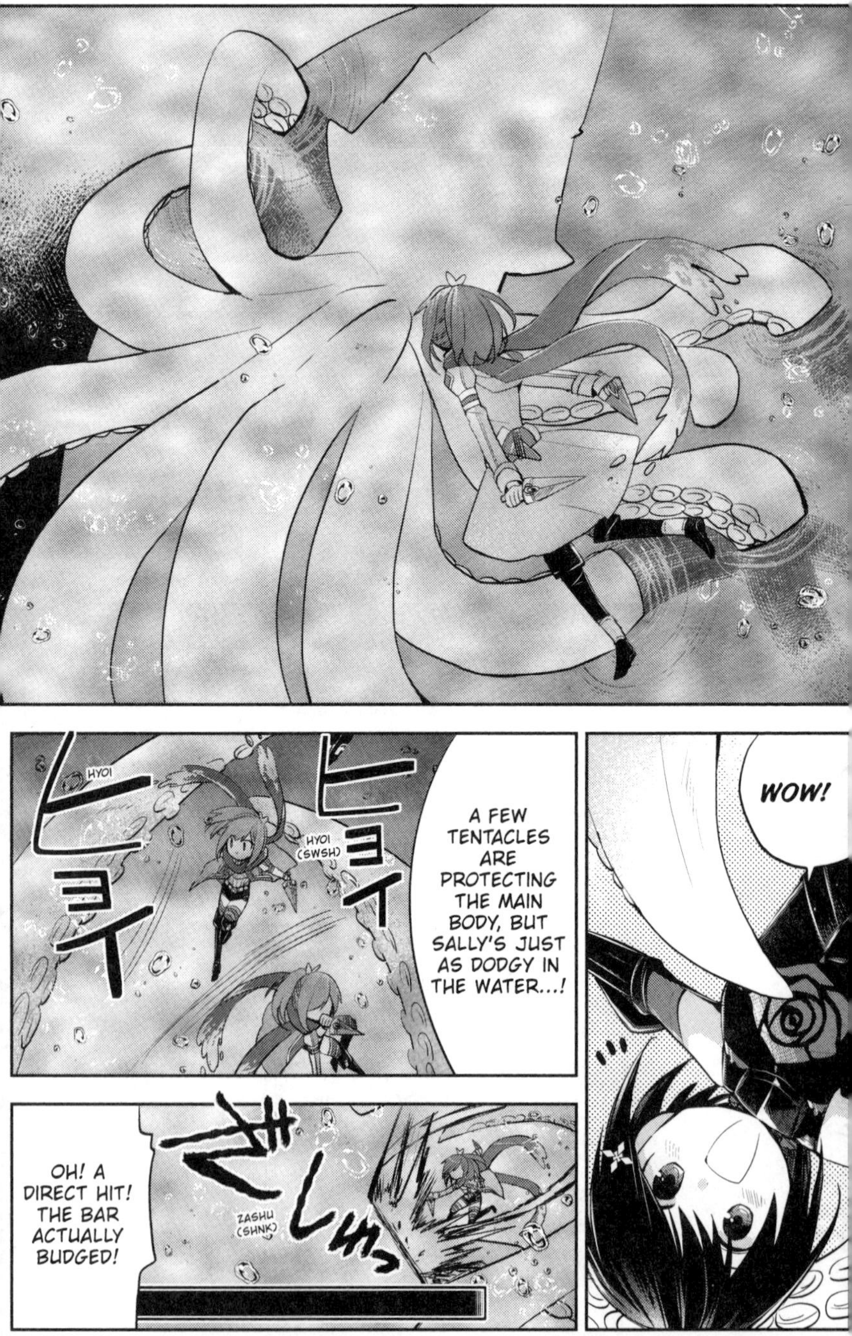

WOW!
...!
A FEW TENTACLES ARE PROTECTING THE MAIN BODY, BUT SALLY'S JUST AS DODGY IN THE WATER...!
ヒョイ
HYOI (SWSH)
HYOI
ヒョイ
ざしゅっ
ZASHU (SHNK)
OH! A DIRECT HIT! THE BAR ACTUALLY BUDGED!

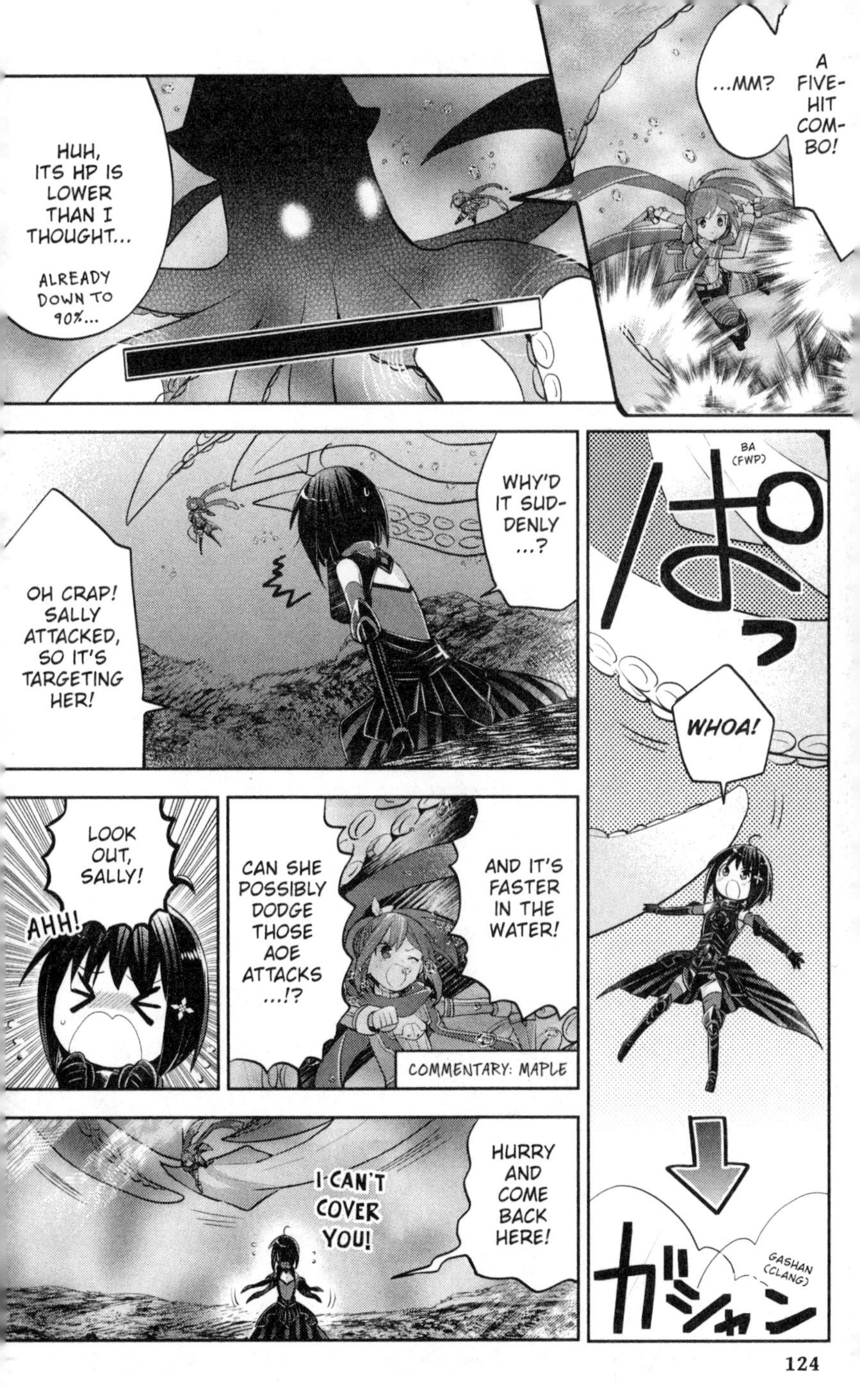

...MM?
A FIVE-HIT COMBO!
HUH, ITS HP IS LOWER THAN I THOUGHT...
ALREADY DOWN TO 90%...
BA (FWP)
WHOA!
GASHAN (CLANG)
WHY'D IT SUD-DENLY ...?
OH CRAP! SALLY ATTACKED, SO IT'S TARGETING HER!
AND IT'S FASTER IN THE WATER!
CAN SHE POSSIBLY DODGE THOSE AOE ATTACKS ...!?
COMMENTARY: MAPLE
LOOK OUT, SALLY!
AHH!
HURRY AND COME BACK HERE!
I CAN'T COVER YOU!

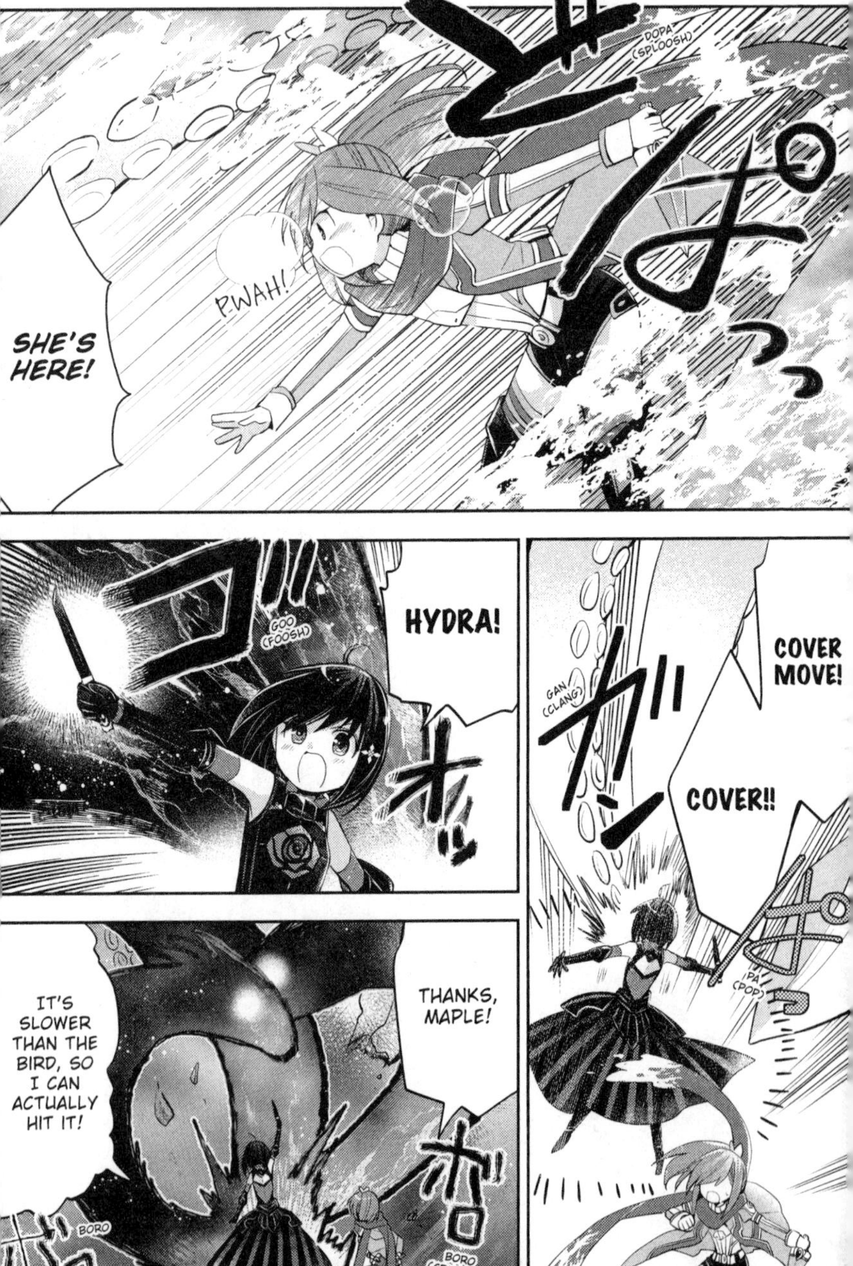
DOPA (SPLOOSH)
PWAH!
SHE'S HERE!
COVER MOVE!
GAN (CLANG)
COVER!!
PA (POP)
HYDRA!
GOO (FOOSH)
THANKS, MAPLE!
IT'S SLOWER THAN THE BIRD, SO I CAN ACTUALLY HIT IT!
BORO (CRUMBLE)
BORO

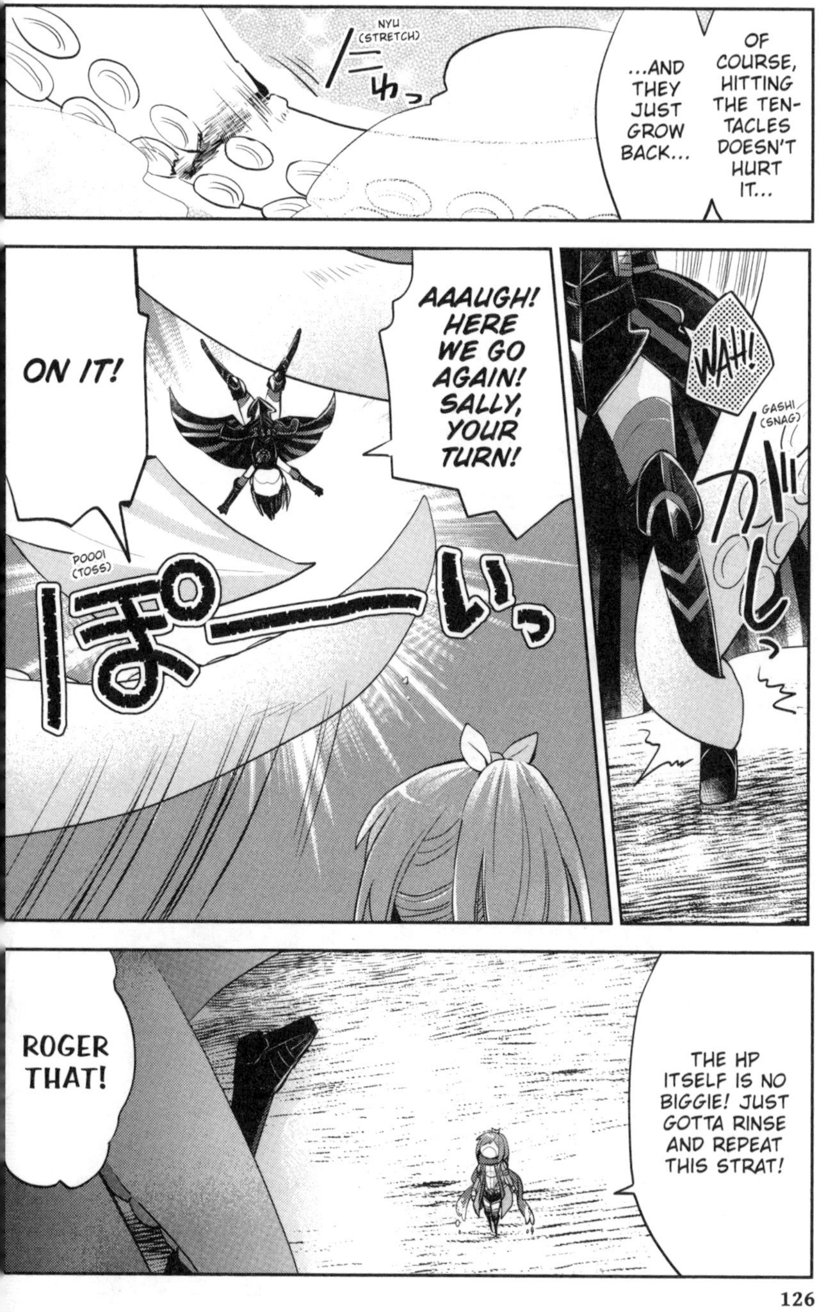
OF COURSE, HITTING THE TEN-TACLES DOESN'T HURT IT...
...AND THEY JUST GROW BACK...
NYU (STRETCH)
ニュっ
WAH!
GASHI (SNAG)
ガシっ
AAAUGH! HERE WE GO AGAIN! SALLY, YOUR TURN!
ON IT!
POOOI (TOSS)
ぽーーーいっ
THE HP ITSELF IS NO BIGGIE! JUST GOTTA RINSE AND REPEAT THIS STRAT!
ROGER THAT!

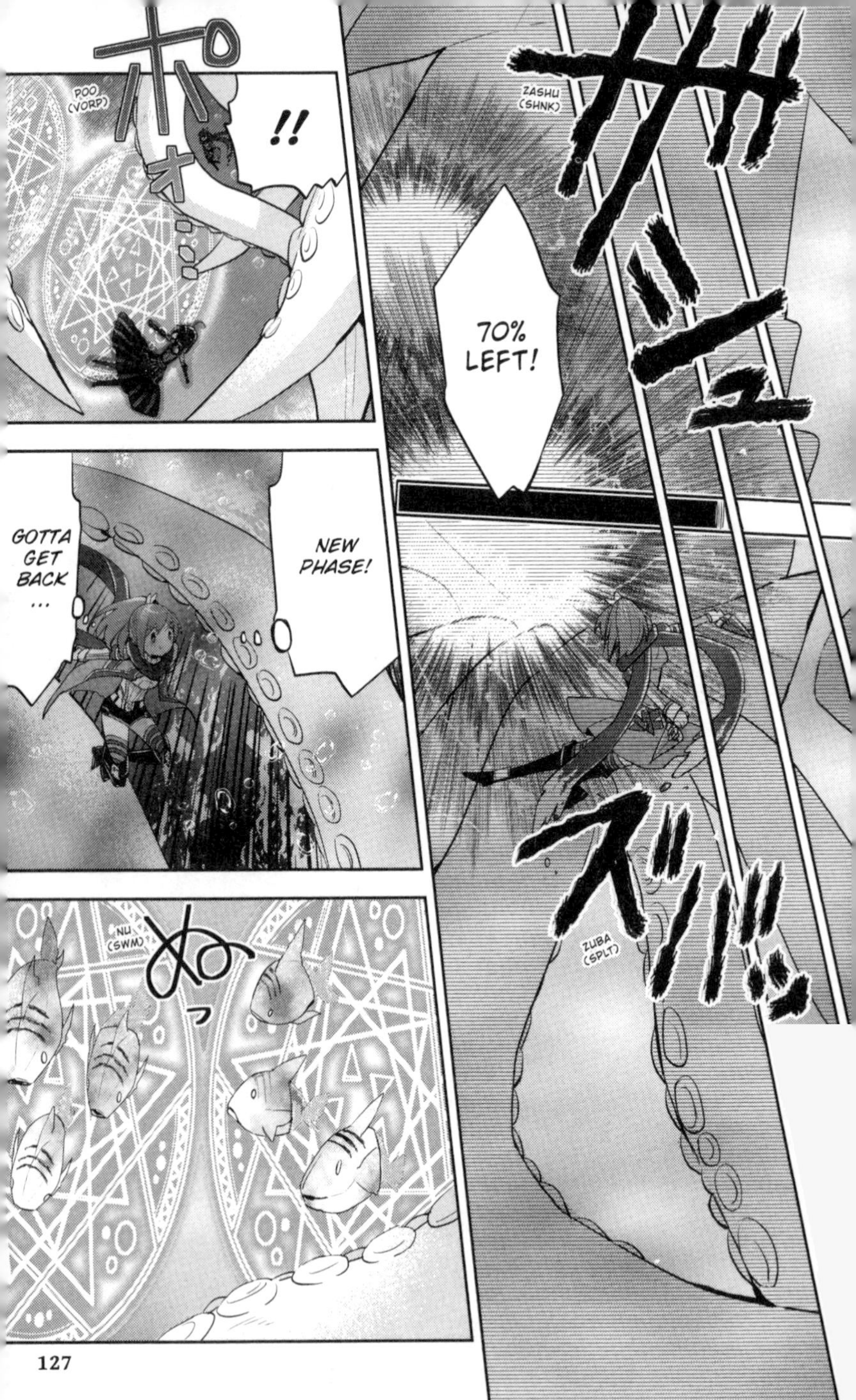
ZASHU (SHNK)
70% LEFT!
ZUBA (SPLT)
POO (VORP)
!!
NEW PHASE!
GOTTA GET BACK...
NU (SWM)

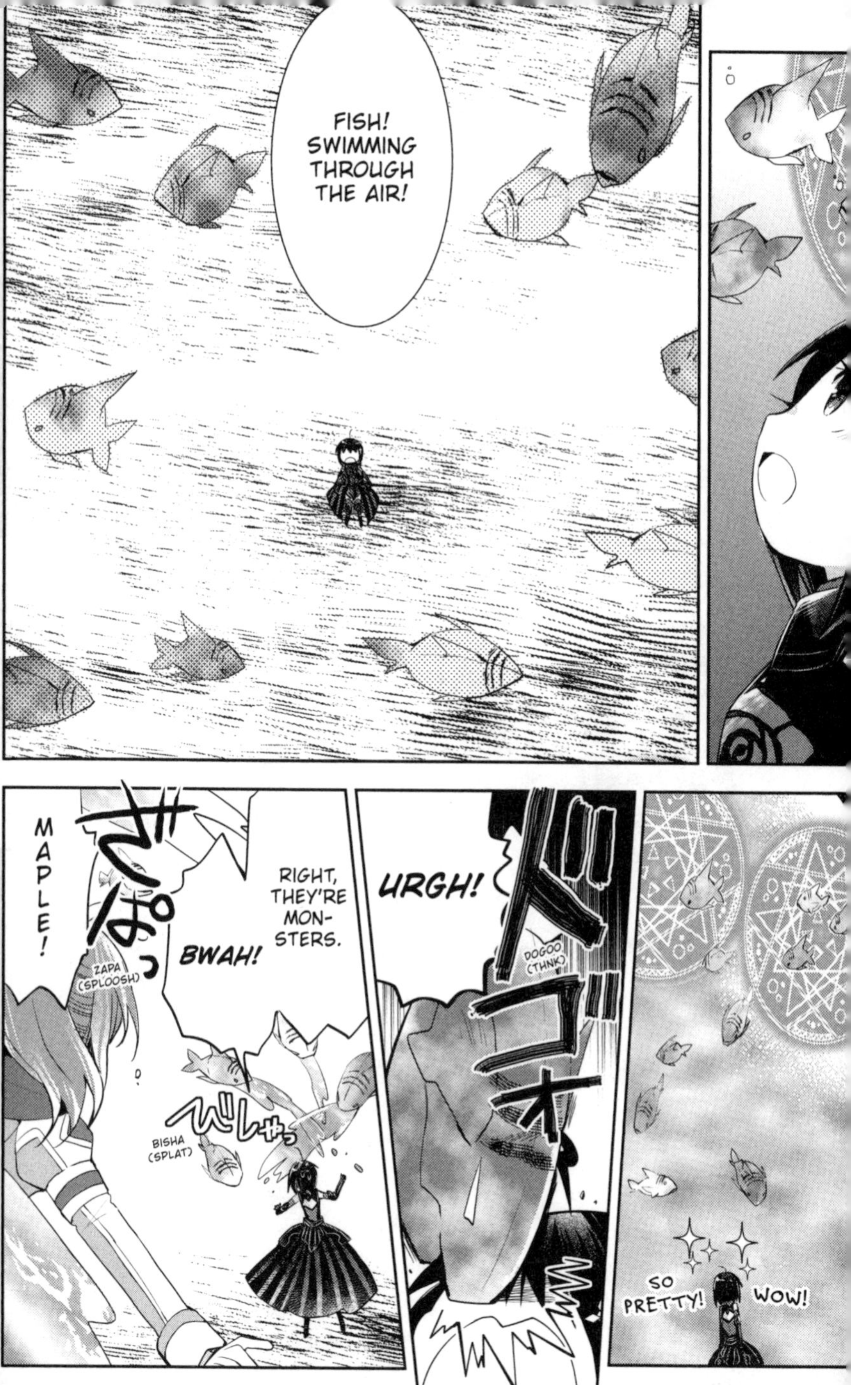
FISH! SWIMMING THROUGH THE AIR!
WOW!
SO PRETTY!
URGH!
DOGOO (THNK)
RIGHT, THEY'RE MON-STERS.
BWAH!
MAPLE!
ZAPA (SPLOOSH)
BISHA (SPLAT)

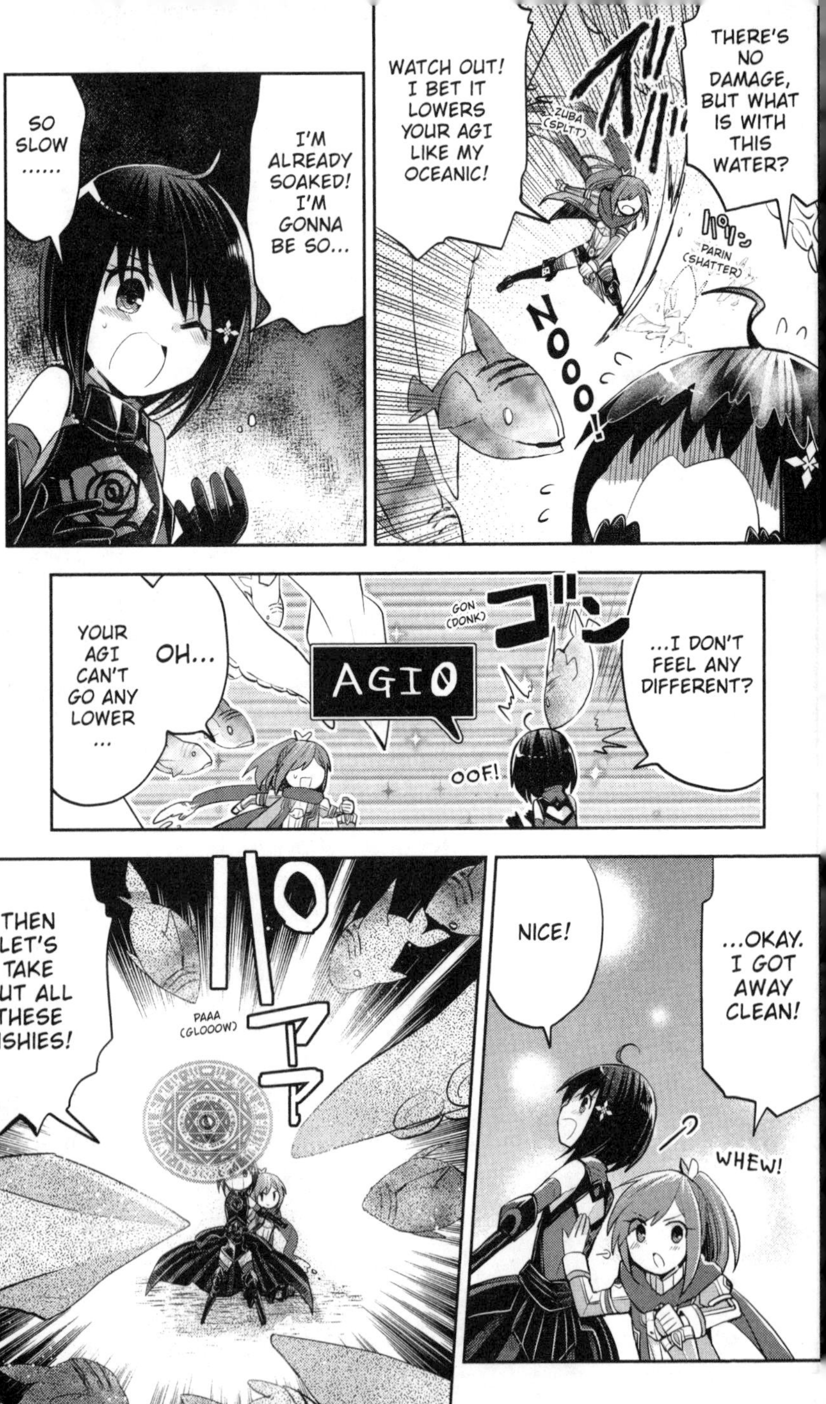
THERE'S NO DAMAGE, BUT WHAT IS WITH THIS WATER?
ZUBA (SPLTT)
WATCH OUT! I BET IT LOWERS YOUR AGI LIKE MY OCEANIC!
PARIN (SHATTER)
NOOOO!
I'M ALREADY SOAKED! I'M GONNA BE SO...
SO SLOW ......
GON (DONK)
...I DON'T FEEL ANY DIFFERENT?
OOF!
AGI 0
OH...
YOUR AGI CAN'T GO ANY LOWER ...
...OKAY. I GOT AWAY CLEAN!
WHEW!
NICE!
THEN LET'S TAKE OUT ALL THESE FISHIES!
PAAA (GLOOOW)

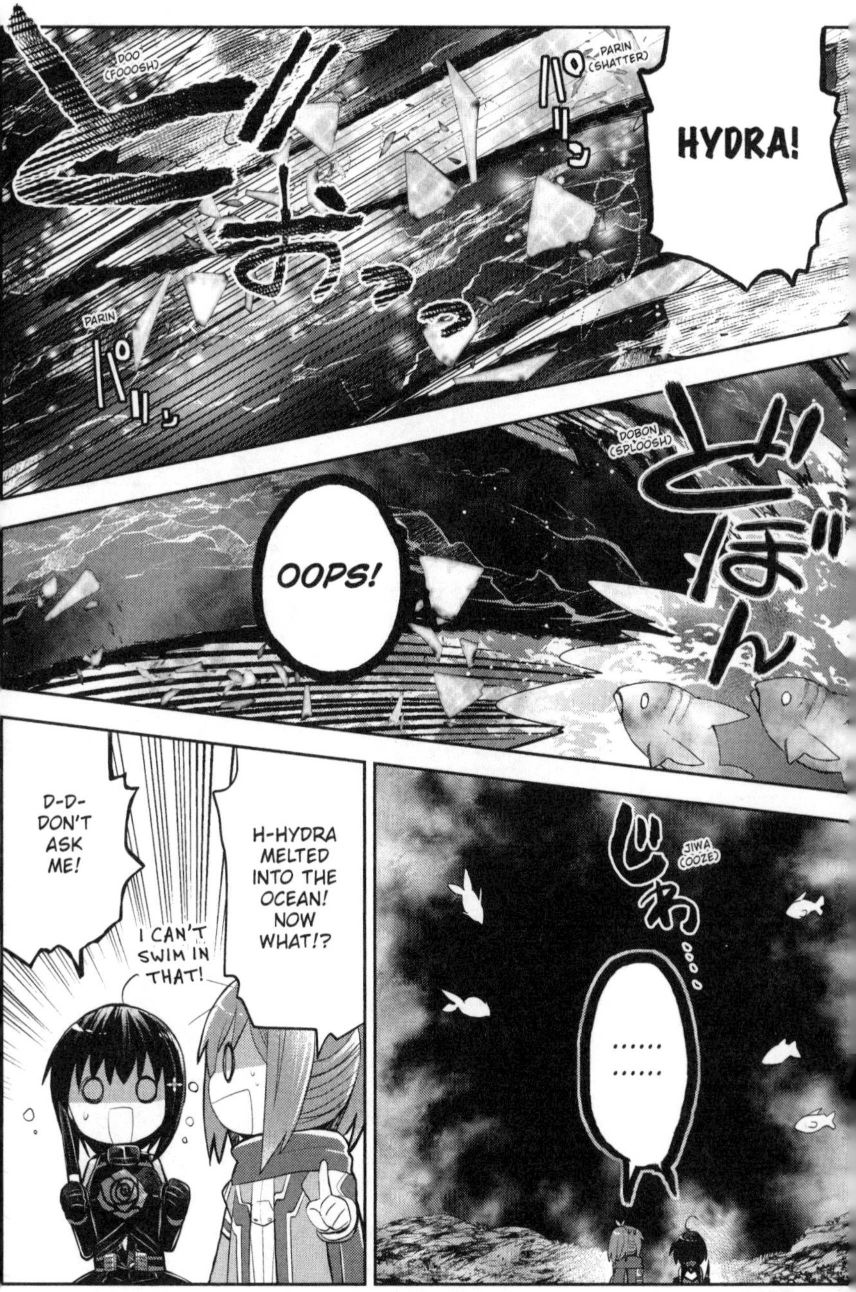
HYDRA!
PARIN (SHATTER)
DOO (FOOOSH)
PARIN
DOBON (SPLOOSH)
OOPS!
JIWA (OOZE)
......
......
H-HYDRA MELTED INTO THE OCEAN! NOW WHAT!?
D-D-DON'T ASK ME!
I CAN'T SWIM IN THAT!

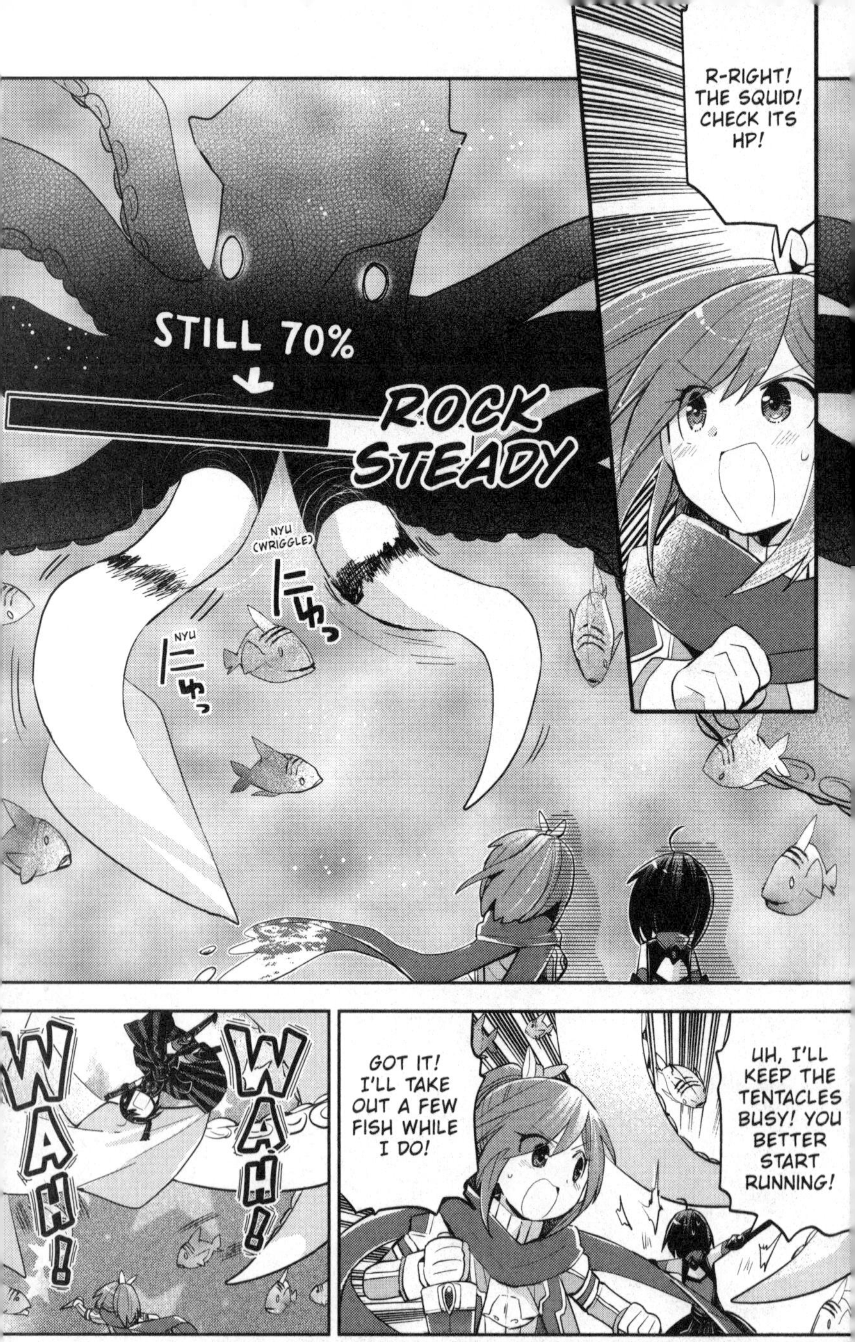
R-RIGHT! THE SQUID! CHECK ITS HP!
STILL 70%
ROCK STEADY
NYU (WRIGGLE)
にゅっ
NYU
にゅっ
UH, I'LL KEEP THE TENTACLES BUSY! YOU BETTER START RUNNING!
GOT IT! I'LL TAKE OUT A FEW FISH WHILE I DO!
WAH!
WAH!

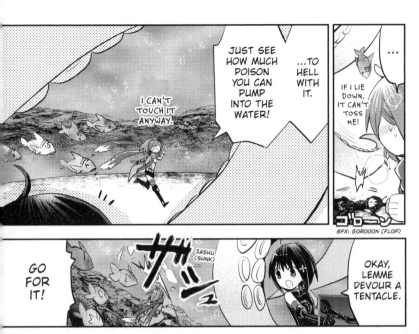

...
IF I LIE DOWN, IT CAN'T TOSS ME!
SFX: GOROOON (FLOP)
...TO HELL WITH IT.
JUST SEE HOW MUCH POISON YOU CAN PUMP INTO THE WATER!
I CAN'T TOUCH IT ANYWAY.
OKAY, LEMME DEVOUR A TENTACLE.
ZASHU (SHNK)
GO FOR IT!
TON (TNK)
ALL RIGHT ...
TAKE THIS!
SHUGOOO (SLUUURP)

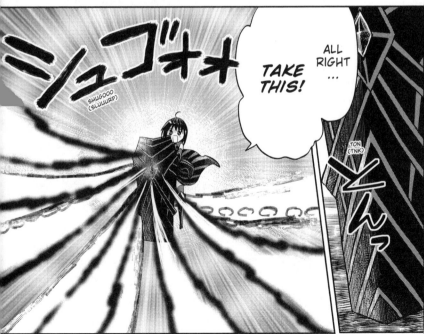

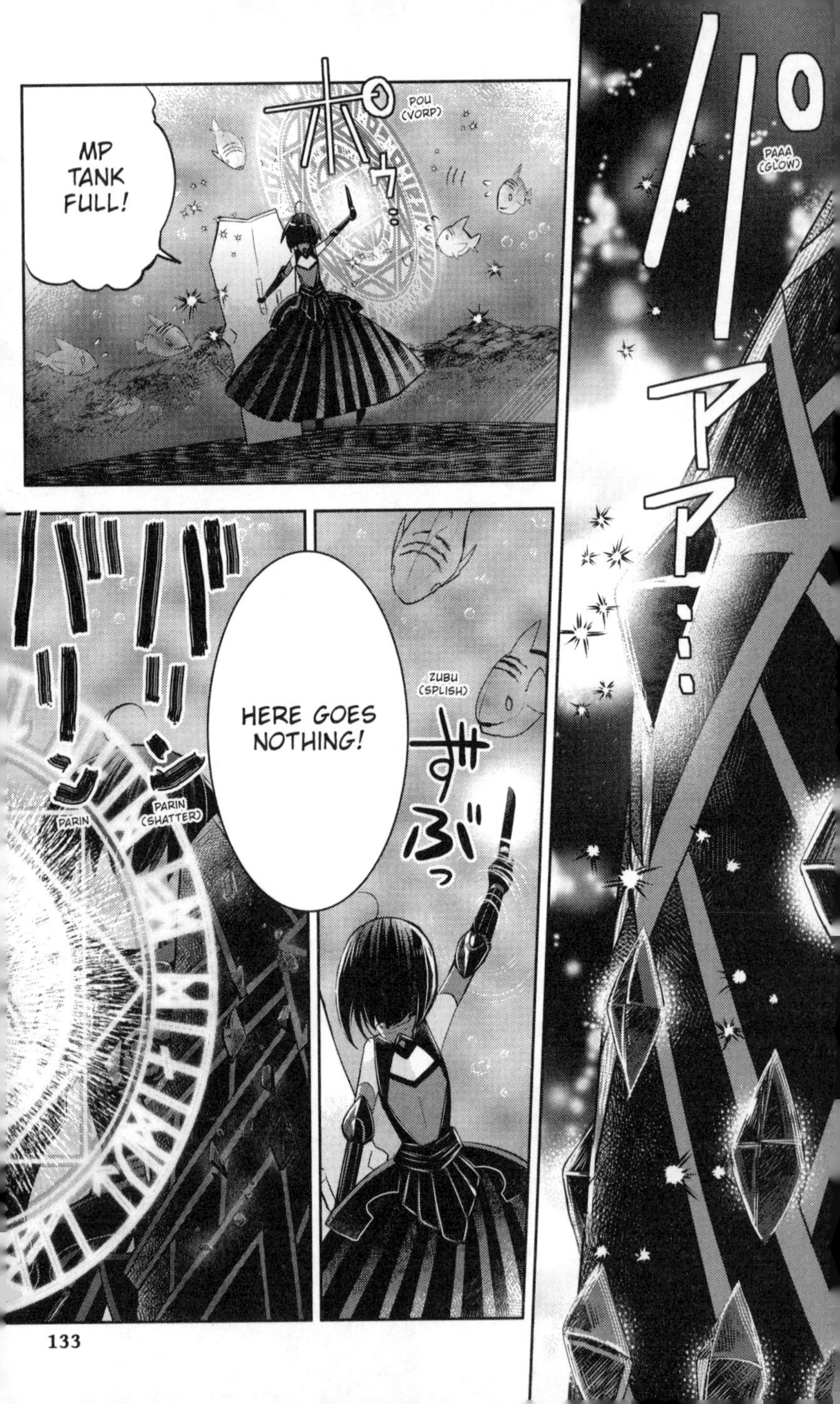
パァァ…
PAAA (GLOW)
ポゥ
POU (VORP)
MP TANK FULL!
HERE GOES NOTHING!
ずぶっ
ZUBU (SPLISH)
PARIN (SHATTER)
PARIN

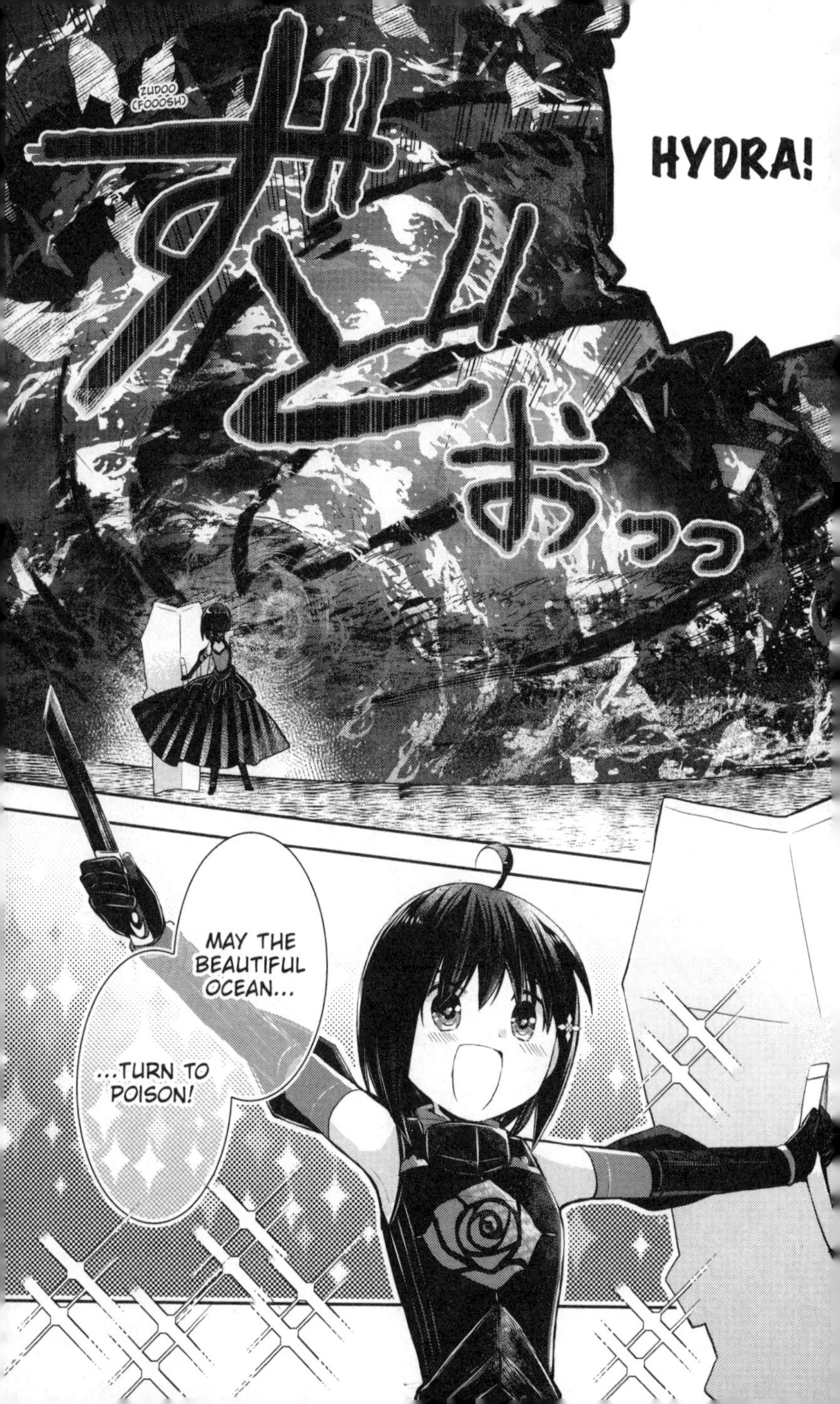
HYDRA!
ZUDOO (FOOOSH)
MAY THE BEAUTIFUL OCEAN...
...TURN TO POISON!

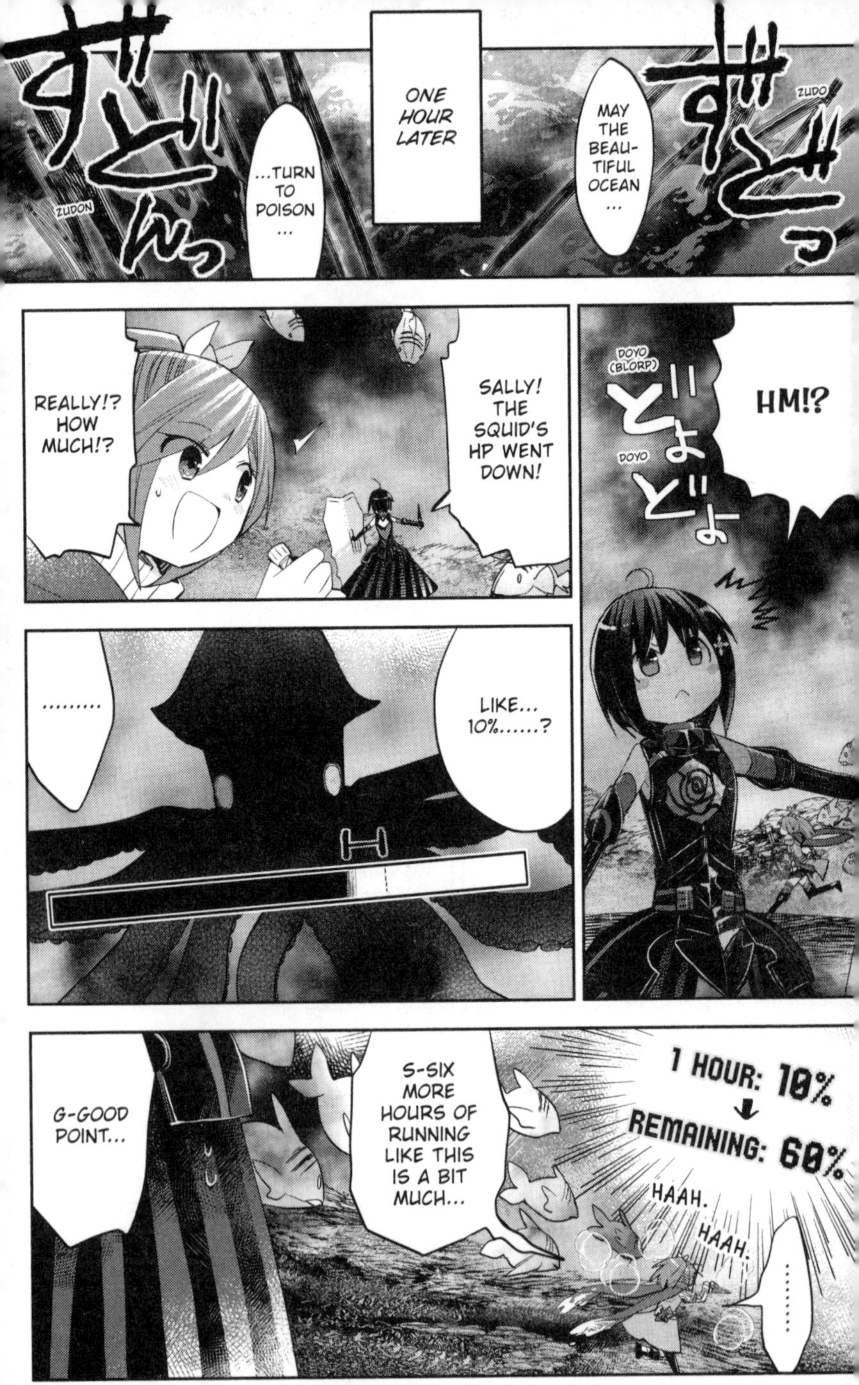
ZUDO
MAY THE BEAUTIFUL OCEAN...
ONE HOUR LATER
...TURN TO POISON...
ZUDON
HM!?
DOYO (BLORP)
DOYO
SALLY! THE SQUID'S HP WENT DOWN!
REALLY!? HOW MUCH!?
LIKE... 10%......?
....
1 HOUR: 10%
REMAINING: 60%
......
HAAH.
HAAH.
S-SIX MORE HOURS OF RUNNING LIKE THIS IS A BIT MUCH...
G-GOOD POINT...

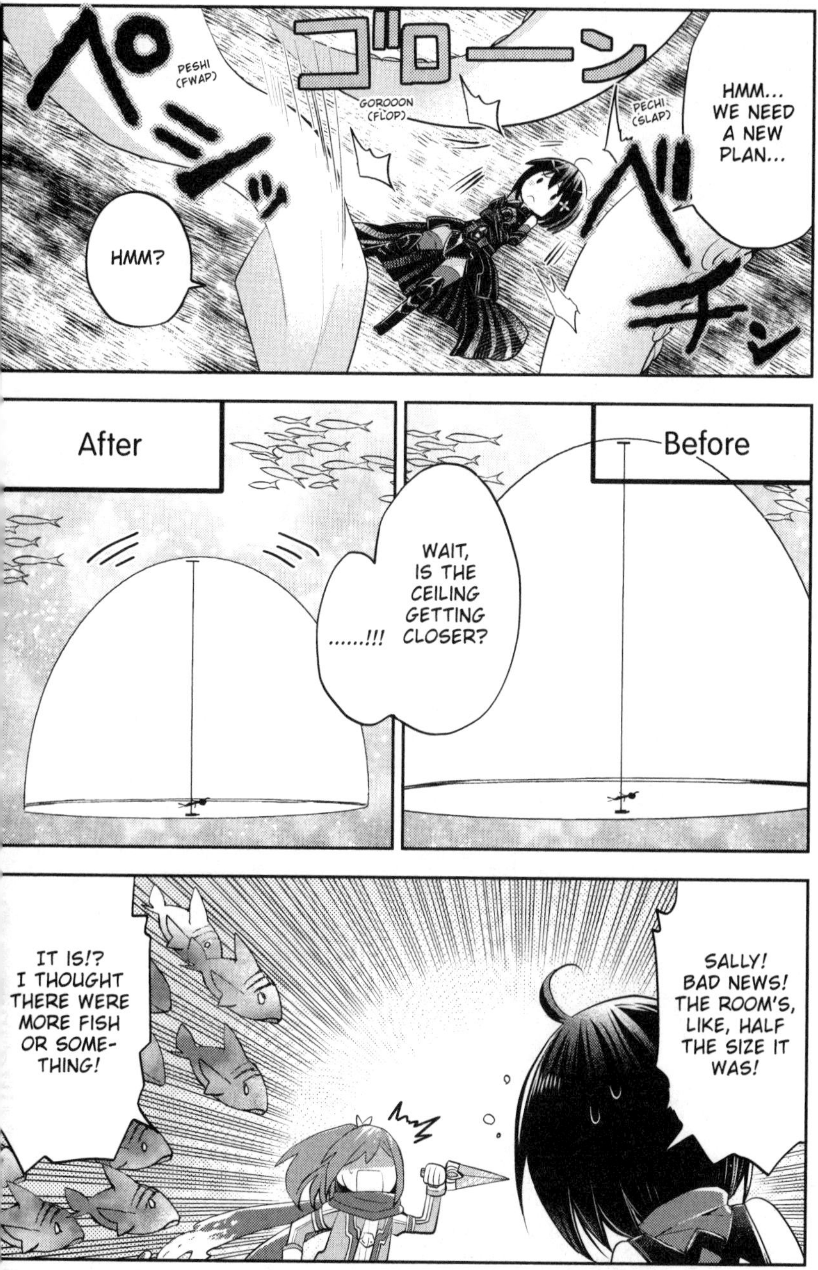
HMM... WE NEED A NEW PLAN...
ベチン
PECHI (SLAP)
ゴローーン
GOROOON (FLOP)
ペシッ
PESHI (FWAP)
HMM?
Before
WAIT, IS THE CEILING GETTING CLOSER?
......!!!
After
SALLY! BAD NEWS! THE ROOM'S, LIKE, HALF THE SIZE IT WAS!
IT IS!? I THOUGHT THERE WERE MORE FISH OR SOME-THING!

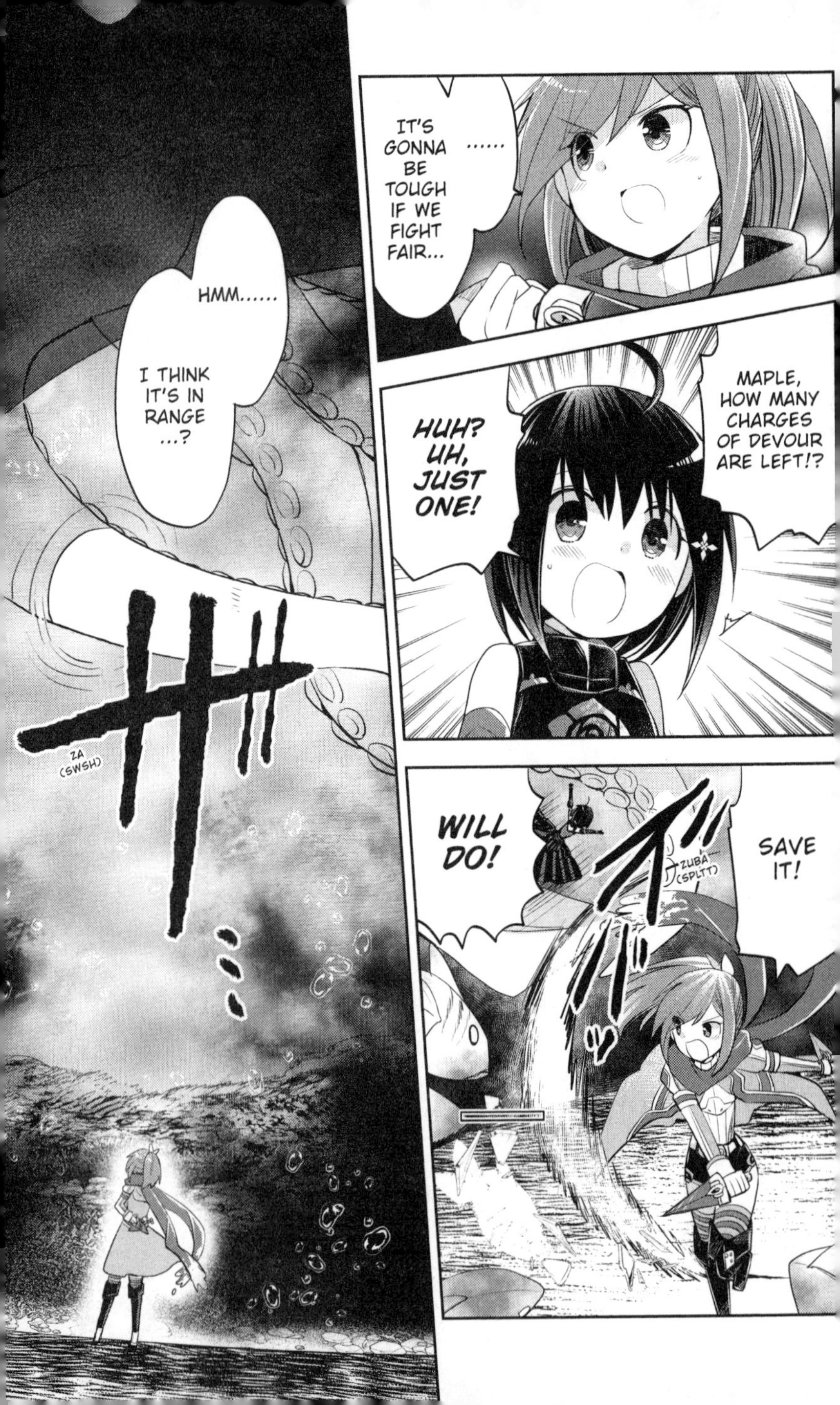

......
IT'S GONNA BE TOUGH IF WE FIGHT FAIR...
MAPLE, HOW MANY CHARGES OF DEVOUR ARE LEFT!?
HUH? UH, JUST ONE!
SAVE IT!
ZUBA (SPLTT)
WILL DO!
HMM......
I THINK IT'S IN RANGE ...?
ZA (SWSH)

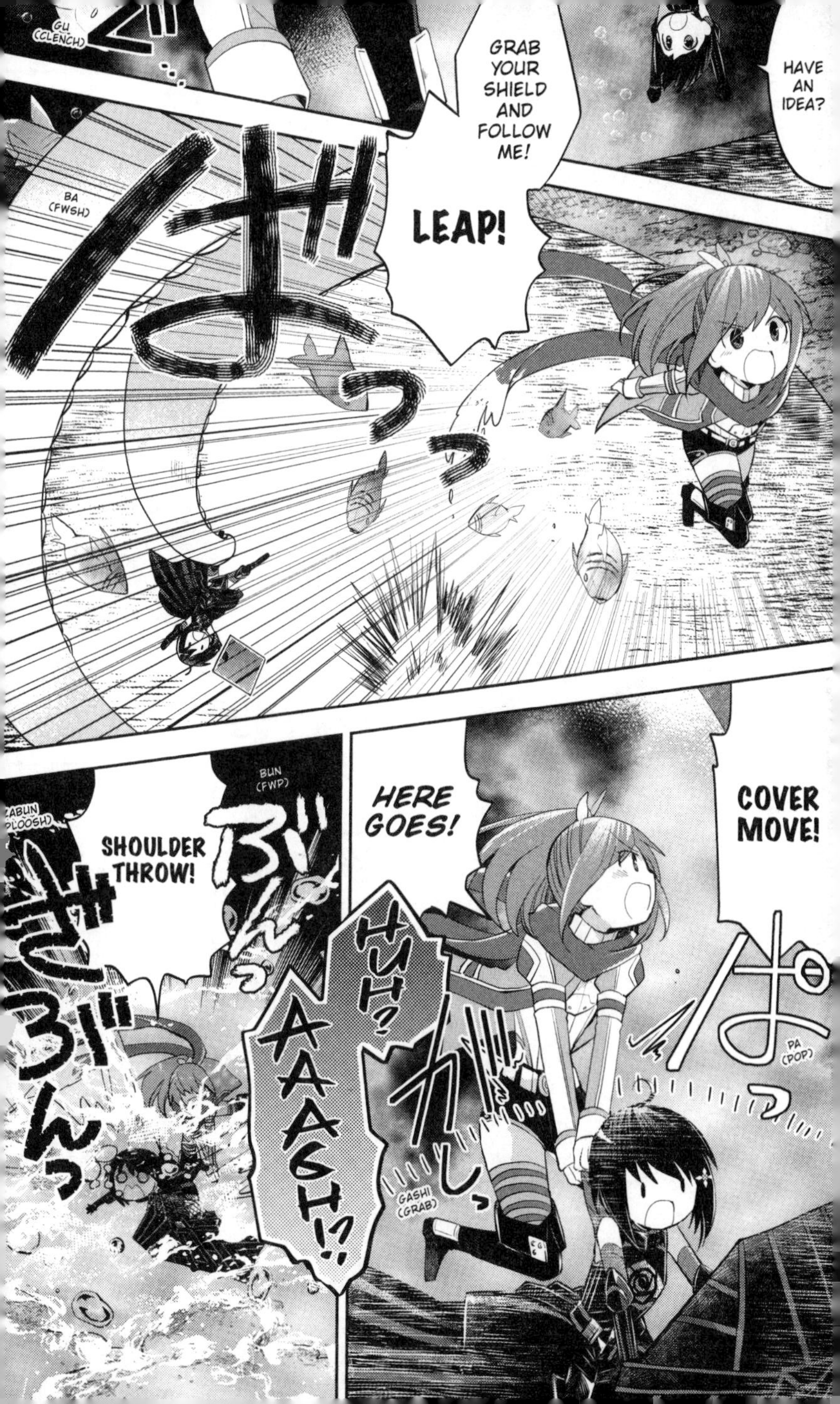

HAVE AN IDEA?
GRAB YOUR SHIELD AND FOLLOW ME!
GU (CLENCH)
LEAP!
BA (FWSH)
COVER MOVE!
HERE GOES!
PA (POP)
GASHI (GRAB)
HUH?! AAAGH!?!
BUN (FWP)
SHOULDER THROW!
ZABUN (SPLOOSH)

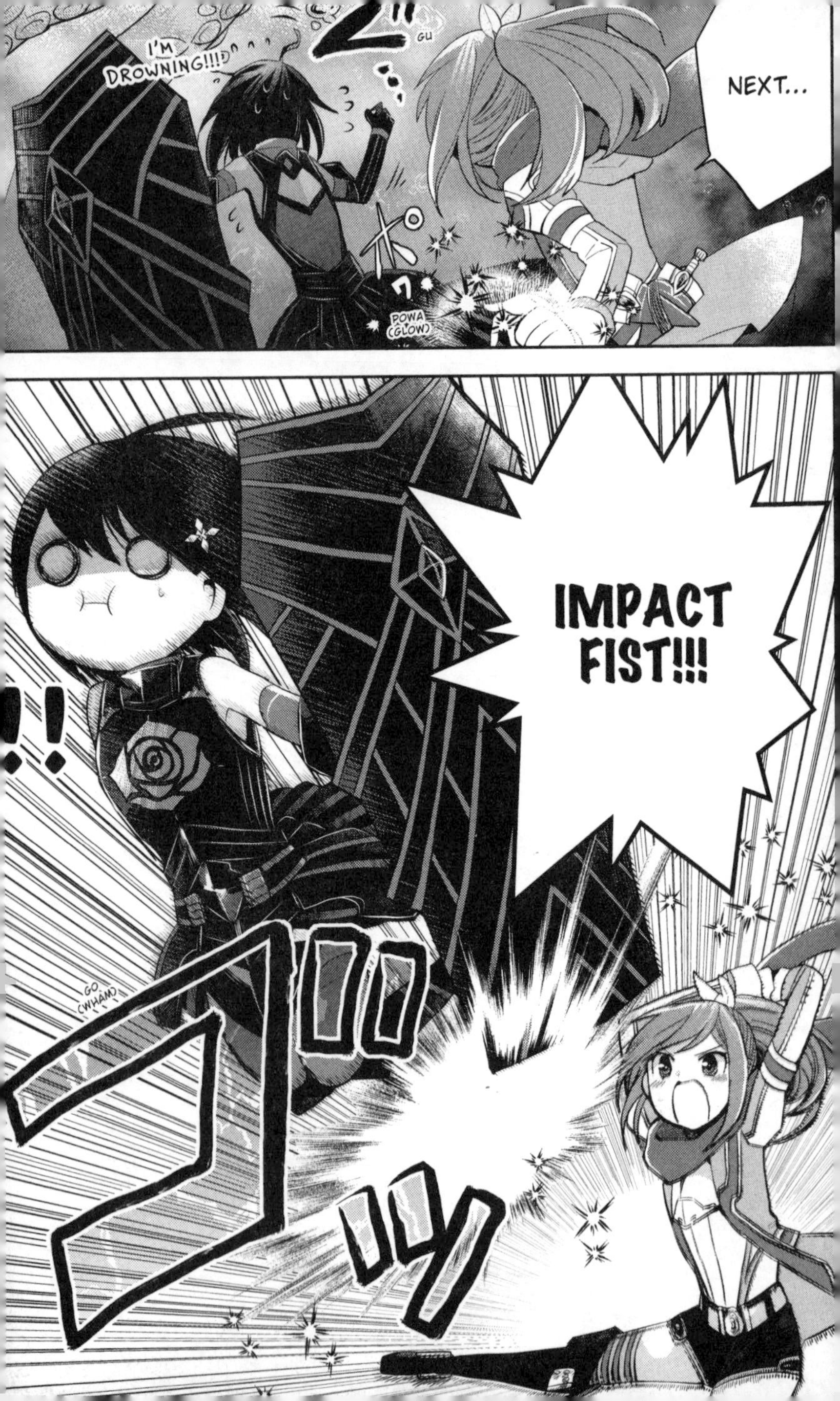
NEXT...
GU
I'M DROWNING!!!
POWA (GLOW)
IMPACT FIST!!!
GO (WHAM)

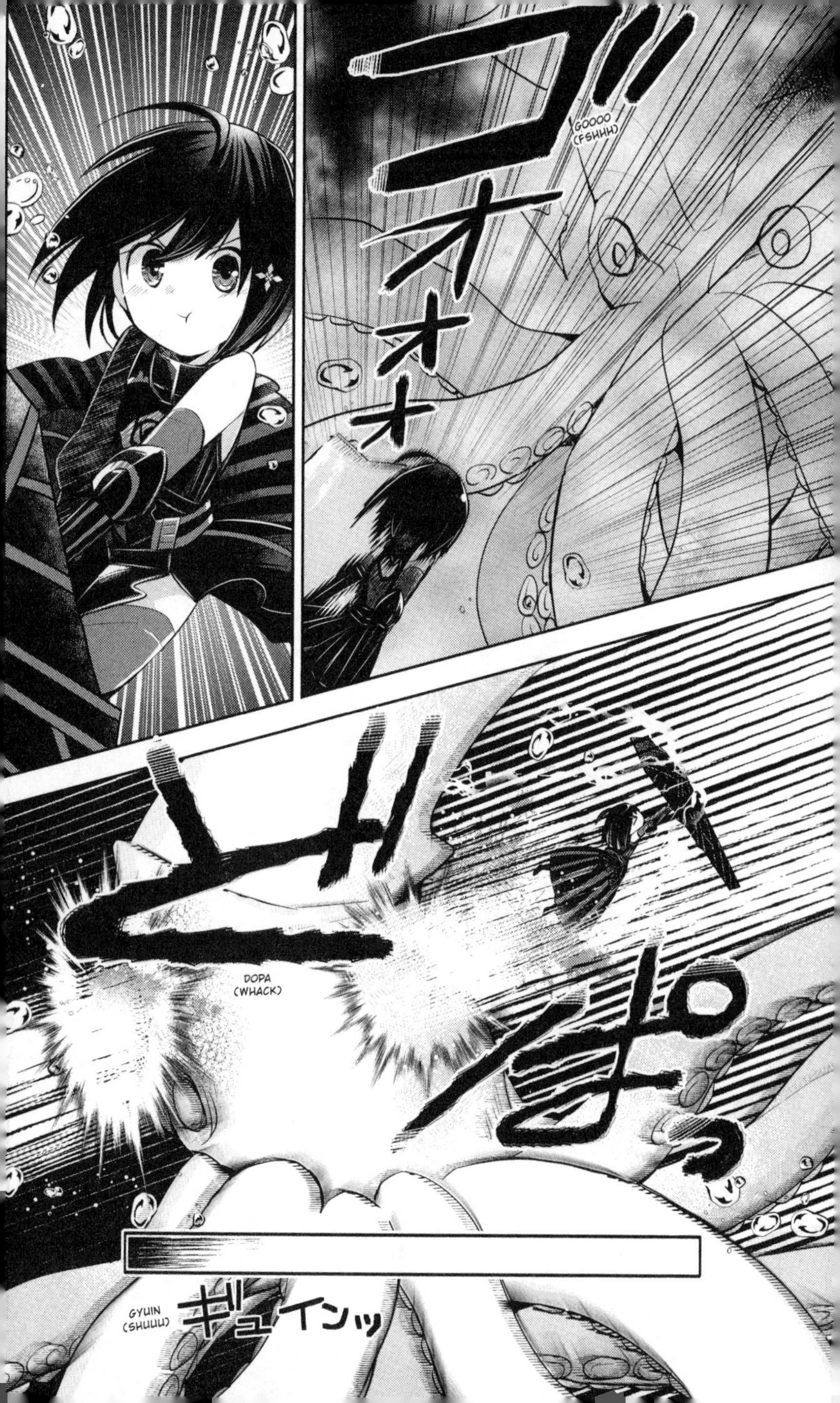

ゴオオォ
GOOOO (FSHHH)
ドパッ
DOPA (WHACK)
ギュインッ
GYUIN (SHUUU)

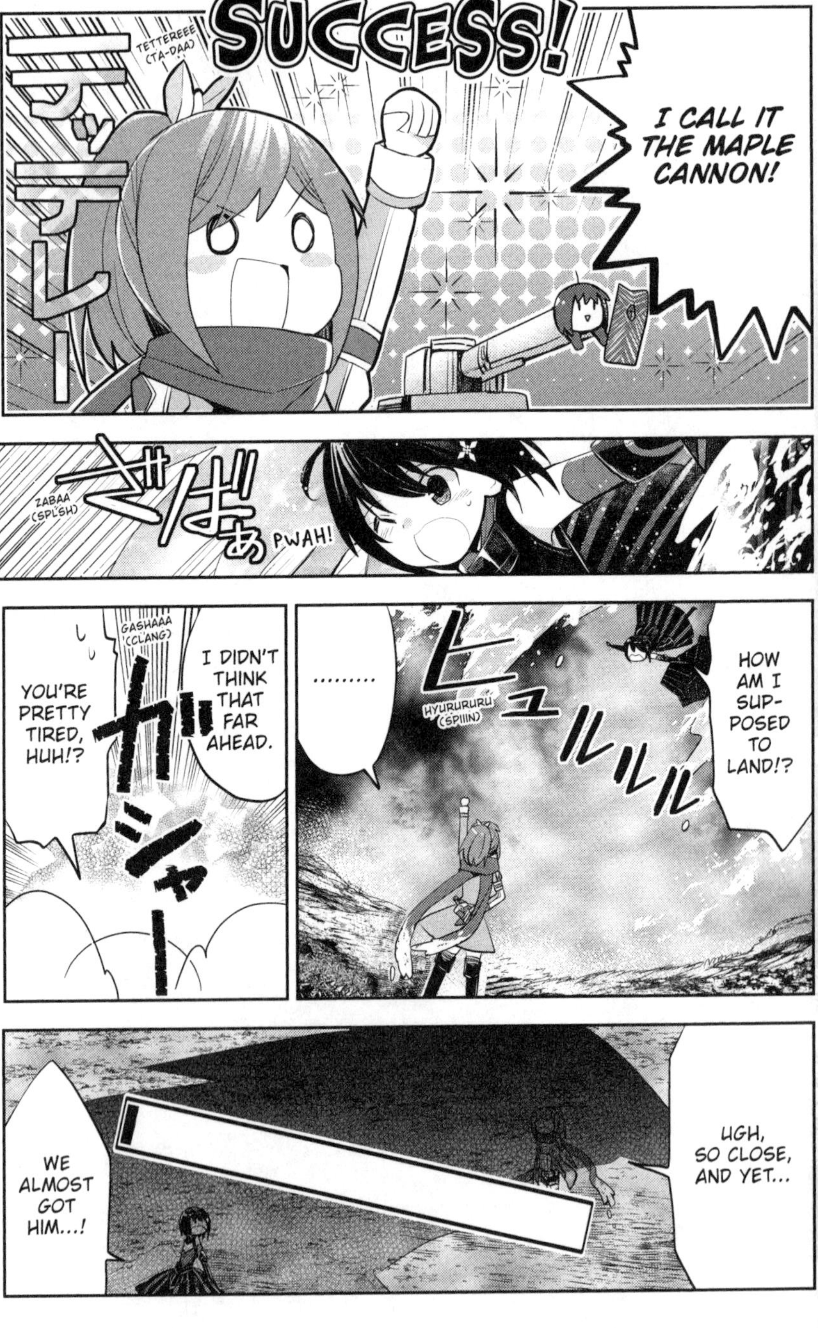
I CALL IT THE MAPLE CANNON!
SUCCESS!
TETTEREEE (TA-DAA)
テッテレー
ざばぁ
ZABAA (SPLSH)
PWAH!
HOW AM I SUP-POSED TO LAND!?
ヒュルルル
HYURURURU (SPIIIN)
....
I DIDN'T THINK THAT FAR AHEAD.
GASHAAA (CLANG)
ガシャー
YOU'RE PRETTY TIRED, HUH!?
UGH, SO CLOSE, AND YET...
WE ALMOST GOT HIM...!

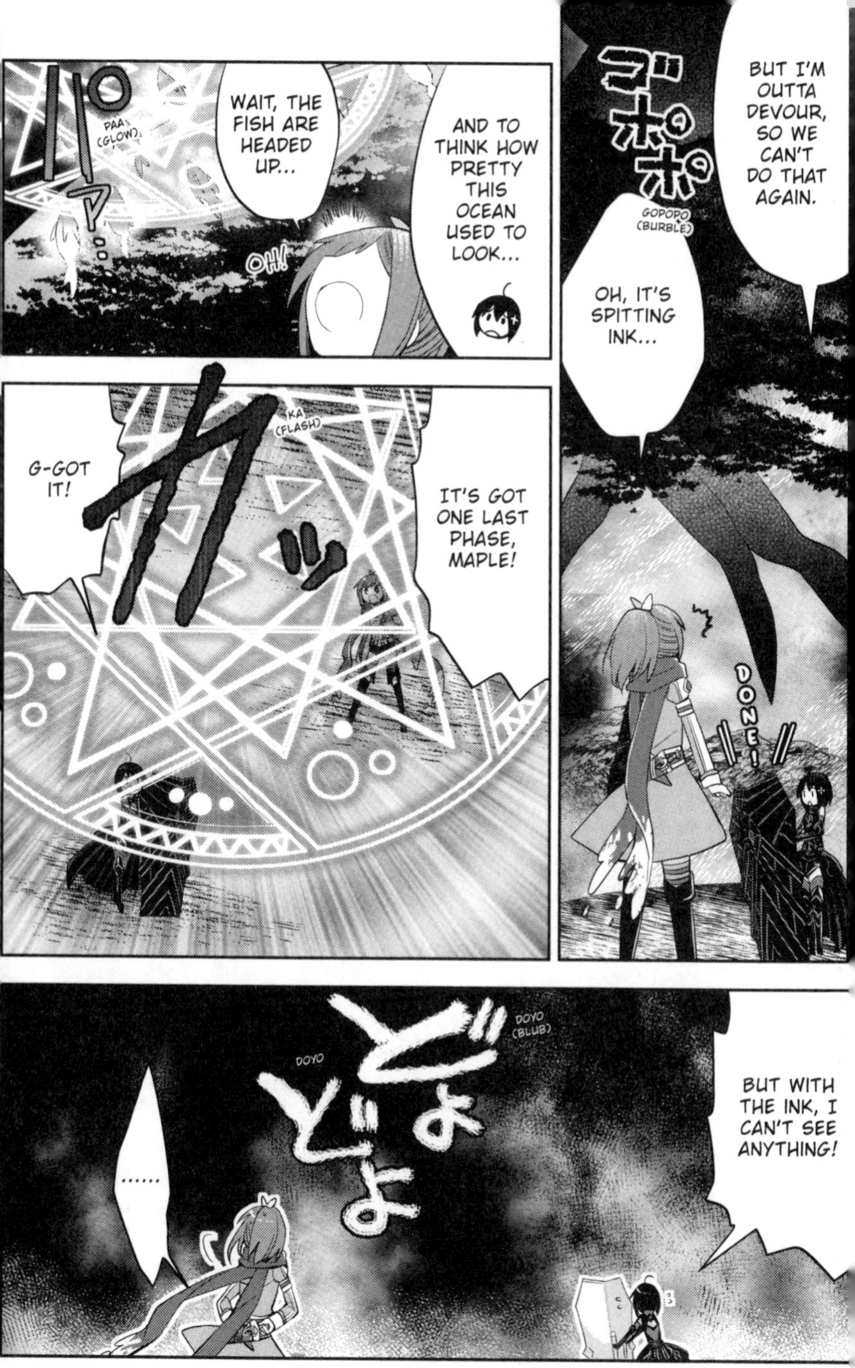
BUT I'M OUTTA DEVOUR, SO WE CAN'T DO THAT AGAIN.
ゴポポ
GOPOPO (BURBLE)
OH, IT'S SPITTING INK...
DONE!
AND TO THINK HOW PRETTY THIS OCEAN USED TO LOOK...
WAIT, THE FISH ARE HEADED UP...
OH!
パァ
PAA (GLOW)
カッ
KA (FLASH)
IT'S GOT ONE LAST PHASE, MAPLE!
G-GOT IT!
BUT WITH THE INK, I CAN'T SEE ANYTHING!
どよどよ
DOYO (BLUB)
DOYO
......

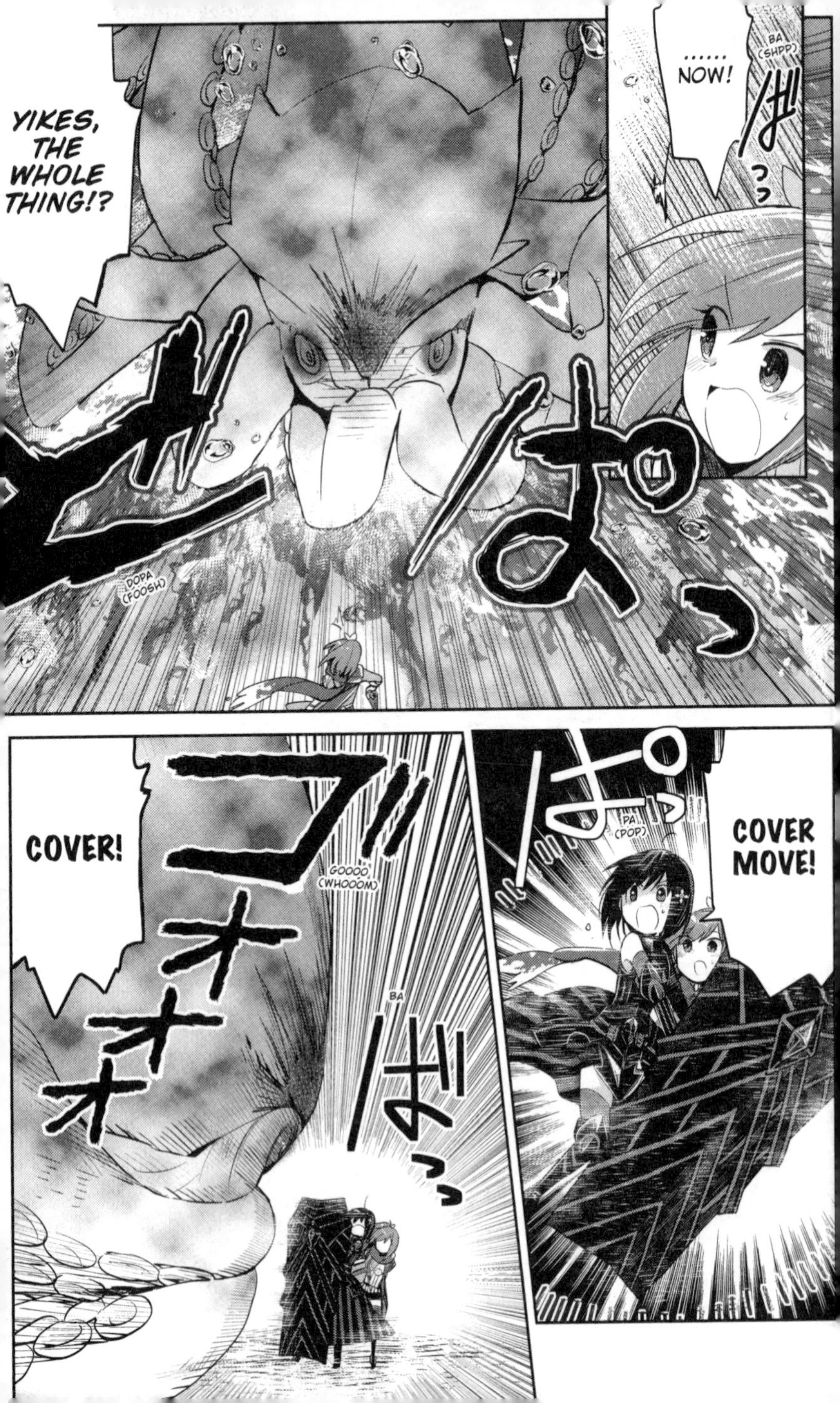

......NOW!
BA (SHPP)
YIKES, THE WHOLE THING!?
DOPA (FOOSH)
COVER MOVE!
PA (POP)
COVER!
GOOOO (WHOOOM)
BA

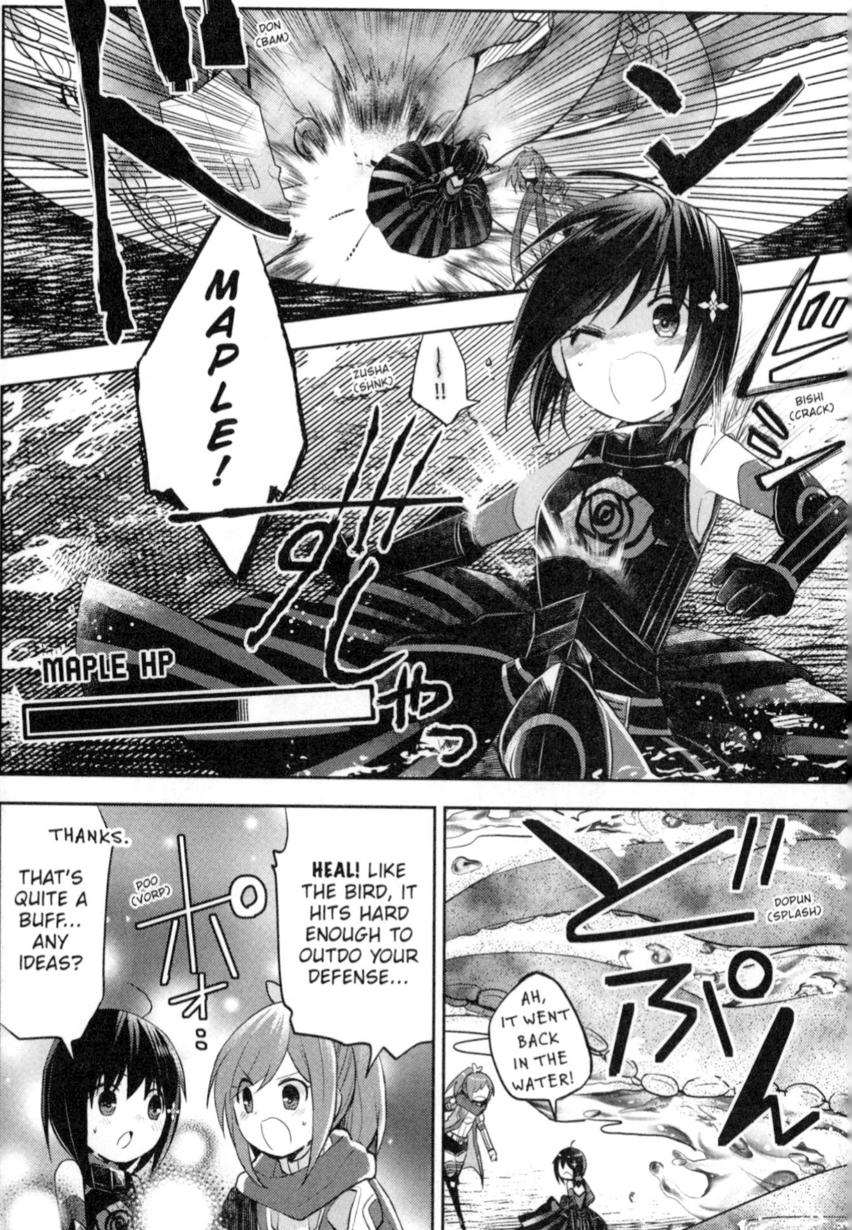
DON (BAM)
BISHI (CRACK)
—!!
ZUSHA (SHNK)
MAPLE!
MAPLE HP
DOPUN (SPLASH)
AH, IT WENT BACK IN THE WATER!
HEAL! LIKE THE BIRD, IT HITS HARD ENOUGH TO OUTDO YOUR DEFENSE...
POO (VORP)
THANKS.
THAT'S QUITE A BUFF... ANY IDEAS?

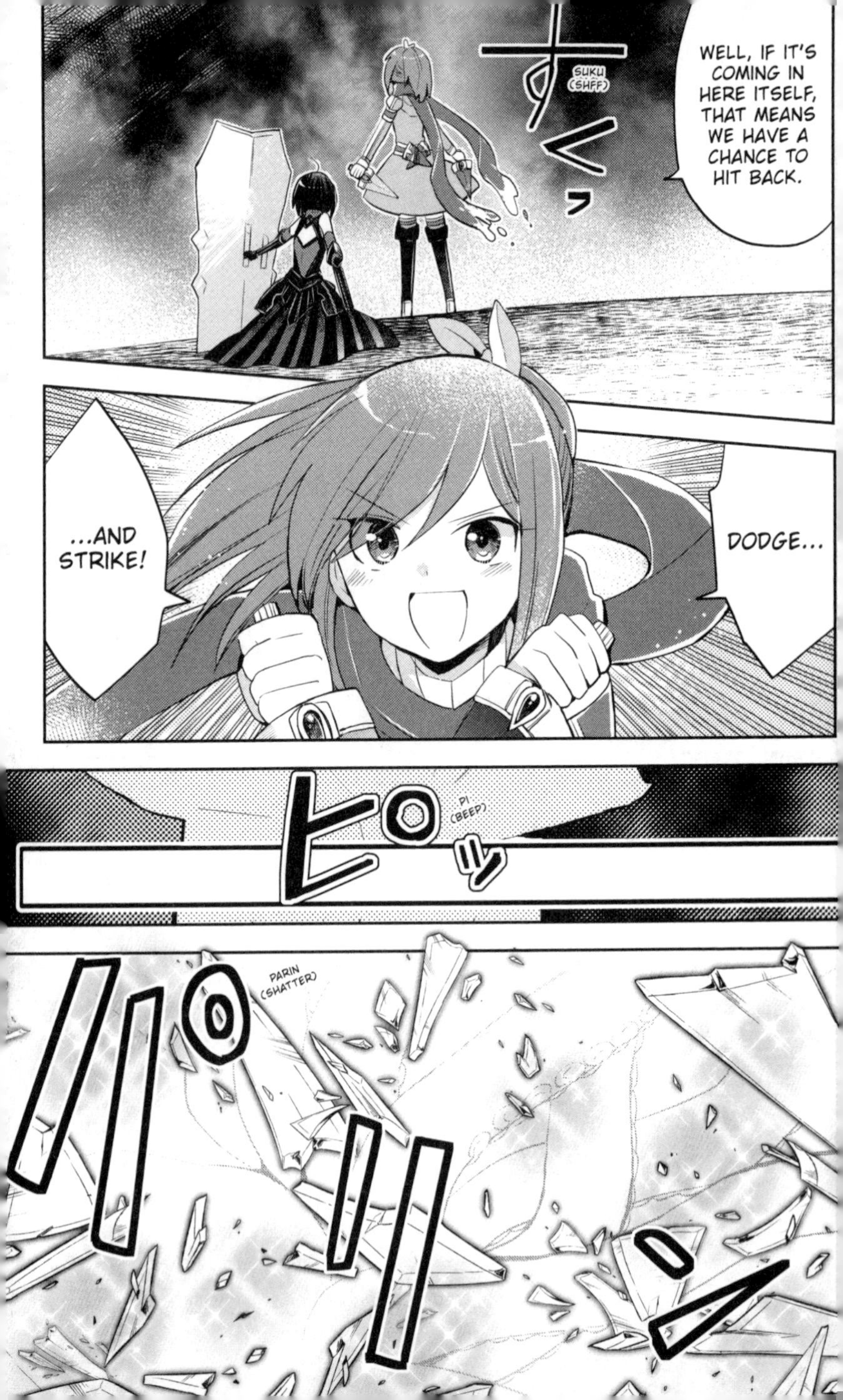
WELL, IF IT'S COMING IN HERE ITSELF, THAT MEANS WE HAVE A CHANCE TO HIT BACK.
SUKU (SHFF)
DODGE...
...AND STRIKE!
PI (BEEP)
PARIN (SHATTER)

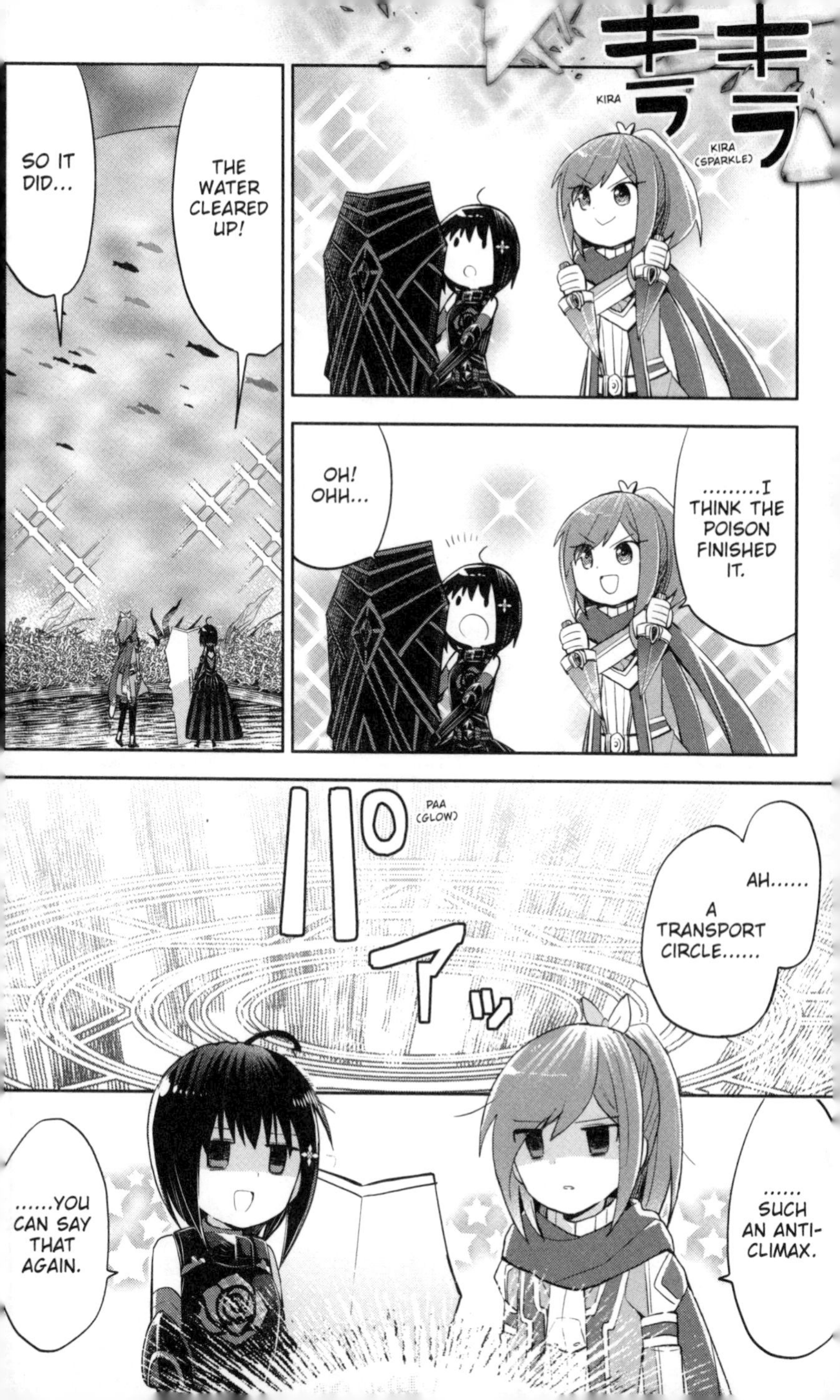
キラ
KIRA
キラ
KIRA (SPARKLE)
.........I THINK THE POISON FINISHED IT.
OH! OHH...
THE WATER CLEARED UP!
SO IT DID...
パアッ
PAA (GLOW)
AH...... A TRANSPORT CIRCLE......
...... SUCH AN ANTI-CLIMAX.
......YOU CAN SAY THAT AGAIN.

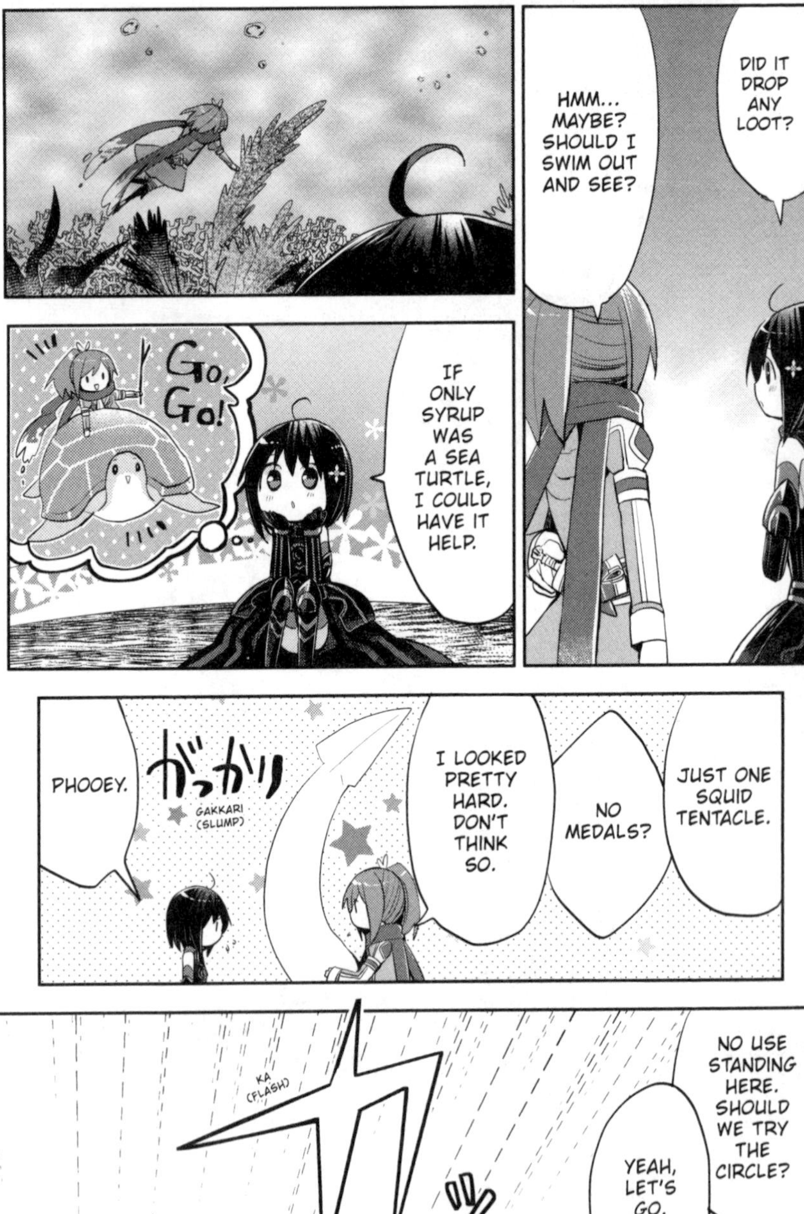
DID IT DROP ANY LOOT?
HMM... MAYBE? SHOULD I SWIM OUT AND SEE?
IF ONLY SYRUP WAS A SEA TURTLE, I COULD HAVE IT HELP.
GO, GO!
JUST ONE SQUID TENTACLE.
NO MEDALS?
I LOOKED PRETTY HARD. DON'T THINK SO.
がっかり
GAKKARI (SLUMP)
PHOOEY.
NO USE STANDING HERE. SHOULD WE TRY THE CIRCLE?
YEAH, LET'S GO.
カッ
KA (FLASH)

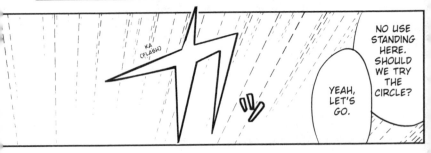

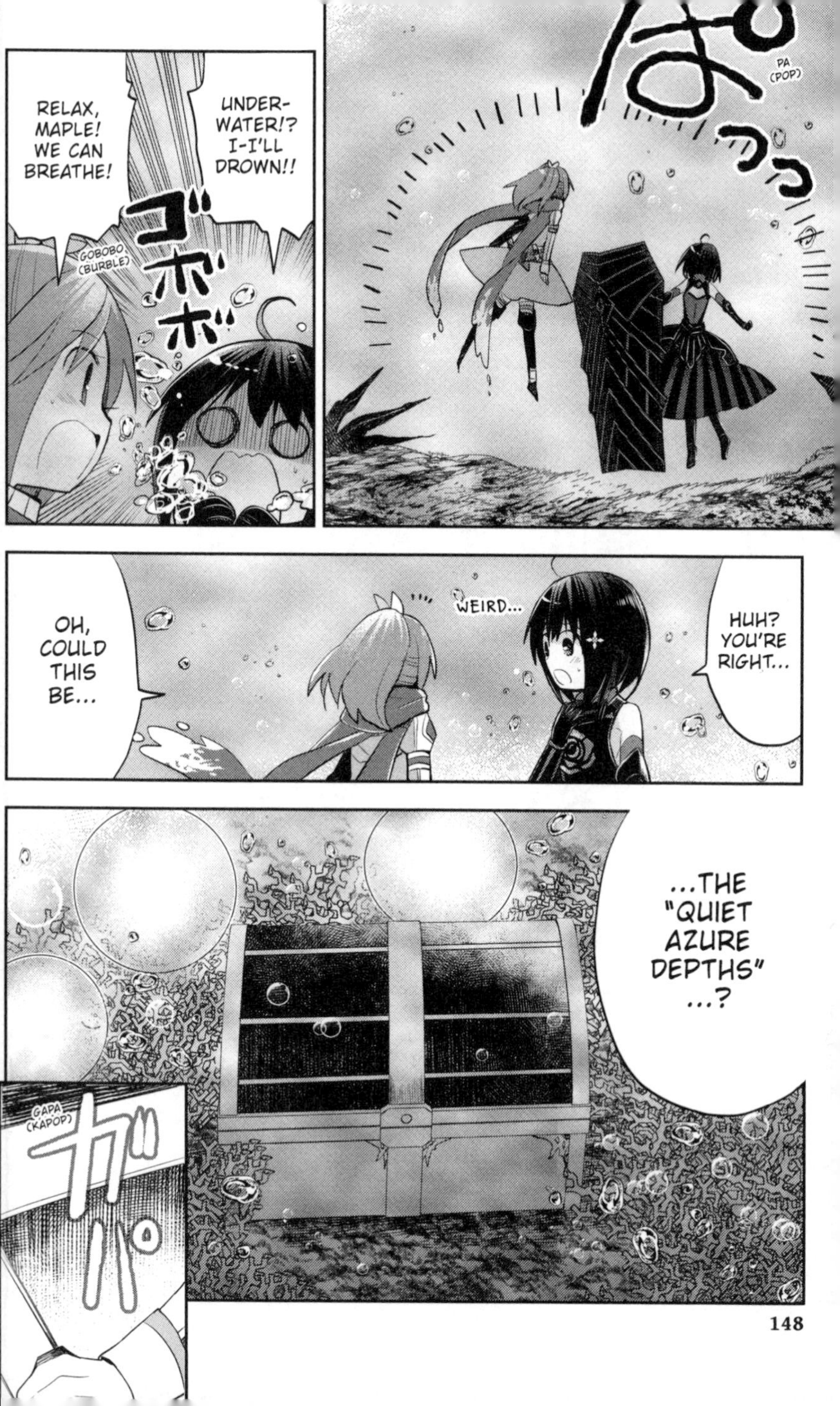
PA (POP)
UNDER-WATER!? I-I'LL DROWN!!
RELAX, MAPLE! WE CAN BREATHE!
GOBOBO (BURBLE)
HUH? YOU'RE RIGHT...
WEIRD...
OH, COULD THIS BE...
..."THE "QUIET AZURE DEPTHS"...?
GAPA (KAPOP)

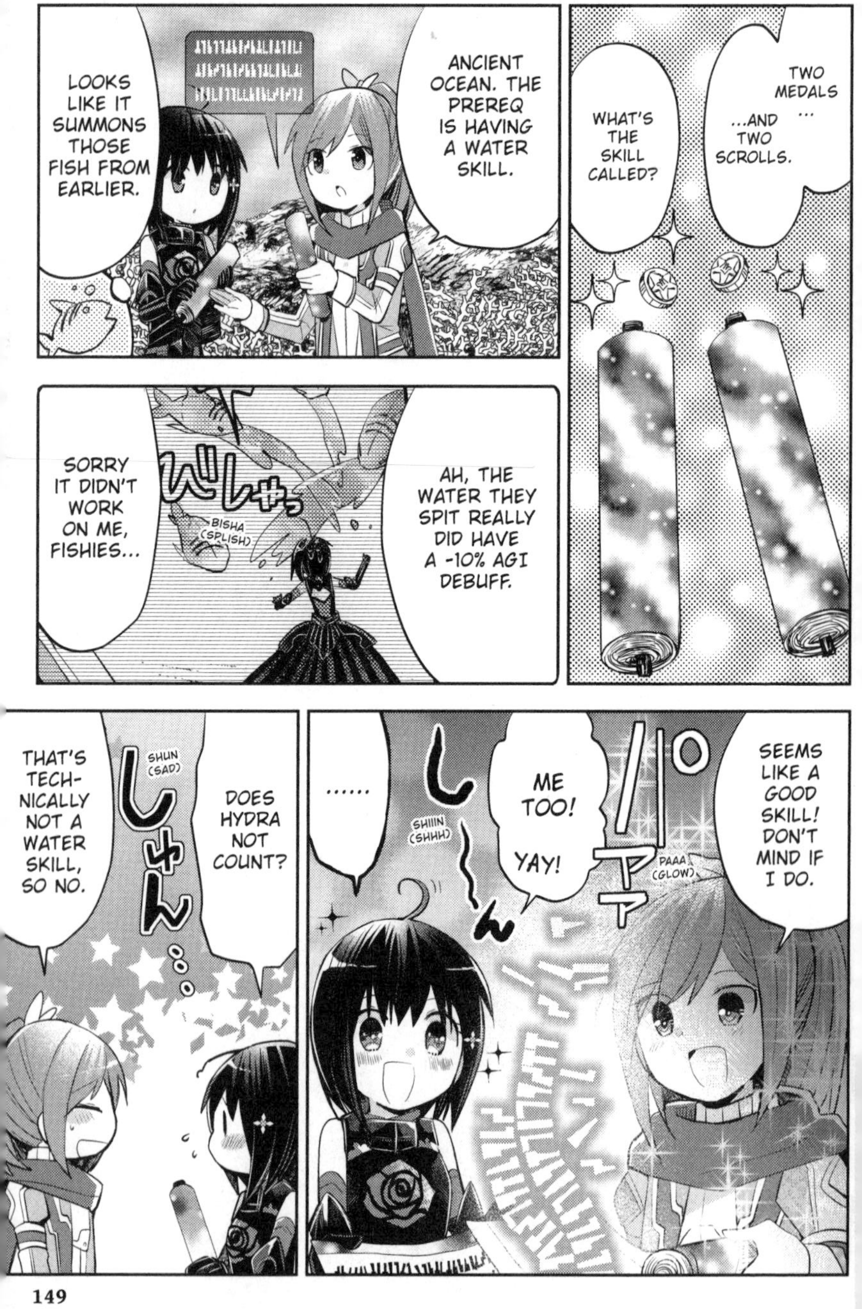
TWO MEDALS ...
...AND TWO SCROLLS.
WHAT'S THE SKILL CALLED?
ANCIENT OCEAN. THE PREREQ IS HAVING A WATER SKILL.
LOOKS LIKE IT SUMMONS THOSE FISH FROM EARLIER.
AH, THE WATER THEY SPIT REALLY DID HAVE A -10% AGI DEBUFF.
BISHA (SPLISH)
SORRY IT DIDN'T WORK ON ME, FISHIES...
SEEMS LIKE A GOOD SKILL! DON'T MIND IF I DO.
PAAA (GLOW)
ME TOO!
YAY!
SHIIIN (SHHH)
......
DOES HYDRA NOT COUNT?
SHUN (SAD)
THAT'S TECH-NICALLY NOT A WATER SKILL, SO NO.

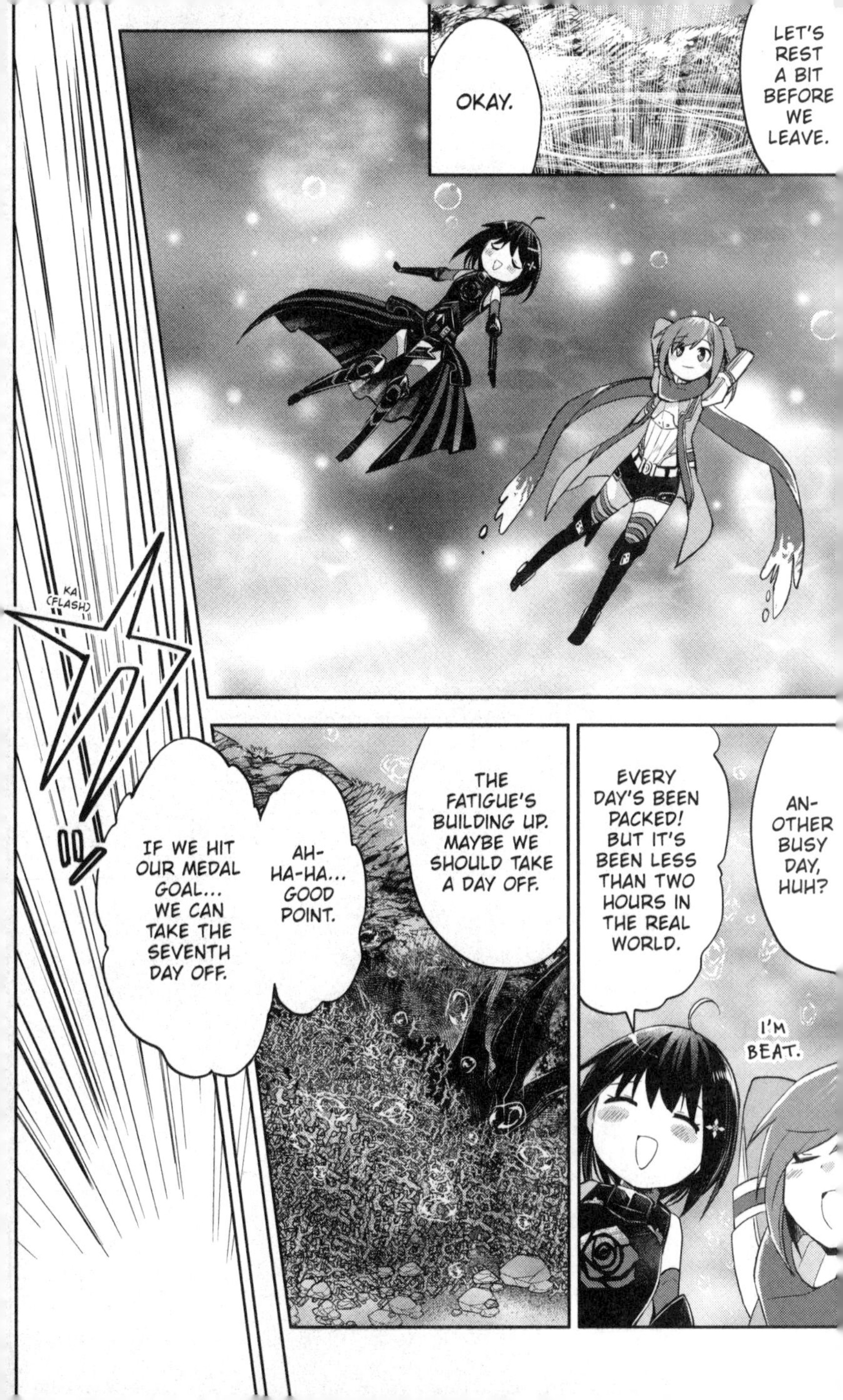
LET'S REST A BIT BEFORE WE LEAVE.
OKAY.
AN-OTHER BUSY DAY, HUH?
I'M BEAT.
EVERY DAY'S BEEN PACKED! BUT IT'S BEEN LESS THAN TWO HOURS IN THE REAL WORLD.
THE FATIGUE'S BUILDING UP. MAYBE WE SHOULD TAKE A DAY OFF.
AH-HA-HA... GOOD POINT.
IF WE HIT OUR MEDAL GOAL... WE CAN TAKE THE SEVENTH DAY OFF.
KA (FLASH)

...WE'RE BACK WHERE WE STARTED?

......

AND THE HOLE IN THE OCEAN'S GONE.

MAPLE, YOU'RE OUT OF DEVOUR, RIGHT?

GASP!

PROBABLY. DIDN'T SEEM LIKE ENOUGH MEDALS, BUT...

...SO WE'RE DONE HERE?

HOLD ON.

YEAH... THEN WE'D BETTER GET MOVING.

ANY DUNGEONS STILL OPEN WILL BE EITHER HARD OR WELL HIDDEN.

YEAH, WE STILL NEED TWO MORE TO HIT TWENTY.

MEDALS OBTAINED

DOPPELS	GOBLIN KING
×2	×2
SEA	BOSS BIRD
×2	×5
PvP	BAMBOO
×3	×1
SQUID	SNAIL DEN
×2	×1

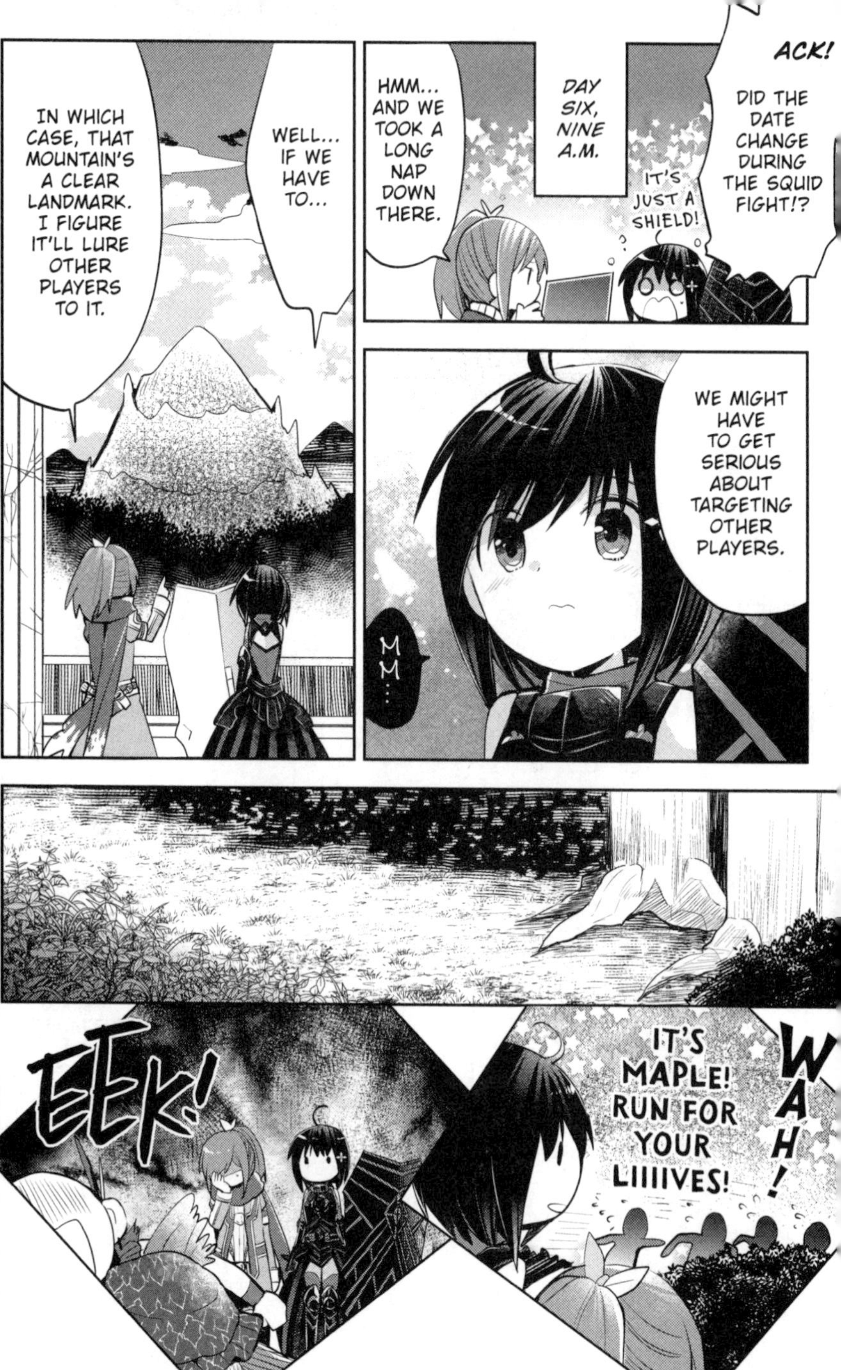
ACK!
DID THE DATE CHANGE DURING THE SQUID FIGHT!?
DAY SIX, NINE A.M.
IT'S JUST A SHIELD!
HMM... AND WE TOOK A LONG NAP DOWN THERE.
WE MIGHT HAVE TO GET SERIOUS ABOUT TARGETING OTHER PLAYERS.
MM...
WELL... IF WE HAVE TO...
IN WHICH CASE, THAT MOUNTAIN'S A CLEAR LANDMARK. I FIGURE IT'LL LURE OTHER PLAYERS TO IT.
WAH!
IT'S MAPLE! RUN FOR YOUR LIIIIVES!
EEK!

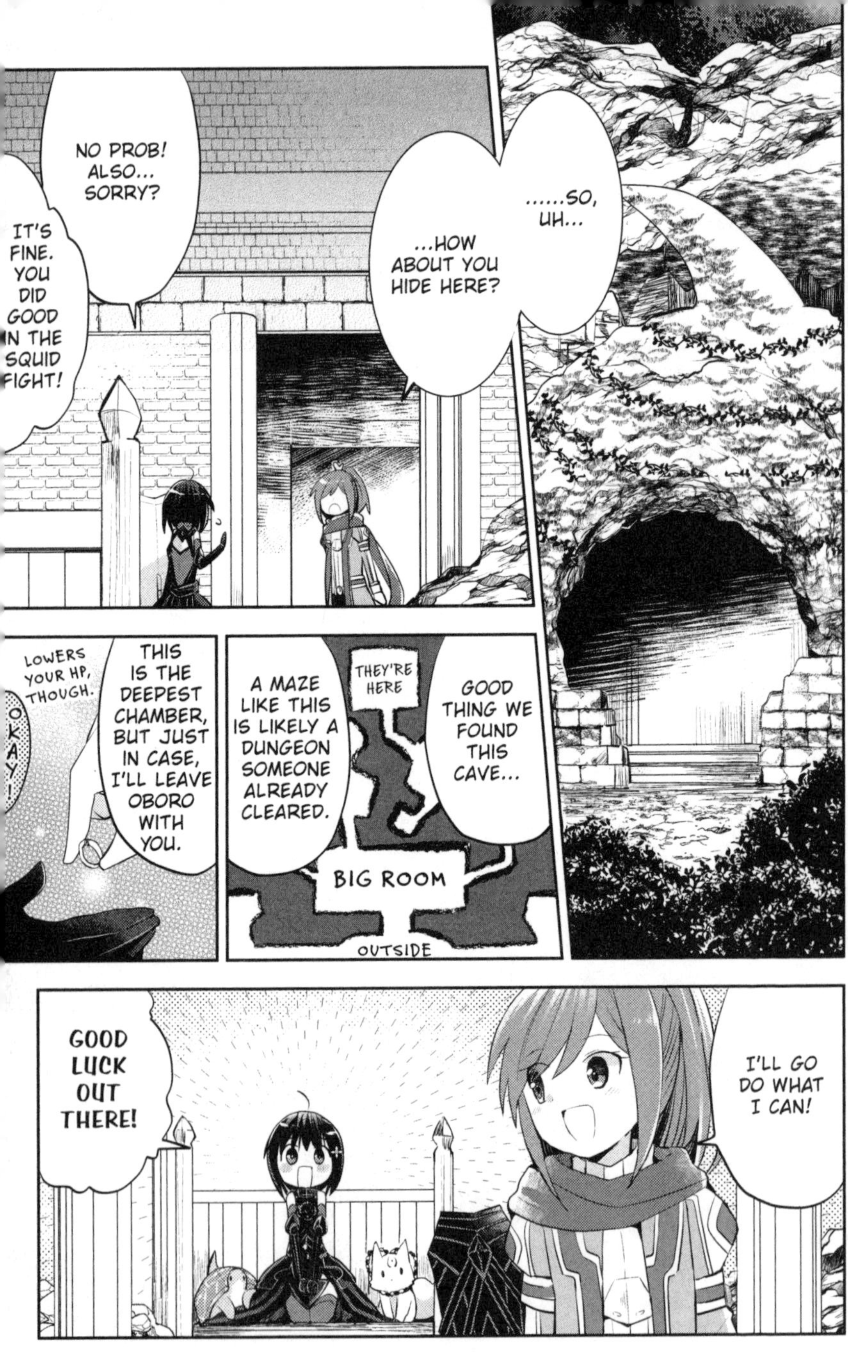

......SO, UH...
...HOW ABOUT YOU HIDE HERE?
NO PROB! ALSO... SORRY?
IT'S FINE. YOU DID GOOD IN THE SQUID FIGHT!
GOOD THING WE FOUND THIS CAVE...
THEY'RE HERE
A MAZE LIKE THIS IS LIKELY A DUNGEON SOMEONE ALREADY CLEARED.
BIG ROOM
OUTSIDE
THIS IS THE DEEPEST CHAMBER, BUT JUST IN CASE, I'LL LEAVE OBORO WITH YOU.
LOWERS YOUR HP, THOUGH.
OKAY!
I'LL GO DO WHAT I CAN!
GOOD LUCK OUT THERE!

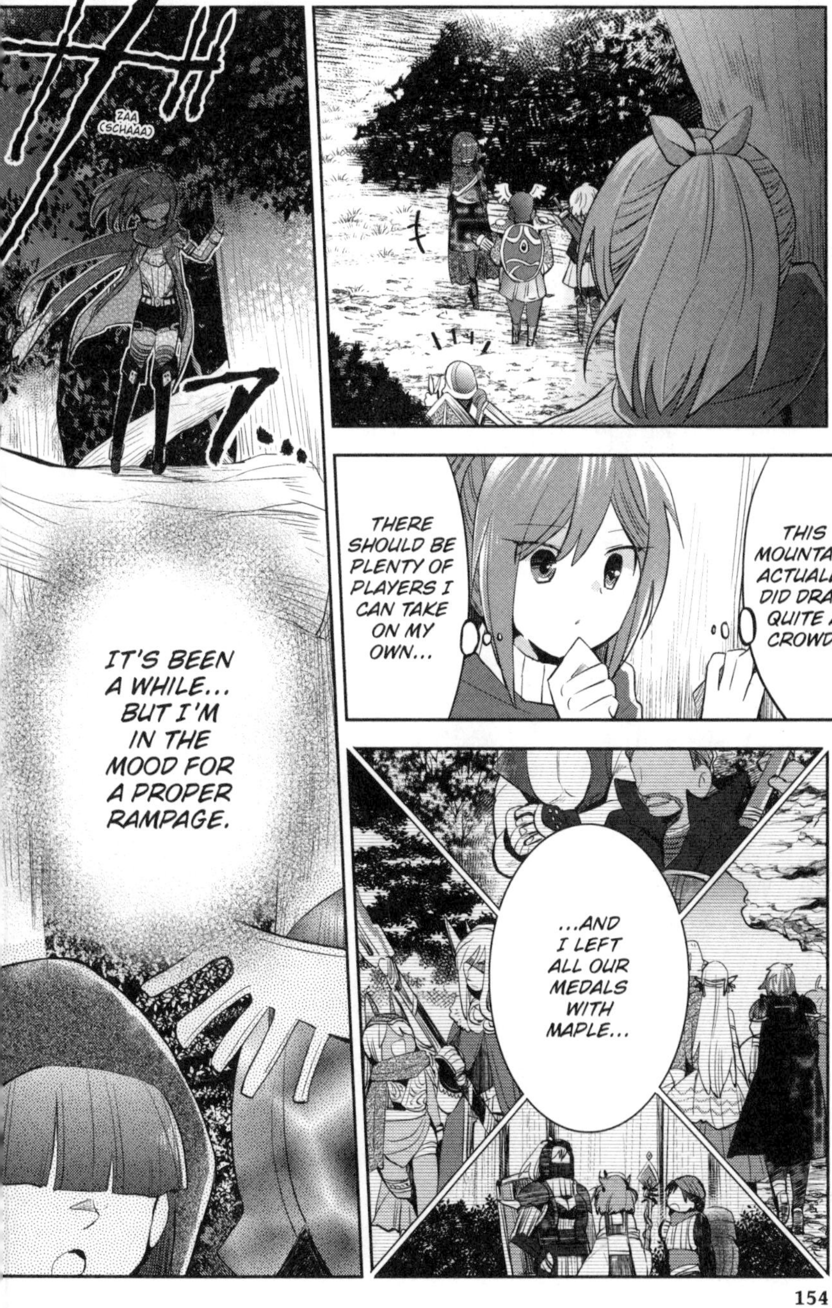

ZAA (SCHAAA)
THIS MOUNTAIN ACTUALLY DID DRAW QUITE A CROWD.
THERE SHOULD BE PLENTY OF PLAYERS I CAN TAKE ON MY OWN...
...AND I LEFT ALL OUR MEDALS WITH MAPLE...
IT'S BEEN A WHILE... BUT I'M IN THE MOOD FOR A PROPER RAMPAGE.

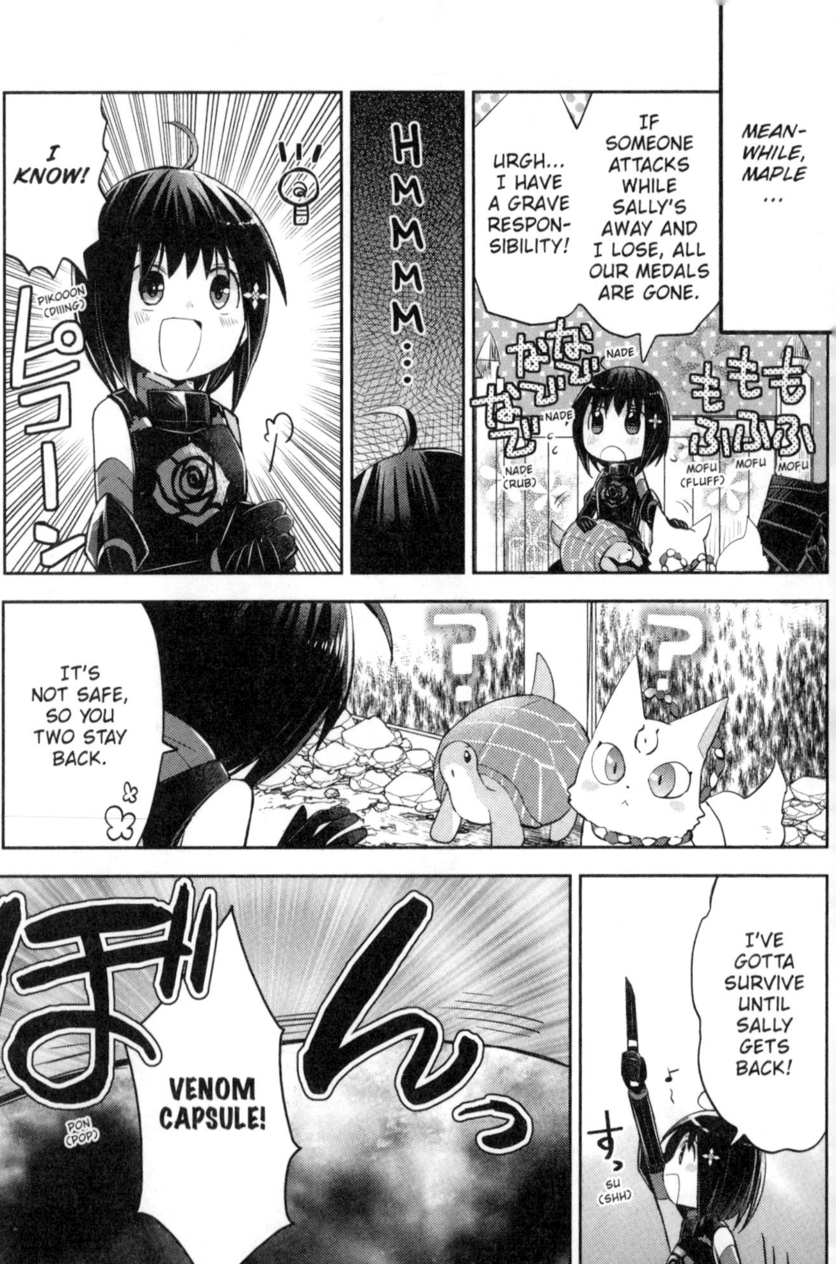
MEAN-WHILE, MAPLE...
IF SOMEONE ATTACKS WHILE SALLY'S AWAY AND I LOSE, ALL OUR MEDALS ARE GONE.
URGH... I HAVE A GRAVE RESPON-SIBILITY!
NADE
NADE
NADE (RUB)
MOFU
MOFU
MOFU (FLUFF)
HMMMM...
I KNOW!
PIKOOON (DIIING)
IT'S NOT SAFE, SO YOU TWO STAY BACK.
I'VE GOTTA SURVIVE UNTIL SALLY GETS BACK!
SU (SHH)
VENOM CAPSULE!
PON (POP)

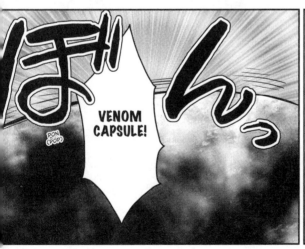

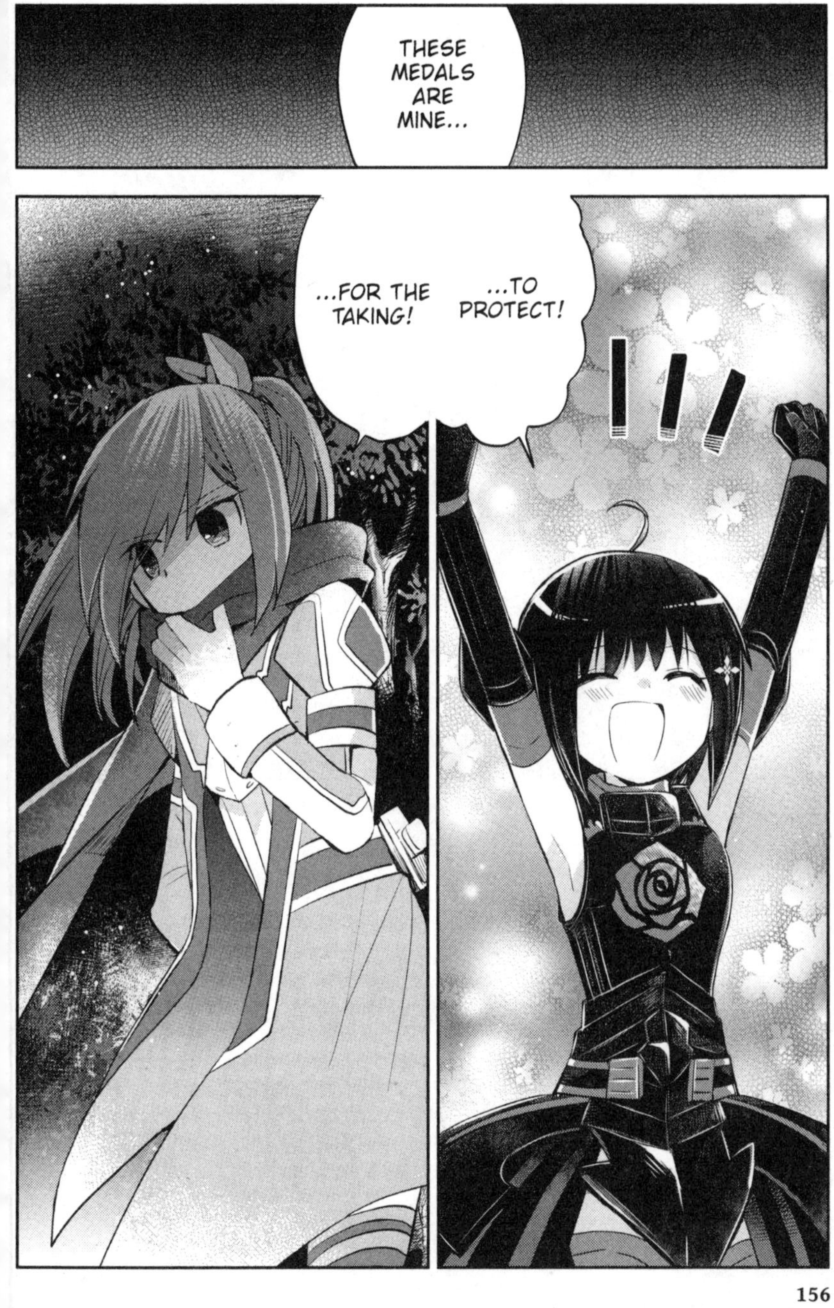
THESE MEDALS ARE MINE...
...TO PROTECT!
...FOR THE TAKING!

Bofuri

I Don't Want to Get Hurt, so I'll Max Out My Defense.

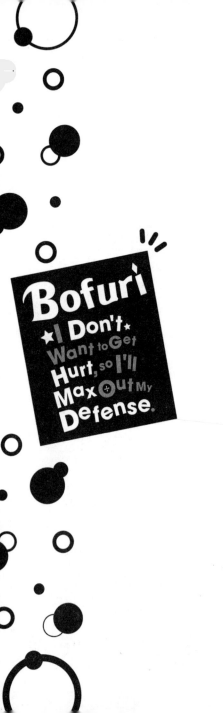

Welcome to
NewWorld Online.

I Don't Want to Get Hurt,

so I'll Max Out My Defense.

presented by: **JIROU OIMOTO & YUUMIKAN**

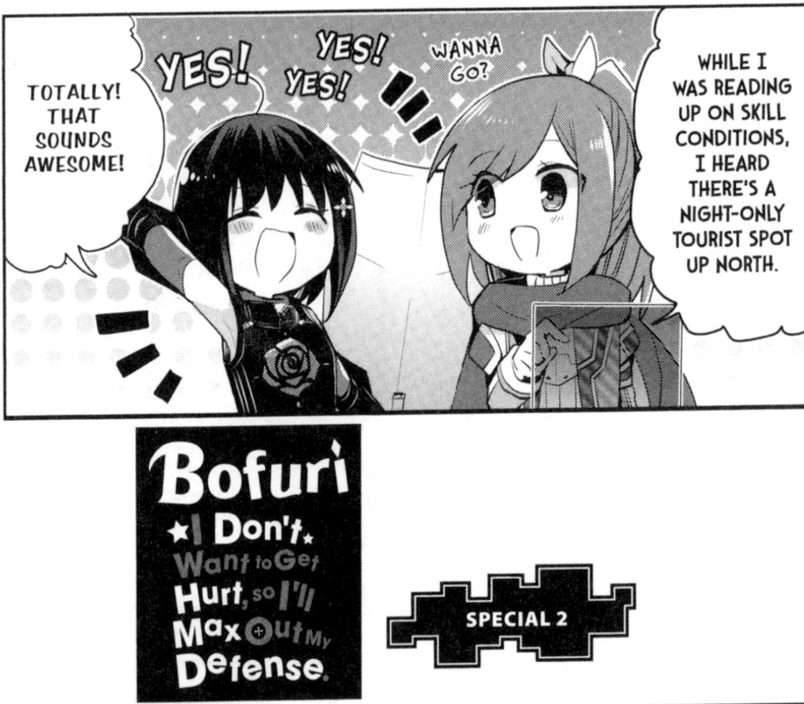
WHILE I WAS READING UP ON SKILL CONDITIONS, I HEARD THERE'S A NIGHT-ONLY TOURIST SPOT UP NORTH.
WANNA GO?
YES! YES!
YES!
TOTALLY! THAT SOUNDS AWESOME!

Bofuri ★I Don't★ Want to Get Hurt, so I'll Max Out My Defense.

SPECIAL 2

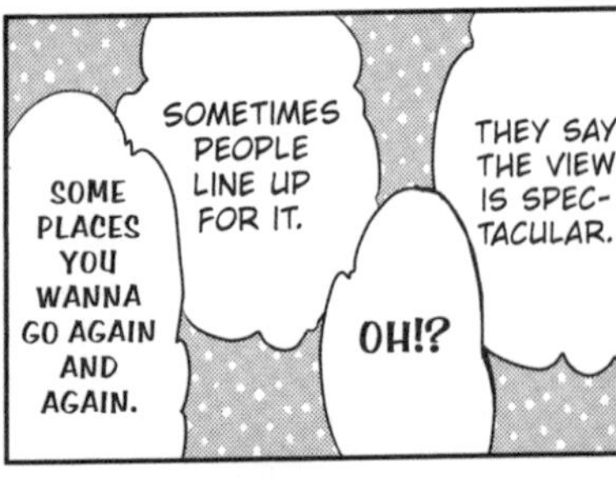
THEY SAY THE VIEW IS SPECTACULAR.
OH!?
SOMETIMES PEOPLE LINE UP FOR IT.
SOME PLACES YOU WANNA GO AGAIN AND AGAIN.

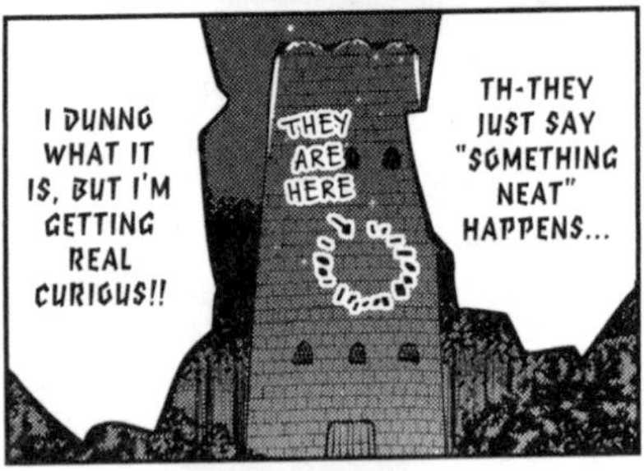
TH-THEY JUST SAY "SOMETHING NEAT" HAPPENS...
THEY ARE HERE
I DUNNO WHAT IT IS, BUT I'M GETTING REAL CURIOUS!!

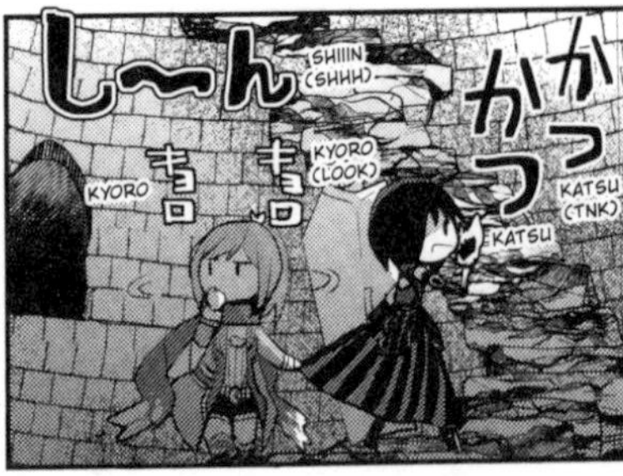
かっ
KATSU (TNK)
KATSU
きょろ
KYORO (LOOK)
きょろ
KYORO
しーん
SHIIIN (SHHH)

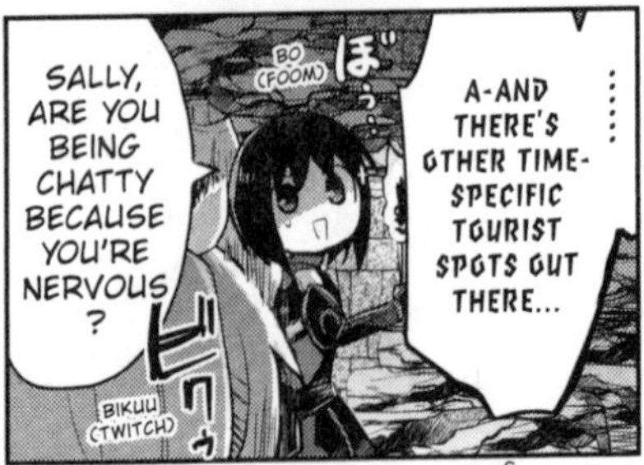
A-AND THERE'S OTHER TIME-SPECIFIC TOURIST SPOTS OUT THERE...
ぼっ
BO (FOOM)
SALLY, ARE YOU BEING CHATTY BECAUSE YOU'RE NERVOUS?
ビクゥ
BIKUU (TWITCH)

SALLY'S AFRAID OF GHOSTS!

GAMER'S INSTINCTS

WOW, THE STARS ARE SO PRETTY!
MM? IS THAT...?
WHEW...
A SIGNIFICANT-LOOKING TABLE AND CHAIRS.
UNLIT CANDLES.
PLACE SETTINGS, BUT NOBODY ELSE HERE.
THE INTEL DIDN'T MENTION TRAPS...
SHOULD WE SIT DOWN?
CLEARLY A SPECIAL EVENT!
LET'S!
SOWA (THROB)
GATA (CLNK)
SOWA

SALLY'S PLAYED TOO MANY GAMES!

FANTASY

PAA (GLOW)
BO (FOOM)
THESE DRINKS ARE LIKE STARRY SKIES!
PRETTY!
KOTO (CLNK)
PACHI (POP)
PACHI
FUWA (HOVER)
FUWA
HUH... THIS SURE IS SOME-THING.
WE'RE NOT GONNA FALL IF WE CHOOSE THE WRONG SILVERWARE, ARE WE?
KNIVES AND FORKS!
I—
I DON'T THINK SO?
HA!

IT'S A LONG WAY DOWN!

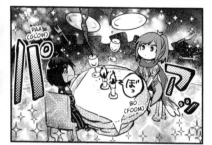

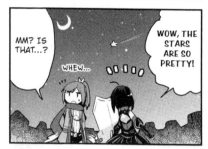

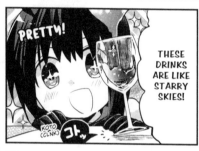

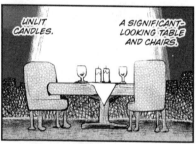

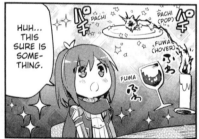

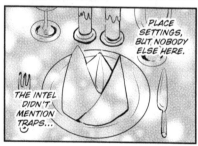

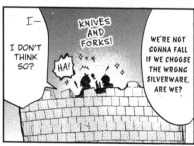

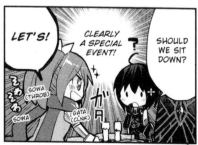

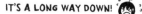

FANCY FOOD

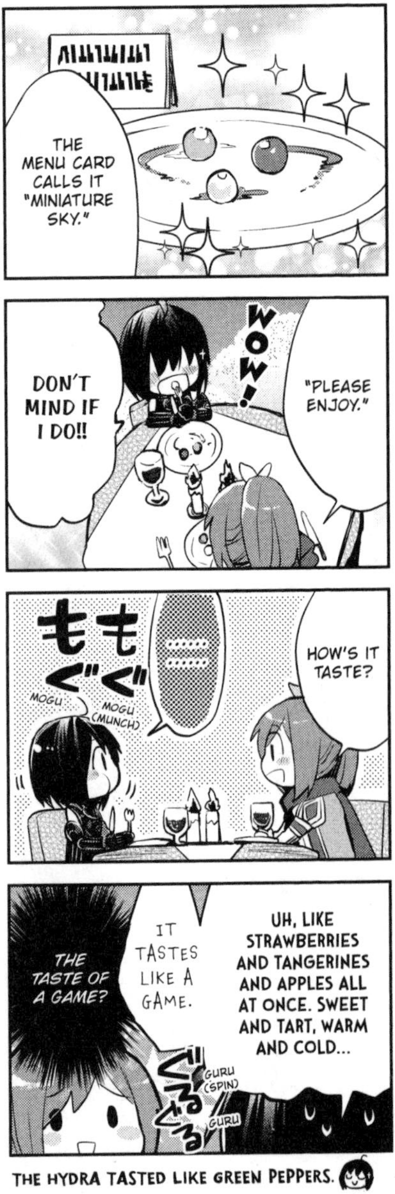
THE MENU CARD CALLS IT "MINIATURE SKY."
"PLEASE ENJOY."
WOW!
DON'T MIND IF I DO!!
HOW'S IT TASTE?
......
MOGU (MUNCH)
MOGU
UH, LIKE STRAWBERRIES AND TANGERINES AND APPLES ALL AT ONCE. SWEET AND TART, WARM AND COLD...
IT TASTES LIKE A GAME.
THE TASTE OF A GAME?
GURU (SPIN)
GURU

THE HYDRA TASTED LIKE GREEN PEPPERS.

ODD-EYE: YES, EVIL EYE: NO

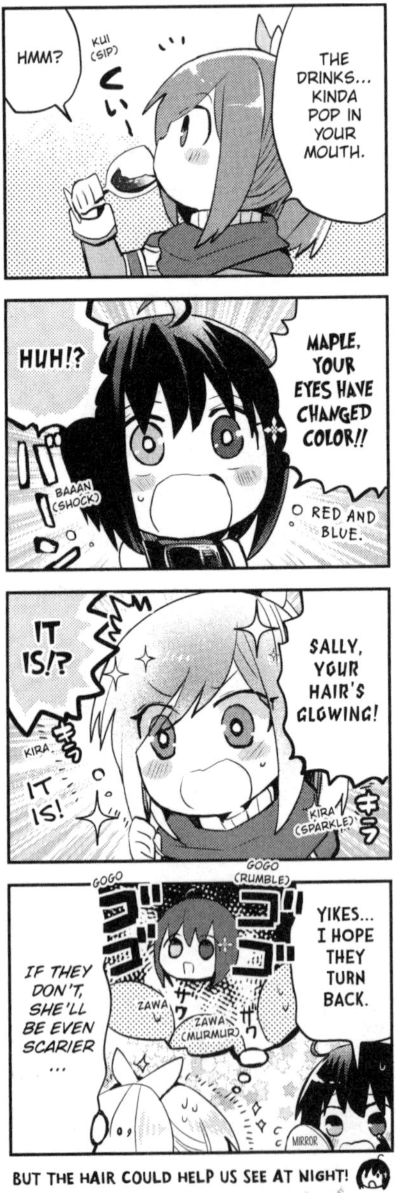
THE DRINKS... KINDA POP IN YOUR MOUTH.
KUI (SIP)
HMM?
MAPLE, YOUR EYES HAVE CHANGED COLOR!!
RED AND BLUE.
HUH!?
BAAAN (SHOCK)
SALLY, YOUR HAIR'S GLOWING!
KIRA (SPARKLE)
IT IS!?
KIRA
IT IS!
GOGO (RUMBLE)
YIKES... I HOPE THEY TURN BACK.
GOGO
IF THEY DON'T, SHE'LL BE EVEN SCARIER ...
ZAWA
ZAWA (MURMUR)
MIRROR

BUT THE HAIR COULD HELP US SEE AT NIGHT!

SUMMON THE CHEF

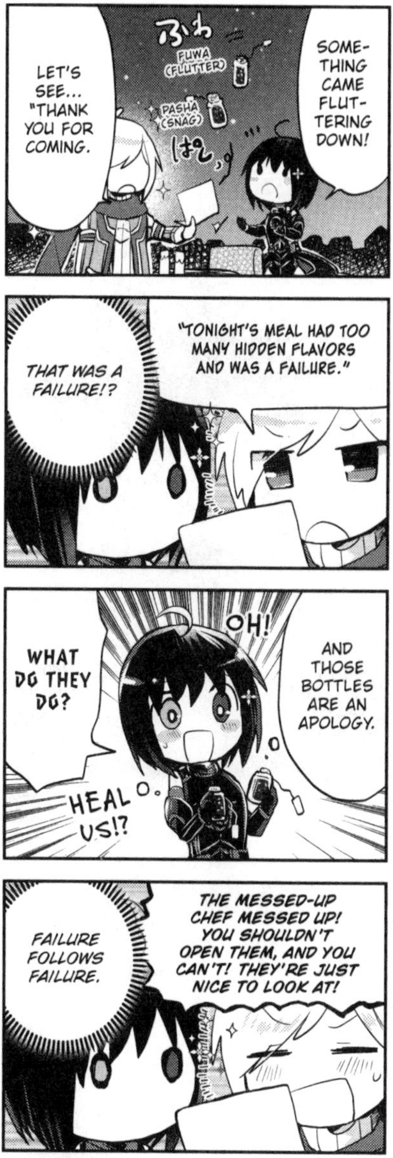
SOMETHING CAME FLUTTERING DOWN!
ふわ
FUWA (FLUTTER)
PASHA (SNAG)
ぱし
LET'S SEE... "THANK YOU FOR COMING.
"TONIGHT'S MEAL HAD TOO MANY HIDDEN FLAVORS AND WAS A FAILURE."
THAT WAS A FAILURE!?
AND THOSE BOTTLES ARE AN APOLOGY.
OH!
WHAT DO THEY DO?
HEAL US!?
THE MESSED-UP CHEF MESSED UP! YOU SHOULDN'T OPEN THEM, AND YOU CAN'T! THEY'RE JUST NICE TO LOOK AT!
FAILURE FOLLOWS FAILURE.

A LITTLE CURIOUS

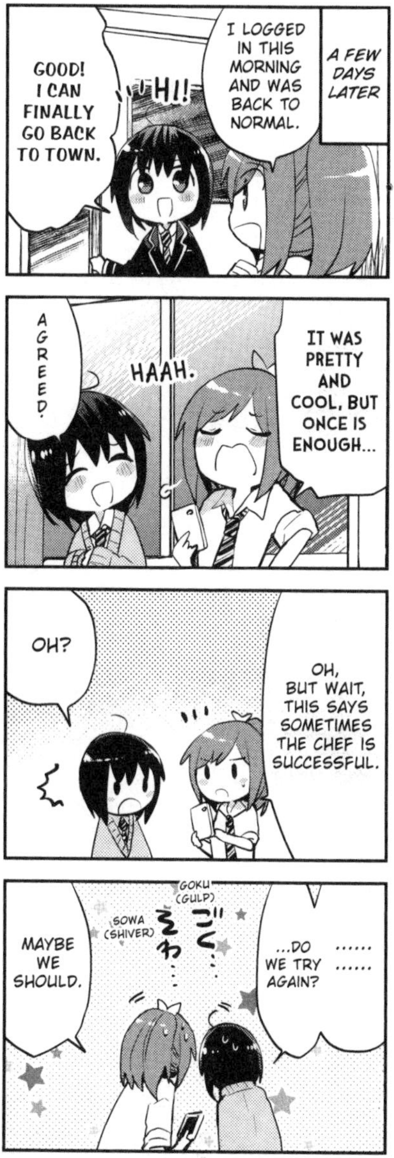
A FEW DAYS LATER
I LOGGED IN THIS MORNING AND WAS BACK TO NORMAL.
HI!
GOOD! I CAN FINALLY GO BACK TO TOWN.
IT WAS PRETTY AND COOL, BUT ONCE IS ENOUGH...
HAAH.
AGREED.
OH, BUT WAIT, THIS SAYS SOMETIMES THE CHEF IS SUCCESSFUL.
OH?
......
...DO WE TRY AGAIN?
GOKU (GULP)
ごく
SOWA (SHIVER)
そわ
MAYBE WE SHOULD.

SEE YOU AGAIN!

Bofuri
I Don't Want to Get Hurt, so I'll Max Out My Defense.

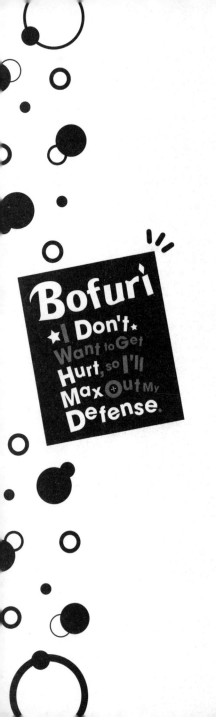

Bofuri ★ I Don't Want to Get Hurt, so I'll Max Out My Defense.

[3]

[Art] **JIROU OIMOTO**
[Original Story] **YUUMIKAN**
[Character Design] **KOIN**

Translation: **Andrew Cunningham** ★ Lettering: **Rochelle Gancio**

This book is a work of fiction. Names, characters, places, and incidents are the product of the author's imagination or are used fictitiously. Any resemblance to actual events, locales, or persons, living or dead, is coincidental.

ITAINO WA IYA NANODE BOGYORYOKU NI KYOKUFURI SHITAITO OMOIMASU Vol. 3
©Jirou Oimoto 2020 ©Yuumikan 2020 ©Koin 2020
First published in Japan in 2020 by KADOKAWA CORPORATION, Tokyo. English translation rights arranged with KADOKAWA CORPORATION, Tokyo through TUTTLE-MORI AGENCY, INC., Tokyo.

English translation © 2022 by Yen Press, LLC

Yen Press
150 West 30th Street, 19th Floor
New York, NY 10001

Visit us!
yenpress.com • facebook.com/yenpress • twitter.com/yenpress
yenpress.tumblr.com • instagram.com/yenpress

First Yen Press Edition: January 2022

Yen Press is an imprint of Yen Press, LLC.
The Yen Press name and logo are trademarks of Yen Press, LLC.

The publisher is not responsible for websites (or their content) that are not owned by the publisher.

Library of Congress Control Number: 2020953028

ISBNs: 978-1-9753-2390-5 (paperback)